UNFINISHED GESTURES

SOUTH ASIA ACROSS THE DISCIPLINES

A series edited by

DIPESH CHAKRABARTY, SHELDON POLLOCK,
AND SANJAY SUBRAHMANYAM

Funded by a grant from the Andrew W. Mellon Foundation and jointly published by the University of California Press, the University of Chicago Press, and Columbia University Press.

The Powerful Ephemeral: Everyday Healing in an Ambiguously Islamic Place
by Carla Bellamy (California)

Extreme Poetry: The South Asian Movement of Simultaneous Narration
by Yigal Bronner (Columbia)

Secularizing Islamists? Jama'at-e-Islami and Jama'at-ud Da'wa Pakistan
by Humeira Iqtidar (Chicago)

The Social Space of Language: Vernacular Culture in British Colonial Punjab
by Farina Mir (California)

Unifying Hinduism: Philosophy and Identity in Indian Intellectual History
by Andrew J. Nicholson (Columbia)

Islam Translated: Literature, Conversion, and the Arabic Cosmopolis of South and Southeast Asia
by Ronit Ricci (Chicago)

South Asia across the Disciplines is a series devoted to publishing first books across a wide range of South Asian studies, including art, history, philology or textual studies, philosophy, religion, and the interpretive social sciences. Series authors all share the goal of opening up new archives and suggesting new methods and approaches, while demonstrating that South Asian scholarship can be at once deep in expertise and broad in appeal.

UNFINISHED GESTURES

Devadāsīs, Memory, and Modernity in South India

DAVESH SONEJI

THE UNIVERSITY OF CHICAGO PRESS
CHICAGO AND LONDON

DAVESH SONEJI is associate professor of South Asian religions at McGill University. He is coeditor of *Performing Pasts: Reinventing the Arts in Modern South India* and editor of *Bharatanatyam: A Reader.*

The University of Chicago Press, Chicago 60637
The University of Chicago Press, Ltd., London

Printed in the United States of America

21 20 19 18 17 16 15 14 13 12   1 2 3 4 5

ISBN-13: 978-0-226-76809-0 (cloth)
ISBN-13: 978-0-226-76810-6 (paper)
ISBN-10: 0-226-76809-0 (cloth)
ISBN-10: 0-226-76810-4 (paper)

Library of Congress Cataloging-in-Publication Data
Soneji, Devesh.
Unfinished gestures : devadasis, memory, and modernity in South India / Davesh Soneji.
p. cm. — (South Asia across the disciplines)
Includes bibliographical references and index.
ISBN-13: 978-0-226-76809-0 (cloth : alk. paper)
ISBN-10: 0-226-76809-0 (cloth : alk. paper)
ISBN-13: 978-0-226-76810-6 (pbk. : alk. paper)
ISBN-10: 0-226-76810-4 (pbk. : alk. paper)
1. Devadasis—India, South. 2. Devadasis—India, South—Social conditions. 3. Dance—Social aspects—India, South. 4. Prostitution—India, South. 5. Social change—India, South. I. Title. II. Series: South Asia across the disciplines.
BL1237.58.D48S66 2011
306.6'94538082—dc23   2011020833

A portion of chapter 2 is a slightly altered version of an essay published in Davesh Soneji, ed., *Bharatanatyam: A Reader* (New Delhi: Oxford University Press, 2010). Reproduced by permission of Oxford University Press India, New Delhi.

♾ This paper meets the requirements of ANSI/NISO Z39.48-1992 (Permanence of Paper).

FOR MY FAMILY,

MUTTUKKANNAMMAL, AND

HYMAVATHI *AKKA*

CONTENTS

ACKNOWLEDGMENTS

This book began as a string of paradoxical and aporetic thoughts around the question of the disappearance of *devadāsīs* from the public life of modern South India. Over a decade ago, I was fortunate to encounter two women—R. Muttukkannammal and Kotipalli Hymavathi—who helped me understand both the complexities and poignancy of women's realities in these communities, and in a very tangible way, forged pathways for the creation of this book. R. Muttukkannammal of Viralimalai in Tamilnadu has shown me limitless affection, openness, and generosity. She has also been a teacher in the fullest possible sense. It was at the home of Kotipalli Hymavathi in Muramanda, Andhra Pradesh, with the blessings of her ailing mother, the late Kotipalli Manikyam, and her sister Kotipalli Sitaramalakshmi (Satyavati), that my work with women on the Telugu-speaking *kalāvantula* communities began. Hymavathi *akka*'s wit, humor, and self-reflexivity run through large portions of this work. As a very small token of my immense gratitude and respect, I dedicate this book to them.

This book would not exist without the contribution of two other individuals: Dr. B. M. Sundaram and Voleti Rangamani. Dr. Sundaram, one of the most generous intellectuals I have ever known, has quite literally "held my hand," guiding me through the dense and often overwhelming amount of cultural and historical data that constitutes the substance of this book. His profound understanding of the history and technique of music and dance in South India is simply unmatched and has never ceased to bewilder me. Dr. Sundaram has also welcomed me into his family, and his nurturing and highly sensitive presence permeates the pages of this book.

My work in Andhra Pradesh would not have been possible without the help, guidance, and warmth of Voleti Rangamani, daughter of the late

C. R. Acharyalu, himself a student of Andhra's courtesan dancers in the early twentieth century. Rangamani *akka* was technically what one could call my "field assistant," but this title by no means does justice to her contribution. For months, she traveled in the Godavari River delta with me and Kotipalli Hymavathi, giving much of her precious time and knowledge for a project to which she remained deeply committed. I am extremely grateful to her for all her help, and for the numerous personal sacrifices I know she made over the course of our fieldwork.

In Muramanda, I was fortunate to meet former members of the late Kotipalli Manikyam's *mēḷam* (troupe), including Kotipalli Somasundaram, Eluru Lakshakasulu, Kotipalli Rajahamsa, and Nayudu Chilakamma. I developed a very close relationship with the late Saride Anusuya, the late Saride Seshachalam, Saride Varahalu, and Saride Mythili (Duvva, West Godavari district), and I thank the women of this family for their passionate and highly erudite self-reflections. I also worked with the late Maddula Venkataratnam, a master artist, for months just before she passed away, and learned a tremendous amount from her improvised performances. Along with Maddula Ramatulasi, I watched for hours and hours as Venkataratnam performed dance and music compositions in the village of Tatipaka, and those are memories that will forever be etched in my mind.

I would like to offer my respectful thanks to the following women in coastal Andhra who openly shared their experiences with me in the most generous and gracious manner: Maddula Mohana, daughter of the late Maddula Lakshminarayana and her family (Manepalli), and the late Saride Manikyamma, along with K. Rukmini, K. Nagamani (Kapileswarapuram), Maddula Janakamma (Manepalli), Anvala Suryakantam, Duggirala Satyavati, Garlanka Pani, Kotipalli Sarasvati, Pendyala Gaggavati, and Pendyala Satyavati (Mandapeta), the late Kola Subrahmanyam and her family (Bommur, outside Rajahmundry), Eluru Krishnaveni (Rajahmundry), and Jakkula Radha (Peddapuram).

The following individuals have also helped me understand the complexities of *kalāvantula* performance in the Godavari delta over the years, and I am sincerely grateful for their time and intellectual generosity: Medinti Achyutaramayya, *hāsya-pātra* artist and singer (Gannavaram), K. Narasimhacharyulu (Vaikhānasa Ācārya, Kuntīmādhava Temple, Pithapuram), P. Purushottamacharyalu (Vaikhānasa Ācārya, Madanagopālasvāmi temple, Ballipadu), the late Arudra (Bhagavatula Sankara Sastri), Nataraja Ramakrishna (Hyderabad), Swapnasundari (New Delhi), and V. A. K. Ranga Rao (Chennai).

I wish to thank the following women from Tamilnadu whose expressions flow in tacit ways through this book: Shanta, granddaughter of the late Subbammal (Pudukkottai); Kumbhakonam Gomati and her family (Oraiyur); Vaideesvarankoyil Kanakambujam and her family (Chidambaram); Thiruvidaimarudur N. Rajalakshmi (Coimbatore); and Nagalakshmi (Thiruvidaimarudur).

I owe a great debt to the late N. Visvanathan, Telugu Pandit at the Sarasvati Mahal Library in Thanjavur, for his guidance and tutelage in Telugu over many years. I am also deeply grateful to the late Thanjavur K. P. Kittappa Pillai; his son, K. P. K. Chandrasekaran; and their family, for allowing me to share in the artistic heritage of the Tanjore Quartet.

In India, the following friends and colleagues have extended much of their time, hospitality, and warmth: S. Babaji Bhonsle Chattrapati (Senior Prince of Thanjavur), Sunil Kothari (Delhi), and Mrinalini and Mallika Sarabhai (Ahmedabad). Ranvir and Nandi Shah, in particular, have looked after me like family in Chennai for over a decade. They have also provided much-needed moral support, and I am indebted to them.

In North America, my work has been inspired and mentored by two individuals to whom I am deeply indebted. Indira Viswanathan Peterson has been a source of inspiration but also a close friend and guide. Her incisive work on colonial modernity in South India and her deep knowledge of multiple languages and literary contexts has played no small part in my own development as scholar, and I am very grateful for the care and rigor with which she has helped me understand so many dimensions of South Indian cultural history. Leslie Orr, whose work on temple women in the Cōḻa inscriptional record has directly impacted the deep questions of *devadāsī* historiography, has played the role of confidante and advisor for well over a decade. Leslie's presence in Montreal has brought much joy to the study of South India in our local context, and I am grateful for the stability and support she has brought to my work. In Montreal, I also wish to thank Katherine K. Young, under whose watchful and nurturing eye the roots of many of the ideas I engage in this book first emerged when I was a Ph.D. student.

Velcheru Narayana Rao, a visionary scholar, has, from a distance, inspired much of this work. His own work on South Indian literary and cultural history prompted me to take the study of Telugu seriously, and over the years, our conversations about *kalāvantula* women in the Telugu-speaking regions have contributed immensely to the ideas I have tried to develop in this book.

The research for this book has been generously supported by grants from the Social Sciences and Humanities Research Council of Canada and

Fonds québécois de la recherche sur la société et la culture. I am also grateful to the following institutions and individuals for their support: the British Library (London), the Victoria and Albert Museum (London), Sri Veeraraghavan and the Sarasvati Mahal Library (Thanjavur), and G. Sundar and the Roja Muthiah Research Library (Chennai).

I am extremely grateful to the editors of the South Asia Across the Disciplines Series, Sheldon Pollock, Dipesh Chakrabarty, and Sanjay Subrahmanyam, for their support of this work, and to the anonymous readers at the University of Chicago Press for their insightful comments. I also thank the staff at the University of Chicago Press, T. David Brent, Laura Avey, Priya Nelson, Maia Rigas, and Carol Saller, for their patience, guidance, and good spirits throughout the production of this book.

Earlier versions of chapters of this book have been presented at invited lectures, seminars, workshops, and conferences in India, the United Kingdom, the United States, and Canada. I thank those who have given me the benefit of their insights on those occasions. Many of these colleagues have continued to be important interlocutors and well-wishers, and I remain grateful to them for our ongoing conversations: Yigal Bronner, Brenda Cantelo, Vasudha Dalmia, Richard Davis, Sascha Ebeling, Kathryn Hansen, Jack Hawley, George and Kauslaya Hart, Steven Hopkins, Robert Hueckstedt, Gene Irschick, Anuradha Jonnalagadda, Padma Kaimal, Philip Lutgendorf, Amelia Maciszewski, Vasudha Narayanan, Regula Qureshi, Himanshu Prabha Ray, Sumathi Ramaswamy, Kristin Rudisill, Adheesh Sathaye, Anna Schultz, David Shulman, Joanne Waghorne, and Margaret Walker.

When I was a teenaged, overzealous student of Karṇāṭak music, I came across Saskia Kersenboom's *Nityasumaṅgalī: Devadāsī Tradition in South India*, which undeniably shaped the trajectory of my entire professional life. To Saskia I owe much—not only for her pathfinding work on *devadāsīs*, but also for her support, warmth, and friendship over a decade and a half, and for our conversations that took place across North America, Europe, and India. I wish to acknowledge my colleagues who have worked on many of the issues surrounding *devadāsīs* that have both informed and challenged my ideas over the years: Matthew Allen, Joep Bor, Sudha Jagannath, Kay Jordan, Douglas Knight, Tiziana Leucci, Avanthi Meduri, Janaki Nair, Srividya Natarajan, Amrit Srinivasan, Lakshmi Subramanian, and Priyadarshini Vijaisri. I wish to thank Janet O'Shea in particular for her sustained and stimulating conversations, and for her friendship and support.

I am grateful to my students, friends, and colleagues in Canada—Lisa Blake, Lara Braitstein, Mohini Datta-Ray, Sujata Ghosh, Meera Kachroo,

Shahin Parhami, Tanisha Ramachandran, Shital Sharma, Chetan Soni, and Elena Young, especially for those "okay, let's talk about something other than *devadāsīs*" moments. I also thank Archana Venkatesan and Layne Little for their long-standing friendship and support of this research.

The always-forgiving, boundless love and energy of my parents Minal and Ranjit Soneji and my sister Sarita have raised my spirits under the most trying circumstances. Their love has supported me in ways that lie far beyond words.

Finally, I owe my utmost gratitude to Hari Krishnan and Rajavairan Rajendran ("Rex")—my closest friends and surrogate family—whose overall support, warmth, patience, criticisms, good humor, and love have been invaluable in sustaining me through the ups and downs of this project, and of life in general. Hari Krishnan's intellectual and artistic camaraderie has supported me for almost two decades, and in so many ways, this research could not be sustained without him.

INTRODUCTION

On Historical, Social, and Aesthetic Borderlands

"REMEMBER ME AS I WAS"

In December 2006, I traveled to the town of Thiruvidaimarudur in the Thanjavur district of Tamil Nadu. Across from the severely dilapidated palace of the Marāṭhā king Amarasiṃha of Tanjore, I was told, lived Thiruvidaimarudur Nagalakshmi, a woman who was an active dancer in the 1930s–1940s. I knocked on the wooden door, but there was no answer. "Ammā?" I inquired. "*Vā* (Come)," replied a faint voice from inside the house. I gently pushed open the door, and there, in the middle of the house, seated on a chair in near-darkness, was eighty-year-old Nagalakshmi. As soon as I introduced myself and told her about my interest in her life, Nagalakshmi invited me to pull up a chair. She apologized that she could not offer me anything to eat or drink, because, quite frankly, she had nothing, she said, gesturing to the emptiness of the house. After an hour-long conversation in which she told me about the Tamil *padam* songs she used to perform, I asked if I could take a photograph of her. "*Vēṇṭām, pā* (No thanks)" she said, handing me a dusty old laminated photo (fig. 0.1). "Take a photo of this photo," she said. "Remember me as I was, not as I am. What would people think if they saw me in this state? This is not how I want to be remembered."

Nagalakshmi comes from a Tamil-speaking *devadāsī* community. Trained in dance by Kuppaiya Nattuvanar (1887–1981), she performed throughout the Thanjavur region in the 1930s—1940s and also toured Ceylon with her troupe. In the 1940s, however, her teacher moved to Bombay (now Mumbai) to teach dance in its reinvented avatar as middle-class, "classical" Bharatanāṭyam, and Nagalakshmi's own opportunities to dance were severely diminished, although she continued to perform

0.1 Tiruvidaimarudur Nagalakshmi, dressed to perform in the *Carapēntira Pūpāla Kuṟavañci* in Thanjavur, c. 1940.

occasionally at weddings and local festivals. She successfully arranged the marriages of her three daughters, none of whom had anything to do with dance or music, and they, together with her grandchildren, continue to provide for her, although she lives alone in Thiruvidaimarudur. Nagalakshmi is not alone in wanting to be remembered for who she *was* rather than who she *is*. Hundreds of unintegrated individuals, mainly women, from *devadāsī* backgrounds in the Tamil- and Telugu-speaking regions of South India contend with this same disenfranchisement. Threaded through this book is an account of this peculiar social, civic, and aesthetic ambiguity, marked by encounters with modernity and voiced through memory.

In this book, I approach the topic of *devadāsī*s over the past two hundred years through slippages, fissures, and movement— Foucauldian "discontinuities that offer history" (1969, 10). This history, like the lives of contemporary women in these communities, is always "in process," pervaded by a profound sense of incompleteness. Despite being the subject of a diverse range of political investments and competing agendas, this history remains critically unfinished. The loose ends of the moralizing projects of colonial and postcolonial modernity, a dance aesthetic that has lost its value, and incipient possibilities of citizenship for *devadāsī*s are all emblems of the unfinished pasts of *devadāsī*s in South India. Attentive to the historical fissures and uneven movements that underwrite the project of cultural modernity in South India, this study of *devadāsī*s critically foregrounds the interface between politics, aesthetics, and sexuality.

From the late sixteenth-century Nāyaka period onward, *devadāsī*s have functioned as courtesans, secular dance artists organized in guilds called *mēḷam*s, and temple workers, some of whom performed in the public spaces of certain Hindu temples. However, these communities have always occupied an ambiguous status in South Indian society. On the one hand, devadāsīs possessed a degree of social agency in that they were not restricted by the norms of patrifocal kinship. They lived in quasi-matrilineal communities, had nonconjugal sexual relationships with upper-caste men, and were literate when most South Indian women were not. On the other hand, records from centers of political power such as the court at Tanjore in Tamil Nadu document the fact that courtesans were commodities regularly bought and sold through the intercession of the court. In other contexts, as the concubines, mistresses, or "second wives" of South Indian elites, they were implicated in a larger world of servitude focused on the fulfillment of male desire. Beginning in the mid-nineteenth century, vociferous social reform movements in South India aimed to dislodge communities of professional dancing women from their hereditary performance practices. Over the next hundred years, their lifestyles were criminalized on the basis of their nonconjugal sexuality, which was understood as prostitution. The Madras Devadasis (Prevention of Dedication) Act, implemented in 1947, officially outlawed the social, ritual, and aesthetic practices of these women.

While the emphasis on the religious lives of *devadāsī*s in some scholarly works has provided a "redemptive" narrative for *devadāsī* history, it has also fixed *devadāsī*s in the past, and in idealizing their practices has shifted attention away from women in contemporary *devadāsī* communities. Arguably, scholarly work on *devadāsī*s in South India has tended to focus on three major issues: (1) the precolonial past, usually a medieval past that focuses almost exclusively on the temple as a center of power (see, for example, Orr 2000; Parasher and Naik 1986; Prasad 1990; Sadasivan 1981, 1993; and others); (2) the period of *devadāsī* reform and its legal interventions (Anandhi 1991, 1997a; Hubel 2005; Jordan 1993, 2003; Kannabiran 1995; Kannabiran and Kannabiran 2003; J. Nair 1994; Parker 1998; Srilata 2003; Sundara Raj 1993; Vijaisri 2004; Whitehead 1998, 2001); and (3) the "dance revival" and the appropriation of *devadāsī* cultural practices by a new class of upper-caste urban performers such as Rukmini Arundale (1904–1986). Indeed, by now, the story of the reinvention of the performing arts under Indian nationalism, the repopulation of hereditary art forms by the urban middle class, and the resignifications these processes effected are well known. Historians, anthropologists, and ethnomusicologists who have worked on music (for example, Bakhle 2005; Neuman 1990; Qureshi 2006; L. Subramanian 2006, 2008; Terada 1992, 2008; Weidman 2006) and those who have worked on dance (for example, Allen 1997; Chakravorty 2008; Gaston 1996; Krishnan 2009; Leucci 2009; Maciszewski 1998, 2006, 2007; Meduri 1996; Srividya Natarajan 1997; O'Shea 2005, 2006, 2007; Sachdeva 2008; A. Srinivasan 1984, 1985, 1998; Walker 2004) have already provided critical and definitive scholarly accounts of these issues. I, too, have been invested in these debates for well over a decade, and a recent volume maps the complexities of this terrain with regard to dance and music in modern South India (Peterson and Soneji 2008).

Many of the questions addressed in this book, however, fall in between these three well-established signposts of *devadāsī* historiography. I focus, for example, on the place of dance in late colonial Tanjore, a quasi-autonomous state eventually brought under complete Company and Crown rule. The place of *devadāsī*s at the Tanjore court—and subsequently the place of Tanjore in the eyes of women from contemporary *devadāsī* communities—complicates received narratives about women's lives prior to the official beginnings of the "anti-nautch" movement at the end of the nineteenth century. It also forces us to examine the connections between colonial modernity and the production of culture in the courtly milieu, a question that has been addressed, for example, by historians such as Janaki Bakhle (2005, 20–49) who have written about music and modernity in princely states in North India. I also focus on dance and the culture of courtesans in late colonial Madras, where the kind of dance that fuels the "anti-nautch" campaign—what I call "salon dance"—lives. Images of *devadāsī*s and their aesthetic and sexual practices circulate through vernacular literature in this period, and these literary tropes about *devadāsī* morality add, in no small measure, to the emergent social reform activity directed toward them. It is these salon performances, and *not* performances inside temples, that ignite the vociferous anti-nautch movement in South India toward the end of the nineteenth century. The anti-nautch movement, which lasts almost half a century, brings discussions of nonconjugal forms of sexuality into the realm of public debate. It also results in the radical restructuring of kinship patterns within *devadāsī* communities and the reinvention of male political subjectivity in these communities through the creation of new caste identities such as *icai vēḷāḷa* (*lit.* "cultivators of music") or *sūryabaḷija* (*lit.* "merchants of the sun dynasty of King Mahābali"). Closely allied with both Congress party politics and the non-Brahmin Self-Respect movement, anti-nautch deliberations promised new avenues of citizenship for "reformed" *devadāsī*s. The legal interventions that actually resulted from such deliberations, however, severely curtailed *devadāsī* women's prospects for the future.

Finally, and perhaps most importantly, this book asks questions about the period following "reform" and "revival," and interrogates the afterlives of these events from within *devadāsī* communities. What happens to women in these communities after 1947? How is the Madras Devadasis Act of 1947 implemented? Do cultural practices survive within *devadāsī* communities today? Are there forms of civic, social, and aesthetic marginality that these women live with on a quotidian basis? How are women from devadāsīs communities—real and imagined—received and "dealt with" in the context of a globalized state and within the capitalist flows of a neoliberal economy? The latter half of this book presents the ethnographic component of this project, engaging over ten different *devadāsī* communities, from the northernmost tip of coastal Andhra Pradesh, to the Tamil-speaking south, in the Pudukkottai district of Tamil Nadu. The ethnography is significant for several reasons. First, it discredits the widespread belief that *devadāsī* communities ceased to exist in South India decades ago. Second, it provides insights grounded in memory, performance, and individual testimony that cannot be recovered from archives or texts. In the last two chapters of this book, I trace the ways in which history, performance, and identity are enmeshed in the mnemonic, focusing on women from both Tamil- and Telugu-speaking regions. Dance and music practices continue to persist here, usually in the form of very private performances held "behind closed doors" within the community. In these chapters, I discuss some of my own encounters with *devadāsī* dance in this milieu and chart narrations of *devadāsī* history through memory and affect. The second half of *Unfinished Gestures* thus challenges us to dwell on the borderline between the embodied present and the historicized past and to oscillate between the two. It makes available a scholarly approach to *devadāsī*s that includes their self-interpretation as a factor in our own critical formulations, and accepts those self-interpretations as ongoing, unfinished gestures.

DEFINITIONS AND DEGENERATION

I wish to preface our exploration of these communities in modern South India by addressing the problematic nature of the term "*devadāsī*." From Wikipedia to popular magazine articles to scholarly writing by academics, today the term "*devadāsī*" is used to index a vast number of communities of women who are generally glossed by English phrases such as "sacred prostitute" or "temple dancer." It collapses a number of regional practices under a singular sign, and the literal translation of the word ("slave of god") is all too often taken as a closed definition of the category.

As Leslie Orr explains, the term *devadāsī* is rarely encountered in Indian literary or inscriptional material prior to the twentieth century, and the idea of a continuous, pan-Indian "*devadāsī* institution"—so pervasive in Indian historical, sociological, and anthropological literature today—simply cannot be sustained through a critical interrogation of literary and religious texts or inscriptional data (2000, 5–8). Thus, as I explain below, we cannot historicize the contemporary use of the term *devadāsī* without reference to imperial knowledge systems and the irreversible epistemic transformations of individuals, communities, and worldviews they engendered in colonial South India.

The mechanisms of empire transformed a range of diverse, localized practices by subjecting them to standardization through administrative processes. Colonial ethnography, the legal surveillance of sexual morality, and the disciplining of sexualized bodies were central to the new order represented by empire. These new "Orientalist sociologies," as Philippa Levine calls them, sought to bring order, hierarchy, and ultimately control to the "melting pot of sexual commerce" in India (Levine 2000, 8). Levine notes that these taxonomic exercises were "fundamentally descriptive and

0.2 *Jogatis* and a *jogappa* in Hospet, Bellary district, north Karnataka, dancing and singing devotional songs for the goddess Yellammā, accompanied by musicians playing the stringed-instrument called *cauṃḍake*. Photograph by Serena Emerson.

empiricist, a mere catalogue of actualities" (ibid, 11). These processes of data collection conditioned the category of the transregional "*devadāsī*" in the colonial order of things. Missionary accounts, imperial anthropology, and eventually the Anglo-Indian legal system all contributed the "objective knowledge" that would define this category in the social, political, and historical imagination of modern India.[1]

In contemporary writings about *devadāsī*s, the practices of Dalit women such as *jogati*s represent one of the most clearly recognizable emblems of civilizational degeneration. *Jogati*s are often defined in scholarly literature as "the last *devadāsī*s" or "contemporary *devadāsī*s" (for example, Evans 1998; Shankar 1994; Tarachand 1991), in a move that posits them as degenerate, residual progeny of the temple dancer of the past and simultaneously enforces the popular notion that communities of South Indian courtesans, such as those who are the subject of this book, no longer exist.[2]

Localized practices of dedicating Dalit girls as *jogati*s to the goddess Reṇukā-Yellammā-Māriyamma are found throughout much of South India (fig. 0.2). The Belgaum district in Karnataka has become extremely well known in the media for these practices, but they are also present in the Telangana region of Andhra Pradesh.[3] Regional variations of these traditions—such as the tradition of dedicating Dalit girls as *mātamma*s or *mātaṅgi*s to the goddess Gaṅgamma in Tirupati, or the dedication of girls to local village goddesses in Villupuram and North Arcot districts in Tamil Nadu—also exist.[4] Similarly, traditions of dedicating young Dalit boys as representatives of the goddess's guardian Poṭurāju, or the dedication of transgendered men as *jogappa*s are found in these regions as well.[5] However, as Dalit practices, their histories are unknown and, to an extent, irretrievable. Hence, the practices of these *jogati*s are only ever discussed with reference to a transregional idea of "the South Indian *devadāsī*," which falsely links them to upper-caste temples, lost art forms, and a sometimes idealized form of sexual difference.

In many of these communities, women undergo a ritual of "dedication," known as "tying beads (*muttu*)" to the village deity, and live by begging for alms (*jogā* or *jogvā*) and singing devotional songs. Until recently in Andhra Pradesh, *jogati*s were also expected to dance at the time of funeral processions in an act that reified their impure status and publicized their sexual availability to upper-caste men. As anthropologist Lucinda Ramberg succinctly puts it, the sexuality of *jogati*s is inevitably "bound up with economies of caste, gender, kinship and rural survival" (2006, 210). These communities began to attract the attention of the global media in the 1980s, when, as Ramberg notes, three significant social movements coalesced around them: (1) the assertion of Dalit party politics that deployed the language of "respectability" and "honour"; (2) local and global feminist mobilizations against forms of gender violence understood as endemic in these communities (these include the prominence of *jogati*s in UN reports related to child prostitution and sex trafficking); and (3) public health initiatives and NGO efforts to curb the spread of HIV among *jogati*s and other sex workers (Ramberg 2006, 10). Legal interventions specifically aimed at Dalit "*devadāsī*" communities are continually ongoing. The Karnataka Devadasis (Prohibition of Dedication) Bill of 1982 has been amended several times throughout the 1980s and 1990s, and most recently, in 2009, an amendment was made that would appoint and empower "Devadasi Dedication Prohibition Officers" who would, among other things, "collect evidence for the effective prosecution of the accused."[6] The Andhra Pradesh Devadasis (Prohibition of Dedication) Act of 1988 is similarly aimed at Dalit groups including "Basavi, Jogini, Parvathi, Mathamma and Thyamma."[7]

In contemporary South India, the term *devadāsī* has become intimately associated with the discourse of development and reform, and these composite historical images of *devadāsī*s travel as much through neoimperial circuits of knowledge as they do through state-endorsed historiographies. In a recent article for the *New Yorker*, for example, William Dalrymple sets out to uncover "the dangerous life of a sacred sex worker." He travels to Saundatti village, and following a description of HIV-positive *jogati*s, proceeds to tell his readers that these women "stand in the direct line of one of the oldest institutions in India." His historical narrative is speckled with dislocated references to *padam* songs danced by courtesans in Telugu-speaking South India and the politics of the anti-nautch movement.[8] Similarly, in a 2004 article for *Tehelka* magazine entitled "Reluctant Inheritors of a Tainted Legacy?" journalist Chinmayee Manjunath, also in search of the "inheritors" of the *devadāsī* tradition, speaks to Dalit *jogati*s in Saundatti:

> The children mill around the camera, fascinated; the women giggle when it is trained on them. I bring up the topic of how *devadasis* used to be, hoping that it will ignite memories. But I end up telling them their own history. The story of how *devadasis* were once accepted in society, how their forms of dance like *sadir* evolved into *bharatnatyam* and how their children inherited property from benefactors. How they were sanctified prostitutes, traded by priests and wealthy patrons. "We never knew that *devadasis* were even respected," gapes Rajeshwari [one of the *jogati*s]. "People don't even talk to us in our village."[9]

These narratives of decline inevitably see rural Dalit *jogati*s, *mātamma*s, and *basavi*s as remnants of the lost "temple dancers" of South India associated with aesthetic practices, matrilineal kinship, and colonial reform movements. These genealogies attempt not only to suture connections between unrelated and distinct groups of women, but also to posit a temple origin for the performing arts in South India, a claim that cannot be substantiated by critical readings of historical material. Contemporary Dalit *jogati*s, on account of the visible ritual dimensions of their lives, are coopted into the "temple narrative" of *devadāsī* historiography. In the piece cited above, the journalist "tells them their own history," sealing these false sutures, and more importantly, violating Dalit subjectivities.

Indeed, among the hundreds of scholarly writings on *jogati*s, rarely have their practices been historicized without reference to a fall from a celebrated, pan-Indian, "high" *devadāsī* tradition. This obfuscates the complexities of Dalit women's experiences and does little in terms of foregrounding issues of gender justice for Dalit women. Although, as the work of Priyadarshini Vijaisri (2004, 2010) has shown, it may be useful to contrast the trajectories of reform discourse between Dalit *jogatis* and non-Dalit courtesan communities in South India, I believe there is more to be gained by examining each on its own terms. This book then, is *not* about *jogatis*, nor should the issues surrounding *jogatis* be read too closely into this project—Dalit women's struggles are fundamentally very different from those experienced by the women described in my work.

The problems with contemporary representations of *devadāsīs* and *devadāsī* history, however, reach far beyond the issue of naming. Scholarly interpretations of *devadāsīs* can be located between two hermeneutic extremes: radical Marxist critiques on the one hand, that dismiss considerations of identity and agency contingent upon aesthetics or affect, and highly romanticized constructions on the other hand, that focus on recovering the image of the generic "temple dancer" in an effort to make contemporary *devadāsīs* "fit" into a civilizational metanarrative. Flowing through both of these interpretive perspectives is a narrative of degeneration that refuses to accept South Indian *devadāsīs* as perpetually ambiguous and controversial social subjects. The discursive frameworks of early twentieth-century reform debates fuel the narrative of degeneration. They use a limited vocabulary—such as that of "temple dedication," which saturates scholarship on the subject—and draw the moral ambiguity of *devadāsīs* to the center of public debate, leaving it open to interpretation and a number of ideological permutations.

In a sense, it is nearly impossible for the modern scholar to speak outside the received language of reform. Throughout this book, however, I supplement my use of the term *devadāsī* with the language of courtesanship, rarely used with reference to professional dancing women in South India. This is part of a larger epistemic agenda, in which I foreground the modernity of *devadāsīs*' social and aesthetic lives not as "temple women" but instead as professional artists in a shifting colonial sexual economy, exceeding the trope of *devadāsīs* as essentially religious subjects. I borrow the English language of courtesanship to strategically align my interpretation with the large, parallel body of critical studies that explore history, identity, and aesthetics in North Indian *tawā'if* or *bāījī* communities (for example, Babiracki 2003; Brown 2000, 2007b, 2007c; Cassio 2005; duPerron 2002, 2007; Maciszewski 1998, 2006, 2007; Oldenburg 1990; Post 1989; Qureshi 2006; V. Rao 1990; Sachdeva 2008; Walker 2004). Indeed, as I note toward the end of chapter 1, there are striking parallels (and perhaps even real historical connections) between these communities and those who are the focus of this book. These similarities extend beyond those around repertoire and aesthetics and permeate discussions of subjectivity and gender justice.[10]

The focus on the temple-based and religious lives of some *devadāsī*s in scholarly and popular writing—the scripting of *devadāsī*s as "temple dancers," in particular—has done much to efface the socioaesthetic realities of these women's lives in the nineteenth and twentieth centuries. Contemporary anthropologists (Marglin 1985; Kersenboom 1987) have deployed structuralist frameworks that have limited interpretations of *devadāsī*s, as Leslie Orr has noted, "almost entirely with reference to abstract, overarching conceptions such as *Śakti* ["sacred power"]or auspiciousness" (2000, 10). These totalizing symbolic and religious interpretations have reified historical narratives about the "degeneration" of *devadāsī*s and, in a sense, have come to justify the politics of revival and the reclamation of a "temple history" for modern Bharatanāṭyam dance by its middle-class, upper-caste practitioners. It is also significant that the temple focus on *devadāsī*s arises only once moral deliberations on these communities come to occupy center stage in twentieth-century Madras.[11] In this period, the South Indian temple emerges as an iconic site for discursive and ideological battles about the relationship between religion and the state, but also about modernity, class, and heritage (Waghorne 2004; Hancock 2008).

Standard historical accounts of *devadāsī*s thus fail to address, for example, salon performances in the homes of elite patrons, even though these are the most common site for *devadāsī* dance in this period. The salon performance, marked in Telugu by the Urdu word *mējuvāṇi* ("performed for a host"), was characterized by a number of heterogeneous dance and music genres that were unabashedly sexual and undeniably modern, and thus could not be mobilized by nationalist historians in their search for the "authentic," religious pasts of dance in South India. In the early twentieth century, with the emergence of popular drama (known as *icai nāṭakam*, or "special" *nāṭakam*) in the Tamil-speaking regions, private performances by *devadāsī*s often deployed hybrid visual and performance elements drawn from the Parsi theater (fig. 0.3). By the 1940s, *mējuvāṇi*-salon performances in the Godavari Delta included the presentation of popular Telugu film songs. As a discomfited emblem of modernity, the salon performance—the South Indian "nautch," in colonial parlance—is posited as *the* sign of the moral and aesthetic degeneration of the "*devadāsī* system."

The recovery of *devadāsī*s from South India's past has also been the result of very specific "archival desires" (Arondekar 2009) that have shaped

0.3 Sikkil Vedavalli and Kottanarvitu Pappa perform a dance drawing from aesthetic influences of the Parsi theater, c. 1920. Standing behind Vedavalli is Sikkil Ramaswami Nattuvanar (1876–1972).

the making of *devadāsī* historiography over the past century and a half. As feminist historian Anjali Arondekar notes in a recent work, "recuperations of the Devadasi are too often simply mimetic and literalizing, their presence materializing subjects of our own historical desire, rather than opening [up] . . . more complex understandings" (2011, 3). She continues, "Devadasis become figures of radical possibility because they hold out the anachronistic promise of a past fashioned from the desires of the present" (ibid., 4). Although I agree with Arondekar's position in terms of the scholarly "recuperation" of radical *devadāsī* pasts, this book argues that a methodology grounded in women's articulatory practices can help us avoid what Arondekar characterizes as the "mimetic and literalizing" scholarly interpretations of *devadāsī* lives. How do women within contemporary *devadāsī* communities stage a historical self-awareness? How are they attentive to the workings of patriarchy at large that resonate with forms of resistance recovered from the archive?

UNFINISHED HISTORIES AND MEMORY

> To articulate the past historically does not mean to recognize it "the way it was." It means to seize hold of a memory as it flashes by at a moment of danger.
> —Walter Benjamin, *Illuminations*

Methodologically, *Unfinished Gestures* stands at the disciplinary borderlands where history and anthropology intersect. At the same time, its theoretical orientations are culled from ethnomusicology, performance studies, dance history, gender and women's studies, and religious studies. The idea for this book emerged out of contemporary encounters with Tamil- and Telugu-speaking *devadāsī*s living on the margins of their communities.[12] I met women like Kotipalli Hymavathi (fig. 0.4), daughter of Kotipalli Manikyam, in the town of Muramanda in the East Godavari district of Andhra Pradesh, who opened up new ways of understanding *devadāsī* history as embedded in bodily habitus. Hymavathi became central to my project, and it was through Hymavathi's own interest in history and aesthetics that I was able to embark on ethnographic work in the *kalāvantula* community of coastal Andhra Pradesh. Women like Hymavathi invited me into self-consciously narrated stories of loss and disenfranchisement in the wake of social reform movements of the twentieth century. They also insisted that aesthetics were central to understanding the past and present from within the communities; nearly all our discussions of the past were punctuated by spontaneous performances of dance and music. Their mnemonic accounts and embodied modalities pointed to significant lacunae in the historicization of *devadāsī*s in the nineteenth and twentieth centuries, and these accounts became the catalyst for many of the arguments I make in this book.

One of my key aims in this book is to move our focus away from discussions of *devadāsī*s that have recovered them solely from within analyses of the structures of power—"the *devadāsī* system"—that complex terrain upon which the forces of indigenous patriarchy, colonialism, and nationalism play out an intense battle over debates between "tradition" and "modernity." In this book I do not wish to rehearse or challenge the fact that women in *devadāsī* communities were, and still are, subject to structural inequalities, and that "agency," understood in contemporary feminist terms, is, and for the most part has been, unavailable to most women in these communities. So while I am conscious of the imbrication of *devadāsī*s in what the feminist historian would identify as problematic

0.4 Kotipalli Hymavathi (b. 1950), Muramanda, East Godavari district, Andhra Pradesh.

structures of power, my ethnographic work within these communities opens up imaginative possibilities for understanding women's resilience under patriarchal constraints. This of course does not alter the structure of power and inequity but certainly foregrounds how individuals inhabit and subsequently cope with the spaces of civic, moral, and cultural margins. In other words, I hope, in parts of this book, to shift our attention away from the systemic to the individual; to examine forms of self-presentation, subjectivity, and autocritique that live among individuals in these communities today. The burdens of the unfinished projects of *devadāsī* reform undeniably fall on the shoulders of women such as those who are the subjects of the second half of this book.

This book has developed over a decade, oscillating between ethnographic work with women in the Kaveri and Godavari River deltas and archival research in Chennai (formerly Madras), Thanjavur, Kumbhakonam, Tiruchirappalli, Pudukkottai, Rajahmundry, Kakinada, Delhi, New York, and London. Its sources have been culled from a range of materials, and one of the great challenges of such a project has been the harmonization of oral, mnemonic materials with those taken from written archives and historiography. To be sure, much of this book is built upon the retrieval of literary and archival material. Chapter 1, for example, represents the first critical engagement with materials related to dance in colonial Tanjore, limited as they are. However, I hope to demonstrate that analyses that foreground only scripted archival sources or "embodied practices" are, on their own, inadequate when it comes to understanding the complex history of *devadāsīs* over the last two hundred years. In this book I demonstrate that a fruitful historicization of *devadāsīs* can only be actualized through rigorous interdisciplinary strategies.

My method bears an imprint of the work of performance studies scholar Diana Taylor, whose book *The Archive and the Repertoire: Performing Cultural Memory in the Americas* (2003) has shaped my understandings of the relationships between archive, ethnography, performance, and memory. In particular, Taylor's attentiveness to the constraints and possibilities of embodied and archival systems of knowledge has demonstrated the ways in which the study of performance must extend beyond "disciplinary preoccupations and methodological limitations" (7). According to Taylor, performance and memory map the gendered practices of individual and collective identity; in the spaces of the marginal or subaltern, "the telling is as important as the writing, the doing as central as the recording, the memory passed down through bodies and mnemonic practices" (35).

I also recognize the dangers in succumbing to the notion that ethnography as memory can answer all our questions, or that it can make up for the absences in the historical record. As Kamala Visweswaran notes, "ethnography, like fiction, no matter its pretense to present a self-contained narrative or cultural whole, remains incomplete and detached from the realms to which it points" (Visweswaran 1994, 1). Rather than approaching ethnographic data, therefore, as a repository of totalizing, counter-hegemonic claims opposed to the "errors" conveyed by written histories, I deploy ethnography to identify slippages; these disclose affective and visceral responses to historical processes that have eluded archival technologies.

Ann Gold and Bhoju Ram Gujar point out that "[m]emory has a 'thick autonomy'; its thickness reveals modes of embodiment, sensuousness, places, materiality, the everyday, and vanished landscapes" (2002, 84). When we think through memory-work with *devadāsīs*, these claims are even more pertinent, because in the evanescent moments of recalling dance, memory and the body are inseparable. To offer a concrete example, in March 2002, I was interviewing a group of five women, all over the age of seventy, from the *kalāvantula* courtesan community in the town of Mandapeta in coastal Andhra Pradesh. They had all performed professionally in a dance troupe in the 1940s. I began to ask them about the kinds of songs they performed in that period. One of the women started to sing a *jāvaḷi* (love lyric) in the *rāga* (tonic scale) Maṇiraṅgu, interpreting it through gesture. Spontaneously, the other four women joined her and, in the manner of Benjamin's mnemonic "flashes," the idea of a professional troupe (*mēḷam*) of courtesans and the performance style it engendered, which until then had only been dimly suggested in archival sources, became visible and tangible through embodiment. This act of recollection did not take the form of a discussion or carefully charted movement through memory; it was eruptive and affective. The memory of bodily habitus, in the form of the repertoire, allows us to perceive connections between history, language, and gestures of the body that would be invisible otherwise, and are impossible to house in the archive. These individual acts of remembering illuminate historical networks and reconfigure pathways for historical study.

The critical possibilities opened up by memory-work among *devadāsī* communities take us back repeatedly to somatic and aesthetic questions. But how can we convincingly account for the place that aesthetic experience holds in the lives of *devadāsī*s without reducing our interpretations to mere aestheticizations? The music and dance repertoire of *devadāsī*-courtesans, I argue, far from being incidental to the larger issue of their economic and political disenfranchisement, is essential to the question of their identities. Indeed, their art is not an ahistorical artifact; it is an embodied form of memory. As Taylor reminds us,

> The repertoire . . . enacts embodied memory: performances, gestures, orality, movement, dance, singing—in short, all those acts usually thought of as ephemeral, nonreproducible knowledge. Repertoire, etymologically "a treasury, an inventory," also allows for individual agency, referring also to "the finder, discoverer," and meaning "to find out." The repertoire requires presence: people participate in the production and reproduction of knowledge by "being there," being part of the transmission . . . The repertoire, like the archive, is mediated. The process of selection, memorization or internalization, and transmission takes place within (and in turn helps constitute) specific systems of representation. Multiple forms of embodied acts are always present, though in a constant state of againness. They reconstitute themselves, transmitting communal memories, and values from one group/generation to the next. (Taylor 2003, 20)

The eruptive and affective moments in my fieldwork that I have described above can perhaps be best understood when we think of the repertoire itself as a *living* site of memory. In his now classic essay "Between Memory and History: *Les Lieux de Mémoire*," Pierre Nora reminds us that "self-consciousness emerges under the sign of that which has already happened, as the fulfillment of something always already begun" (1989, 7)—in other words, as the unfinished. Nora places before us two modes of thinking about memory. The first is what he terms *milieux de mémoire* ("real environments of memory"), residing in "gestures and habits, in skills passed down by unspoken traditions, in the body's inherent self-knowledge, in unstudied reflexes and ingrained memories" (13). This is the realm of pure memory, unmediated, absolute, and spontaneous. The other is *lieux de mémoire* ("sites of memory"), which exist because *mileux de mémoire* have disappeared and are essentially fictional, mediated, and relative. *Lieux de mémoire* are commemorative of memory but can never substitute for it, and hence move us from the realm of pure memory into that of history. For Nora, "true memory" and "history" are the opposing ends of a binary, existing in a dialectic represented by the past and the present. *Lieux de mémoire* demand that "we must deliberately create archives, maintain anniversaries, organize celebrations . . . because such activities no longer occur naturally" (12).

When we examine acts of remembering in contemporary *devadāsī* communities, which rely so heavily on repertoire and spontaneous, embodied performance, they appear to lie in between Nora's categories. On the one hand, dance and music repertoire could easily be seen as a near-perfect *milieu de mémoire*. In their very personal acts of remembering, *devadāsī*s enter the realm of pure memory, a memory that lives through the body and affect. On the other hand, these mnemonic journeys could also be understood as "sites" that commemorate, through nostalgia, a past that no longer exists and an aesthetic that is no longer viable. Part of the difficulty when it comes to thinking about performance in the context of contemporary memory theory has been articulated by Taylor, and her insights are significant here. Taylor notes that Nora's differentiation "falls into a temporal before and after, a rift between past . . . and present" (Taylor 2003, 22). My work affirms Taylor's critique of Nora. Thinking through *memory as performance* and *performance as memory* reveals another kind of mnemonic culture that forces us to reconsider the temporal dimensions of Nora's *milieux* and *lieux*. Remembering is what connects *devadāsī* women to the past; it is a potent medium for *communitas*. A sequential construction of memory as *milieux* and *lieux* cannot capture the ways in which memory simultaneously functions as embodied present and a memorialized past. The embodied iteration of repertoire by *devadāsīs* also clearly traces the contexts of its emergence—histories of the colonial experience and marginality, for example, live in this repertoire. Indeed, performance is itself a way of making knowledge present, of dramatizing the subaltern experience. As an active site of memory, *devadāsī* repertoire need not always function as an emblem of social or political constraint. Repertoire, therefore, has a privileged place in this book, as both the catalyst for the memories of living *devadāsīs* and as the object that reconfigures our impression of what dance was like in prereform South India.

Memory-work discloses some of the real effects that social reform had in these communities. While several important works on the "official," recorded, and archival debates around anti-*devadāsī* legislation have been produced over the past three decades (for example, Hubel 2005; Inoue 2005; Jordan 1989; Kannabiran and Kannabiran 2003; Meduri 1996; Natarajan 1997; A. Srinivasan 1984; Sundara Raj 1993; Vijaisri 2004; Whitehead 1998, 2001), none of these has allowed us to understand exactly how public moral debates and the subsequent criminalization of women's lifestyles worked "on the ground." Mnemonic narratives reveal the undocumented side of these debates, at times deeply affecting and troublesome. Various parts of this book follow up on some of these unanswered questions: Were women prosecuted under the new legislation of 1947? How did individual women cope with these radical systemic transformations? A significant aim of this work, therefore, is to illuminate the unforeseen consequence and lingering signs of reform—such as the restitution of patriliny—in these communities.

These questions, however, cannot be answered only through memory-work with living *devadāsīs*. Substantial archives, some of which have remained unexplored, call out to be interpreted alongside the data gathered from ethnographic encounters. The archival sources deployed in *Unfinished Gestures* range from Marathi court records in Moḍi script from colonial Tanjore, to Tamil and Telugu literary materials that circulated in the early print culture of South India, to the personal files of reformer Muthulakshmi Reddy. These material collections, I contend, are also "unfinished" in the sense that they are bound by limitations in a manner parallel to that of performance and memory. The political and gendered subjectifications they house also require supplementation and, I would argue, meet their historical potential only when they are read together with sources that lie beyond them.

UNFINISHED CITIZENSHIP

> I appeal to you who are mothers to make the future of your children bright, happy, and glorious and make them respectable and useful citizens.
> —Muthulakshmi Reddy (1932, 614)

Another dimension of this book deals with issues of modernity and reform. The near-half-century-long public deliberations and two-decade-long legislative debates on *devadāsī*s in Madras resulted in the state-endorsed criminalization of their lifestyle through the Madras Devadasis Act of 1947. At stake in the contest over the status of *devadāsī*s was the tension between the archaic sign represented by recalcitrant *devadāsī* practices—the ritual of "dedication" (*poṭṭukkaṭṭutal*) and the mode of institutionalized concubinage, in particular—and the new sexual and moral economy represented by colonial and nationalist modernities. *Devadāsī*s, and especially the ritual of *poṭṭukkaṭṭutal*, were projected onto what Anne McClintock calls "anachronistic space: prehistoric, atavistic and irrational, inherently out of place in the historical time of modernity" (1995, 40). The *devadāsī* question was thus framed by a much larger reordering of sociopolitical agendas in the emergent nation-state, which by the beginning of the twentieth century included women as key emissaries of change. As Mrinalini Sinha points out, "the universalizing ambition in making women into a political constituency on the basis of their gender worked in . . . complex ways. It required the incorporation of the poor and of the working-class woman—even the female sex worker—to mobilize a construction of women as *both* the agents *and* the objects of reform" (2006, 191). The logic of reform, often articulated by women reformers, was ubiquitously couched in the language of a nationalist patriarchy that naturalized female chastity and marital fidelity and rendered it "part of the 'common sense' of the middle class" (J. Nair 1996, 148). This logic worked through the renegotiation of the public and private spheres, extending, through legal intervention, an accumulative intrusion of criminal law into the realm of sexuality.

And so at the core of *devadāsī* reform lies the pervasive class-inflected irony of Indian nationalism and early Indian feminism (Sarkar 2001; Sinha 1999, 2006). *Devadāsī* reform was necessarily an altruistic act, and in the discourse of "rescue," *devadāsī*s could only be marked as "victims."[13] As Srividya Natarajan observes,

> The women campaigners of the late nineteenth and early twentieth centuries thus became simultaneously symbols of freedom and self-determination (since most of them were highly educated and articulate) *and* norm-enforcing exemplars. They endorsed middle-class and patriarchal values, though they spent much of their lives mobilizing sympathy or aid for non-middle-class women. There is, consequently, a palpable tension between class and gender positions in most of the debates around the woman questions, especially in the debates on prostitution and on the *devadasi*s. The gender of the women campaigners allowed them—it was believed—to *feel* for the supposedly miserable *devadasis*; but since they were anchored to their superior caste/class position by their impeccable morals . . . this sympathy was prevented from becoming *identification*. The result was their attitude to the object of their altruism was invariably patronizing or censorious. (1997, 131; emphasis in the original)

The legal and bureaucratic regulation of *devadāsī* sexuality brought with it promises of a wholeness, a restructuring of the self based on middle-class sexual ethics. "Reformed" *devadāsī*s, those who were made into "good, pure, and respectable women," in Reddy's words, would be able to fully participate in the incipient modernity of the nation as citizens. *Devadāsī* reform certainly worked to consolidate a new nationalist modernity for middle-class women by setting up the *devadāsī* as the marked other, but it offered little to women within *devadāsī* communities. Each of the reformers I discuss in chapter 3, for example, go to great lengths to document and make public the names of "reformed" *devadāsī*s in the 1920s–1930s, likely because there were only a handful of such women. Many of the women who made "good wives" were singled out as exemplary *devadāsī*s (as in the case of the popular singer M. S. Subbulakshmi, for example) but the vast majority of *devadāsī*s did not, indeed could not, be integrated into the moral economy of the middle class. In the families of such unintegrated individuals, we encounter women's marginalization with all its complexities: some women are commercial sex workers in cities such as Chennai (Sariola 2010); some continue to live as the "second wives" of members of the civic elite; some settle into endogamous marriages; and the older generation of women who lived through the period of radical social reform, many of whom are the focus of this book, invariably see themselves as inhabiting the borderlands of modern citizenship.

The legacy of the failure of *devadāsī* reform and its subterfuges of respectability, I would argue, is visible in the "shame of not belonging" so evident in these communities today. Like the Tamil drama actresses who are the subjects of Susan Seizer's work, women in *devadāsī* communities today are almost wholly characterized by an "excess born of lack" (2005, 334). They are understood to embody a sexual "abundance that is primarily met with suspicion" (ibid.). Large numbers of these women live in a kind of social and civil limbo. In the Tamil-speaking regions, it is difficult for them to publicly claim caste status as "*icai vēḷāḷar* women" in schools, for example. Unlike the men in this community, women cannot invoke this caste position without it being understood as a euphemism. As I demonstrate in chapter 3, new caste identities provide social mobilization for men in the wake of *devadāsī* reform, usually at the expense of women. Nor are women sufficiently integrated into the social mainstream to be able to "pass" as non-*devadāsī*s. For the "first generation"—women who lived through social reform themselves—and usually also the second generation, "passing" is simply an impossibility—everyone seems to know who they *were*, and consequently, who they *are*. Women from *devadāsī* communities are particularly subject to moral suspicion and harassed in schools and other public spaces. These women are often accused of promiscuity and are the objects of name-calling; the public use of the Tamil words *tāci* or *tēvaṭiyāḷ* (terms that both denote "whore" and also index the *devadāsī* community) as insults are part of the quotidian negotiation of identity, stigma, and social discrimination that young women contend with in these communities. Their future prospects are almost always restricted to endogamous, arranged marriages, and these occur at a young age—usually as soon as the first available groom presents himself—in a kind of social paranoia about ensuring that girls do not "miss an opportunity" to become socially integrated.

The failure of reform and the spaces of social isolation it engendered for *devadāsī*s foreclosed possibilities for these women in other allied professions that they had only recently entered in the early twentieth century. Figures like Tirugokarnam Kanakambujam (1908–1973), a *devadāsī* from the Pudukkottai region, for example, became one of the first women to enter the largely male- and Brahmin-dominated field of public devotional oratory and singing known as *harikathā* or *kathākālakṣepam* (fig. 0.5), because it was professionally risky for her to continue with her dance training.[14] By the 1920s, a number of *devadāsī*s had joined the emergent world of popular Tamil drama, known variously as *icai nāṭakam, tamiḻ nāṭakam,* or "special" *nāṭakam*. Balamani Ammal, born into the *kavarai* merchant community near Kumbhakonam in Thanjavur district, for example, created the first all-woman theater company in Tamil Nadu in the first two decades of the twentieth century. Along with her sister Rajambal, she led the Balamani Drama Company, which created jobs for a number of disenfranchised *devadāsī*s at the height of public debates on social reform (fig. 0.6).[15]

Spaces such as Balamani's drama company and the new culture of gramophone recording opened up possibilities for *devadāsī* women in the early years of cinema. Almost all of the earliest female stars of Tamil cinema—T. R. Rajakumari, Sayi-Subbulakshmi, S. P. L. Dhanalakshmi, N. Rajalakshmi, Tiruvelveli Papa, and others—came from *devadāsī* families. Later, of course, they gave way to upper-caste, specifically Brahmin, women, in a move remarkably parallel to the dance "revival" for the 1930s–1940s, as M. S. S. Pandian noted well in a monumental essay on Tamil elites and cinema over a decade ago (Pandian 1996). Traces of *devadāsī*s as actresses remain in cinema today. Women from *devadāsī* backgrounds in the South Indian film industry are for the most part stigmatized and vilified by their peers in the field. Women such as Jyothilakshmi and Jayamalini, descendants of Tanjore Bhavani and her daughter Kuchalambal (who were among the last performers in the princely state), for example, entered South Indian cinema at a time when Brahmin women were already holding the reins, and were typecast as whores, vamps, and "item-dancers." By the 1950s, women from *devadāsī* families could simply no longer "make it" in the world of cinema, just as they could not in the new world of dance.

In this book, I am not concerned with those "exceptional" *devadāsī*s—

0.5 Tirugokarnam Kanakambujam (1908–1973) performing *harikathā* with her troupe. Photograph courtesy of Dr. B. M. Sundaram.

0.6 Balamani Ammal together with K. Rukmini (seated) in drama costume. Rukmini was from a Tamil-speaking *devadāsī* community of Pudukkottai and one of the prominent members of the Balamani Drama Company. Photograph courtesy of Dr. B. M. Sundaram.

the singers Bangalore Nagarathnam, M. S. Subbulakshmi, and M. L. Vasanthakumari or dancer T. Balasaraswati, for example—who achieved iconic status through the endorsement of their aesthetic value by the state and Madras's bourgeoisie. Rather, I turn my attention to women who did not enter the world of theater, gramophone recording, or cinema and certainly did not become performers of dance or music on the new, urban, middle-class stage. These are the women for whom postreform "respectability" was impossible in any shape or form.

UNFINISHED AESTHETICS

> Why should I show anyone this dance? What's the use? I *know* that no one can appreciate it today.
> —Jakkula Radha, Peddapuram

Much of this book is deeply influenced by perspectives drawn from the work of Partha Chatterjee, Ranajit Guha, and other members of the Subaltern Studies collective. Their work has drawn attention to the inventive agency of the colonized and has shaped our discussions of colonial modernity in significant ways. Sustained discussion of *devadāsīs* as subalterns first appeared in the work of Avanthi Meduri (1996), and this compelling and highly cogent study has left a long-standing impression on subsequent works, including my own. In this book, however, I wish to move beyond simply locating *devadāsīs* in the spaces of subalternity, advancing instead a hermeneutic mode that allows us to address the place of aesthetics in the subaltern consciousness. In contrast to Meduri, who thinks of performance as a totalizing experience in which "the *devadāsī* learned to empty her subjectivity" (1996, 22), ethnography with contemporary *devadāsī* women forces us to reconsider the role of performance in fashioning subjectivity. *Unfinished Gestures* follows the orientation of Amelia Maciszewski's ethnography with *tawā'if* courtesans in North India. In her account, "[the performer] is both an object of the (male) gaze and purveyor of her own artistic (and professional) gaze—thus simultaneously subsuming her individual identity into the extant artistic form *and* deploying her creative agency within it" (1998, 88). So without losing sight of the patriarchal location of *devadāsī* culture or the fact that it is nearly impossible to speak of a "pure aesthetics" in modern South India outside the space of politics, I think of performance as a key modality of subaltern self-presentation and self-consciousness. For devadāsīs, performance is both the *subject* of their history and the *medium* through which they express it. Their performances have aesthetic, mnemonic, and affective values that demand our attention. In other words, my analyses of genre and movement do not represent mere evaluative judgments of artworks, but rather a means of taking *devadāsī* performance practices seriously as embodied history. These practices both reference reform's expurgations and preserve a performance style—sexually explicit, casual, "unclassical"—that is not palatable to the urban middle class. It is this *present* historicity, available only through the performance itself, that cuts through the many layers of idealized representation and enables us to address stigma, history, and *devadāsī* identity itself in more productive ways.

I want to suggest that the disappearance of *devadāsī* dance from the public sphere has to be understood in the context of specific taste hierarchies that were created in the early part of the twentieth century. Although a number of scholars have described the caste politics that undergirded the so-called "dance revival" of the mid-twentieth century, very rarely has this been discussed in terms of the cultivation of specific taste habits among the elites of Madras. Historians and theorists of popular culture in North America have noted that a key marker of the postmodern condition is the blurring of visual and social boundaries between "high" and "low" culture. While critiques against this Pierre Bourdieu–style class-based bifurcation of taste could certainly be applied when we talk about some forms of popular culture in India (here, I am thinking specifically of commercial cinema, for example), this is not the case with arts that have been marked as "classical" by the Indian state. These arts, by their very social and political constitution, were trapped in class- and caste-inflected stratifications of taste. Upper-caste, nationalist reinventions of Bharatanāṭyam combined social power with cultural capital and highbrow taste. While non-Brahmin individuals do marginally participate in the professional world of Bharatanāṭyam today, it is almost always to reify and even valorize the aesthetic parameters of Brahmin aspirations. The construction of what Kristen Rudisill (2007) in her study of modern Tamil theater has called "Brahmin taste" is significant in terms of its implications for twentieth-century dance history as well.

The South Indian cultural bourgeoisie, and practitioners of Bharatanāṭyam in particular, are quick to assess the past in terms of this hierarchy of taste. In the popular imagination, *devadāsī* dance is understood as both aesthetically impoverished and morally dubious. Loose limbs, footwork, and *mudrā*s, or unstructured improvisation, explicit and excessive eroticism (articulated by the Tamil-speaking middle class as *paccai ciṅkāram*, "raw eroticism"), lack of emphasis on "proper" *rāga* and *tāla* (rhythm)—these are the aspects of *devadāsī* performance that were and continue to be configured as "in bad taste." The perceived aesthetic falsehood of *devadāsī* dance in particular is trumped by the supposed antiquity and universality of religious values that appear embedded in modern Bharatanāṭyam. *Devadāsī*s are an embarrassing sign of India's feudal past for the middle class, even as the reinvented Bharatanāṭyam is constructed as an enabling, "classical" tradition. Just as *devadāsī*s could not be accommodated as citizens by the modern nation-state on account of their nonconjugal sexuality and caste location, their aesthetic practices, constructed in opposition to the taste habits of the nation, cannot be accommodated today. As a living sign of the past, the persistence of dance in contemporary *devadāsī* communities *despite* the efforts of reform forces us to reconsider the loose ends of the anti-nautch movement and the horizons of modernity and citizenship it promised for *devadāsī*s. Located on the borderline between the demise of colonial courtly culture and the industry of "classical" dance in the twentieth century, these performance practices, like the social location of *devadāsī*s, elude obvious categories. Suspended, hybrid, and polysemous, I understand *devadāsī* subjectivity as symptomatic of what Antoinette Burton (1999) has called the "unfinished business of colonial modernity."

CHAPTER ONE

Producing Dance in Colonial Tanjore

Tanjore possesses the distinction of being the original home of the Indian Nautch, born in the shadow of the great Pagoda, and still blending the religious associations of the mystic past with the passionate imagery of love, sorrow, and despair, woven into a thousand forms by the symbolical poetry of motion. The Nautch girls of Tanjore stand at the head of their profession, and no important function of the native Courts is considered complete without the presence of these ideal dancers, clad in filmy muslins and golden tissues clasped with jewels and roped with pearls, the costly tribute paid to their irresistible charms.
—Anonymous British writer, 1894[1]

You know why I can dance like this? My father's teacher was Kumarasvami Nattuvanar of Tanjore!
—R. Muttukkannammal, Viralimalai

The relationship between dance and colonial Tanjore looms large in both the European and Indian imagination. In European contexts, dancing in Tanjore has been commented upon since at least 1661, when the Icelandic sailor-soldier Jon Olafsson arrived at the city and wrote about *devadāsī*s and *naṭṭuvaṉār*s (Tamil for "dance masters") during the rule of King Raghunātha Nāyaka (r. 1612–1634) in his memoirs.[2] Since then, professional dancing women from Tanjore have almost universally been understood in European writings as the most accomplished "nautch girls" of South India. Contemporary *devadāsī*s living as far away as coastal Andhra remember *salām-daruvu*s (songs of "salutation") dedicated to the Marāṭhā kings of Tanjore such as Pratāpasiṃha, Tuḷajā, and Serfoji.[3] *Devadāsī*s in Pudukkottai, a nearby Tamil-speaking region, nostalgically celebrate the achievements of their teachers who were trained by masters from Tanjore. Both groups attribute the complexity and rigor of their training and repertoire to the development of the dance under the patronage of the Marāṭhā kings at Tanjore, and inevitably commit to memory aesthetic genealogies that reach back into the late eighteenth and nineteenth centuries.

Unfinished Gestures begins, therefore, with a discussion of dance in colonial Tanjore. In nearly all writing on *devadāsī*s—from colonial accounts to contemporary nationalist historiographies—this location emerges as the cultural epicenter of South India. Although contemporary dance historians and historiographers privilege Tanjore's centrality in their narratives, and several scholarly works have addressed the issues raised by its music (Seetha 1981; L. Subramanian 2006; Weidman 2006), a critical examination of its courtly dance practices is almost entirely lacking.[4] This chapter thus attempts to unpack the complexities of performance at the nineteenth-century Tanjore court. It winds through the social and aesthetic topography of Tanjore performance culture, mapping the domain using court records and literary sources.

Motivated by ethnographic encounters in which Tanjore is imagined as a site of remembrance, I turn to the archive to assess what kinds of identities and subjectivities colonial Tanjore made available to *devadāsī*s. What emerges in this chapter is a picture of professional dancing women embedded in complex political and aesthetic economies. "*Devadāsī*" proves not to be as stable a category of identity as scholars have thought. Indeed, the word does not appear anywhere in the Marathi court records themselves. Instead, we can discern considerable slippage between a number of social categories—dancing woman, concubine, and court servant, for example—a fact that emphasizes the contentious status of women in nonconjugal roles. In terms of aesthetics, identifying consistent practices for *devadāsī*s (in terms of genre, language, musical style and occasion) is even more difficult, given the radical eclecticism of art produced in Tanjore. Such eclecticism, and the accelerated cultural production to which it gave rise, become *the* mark of modernity in this context. This unique moment in the history of Indian dance was in many ways made possible by a unique Tanjorean cosmopolitanism directed by the distinctly modern figure King Serfoji II (1798–1832). As Indira Peterson has noted, Serfoji cultivated a "personal style" of kingship deploying improvisational strategies that enabled multiple modes of representation and historical agency (1998b; 2002).

The court produced a peculiar, syncretic culture that integrated aspects of indigenous Tamil and Telugu literary material, the new Mughal-style Marāṭhā courtly practices from Maharashtra, and the modernity of the European Enlightenment. Serfoji II and his heir Śivājī II (r. 1832–1855) deployed courtesan dancers in their rituals of display, casting themselves as rulers who, though incrementally divested of political authority by the British, were nevertheless effective, modern patrons of culture. The Tanjore court thus exemplifies the ways in which *devadāsī*s were instrumentalized as emblems of cultural capital in the context of an emergent colonial modernity. The presence of a Western-style band, North Indian (Hindustāni) musicians of a high caliber, and the integration of Western music into the dance repertoire, distinguished Serfoji's court as an early theater of cultural experimentation.

It is significant, however, that Tanjore was different from other princely states in several regards. As Peterson (2010) has pointed out, Tanjore had a distinct relationship with the colonial state, and as Serfoji's own career indicates, Tanjore was also among the earliest states to improvise a culture of what Manu Bhagavan has called "princely modernity" (2003). The interventions made by rulers in the better-known princely states of Mysore and Baroda follow those forged by Serfoji and Śivājī II in late eighteenth- and early nineteenth-century Tanjore. Peterson points out that Tanjore's relationship with the colonial state and with the emergent culture of nationalism was quite different than that of the other princely states. Peterson has demonstrated in more than one instance how Serfoji's very individualistic improvisations on cultural patronage and bureaucracy "underscore the importance of attending to the multiplicity of discourses and conversations among diverse agendas embodied in the construction of princely modernity" (Peterson 2010, 5).

Devadāsī dance, as we understand it, emerges in this already-modern milieu. In the early nineteenth century, the dance is already participating in global circuits of culture. The moment celebrated by nationalist historians as the "golden age" of dance at Tanjore—usually the time of the famed dance masters known as the "Tanjore Quartet" (1802–1864)—is contemporaneous with the transnational movement of dancers across imperial axes. In 1838, a troupe of *devadāsī*s from Tiruvendipuram, just outside Pondicherry, was brought to Europe by French impresario E. C. Tardivel (Bor 2007). As the celebrated *naṭṭuvaṉār*s and *devadāsī*s of Serfoji's court are shaping their illustrious dances, other *devadāsī*s are billed as "Hindoo slaves of the gods" on elite stages in London, Brighton, Brussels, Frankfurt, Munich, Berlin, and Vienna.

DANCE IN PRE-MARĀṬHĀ TANJORE

Indologists and nationalist historiographers advance the claim that today's Bharatanāṭyam, as a descendant of *devadāsī* dance, has its origins in the Tamil Caṅkam age (c. 300 BCE to 300 CE). A critical reading of courtesan dance, however, can only begin with the Telugu-speaking Nāyaka courts at Tanjore and Madurai in the late sixteenth and seventeenth centuries. To be sure, professional dancing women, courtesans, prostitutes, and temple women are found throughout South India's literary, epigraphic, and oral histories. The female bards (*viṟali*) of the ancient Tamil Caṅkam poems, the courtesan Mātavi of the Tamil epic *Cilappatikāram*, the temple woman Paravaiyār of the Tamil Śaiva *bhakti* tradition, the four hundred "women of the temple quarter" (*taliccēri peṇṭukaḷ*) mentioned in King Rājarāja Cōḻa's famous eleventh-century inscription at the Bṛhadīśvara temple in Tanjore—these could all be construed as predecessors of eighteenth- and nineteenth-century *devadāsī*-courtesans.[5] For our purposes, however, it is important that these scattered and fragmentary references to temple women, court dancers, and other "public women" only coalesce in the Nāyaka period, when these hitherto independent roles are fully collapsed and the identity of the "*devadāsī*," as I see it—with simultaneous investments in temple, courtly, and public cultures, complex dance and music practices, and matrifocal kinship structures—emerges (Narayana Rao, Shulman, and Subrahmanyam 1992, 187). In the Nāyaka period, the *devadāsī*-courtesan appears as a distinct cultural presence, inextricably linked to sophisticated articulations of courtly eroticism. Narayana Rao, Shulman, and Subrahmanyam characterize the culture of the Nāyaka court as directed toward the telos of *bhoga*, or enjoyment (57). This culture of *bhoga*, of erotic longing and fulfillment, is one in which the boundaries between courtesans (*bhoga-strī, veśyā*) and temple women have become indistinguishable. Their new role as artists who performed at both temple and court allowed these women to be imaged as mistresses, wives, or even queens at the Nāyaka court (187).

The Nāyaka court at Tanjore also supported creative writing by courtesans; works by Rāmabhadrāmba and Raṅgājamma, for example, are considered among the crowning literary pieces from this period.[6] This is also the period when the erotic poems (*padams*) of Kṣetrayya were composed, perhaps partially under the patronage of King Vijayarāghava Nāyaka (r. 1634–1673). The *padams* of Kṣetrayya, which continue to survive in the repertoire of the Telugu *devadāsī* community today, reflect innovative images of womanhood and a unique world of fully eroticized aesthetic practices. Many of these songs express female desire and are completely unabashed in their representations of the corporeality of sexual experience. It is against this backdrop that we find the names of a number of professional dancing women at the Nāyaka *darbār* in Tanjore.[7] Most significantly, however, the *substance* of the surviving aesthetic practices of *devadāsīs*—the lyric genre of *padam*, a lineage of hereditary male dance masters (*naṭṭuvaṉārs*), and musical genres such as *śabdam* (usually in praise of royal patrons or localized deities)—can only be traced as far back as the Nāyaka period.

MARĀṬHĀ-PERIOD TANJORE AND THE TANJORE MOḌI RECORDS

Marāṭhā rule in South India succeeded that of the Nāyakas. On January 12, 1676, Veṅkojī Bhosale, the half-brother of Chatrapati Śivājī (1627–1680), ascended the throne of Tanjore. Veṅkojī was succeeded by his sons, Śāhajī (r. 1684–1712); Śarabhojī [Serfoji] I (r. 1712–1728); Tuḷajā I (r. 1728–1736), and later by Veṅkojī II (also known as Bāvā Sāheb, r. 1736–1739), son of Tuḷajā I. By the time Pratāpasiṃha (1739–1763), another son of Tuḷajā, came to power, Tanjore found itself slipping into fiscal decline, under pressure from both the Nawab of Arcot and the East India Company, a development that has been meticulously mapped by Sanjay Subrahmanyam (2001). Following Pratāpasiṃha's death in 1763, his son Tuḷajā II (r. 1763–1787) ascended the throne. Tuḷajā ruled until 1787 when, on his deathbed, he adopted a young boy, Serfoji II. Upon the death of Tuḷajā II, however, a controversy arose regarding the legitimacy of the adopted boy-prince Serfoji's right to rule Tanjore. With the aid of a group of *pandit*s, Amarasiṃha (r. 1787–1798), Tuḷajā's half-brother, ascertained that the adopted son could not be the heir, and installed himself on the throne in 1788. Serfoji and two of Tuḷajā's queens were exiled to Madras, where Serfoji was educated by Wilhelm Gericke of the Lutheran Mission. Through appeals to the court of the Board of Directors in England and the interventions of the German missionary Christian Frederick Schwartz (1726–1798), Serfoji was eventually restored to Tanjore. He ascended the throne on October 25, 1799, after signing a treaty that handed all administrative control of the Tanjore kingdom to the British, in return for which the king and his family retained control over the Tanjore fort and some of its secondary institutions (temples and choultries, for example), received an annual stipend of 350,000 Company rupees, and could claim a right to one-fifth of the net revenues of the kingdom. Serfoji II died on March 8, 1832, and was succeeded by his son Śivājī II, who ruled until 1855. It is during the rule of Serfoji and Śivājī that Tanjore develops its unique cosmopolitanism in the context of what Nicholas Dirks has termed a "hollow" kingship (1993), actualized largely through display and performative practices.[8] Śivājī died on October 29, 1855, and in April of 1856, the title of "raja of Tanjore" was declared extinct for lack of a male heir as per the government's Doctrine of Lapse, and the Tanjore Raj was annexed to the British government. On October 18, 1856, Gordon Forbes, the commissioner of Tanjore, took possession of the Fort of Tanjore, and the lands held by the late raja Śivājī. Backed by public sympathy in the form of petitions from the Madras Native Association, Kāmākṣī Ambā Bāī Sāheb (d. 1892), a senior widow of Śivājī, and her agent, John Bruce Norton (1815–1883), fought a seven-year-long legal battle against the colonial government. On August 21, 1862, the Madras government granted the palace estate back to Kāmākṣī Bāī.

The official records of Marāṭhā rule in Tanjore are written in Moḍi script, which likely evolved as a "shorthand" form of Bālabodha (Devanāgari), in a manner similar to the development of Shikasta script out of Nastaliq for Persian (Strandberg 1983, 24–25).[9] The records provide a number of important details about the fiscal, political, and cultural developments in Tanjore under the Marāṭhā rule. In the middle of the twentieth century, the Tanjore Moḍi documents were divided, rather haphazardly, into three collections: one very small one held by the Sarasvati Mahal Library; one held by the Tamil University, Thanjavur; and a third held by the Tamil Nadu State Government Archives at Egmore, Chennai.[10] Of these, the set from Tamil University has been translated into Tamil and published in three volumes (Venkataramaiya and Vivekanandagopal 1984; Venkataramaiya 1985). Selections from the set at Sarasvati Mahal have been summarized (Shelvankar 1933), and a small number have recently been translated (Vivekanandagopal 1999). For the purposes of this study, I will also be referring to an unpublished selection of the Sarasvati Mahal Library set, transcribed by the library's Marāṭhī *pandit* G. Nagaraja Rao (1902–1973) and musicologist B. M. Sundaram in 1955.[11]

WOMEN AND THE PRODUCTION OF CULTURE

In order to understand the conditions of professional dancing women at Tanjore, we must delineate the roles afforded to women in the courtly milieu. All women at the Tanjore court, from the official queens (*mahārāṇīs*) to the servant-girls of concubines, were implicated in a symbolic order that attempted to exhibit the power of courtly culture to colonial audiences and beyond. In many cases, women's agency was severely curtailed in this process—women and young girls were regularly bought and sold through the intercession of the court, for example—but in other cases, elite courtly women exercised a degree of administrative and cultural power, as we shall see in some of the examples below. Roles for palace women were diverse and hierarchically organized at the Tanjore court in the nineteenth century. In the section that follows, I delineate the four major categories of palace women as we encounter them in the Moḍi records: queens, concubines, servants of the concubines, and entertainers. Even within each of these categories, there is a great deal of variation in terms of the privileges such women were afforded and the constraints under which they lived. Courtesans bear important resemblances to queens, concubines, and slaves, resemblances that underscore the fact that they inhabited positions whose social purposes were never fully elaborated.

The Marāṭhā Queens (Bāī Sāheb)

Much has been written about the orthodox and conservative paradigms of womanhood that were fostered at Tanjore among the queens (Leslie 1989). Undoubtedly, as elite women, the Tanjore queens were subject to a rigorous code of conduct, which included living in near-complete purdah, known among the Tanjore Marāṭhās as *kośa* or *rāphtā*. We also know that women such as Sulakṣaṇāmbā Bāī and Rājasā Bāī, the wives of king Pratāpasiṃha, committed sati in Tanjore (Venkataramaiya 1984, 317–320).[12] Polygamy and concubinage were also key dimensions of courtly life at Tanjore during the eighteenth and nineteenth centuries, and it is often difficult to distinguish one from the other, since courtly concubinage at Tanjore was solemnized by a ceremony of marriage known as *katti kalyāṇam*, which I discuss below. Śivājī II did not father any fully legitimate male children, and so to ensure that he would produce an heir, eighteen young women from Maharashtra were brought to Tanjore to become his queens in 1852, just three years before he died. Senā Dhuraṅdhara Ṛturāja Ānandarāja Jādav, a high-ranking court official, was sent to Maharashtra to procure these women.

Despite these images of elite forms of extreme subjugation, two queens—Sujan Bāī (from the eighteenth century) and Kāmākṣī Bāī (from the nineteenth century)—stand out because of their political enfranchisement. Why these women attained political sovereignty remains an open question. Sujan Bāī (r. 1737–1740) succeeded her husband, Veṅkojī II [Bāvā Sāheb], as queen of Tanjore for a period of three years. Little is known about her, but she was cited by Kāmākṣī Bāī in the latter's bid to gain the title of heir to the Tanjore kingdom, following the death of her husband, Śivājī II, in 1855. Kāmākṣī Bāī took the colonial government to task for denying her the title of heir, and for the roughly £700,000 that was attached to the Tanjore kingdom (Norton 1858, 162). She took her suit to the Supreme Court in London, arguing that women could claim succession in the absence of a male heir.

Morganatic Wives: The Concubines of Kalyāṇa Mahal and Maṅgala Vilāsam

Between roughly 1824 and 1845, Serfoji II and his son Śivājī II built large seraglios called Kalyāṇa Mahal and Maṅgala Vilāsam, respectively, that housed dozens of concubines who bore the titles *bāī* or *ammāḷ* ("respected lady"). The seraglio of Serfoji II was known as Kalyāṇa Mahal and was built in 1824 on the banks of the Kaveri River in Tiruvaiyaru (fig. 1.1). Maṅgala Vilāsam is the name given to a structure that housed the concubines of Śivājī on South Main Street in Tanjore city (fig. 1.2). Both structures are made up of several dozen rooms and other chambers. The concubines, whose relationships with the kings were solemnized through a "sword marriage" (*katti kalyāṇam*), came from a strikingly diverse range of caste and regional backgrounds, and in Śivājī's time included Tamil Christian women, Tamil Brahmin women from the *ayyaṅkār* or Vaiṣṇava community, and various groups of Maharashtrian women. Although the tradition of maintaining "sword wives" is known to have existed at least since the rule of Tuḷajā I (1728–1736), the most detailed accounts of these women come from the records of Śivājī's rule. The women are known, as are the Marāṭhā queens, by the Marathi honorific, *bāī* ("respected lady"). These wives were distinguished by the *kattikaṭṭi vivākam* ("marriage to the dagger"), also called *katti kalyāṇam, khaḍga vivāham*, or *talvār lagna* a rite that guaranteed them status as Śivājī's morganatic wives but did not confer upon them the title of *mahārāṇī*.

This *katti kalyāṇam* is significant for several reasons. Some professional dancing women underwent a similar rite called *poṭṭukkaṭṭutal* (tying of the *poṭṭu* [pendant]) in which they were "dedicated" to daggers in temple contexts. As I will argue later, the *poṭṭukkaṭṭu* ceremony for dancing women needs to be understood in relation to the *katti kalyāṇam* ritual of palace concubines (even those in smaller kingdoms, or *zamīndāris*), instead of being glossed as a "marriage" to a temple deity. Both ceremonies mark women as set aside for nonconjugal sexual roles, primarily as

1.1 Kalyāṇa Mahal, the seraglio of King Serfoji II, on the banks of the Kaveri at Tiruvaiyaru. Photograph by the author.

1.2 Maṅgala Vilāsam, the seraglio of King Śivājī II, on South Main Street in Tanjore. Photograph by the author.

concubines. Seen in this manner, the "dedication" rituals so fetishized in scholarship on *devadāsīs* has less to do with theological symbolism than it does with economic investments. The *poṭṭukkaṭṭutal* is fundamentally a lifecycle ritual that binds a woman to the sexual economy of the courtesan lifestyle, and for the women of the Tanjore seraglios, the *katti kalyāṇam* had the same significance.[13]

Palace Servants (akkā, akkāmār, akkā kūṭṭam)

There is no doubt that slavery was a major part of the economy of the Tanjore Marāṭhā kingdom. Female servants of the *mahārāṇīs* and concubines are referred to as *akkā* ("elder sister"). Their significance here has to do with the fact that they, like professional dancing women, were regularly bought and sold through the intercession of the court. The mechanisms for obtaining slaves, dancers, and perhaps even concubines were the same (Venkataramaiya 1985, 326–328). Young girls who were orphaned or destitute were often bought by the court in order to have a *poṭṭu* tied and then given to a courtesan household, or simply brought to work as the servants of other palace women. Many also lived with the concubines in the seraglios.

The similarity between courtesans and other palace servants has to do with the severe restrictions placed on their behavior. While courtesans enjoyed certain liberties not afforded to other women (literacy, for example), their lives were subject to administration and surveillance by court authorities. A number of Moḍi records point to punishments and restrictions for court performers. In 1825, for example, Nāgu, the daughter of a *dāsī* named Aṟiku, was fined when her bullock cart crossed in front of the cart of the British resident who was on his way to inspect damage caused by floods in the area.[14] During the reign of Serfoji, an extensive Moḍ i document enumerates the restrictions placed on clothing and accessories worn by courtesans and male dance masters (*naṭṭuvaṉārs*; Shelvankar 1933; Radhika 1996). In this regard, the restrictions on courtesans at Tanjore bear striking resemblance to those imposed on women who worked as part of the *kaḷāvant khāta* or *karkhānā* ("artist's workshop") in the service of the Gaekwad rulers of Baroda.[15] As Bakhle (2005, 22–49) has demonstrated, in the late nineteenth century, as part of a bureaucratic overhaul that sought to replicate the administration of a British district, Maharaja Sayajirao Gaekwad III codified rules for the behavior of performing artists, including courtesans, through the creation of official manuals such as *Kaḷāvant Khātyāce Niyam* (Rules for the Artists' Department). Although these developments at Baroda are considerably later than those at Tanjore, they foreground the fact that artists in the princely states were severely monitored and controlled by the state. Courtesans, perhaps even more so, were understood as ornaments of palace life. They were undoubtedly involved in patriarchal sexual economies and were also clearly regarded as property that could be given, sold, or exchanged. Given the hierarchies of servitude at work in colonial Tanjore, it is safe to say that "slavery" in this context covered a range of occupational positions attended by varying levels of constraint.

IDENTIFYING PROFESSIONAL DANCERS IN THE MOḌI RECORDS

Professional dancing women are identified by three terms in the Moḍi records: (1) *dāsī*; (2) *kalāvantīṇ* or *kalāvant*; and (3) *sūḷe* or its derivative *sūḷyā*. The presence of professional dancers in the Moḍi records is matched by the rather ubiquitous presence of male dance masters known in Tamil as *naṭṭuvaṉār*s but who commonly appear in the records as *naṭavā* or *naṭhamuṭhagāra*. However, I will defer discussion of these figures to the latter part of this chapter. The term *dāsī* ("servant, slave") is normally prefixed to the given name of a woman—*dāsī* Kāvēri, *dāsī* Ciṉṉikuṭṭi. It is used specifically with reference to women who have had the *poṭṭu* tied, almost always at one of the local temples that fall within the purview of the Tanjore palace *devasthānam*, which controlled about ninety temples in and around the city.

The terms *kalāvantīṇ* and *kalāvant* ("embodiment of art") were widely used in Maharashtra in the eighteenth century to refer to courtesans and professional dancers, and they are frequently used in Tanjore.[16] Their presence in the Moḍi records is a reminder of the legacy of courtesan performance among elites in Maharashtra. In eighteenth-century Maharashtra, under the rule of figures such as Peśvā Bājīrāv I (r. 1720–1740)[17] and Peśvā Bājīrāv II (r. 1796–1818), professional dancers called *kalāvantīṇ* regularly performed music and dance at the court, and some of these women, such as Veṅkaṭ Narsī Karṇāṭakī, were of South Indian origin.[18] Similarly, the names of Marathi-speaking courtesans such as *dāsī* Hīrā appear in the Moḍi records of Tanjore.[19] As we shall see later, the performance practices of the Maharashtrian *kalāvantīṇ*—such as North Indian ("Hindustānī") music and dance, and uniquely Marathi genres such as *lāvaṇī*—were key components of courtesan performance in Tanjore.

The term *sūḷe* or *sūḷyā* is likely from the Sanskrit *śūlā*, meaning prostitute. The term is very common in Kannada and frequently occurred in early medieval Kannada inscriptions (Parasher and Naik 1986).[20] A few Moḍi documents refer to *devadāsī* performance as *sūḷyā meḷa* (a *mēḷam* or troupe of *sūḷe*), and this term can be understood to index the sexual availability of the women. The extant records, unfortunately, do not furnish details about the sexual activity of courtesans who are implicated in systems of institutionalized concubinage. The archive, on this front, fails us, and this is a significant issue that can only be addressed through personal narratives and ethnography. The women who are the subjects of chapters 4 and 5 provide rich accounts of the relationships they had with men and the ways in which they represented the erotic in their professional lives.

It is significant that the vocabulary that contemporary scholars tend to associate with performance in nineteenth-century Tanjore—such as *devadāsī*, *catir*, or *ciṉṉamēḷam* (both Tamil terms that refer to dancing by courtesans)—is not found in the Moḍi documents. I would suggest that these were South Indian vernacular terms that did not find a place in the "official" state records that employed a somewhat formulaic style borrowed from the courtly records of seventeenth-century Maharashtra (Strandberg 1983). Typically, Moḍi records referring to dance provide us with the names of dancing women and their musical accompanists. Most also refer specifically to economic transactions or simply list the fees paid to the artists. Cash payments are usually in the form of *cakram*s, small coins worth approximately one and three-quarters of a Company rupee, and *paṇam*s, worth approximately one-sixth of a Company rupee. Figure 1.3 represents a fragment from a Moḍi record from 1797 about dance from the time of Serfoji II. The text of the record reads as follows:

> Order from a lower rank (*yāde*): The following *sūḷe* and their troupe are sent to perform dance in fulfillment of the endowment (*kaṭṭaḷai*) to the Lord at Tiruvaiyāṟu during the full moon (*pūrṇimā*) festival in the month of Sha'ban [March–April] 1797: Ciṉṉakkuṭṭi, Koḻantai, and Ciṉṉamuttu, with the *naṭṭuvaṉ* Rāmasvāmi, vocalist Nārāyaṇa, drummer Nāgaliṅgam, Pañcanadi of Palakkarai [presumably the flutist], and the drone-keeper (*tutti*) Muttukkaruppaṉ. These eight persons should be given 11.5 *cakram*s in addition to food, etc., [while they are] at Tiruvaiyāṟu. Signed Lakṣmaṇa Rāv Bhoṃsale, witnessed by Rāmasvāmi.
>
> [yāde: trivādī devasthānī śrī svāmī kaṭale kī saundarapāṃḍika bhāṇḍāraka sū samāna tīsaina mayā alaja ḍāra sīmagī paurṇimā badala deula bhārapaikī *sūḷyā* va meḷa hiśā cha 3 śābāna hajara kela asa ā sūḷyā 1 sīnakuṭṭī, 1 koḷaṃde, 1 sīnamutu, meḷa ātā 1 naṭavā

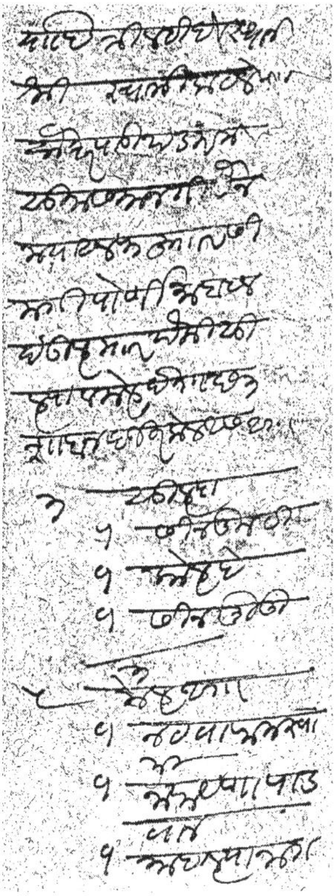

1.3 Moḍi record (TSML 101-5/15 1797) dated 1797.

rāmasvāmī 1 nārāyaṇā pāḍavāna, 1 māhaḷyā nāgaliṃgam 1 pālekarī paṃcenadī 1 tutivālā mutūkarapan padara asi dara 8 || pā ā 8 dara 11. ṣā yeśā ā 8 sa
hastākṣara
Lakṣmaṇa Rāv Bhoṃsale
jabāni
Rāmasvāmi
cār śābāna]

PROFESSIONAL DANCERS, TEMPLES, AND *POṬṬUKKAṬṬUTAL* IN COLONIAL TANJORE

Some women who performed dance at the court underwent a rite of passage known as *poṭṭukkaṭṭutal*, the tying of the *poṭṭu* emblem. Perhaps because it occasionally took place in a temple, the ceremony is commonly understood as a "marriage to god." As I have argued elsewhere (Soneji 2008), it is important to understand that while "temple dedication" authorized participation in daily rituals (*nityapūjā*) in temples, this was only *one* role that professional dancers could enact in nineteenth-century South India. A large number of women within courtesan communities did not undergo such rituals but still participated in the aesthetic practices and nonconjugal sexual lifestyles associated with these communities. My analysis thus highlights the material and aesthetic concerns of women's lives rather than isolating them in epistemological frameworks based on notions of divine power (*śakti*) or auspiciousness (*saubhāgya*), categories that tend to elude historicization.

Instead of thinking about *poṭṭukkaṭṭutal* as a ceremony that carries the lofty religious resonances of "theogamy," it is more fruitful to think of the ritual as a way of marking a woman's inscription into an alternative nonconjugal lifestyle. Although in the discourse of social reform the *poṭṭukkaṭṭutal* is glossed as "*temple* dedication," in the nineteenth century, this ritual was commonly performed in the homes of *devadāsī*s. It is significant that references to the religious symbolisms of *poṭṭukkaṭṭutal* are nowhere to be found in the Moḍi records, or in any eighteenth- and nineteenth-century writing in Tamil or Telugu. The interpretation of the *dāsī* as the "wife of the god" does not surface in Tamil and Telugu literary materials as it does in English writings from roughly the same period. As Amrit Srinivasan has noted, "conscious economic motivations" were at the heart of *poṭṭukkaṭṭutal* in *dāsī* communities (A. Srinivasan 1985, 1871). Mytheli Sreenivas, in her recent work on the Saptur *zamīndāri* in Madurai district, demonstrates that the "dagger" (*kaṭṭāri*) marriage was also a way of marking women as "official" concubines with limited legal and personal rights (Sreenivas 2008, 32). I would argue that it is important to understand the *poṭṭu*-tying ceremony of professional dancing women in these terms. In many parts of South India, including Tanjore district and coastal Andhra Pradesh, *poṭṭukkaṭṭu* was literally performed as a "dagger marriage," with a dagger placed over the *dāsī*'s right shoulder while the *poṭṭu* was tied. Although the *poṭṭukkaṭṭutal* is often imagined as a marriage to the deity himself, we should understand it as a metonymic act. A *dāsī* does not marry the god Murukaṉ, for example, but marries his spear, just as a concubine does not marry King Śivājī, but his sword. Thinking through "dedication" in this way allows us to see it as part of a larger category of atypical rites of passage that take the place of marriage in a woman's life and also mark her as socially and sexually exceptional. I will now turn to representations of *poṭṭukkaṭṭu* in the Moḍi records.

Women who had *poṭṭukkaṭṭutal* performed at temples in and around Tanjore were invited to perform at the palace on occasions such as calendrical festivals and visits by officials of the British government. They would often be given homes on the lanes surrounding the temple at which they had the *poṭṭukkaṭṭutal*. Although it is commonplace to think of these women as "attached" to these temples—that is, regularly performing daily (*nityapūjā*) rituals in these places—the Moḍi records do not mention any such provisions. They simply refer to temples as the places where *poṭṭukkaṭṭutal* was performed. It was, however, understood that some of these women were professionally bound to the court and, unless they had secured permission from court authorities, were unable to perform in other contexts. In 1847, during the reign of Śivājī, for example, a dancer named Periya Vīralakṣmī Maṇi who had *poṭṭukkaṭṭutal* performed at the Bṛhadīśvara temple was fined for performing at a private event outside the court without permission.[21]

In the Moḍi records at the Sarasvati Mahal Library, we find several references to women having *poṭṭukkaṭṭutal* performed with the support of the court during the rule of Serfoji and Śivājī. The temples at which *poṭṭukkaṭṭutal* was performed include the Bṛhadīśvara and Prasanna Veṅkaṭeśa Perumāḷ temples in the heart of the city, the Santānarāma temple at Nidamangalam (known in the records as Yamunambapuram), the Cidambareśvara temple at Saluvanayakanpattinam (Sarbhendrarajapattanam), the Kāśī Viśvanātha temple at Orathanadu (Muktambapuram), and the Netrārpaṇeśvara temple at Tiruvizhimizhalai. In most of the records, references to *poṭṭukkaṭṭutal* are inevitably bound up with some kind of economic agreement or transaction. For example, in 1842, during the reign of Śivājī, a *dāsī* named Aṉṉam had her *poṭṭu* tied at the age of ten at the Santānarāma temple. The record states that she is to be given one *kaḷam* of paddy every month and one-and-a-half handfuls of cooked rice a day. A few years later, the court records a petition submitted by an unnamed *dāsī* who had her *poṭṭu* tied at the Bṛhadīśvara temple to request that the court authorities to allow her daughter Kṛṣṇā to have *poṭṭukkaṭṭu* performed as soon as possible:

> I have only one daughter, named Kṛṣṇā. For the past two years, I have requested [the authorities] to have the *poṭṭu* tied for her, but the *devasthānam* [temple committee] has consistently delayed this. Additionally, officials accused me of protesting against *sarkār*. An inquiry was made and I was later acquitted of these charges. All of my subsequent petitions have been dismissed. I beg to be excused if there is any

fault on my part, and request *sarkār* to order my daughter's *poṭṭukkaṭṭu*, if not in this temple, then at another place.[22]

Even after the full annexation of Tanjore to the British in 1856, *poṭṭukkaṭṭutal* continued in several temples administered by the palace *devasthānam*, especially the Prasanna Veṅkaṭeśa Perumāḷ temple and the Rājagopālasvāmi temple.[23] As late as 1882, two young *dāsīs*, Kuḷivāy (twelve years old) and Kampālayam (ten years old), who had their *poṭṭukkaṭṭu* performed at the Baṅgāru Kāmākṣī temple on West Main Street, had another *poṭṭukkaṭṭu* ceremony at the Bṛhadīśvara temple, and 46 rupees were paid by the palace to cover the expenses.[24] This reiterates that *poṭṭukkaṭṭu* was clearly *not* understood as a "religious marriage" but rather as a transaction that secured a girl's commitment to local economies of land and guaranteed her sexual and aesthetic labor. Thus, in Tanjore, the *poṭṭukkaṭṭu* could be repeated more than once if a woman was to be "transferred," as we see here, through the intercession of the Tanjore court.

DEPLOYING DANCE: WOMEN AND CULTURAL DISPLAY

What kinds of occasions called for the participation of dancers in nineteenth-century Tanjore, and how did such performances underwrite the cultural authority of kings divested of political power? Court dancers occupy an ambivalent position insofar as they are deployed as signs of the past and, at the same time, mark one point of entry into a new, cosmopolitan modernity. In this section, I present some specific instances in which kings use *devadāsīs* as markers of traditional Indian kingship. Later I explore the cosmopolitan nature of their performance practices by reading *devadāsī* dance at the intersection of North Indian and Western aesthetic influxes.

The Moḍi records provide us with four major contexts for the performance of dance by *dāsīs* that traverse courtly, temple, and private spaces: (1) calendrical festivals, (2) festivals at temples administered by the Tanjore court (such as the one described by the Moḍi record in fig. 1.3), (3) *darbārs* held in honor of visiting company officials, and (4) private celebrations for members of the royal household.

Calendrical festivals, such as Vasanta Pañcamī, Vināyaka Caturthī, Navarātrī, Dīpāvalī, Saṅkrāntī, and Guḍhīpāḍavā (Marāṭhā New Year), required dancers to perform rituals and entertain guests. The records make several references to an annual royal ritual, *sīmollaṅghana*, at which dancing played a central role. *Sīmollaṅghana*, "crossing the boundary [of the kingdom]," was a ritual in which the king and his retinue would travel to the extremity of the kingdom and ritually overstep its boundary. As a mark of aggression and defensiveness, the ritual dramatized both a willingness to engage in battle, and the protective surveillance of the limits of the kingdom by its sovereign. As in many other South Indian kingdoms and *zamīndāris*, *sīmollaṅghana* at Tanjore always took place on Vijayādaśamī, the tenth day of Navarātrī, which has for centuries carried imperial significance (Biardeau 2004). After the king returned from the *sīmollaṅghana*, courtesans would wave a lamp before him (*ārati*) to ward off the evil eye (*dṛṣṭi-pariharaṇa*), and a dance performance would follow.

During the reign of Serfoji II, the name of one courtesan—Sundarī—stands out in the Moḍi records. It was Sundarī who had the privilege to perform the *ārati* when Serfoji returned after performing the *sīmollaṅghana* ritual. She would receive a large remuneration for her dance performance on that day, in addition to an expensive shawl given to her from the palace cloth treasury (*jāmdārkhānā*). During the reign of both Serfoji and Śivājī, the average payment allotted to courtesans for a single performance ranged from 2 to 5 *cakrams*. On important days—the sacred thread ceremony (*upanayana*) of Śivājī in 1811, for example—the payment would be closer to five *cakrams*.[25] Sundarī, however, was allotted the exceptionally high payment of 15 *cakrams* on all days except Vijayādaśamī, when she would receive 20 *cakrams*.[26] It is interesting to speculate on how Sundarī achieved such pride of place during Serfoji's rule; oral tradition in Tanjore understands Sundarī as Serfoji's most beloved courtesan.

Serfoji's engagements with ritual sovereignty took many forms. As Peterson has demonstrated, many of these activities centered on the reclamation and revivification of the Bṛhadīśvara temple at Tanjore as a "royal temple" (Peterson 2006). Originally built in the year 1010 under the patronage of Rājarāja Cōḻa I, the temple did not receive sustained state patronage in the periods that followed, except when some building activity occurred at the hands of the Nāyakas. In 1803, Serfoji performed a massive reconsecration ceremony (*aṣṭabandhana kumbhābhiṣekam*) for the temple,[27] and had a long Marathi genealogical narrative entitled *Bhoṃsale Vaṃśa Carita* ("History of the Bhosala Dynasty") etched in Devanāgari script on the outer walls of the temple. He also had a Tamil translation of a Sanskrit text about the temple—the *Bṛhadīśvaramāhātmya*—prepared by his court poets.[28] He rebuilt the entire shrine to Gaṇeśa, and consecrated 108 *liṅga* icons of Śiva along the outer corridor (*tiruccuṟṟumālikai*) of the temple. Indeed, Tanjore's resident dance masters (*naṭṭuvaṉārs*) also participated in what Peterson has called Serfoji's "new cult of Bṛhadīśa" by composing several songs in the *varṇam, śabdam, kīrtana,* and *tillānā* genres in honor of the deity and his consort.[29]

Sometime in the 1820s, Serfoji commissioned two Tamil literary works from his court poet Koṭṭaiyūr Civakkoḻuntu Tēcikar: the *Tañcai Peruvuṭaiyar Ulā* and the *Carapēntira Pūpāla Kuṟavañci.*[30] The first of these is a work in the Tamil literary genre of *ulā,* which provides a highly aestheticized description of the god Śiva-Bṛhadīśa in procession. The *Carapēntira Pūpāla Kuṟavañci,* a text specifically meant for performance, is based on a similar motif and is thought to have been set to music by the *naṭṭuvaṉār* Poṉṉaiya (one of the "Tanjore Quartet").[31] The heroine, Mataṉavalli, sees King Serfoji in procession, falls in love with him, and through the divinations of a fortune-telling woman of the Kuṟa tribe, is assured that she will be united with him. Serfoji had a special stage, known locally as *kuṟavañci mēṭai,* built for the performance of this text at the entrance to the Bṛhadīśvara temple. *Devadāsīs* danced the parts of Mataṉavalli, her friends, and the fortune-teller, while a male *naṭṭuvaṉār* would be the *kaṭṭiyakkāraṉ,* or narrator. The performance would take place once a year on the ninth day of the eighteen-day-long temple festival (*brahmotsavam*) in the Tamil month of Cittirai (April–May). On this day, known as *aṣṭakkoṭi,* eight flags (*koṭi*) would be hoisted to mark the high point of the ritual festivities.

The coordination and training of *devadāsīs* for this annual performance appear to have been entrusted to the family of the Tanjore Quartet. It was this family's responsibility to ensure that rehearsals for the *kuṟavañci* took place two days before the performance on the *aṣṭakkoṭi* day (figs. 1.4 and 1.5).[32] It is significant that the performers in the *kuṟavañci* need not have had any formal association with the Tanjore palace. Dancers were recruited to perform in the *kuṟavañci* by the Quartet's family. These *naṭṭuvaṉārs* were allowed to train and recruit professionals from outside the pool of dancers officially linked to the court. The performance of the *Carapēntira Pūpāla Kuṟavañci* in the month of Cittirai was one of the most important public events at the temple in the late nineteenth and early twentieth centuries. In 1930, Thomas Lowell, an American traveler, noted that the "Davidasis, or temple-girls, who are dedicated to the rites of Siva . . . dance during the full moon of April" (Lowell 1930, 77). This tradition persisted until the late 1940s, when it was discontinued because of pressures from the public to end all performances by women from *devadāsī* communities.

Kuṟavañci dramas were enacted in a few temples in the Kaveri Delta region, and unlike courtly or private performances by *devadāsīs,* they

1.4 Dancers with *naṭṭuvaṉār* Picchaiya Pillai (1880–1945), a descendant of the Tanjore Quartet, after a rehearsal of the *kuṟavañci*, outside the home of the Quartet on West Main Street in Tanjore. Collection of the author.

1.5 The *Carapēntira Pūpāla Kuṟavañci* being performed in front of the *kuṟavañci mēṭai* at the Bṛhadīśvara temple, c. 1946. This image likely captures the performance of the song *cakivantāḷaiyā* ("Here come the friends [of Mataṉavalli]") in the *rāga* Sāveri. The dancers are accompanied by singers, the *naṭṭuvaṉār* Picchaiya Pillai, a drummer, and a clarinet player who stand in a row behind the dancers. Collection of the author.

belonged to the realm of public spectacle. Slightly different in form from the cyclical love poetry performed by *devadāsīs* in other contexts, *kuṟavañci* performances were based on a linear narrative, with the performers enacting "roles" in a manner parallel to the *bhāgavata mēḷa* traditions of Brahmin drama in this region.

The text of the *kuṟavañci* itself is marked by passages that carry the imprint of the cosmopolitanism of Serfoji's court. When the Kuṟa woman comes to read the heroine Mataṉavalli's fortune, she narrates her travels and fortune-telling "appointments" with women from various linguistic backgrounds, including an Englishwoman, in the song "CONNA kuṟikaḷum," translated here by Indira Peterson:

> There a Telugu beauty said to me: "nā cey cūḍu." [Telugu]
> I divined a good fortune for her, and she gave me this nose-ring.
> A lovely Maratha lady said, "maja hāt pahāv ge," [Marathi]
> and for the fitting fortune I divined from her palm,
> she gave me a diamond necklace.
> A Kannada maiden said, "nana kaiyina nōḍe." [Kannada]
> For the agreeable fortune I told her, she gave me earrings.
> A charming Turk damsel said: "me hāth dekh kar bolnā." [Hindi]
> When I read her palm, she gave me a glittering chain.
> An English lady with a bright brow said, "Look my hand!" [English]
> I read the lines on her palm, and she rewarded me with this girdle.
> (Peterson forthcoming, 32)

The performance of the *kuṟavañci* was one more way of making Serfoji's "personal style" of kingship public. *Devadāsīs* were deployed here too in "traditional" roles as lovers and attendants of king; as we see in the passage above, however, nearly all of Serfoji's displays of kingship bore the stamp of hybridity and innovation.

Beyond these large-scale public forms of display, dance performances would generally take place in the main "darbār hall" (called Śivasaudha, built in 1684 by Śāhajī), and at a couple of other smaller spaces on the palace grounds. Both men and women of the court would view these public dance performances, although palace women, including queens and concubines, watched from closed quarters, usually the balcony spaces. Private performances, usually to mark important occasions in the royal household, also occurred. Some Moḍi records describe courtesan dance taking place in the women's private quarters. One such record from 1801 notes that a dancer named Veṅkaṭalakṣmī danced in the presence of Bhavānī Bāī

Sāheb and Pārvatī Bāī Sāheb, both wives of Amarasiṃha (r. 1787–1798), and was paid 2 ½ *cakrams*.[33] Later, in 1841, music and dance were performed by a troupe of courtesans in the Vijaya Vilāsa Mahal before the pregnant queen Rājasā Bāī Ammaṇi Rāje Sāheb, the daughter of Śivājī and his consort Saidāmbā Bāī. Finally, a document dated 1842 lists a number of North Indian instruments (including *svarabat, sāraṅgī,* and *sitār*) and Western instruments (violin, dulcimer, and guitar) lent for a private performance of music and dance for Śivājī's wife Saidāmbā Bāī in the Kṛṣṇa Vilāsa chamber of the palace.[34]

Courtesan dance was also provided as entertainment for palace officials, particularly when special events were held for European visitors. In March 1845, for example, the court sent four dancers from the "Huzūr Nāṭyaśālā" (presumably an institution for courtesans who trained and performed at the palace, or perhaps the home of the dance-masters known as the "Tanjore Quartet"), to perform at an event in the Sivagangai Garden, just outside the Bṛhadīśvara temple.[35] The event was hosted by the East India Company, and the Moḍi record notes that each dancer was paid 10 rupees by Company officials.[36] In the following section, as well as in chapter 4, I discuss the significant influence of European music on the presentation and content of dance performed in *dāsī* communities well into the twentieth century. For now, it is enough to note that rulers had uses for *dāsī*s that connected them with the South Indian past, a past that in colonial Tanjore was made to serve present political ends.

PERFORMANCE ECOLOGY

As I have already suggested, music and dance in this period undergo a radical transformation that permanently alters the course of the performing arts in modern South India. It is difficult to overstate the role that nineteenth-century Tanjore plays in the formation of the genres and styles of music and dance that persist today and are often glossed by the term "classical." Dance performances at the Tanjore court in the nineteenth century must be understood in the wider context of aesthetic practices patronized by the state. Historians and writers on dance often construct *devadāsī* dance as a discrete artistic practice that emerges out of unilateral economic relationships with courtly patrons. What the evidence suggests is that *devadāsī*-courtesans represent one point in a shifting network of artists, genres, patrons, and venues. Many of the following practices were already allied with courtesan music and dance, while others came to influence it. Besides the dance and music practiced by courtesans, five major types of performance were regularly patronized by the Tanjore court until the beginning of the twentieth century: (1) drama, which included *bhāgavata mēḷa nāṭaka*, a Telugu-language theater performed largely by *smārta* Brahmin men; (2) *lāvaṇī*, a Marathi literary genre of love songs interpreted through music and dance; (3) *gondhaḷa* or *gondhaḷī*, a Maharashtrian form of ritual music and drumming, which in Tanjore was performed by men during palace functions; (4) North Indian (Hindustānī) music and dance; and (5) Western music and dance practices. Undergirding this complex ecology of performance practices is the accelerated and innovative growth of South Indian music at the court, which has already been the subject of many scholarly works (Seetha 1981; L. Subramanian 2006; Weidman 2006).

Drama had been a vital and dynamic part of the courtly aesthetics of Tanjore since the Nāyaka period, when an innovative Telugu literary form, the *yakṣagāna*, emerges and permanently blurs the boundaries between literature and performance at the court, anticipating, in some ways, the imbrication of poetics and movement that come to characterize courtesan dance. The structure of Nāyaka *yakṣagāna* dramas becomes paradigmatic and gives rise to a number of innovative literary and performance genres (Soneji 2004, 51–61). By the time of Marāṭhā kings such as Śāhajī (r. 1683–1711) and Pratāpasiṃha (r. 1740–1763), the *yakṣagāna* drama had become a fixture at the Tanjore court.[37] The *bhāgavata mēḷa nāṭaka* drama, a form of ritual theater dedicated to Viṣṇu, evolved out of the Nāyaka-Marāṭhā courtly milieu, and in the late Marāṭhā period was patronized as one of the most prominent performance genres of the palace.[38] Like the *yakṣagāna* drama, *bhāgavata mēḷa* is structured in the form of songs (called *daruvu*s) that are linked by prose and short poems (*vacana*s and *padyam*s). The performance is always structured in the form of a straightforward linear narrative, and the audience consists of a range of caste groups. The Moḍi records furnish extensive information about *bhāgavata mēḷa* performances at the court, and some of this material has recently been discussed by Takako Inoue (2008). It is significant for us that nineteenth-century *bhāgavata mēḷa* performers employed "dance" in their performances, and the vocabulary for this dance clearly came from the courtesan dance tradition. In Tanjore, the interface between *devadāsīs* and the Brahmin artists of *bhāgavata mēḷa* troupes is well documented, even into the middle of the twentieth century. One undated Moḍi record in particular notes that male actors of *bhāgavata mēḷa* lent their dancing bells to the courtesans,[39] and it is clear that these communities regularly exchanged repertoire and technique.

Lāvaṇī is a genre of poetry, music, and dance typically associated with Marathi-speaking women artists from lower-caste groups such as Kolhātis,

Mahars, and Mangs (Rege 1996; Kadam 1998; Rao 1985). The genre is known to have existed in the late Peśvā period (c. 1796–1818) in Maharashtra, and then later became an indispensible component of Marathi popular theater (*tamāśā*) in the nineteenth century. The texts of many *lāvaṇī* songs are highly salacious (there is, in fact, a subgenre called "erotic" or *śṛṅgārik lāvaṇī*), making frequent reference to sexuality in the manner of songs performed by courtesans. Unlike in Maharashtra, where *lāvaṇī* was the preserve of female performers, in Tanjore it seems to have been largely the purview of men. *Lāvaṇī* appears to have been established in Tanjore by three figures, Hindu and Muslim, in the late eighteenth and early nineteenth centuries: Tukkan Gīr (1750–1815), Sayyad Umar Sāheb (1755–1824), and Hīrojī Rāv (1762–1840). In addition to these, Veṅkaṭ Rāv (c. 1833–1855) was a prolific composer of *lāvaṇī*s during the rule of Śivājī II (Sundaram n.d., 1994). *Lāvaṇī* in Tanjore was performed in public at *darbār* events, for example, and also in private, particularly in the closed quarters of the *bāīsāheb*s, the queens or concubines. One rather anomalous Moḍi record from 1814 tells us that Brahmin women performed *lāvaṇī*s at the court,[40] but this appears to be an exception rather than a rule. Another record from 1811 notes that female dancers associated with temples in Tiruvaiyaru, Tiruvarur, and Kumbhakonam were invited to the court to perform *lāvaṇī* songs during the erotic festival of Holī (*kāmaṉ paṇṭikai* in Tamil).[41] *Lāvaṇī* was also performed at the time of the birth of a child in Marāṭhā households in Tanjore, usually on the fifth, seventh, and eighth nights following childbirth. Two manuscripts in the Sarasvati Mahal Library preserve *lāvaṇī*s attributed to a number of local *lāvaṇīkār*s with names such as Vandakar, Kāsā Huseni, and Kāśinātha.[42]

Gondhaḷa, a form of ritual song and drumming, was performed occasionally, like courtesan dance, during rites of passage ceremonies and during calendrical festivals (such as *pūjā* cycles for the clan goddess Tuḷajā-Bhavānī). *Gondhaḷa* refers to a drum played to the accompaniment of a single-stringed instrument called *ektārā*. Praise-poems to goddesses such as Bhavānī or Reṇukā are sung or recited as the *gondhaḷa*, *ektārā*, and the circular drum (*ḍep*) are played. *Gondhaḷa* is performed in many parts of Maharashtra, and its performers traditionally claim to form a separate caste.[43] Sometimes *gondhaḷa* would be accompanied by a kind of dance performed by the men who sing the songs. In both royal and elite nonroyal households in Tanjore, *gondhaḷa* performance, which was also known locally as *sama mēḷa*, was most commonly seen at the birth of a child. To protect the mother and newborn from ghouls, the evil eye, and other malignant forces, *gondhaḷa* would be played in the home on the tenth night following childbirth, and a goddess named Jīvatī would be propitiated.[44]

1.6 Company paintings of a *devadāsī* dance performance and a *gondhaḷa* performance in Tanjore. © The British Library Board (AddOr No. 3924 and 3925).

At the end of this performance, the *gondhaḷa* would sing lullabies (*pāḷanā*) with the participation of the new mother and her family, and this would mark the end of their ten-day observance of birth pollution. The British Library preserves a set of nineteenth-century Company paintings (fig. 1.6) from Tanjore that depict a courtesan dance troupe and a *gondhaḷa* troupe in exactly the same pose, indicating the ways in which both were understood as part of a common culture of performance sponsored by the court. In today's context, *devadāsī* dance has been reworked as Bharatanāṭyam, a "high" art form whose classicism is endorsed by the state. *Gondhaḷa*, which is now extinct in Tanjore, continues to flourish in rural Maharashtra, but the state and its cultural agencies inevitably classify it as a "folk" art. In the visual practices of contemporary India, one would be hard-pressed to find Bharatanāṭyam and *gondhaḷa* represented symmetrically as they are in the image from colonial Tanjore.

A key feature of courtesan dance at Tanjore was the presence of North Indian (Hindustānī) musical forms in the dance repertoire. Musicians brought from North India would have found courtesan culture recognizable, and the Moḍi records preserve a number of concrete examples of collaboration between northern and southern forms. Many such musicians were specifically hired out of Gwalior, founded in the eighteenth century as part of the Marāṭhā confederacy and later one of the key princely states in British India. The Moḍi records mention several musicians by name—Ghulām Hussain (1801), Mīr Rahmān (1811), and Dilvar Ali (1814), for example. In 1819, six musicians—Bilāval Ali, Mirzābakar Ali, Allauddin, Hussain Khān, Govindarāj Rāmjī Bove, and Govinda Rāv Bove—signed a contract with the court indicating that they would not teach North Indian musical forms such as *dhrupad*, k̲h̲yāl, and *tappā* to anyone other than professional dancing women of the court.[45] In 1829, a North Indian Brahmin stayed in the home of the Brahmin court musician Varāhappayya, and was paid 2 Company rupees for composing a treatise on South Indian music.[46] In 1837, a second wave of Gwalior musicians arrived, among them Kalyāṇ Singh, Dildār Ali, and Lakhā Rām.[47] Apart from these references to music, it is also clear that North Indian forms of dance were actively performed at the court. These forms of dance are glossed as "Hindustānī" in the Moḍi records, but occasionally the word "*kiñjin*" is also mentioned. The term *kñin* likely comes from the word *kañcan* ("golden") or *kañcanī*, used in North India to refer to courtesans. The term *kañcanī* is found in late Mughal literary sources and also in colonial ethnographies from North India to refer to courtesans who are professional dancers (Brown 2000; Sachdeva 2008; Walker 2004). In Tamil Nadu, the word *kiñjin* came to reference courtly dance performed in the North Indian style.[48] A fascinating but unfortunately undated Moḍi record gives us the following information: "Hussain Khān performed female roles and also performed the art of *kiñjin*. He was taught this art by a *dāsī*. For having visited the *dāsī*'s house, Hussain Khān was fined 12 coconuts."[49] Not only was *kiñjin* dance performed at the court by *dāsī*s, it was also performed through gynemimetic conventions (*strī veṣam*) by at least one Muslim man.[50]

Given the presence of Hindustānī music and musicians at Tanjore and the considerable influence they wielded, it is not improbable that courtesans from North India were also present in this milieu. Certainly by the nineteenth century, "Hindustānī" dance was being taught to local dancers by court *naṭṭuvaṉār*s. A Moḍi letter from Civāṉanta Naṭṭuvaṉār dated 1844 records a complaint to King Śivājī in which the *naṭṭuvaṉār* states that he has trained two girls in "Hindustānī" dance and wants to present them before the king, but the temple officials (*madhyastha*s) are not permitting him to do so.[51] Clues from visual culture also substantiate the presence of North Indian courtesans at Tanjore. For example, a late nineteenth-century painting inside the Bṛhadīśvara temple (in the pavilion known as "Rājā Maṇḍapa" adjoining the Subrahmaṇya shrine) depicts two types of

1.7 "Hindustani" dancers and musicians, including a *muṭṭu* drummer and *naṭṭuvaṉār*, Tanjore, c. 1828. The English inscription below reads "Hindoostany Natch." © Victoria and Albert Museum, London (IS.39:24-1987)

courtly performers, one a South Indian *dāsī*-courtesan, decked in a sari and traditional jewels, and the other, a North Indian courtesan wearing a Mughal-style dress. This is consistent with another Tanjore Company painting from the Victoria and Albert Museum (fig. 1.7) that dates to the rule of Serfoji II, which depicts a "North Indian" courtesan and her troupe, including two instrumentalists playing the North Indian bowed instrument *sāraṅgī*, but also a South Indian *muṭṭu* or *mṛdaṅgam* drummer, and a man playing cymbals, likely a South Indian *naṭṭuvaṉār*.[52]

It is tempting to suggest that the entire culture of salon-style (or "chamber"-style) courtesan performance in South India originates with the movement of personnel between Maharashtra and Tanjore. Margaret Walker and Shweta Sachdeva have demonstrated that North Indian courtesan practices (later referred to as "nautch") attained a level of sophistication and development under Mughul and Marāṭhā patronage long before such practices can be detected in the south. For the Tanjore Marāṭhā kings, Maharashtra and Gwalior represent stores of culture to be mined and mobilized for their own purposes. North Indian music and dance were seen as virtuosic, worthy of emulation, and thus it is not surprising that the radical shifts in dance technique in the south (the subject of the next section) coincide with the importation of northern artistry.

Still more intriguing is the cultivation of Western music and taste habits by Tanjore rulers, especially Serfoji. As early as 1770, during the reign of Tuḷajā II (r. 1764–1789), the Moḍi records indicate that one Mister Anthony was paid 5 Company rupees for playing the sackbut.[53] There are a significant number of Moḍi records that refer to the sackbut, Irish pipe, harp, clarinet, French horn, trumpet, fiddle, and piano being played, bought, and even manufactured in Tanjore for the court. On March 28, 1826, Bishop Heber and others were entertained by two Brahmin musicians on the piano who sight read Handel's "Overture to Samson" (Robinson 1831, 120). Serfoji encouraged the use of Western music in his royal rituals of display by instituting the Tanjore Palace Band as a permanent fixture at the Marāṭhā *darbār*, which was the earliest known nonmilitary European-style ensemble in South Asia (fig.1.8). As Gregory Booth (1996; 2005) has shown, this courtly South Indian band was the precursor of the brass bands later employed by elites during wedding processions in various parts of India.

In chapter 4, we will investigate the significance of the indigenization of Western forms among *dāsī*s in the Tanjore region, paying particular attention to the repertoire of R. Muttukkannammal, which preserves a unique hybrid genre, *noṭṭusvaram*. During the reign of Serfoji II, we see

1.8 A parchment manuscript entitled "Musical Pieces Played by the Band of Maharaja Sarfoji, Tanjore." Accessed courtesy S. Babaji Rajah Bhonsle, Thanjavur, photographed by Cylla von Tiedemann.

the indigenization of marching band tunes in projects such as those of Muttusvāmi Dīkṣitar (1775–1835), who is known to have composed over forty songs based on Western melodies. These are generally known as *noṭṭusvaram* (the root *noṭṭu* here refers to the English word "note").[54] One of the compositions attributed to Dīkṣitar in this period is "santatam pāhimām saṅgīta śyāmale," a Sanskrit song dedicated to the goddess Sarasvatī. This is actually "God Save the King," overlaid with Sanskrit lyrics. In the year 1848, the *devadāsīs* of the Tanjore court are known to have danced to Western music, including "God Save the King," taught to them by one Mr. Edward who was on the palace payroll (Seetha 1981, 120). Social dancing—the waltz, for example—appears to have been performed regularly at the Marāṭhā *darbār* during the rule of both Serfoji and Śivājī. A Moḍi record dated 1855 mentions a certain english social dancing "Lady Catherine Encee" who was paid a salary of five Company rupees for teaching to palace officials (Seetha 1981, 120).

These examples affirm the experimental nature of the culture produced in the cosmopolitan world of colonial Tanjore. As we have seen, courtesan dance must be defined by its engagement not only with a network of indigenous ritual and aesthetic practices, but also with political theater, North Indian cultural forms, and colonial systems of knowledge.

THE TANJORE QUARTET AND AESTHETIC INNOVATION

We have now surveyed the matrix of practices in which the courtesan dance emerged and thrived. It is now incumbent to describe the nature of the dance courtesans themselves were practicing in Tanjore. By the beginning of the twentieth century, a formalized, virtuosic style of courtly dance had been developed and refined by hereditary dancers and dance masters, a style that would be eclipsed suddenly by the vociferous antinautch movement that emerged almost simultaneously with the art form it opposed. The twentieth-century movement to transform *devadāsī* dance into Bharatanāṭyam involved the repopulation of the art by nonhereditary (mostly Brahmin) women. The so-called dance revivalists narrated a history of Indian dance that cast the nineteenth century as a moment of sheer degeneration, a lapse that followed a moral "golden age" in which dance was used only in the service of Hinduism. The irony is that the "degenerate" form of South Indian dance so denigrated by dance revivalists actually represents that form in its first major instantiation.[55] Below I describe the development of the dance at the hands of its most prolific makers. The *tañcai nālvar* (hereafter the Tanjore Quartet) was responsible for many of the genres, compositions, and choreographies that both inspired and repulsed twentieth-century observers, those reformers who would reinscribe this art as an urban, middle-class practice.

Dance masters, known as *naṭṭuvaṉārs*, *naṭṭuvaṉs*, or *naṭṭumuṭṭukāraṉs*, were key players in performances at the Tanjore court. For the most part they appear to have been provided for by the court, and the names of a number of *naṭṭuvaṉārs* occur in the Moḍi records. In the records they are usually known as *naṭava* (*naṭṭuvaṉ*, "dance-master"), *naṭhamūṭhagāra* (*naṭṭumuṭṭukārar*, "dance-master and drummer pair"), or occasionally *kaḷāvanta* ("artist"). In modern historical and historiographic writing on dance in South India, the four brothers known popularly as the Tanjore Quartet have been celebrated as radical aesthetic innovators who made significant contributions to the culture of courtly dance in the nineteenth century. The brothers—Ciṉṉaiyā (1802–1856), Poṉṉaiyā (1804–1864), Civāṉantam (1808–1863), and Vaṭivēl (1810–1847)—each composed lyrics, music, and choreographies for performances in colonial Tanjore and beyond (fig. 1.9).[56] Although historians of dance have been somewhat preoccupied with the achievements of these brothers, there were in reality at

1.9 Marāṭhā-style portraits of Ciṉṉaiyā and Poṉṉaiyā, the eldest brothers of the Tanjore Quartet. This image is currently housed in the ancestral home of the brothers on West Main Street in Tanjore. Photograph by Cylla von Tiedemann.

least three active lineages of *naṭṭuvaṉār*s whose services were employed by the Tanjore court during the time of Serfoji and Śivājī. These included not only the family of the Tanjore Quartet, but also the families of Rāmu Naṭṭuvaṉār and Veṅkaṭakiruṣṇa Naṭṭuvaṉār.[57] In addition, the Moḍi records mention a number of *naṭṭuvaṉār*s at the court whose identities are unclear—for example, Sabhāpati Naṭṭuvaṉār (1831) and Gopāla Nārāyaṇa and Śivarāma Subbayya (1845).

If nationalist historians merely celebrate the artistic achievements of the Tanjore Quartet and iconize them for their radical aesthetic innovations, some feminist historians, drawing on these same nationalist histories, interpret their achievements as the beginning of the end of "*devadāsī* matriliny." Avanthi Meduri, for example, writes that the brothers inscribed the dance "in a patrilineal history or lineage" (Meduri 1996, 46–47). Anupama Taranath, citing only Meduri, reiterates this point. She posits that "the four brothers were instrumental in textualizing the dance and musical craft of temple dancing women" (Taranath 2000, 106). She continues:

> Making links to the sacred texts of India ensured that the Quartet's life work could be acknowledged and recognized by the growing numbers of Orientalist scholars who were interested in such artistic links. Sanskritizing and formalizing the cultural practices of dancing women, then, were ways in which Orientalist rhetorical practices and Indian patriarchal formations converged upon the dancing woman's body, leaving little room for her own voice and story to emerge. (109)

Making such interpretive claims about the Quartet is specious at best. While it is important to recognize the fact that the Quartet maintained the patriarchal order of performance in colonial Tanjore, glossing them as "Sanskritizing patriarchs" severely limits the interpretive possibilities that the textual and oral archives make available. I would argue that a significant element of this entire discussion turns on a concrete historical fact. The family had actually *left* Tanjore in the early phase of Marāṭhā rule, only to be invited back by Tuḷajā II (father of Serfoji II), at approximately the same time that he entered complex negotiations with the East India Company regarding the political status and governance of the Tanjore kingdom. Tuḷajā's invitation that the family return to Tanjore at this moment signals his investment in promoting an innovative, contemporary dance ("nautch") similar to that patronized by the Company and native elites in urban settings such as Calcutta and Madras.[58]

The evidence for the movement of the family and its genealogy

1.10 The home of the Quartet on West Main Street, given to their father by King Tuḷajā II. Photograph by the author.

comes from the work of B. M. Sundaram, who discovered a set of manuscripts from Thiruthuraipoondi (Thiruvarur district) that contain the horoscopes and birth and death dates of all male members in the family up to the present (1997, 30–31).[59] When the family returned to Tanjore around 1779, King Tuḷajā II granted them land and a house on West Main Street (fig. 1.10).[60] Known in Tanjore by epithets such as "the house of the great *naṭṭuvaṉārs*" (*periya naṭṭuvaṉār vīṭu*) or "[dance] practice hall" (*cilampakūṭam*), this house became famous as a rehearsal space and training center for *devadāsīs* well into the twentieth century. A single Moḍi record dated 1780 provides us with a reference to Cupparāya Naṭṭuvaṉār (1758–1814), father of the Quartet, and outlines the patronage extended to him by King Tuḷajā II on the occasion of *sīmollaṅghana*:

> Royal Order of Mahārāja Tuḷajā Rāje Sāheb: Given to the artist (*kalāvanta*) Subbarāya, leader of the female artists (*kaḷāvantiṇī*) and *naṭṭumuṭṭukāras* (*naṭhamūṭhagāra*). Whenever His Highness (*hujūr*) returns from *sīmollaṅghana*, they must perform [dance and music] in his presence. As payment (literally, "to fill their bellies," *poṭagī*), they must be given 9 *phaḷam*, weighed against the measuring rod every day. This should be enforced on a daily basis until the full moon day in the month of the *sīmollaṅghana*.[61]

Historical data on the Quartet is severely lacking. There are two major categories of evidence: the oral and material artifacts preserved by the Quartet's descendants and other hereditary families of dance practitioners, and aesthetic artifacts in the form of manuscripts that capture their prolific output. A third category of evidence is represented only by a single, contentious document in the Moḍi records that we have already referred to above.[62] This is the letter dated 1844 by a *naṭṭuvaṉār* named Civāṉantam petitioning that he be allowed to present before Sivaji II two dancers he has trained in "*Hindustānī* dance." Confusingly, the document exists in two versions, one that identifies Civāṉantam as one among the Quartet, and another that places him in another lineage.[63] If we accept that the first version does indeed refer to Civāṉantam of the Quartet, we have here the only reference to the brothers in the entire corpus of Moḍi records.

Of the manuscripts related to the Quartet at Sarasvati Mahal, two are relevant to our discussion. The first is a theoretical work called *Abhinaya Lakṣaṇamu*, attributed to Ciṉṉaiyā (B.11518A and B.11518B). The colophon reads "as dictated by Subbarāya," most likely a reference to Cupparāya Naṭṭuvaṉār, father of the members of the Quartet. This work, a Telugu transcreation of the medieval Sanskrit text *Abhinayadarpaṇa*, focuses on the types of gestures of the eyes, hands, and limbs that evoke moods and index ideas in the performance of *abhinaya*. The second, perhaps more important manuscript, entitled *Varṇa Svara Jati* (B.11616B), has recently been edited by B. M. Sundaram (2002b).[64] It consists only of compositions meant for courtly dance performances, and contains a number of pieces that are also part of the oral repertoire remembered by descendants of the Quartet.

The Tanjore Quartet is usually credited with one major aesthetic innovation, that of the creation of a sevenfold sequence of presenting genres of courtly dance. This program or suite (sometimes referred to today as *mārgam*, "path") still persists in the solo presentation of modern Bharatanāṭyam dance. The suite consists of genres known as *alārippu, jatisvaram, śabdam, varṇam, padam, tillānā*, and *śloka*.[65] While it is widely accepted that the Quartet is responsible for configuring this suite, the evidence only derives from the oral tradition of the family's descendants.[66] These descendants also preserve the repertoire itself in practice, and have been the primary disseminators of colonial Tanjore's dance traditions over the last hundred years or so. In addition, the family is also in possession of manuscripts and notebooks attributed to the Quartet and their early descendants. It is from these manuscripts—both palm leaf and paper—that printed anthologies of the Quartet's repertoire were made available to urban, middle-class

Bharatanāṭyam dancers in the mid-twentieth century. Approximately ten such manuscripts are currently available, and these are in the personal collection of S. Sivakumar, son of K. P. Sivanandam, a descendant of the Quartet. It is likely that many of these compilations were made after the time of the Quartet, since some of them contain songs dedicated to local *zamīndārs* who lived long after the Quartet.[67]

Among the more important of these manuscripts is a paper notebook that bears the label "Nellaiyappa Naṭṭuvaṉār Parata Puttakam" (fig. 1.11), the personal notebook of Nellaiyappa Naṭṭuvaṉār (1859–1905), grandson of Poṉṉaiyā of the Quartet, who moved to Madras around 1880, establishing himself as one of the most prominent dance masters in the city. Nellaiyappa appears to have preserved one of the most extensive collections of compositions attributed to the Quartet, consisting of pieces in the *jatisvaram, śabdam, varṇam, svarajati,* and *tillānā* genres. The movement of the compositions and the new "suite" of the Quartet out of Tanjore and into Madras is a process that shapes the culture of "nautch" in a significant way, and this will be fully elaborated in the following chapter.

Other biographical information that comes to us from oral sources tells us that the brothers trained under the Brahmin musician Muttusvāmi Dīkṣitar (1775–1835).[68] In the 1950s, Pandanallur Meenakshisundaram Pillai (1869–1954), a descendant of the brothers, narrated the following incident about them to musicologist B. M. Sundaram. The anecdote accounts for their patronage at the courts of Mysore and Travancore:

> On one occasion, Serfoji sent for the Quartet and declared that he planned to appoint a person for daily service in the Brihadeesvara temple in addition to them. The person was none other than the son of Serfoji's concubine and trained, to some extent, by the brothers themselves. The brothers submitted that the Raja should keep in mind the age and talents of the appointee before taking a decision. But Serfoji promulgated a *firman* [official order] by which the new incumbent would not only be appointed in the temple, but would also have exclusive right to temple honours such as *parivattam* [the ritual honor of wearing the cloth of the deity around one's head]. This was an insult to the brothers so they left Tanjavur. (Sundaram 1997, 34)

Sundaram goes on to say that Poṉṉaiyā and Civāṉantam returned to Tanjore once Śivājī II ascended the throne in 1832 (ibid.). This narrative also suggests that the brothers performed "daily service" at the Bṛhadīśvara

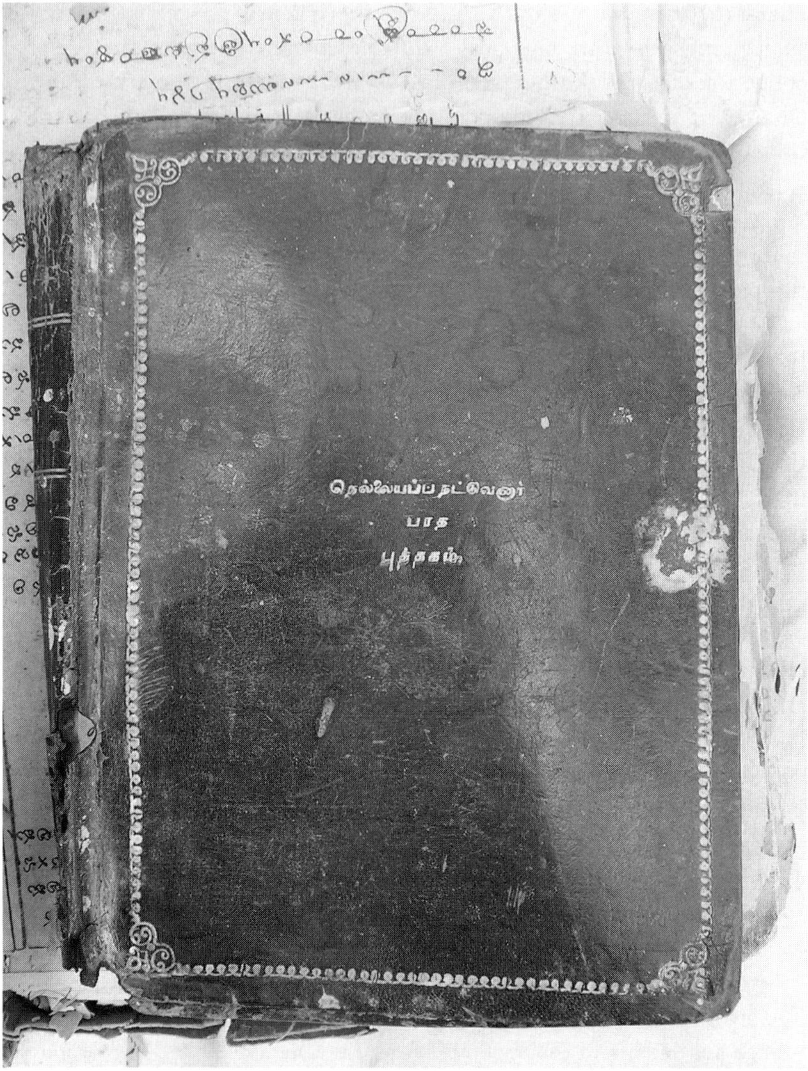

1.11 Notebook of Chennai Nellaiyappa Naṭṭuvaṉār (1859–1905), grandson of Poṉṉaiyā of the Quartet, in Telugu script. Notations for the Quartet's compositions survive today largely because of the existence of this text. The contemporary printed editions of the compositions were sourced from this book by K. Ponnaiya Pillai and his family in 1940s and 50s. Photo by the author.

temple, although at this point such a suggestion remains unverifiable. Other oral narratives among the descendants of the family tell of the brothers training *devadāsīs* such as Mīnākṣī of Mannargudi and Ammāḷu of Pudukkottai (Sundaram 1997, 32).[69] The Quartet thus comes to occupy iconic status among traditional non-Brahmin musicians, and their standing rests upon the reconfiguration of *devadāsī* dance thought to have occurred under their supervision. In these aesthetic metamorphoses, as I demonstrate below, lyric eroticism is supplemented by an emphasis on virtuosity, training, and presentation.

A GENEALOGY FOR THE TANJORE DANCE REPERTOIRE

The innovations focused and formalized by the Quartet begin much earlier and represent the culmination of aesthetic experiments with movement, text, language, and music that were patronized by the Marāṭhā kings explicitly as forms of courtly entertainment. Far from representing a nineteenth-century "degeneration" of dance, the moment of the Quartet's ascendency signals a self-conscious focus on three imperatives—the display of virtuosity, practice, and staging—that come to redefine courtly dance in this period. As Lakshmi Subramanian notes, the late eighteenth- and early nineteenth-century Tanjore court displayed an interest not only in patronizing music, but also in formulating "conventions and guidelines for training, practice, and presentation" (2006, 37). Practice and presentation, I would argue, were also key concerns when it came to dance. The Quartet's family, for example, is entrusted with the responsibility of recruiting, rehearsing, and presenting dancers at the court and for the annual performance of the *Carapēntira Pūpāla Kuṟavañci* in the month of Cittirai. The rehearsals for the *kuṟavañci* are given specific names, and temple and court officials also regulate and mediate the training of women who are to perform at the court. Inevitably, women performers are instrumentalized in this process. Most of the women who perform at the court or in the *kuṟavañci* are officially bound to the court through the palace temple board *(devasthānam)*, which administered the temples at which they were dedicated. I would argue that it is in the context of this preoccupation with "staging" dance as a vital courtly practice that virtuosic forms such as the *svarajati* and *varṇam*, which I discuss briefly below, emerge as the central elements of courtly dance practice.

For the most part, court dance in colonial Tanjore coalesced around the interpretation of lyric poetry. Like most forms of dance practiced by *devadāsīs*, this was in fact not linear "storytelling" as much as a cyclical, almost abstract visualization of poetic text. Courtesans would sing these lyrical texts and bring them to life through improvised gestural interpretation (*abhinaya*). The origins of this lyric vocabulary for court dance can be traced to the Telugu song genre known as *padam* crystallized in the seventeenth century, perhaps even at the Tanjore Nāyaka court (Allen 1992, 43–48; Ramanujan, Narayana Rao, and Shulman 1994; Seetha 1981). *Padams*, such as those of the seventeenth-century poet Kṣetrayya, were primarily couched in the language of erotic devotion, and as Ramanujan, Narayana Rao, and Shulman (1994) have demonstrated, the content of these *padams* mirrors the new telos of pleasure (*bhoga*) that permeated the courtly cultures of seventeenth-century South India. Dance at the Tanjore Marāṭhā court is characterized, right up to the early twentieth century, by the persistence of the eroticism of the early Telugu *padam* tradition. Indeed, these early *padams* never disappear from the court dance repertoire, but are augmented, as we shall see below, by a number of virtuosic dance forms that remain embedded in the poetic world of erotic lyricism.[70]

In the early period of Marāṭhā rule at Tanjore, the lyrical dimensions of court dance are evident in three genres: *padas* and *śabdas*, lyrical songs and benedictory songs, similar to those from the Nāyaka period; *yakṣagāna*-style plays in Telugu, Sanskrit, and Marathi that evoked a number of religious and secular themes, modeled after those of the Nāyaka period; and the emergent Tamil *kuṟavañci* dramas.[71] During the reign of Śāhajī (1684–1712), we see a large number of important innovations in literature and performance. Hundreds of Telugu and Marathi *padams* are composed in praise of the king's chosen deity, Śiva-Tyāgarāja of Tiruvarur.[72] Śāhajī's court was also adorned by two Brahmin dance masters of the *bhāgavata mēḷa* tradition, Bharatam Kāśināthayya (c. 1690–1764) and Bharatam Nāraṇa Kavi, both of whom composed a large number of *śabdas* in praise of the Marāṭhā kings and local deities. Śāhajī also commissioned a number of *yakṣagāna* dramas in a variety of languages, and these consisted almost entirely of songs called *daru* or *daruvu*.[73] Significantly, some of these dramas contain other song-types and musical forms clearly meant for dance (such as *kavuttuvam*, *korvai*, *jakkiṇi*, and *abhinaya-pada*), and so these dramas were undoubtedly meant to be performed by court dance masters and courtesan-dancers. As characters, courtesans continue to occupy a central place in many of the *yakṣagānas* and other performance-poems of this period, as they did in the earlier Nāyaka-period texts. A Sanskrit poem entitled *Śāhavilāsa Gītam*, based on the twelfth-century *Gītagovinda* of Jayadeva, for example, is about the love between Śāhajī and a courtesan named Līlāvatī.[74] It is also during the reign of Śāhajī that one of the earliest extant Tamil *kuṟavañci* texts, the *Tiyākēcar Kuṟavañci*, was apparently composed.[75] Similarly, the majority of dance-related textual materials from the reign of the subsequent Marāṭhā kings Serfoji I, Tuḷajā I, and Ekojī II are either in the form of *padams* or *yakṣagāna* plays.[76]

Over and above these lyric genres of literature meant to be interpreted through dance, the Marāṭhā court at Tanjore also patronizes a number of theoretical texts that deal with the technique of dance. One of the most striking examples is the Sanskrit text entitled *Saṅgīta Sārāmṛta* ("Ambrosia of the Essence of Music") composed during the rule of Tuḷajā I. The *Saṅgīta Sārāmṛta*, as Hari Krishnan has noted in a recent essay, represents "an attempt to reconcile the local traditions of dance with the Sanskrit textual tradition" (2008, 73). In a section of the text entitled *śramavidhi* ("directions for practice"), for example, the text lays out the basic units of abstract dance movement (known in Telugu as *aḍavu*) and replaces the Tamil and Telugu names of the movements with Sanskrit ones. Remarkably, this text lays out the basic structure and sequence of the *aḍavus* as they continue to be practiced in courtesan communities today. The *Saṅgīta Sārāmṛta* is thus significant not only for its attempts to forge a uniquely localized Sanskrit dance theory, but also for its early codification of movement patterns that form the basis of courtesan dance into the present.

It is during the rule of King Pratāpasiṃha (r. 1739–1763) and his second son Tuḷajā II (r. 1763–1787) that a significant metamorphosis of court dance begins.[77] This change was characterized by the development of technical and virtuosic dance compositions such as the *svarajati*, specifically meant for the solo female dancer, which differed from the existing repertoire of *padas*, *śabdas*, and other genres of court dance. Virtuosic forms such as the *svarajati* integrated all the elements of courtly musical style (lyrics, spoken rhythms, sung rhythms, solfège [*svaras*]) and brought together abstract and lyrical dance in a single, albeit very lengthy, composition. The chief architects of these virtuosic forms were musicians and dance masters. The *svarajati*, for example, was thought to have been invented by the Telugu Brahmin composer Melattur Vīrabhadrayya (early eighteenth century), who is mentioned in the Moḍi records as receiving a land grant (*sarvamāṉiyam*) from Tuḷajā II in 1776 (Sundaram 2002b, 28).[78] Vīrabhadrayya's most famous composition, a Telugu *svarajati* in the *rāga* Huseni, is addressed to a relative of the Marāṭhā ruling house, Mallārjī Gāḍerāv Sāheb, who married King Pratāpasiṃha's younger sister Śyāmalā Bāī (ibid. 2002b, 49). In a manner continuous with the *padam*, the *svarajati* also stages the lyric subjectivity of the *devadāsī*-courtesan as an eroticized character. The first few lines of the Huseni *svarajati* "e māyalāḍirā" run as follows:

Who is that cunning woman
and how has she convinced you?
In this world, you are the great Mallārjī, son of Dattajendra.
Listen: How is it
that you have forgotten my love?
A love I cannot even think?
I thought you were a great person,
but now you refuse to come to me!
Ah! That lotus-eyed woman has ensnared you
in the web of her love,
and you've forgotten all my affection!
You said, "I won't even look at another,"
but when she enticed you,
you just gave your heart to her.

In performance, the text would be punctuated with complex passages of rhythmically oriented patterns of abstract dance (known as *aṭavus*, *kōṟvais*, and *tīrmāṉams*), and the interpretation would thus alternate between the gestural interpretation of the lyric and sequences of nonrepresentational dance. From the time of the composition of this piece, solo dance at the Tanjore court becomes the site for a number of important aesthetic experiments and innovations. This *svarajati* is remembered in palace manuscripts and the personal notebooks of dance masters for generations to come, and its iconic status indexes a new, reflexive approach to making, performing, and remembering the dance art of the courtesan.[79]

Over the next hundred years or so, court officials went to great lengths to incorporate courtesan performances into their rituals of display, and no doubt the growing European fascination with "nautch" dancing in Calcutta and Madras continued to this development. As we have already seen, it is during the rule of Tuḷajā II that the Quartet's family moved back to Tanjore and established the main "training centre" for professional dancers in the city. It would not, therefore, be unreasonable to suggest that the Quartet's new "suite" for the dance, which combined the established idioms of erotic, lyric poetry and rhythmic virtuosity in a balanced manner, was self-consciously styled for courtly performances that were understood as "nautch," that is, as a performance meant to circulate as entertainment by professional female dancers for native and colonial elites. Certainly, the Quartet's professionalization of the training, practice, and presentation of dance seems to support this interpretation.

The Quartet composed a number of songs in a variety of genres including *svarajati* and its offshoot, *varṇam*. Many of these were dedicated to deities in temples associated with the courts of Tanjore or Travancore, such as Śiva-Bṛhadīśvara of Tanjore, Kṛṣṇa-Rājagopāla of Mannargudi, or Viṣṇu-Padmanābha at Travancore. Others, indeed, the vast majority, are composed in praise of royal patrons including Serfoji II, Śivājī II, and Kṛṣṇarāja Uḍaiyār III. In the collections of these compositions preserved by the Quartet's descendants, the same composition often had two alternate sets of texts—one in praise of a royal patron and the other in praise of a deity. An example is the *varṇam* in Bhairavī *rāga*, which exists in two versions: one in Telugu dedicated to Serfoji II (likely an actual composition of Poṉṉaiyā), and another (later) one in Tamil dedicated to Śiva-Tyāgarāja of Tiruvarur.[80] The Telugu version, "nī sāṭi dora", survives today among the Telugu-speaking *kalāvantula* courtesans in the East Godavari district of Andhra Pradesh. Along with two other compositions by the Quartet, it was among the "five great *varṇams*" (*peddaidu varṇālu*) that were central to performances of salon dance in this region in the early twentieth century. As we will see below, Tanjore's courtly repertoire lived largely through the salon performances of the late nineteenth and early twentieth century in both the Tamil- and Telugu-speaking regions. The following translation was compiled from the version preserved by Kola Subrahmanyam, a woman from the *kalāvantula* community in Bommur, a suburb of Rajahmundry:

> *Pallavī*:
> I believed there was no king to equal you.
> Listen to me now, my Lord.
> *Anupallavī*:
> Śarabhendra, Scion of the Bhosala clan, son of King Tuḷajā,
> who revels in pleasure (*bhoga*) like the king of the gods.
> *Muktāyī Svara-sāhitya*:
> [I thought] I was a befitting woman for you,
> so I came into your presence.
> Now you must protect and look after me.
> I am in love with you, I can't afford to be tired;
> I can't be separated from you for even a minute.
> Great Lover, I've come to act out
> the books of love (*madanaśāstra*) with you!
> *Caraṇam*:
> Look, the God of Desire has descended upon me, I can't bear it.
> *Caraṇa Svara-sāhitya*:

He has unleashed his flowery arrows upon my breast.
Now the cool beams of the moon hurt,
Kokila birds are incessantly cooing.
This is the time for union,
Don't be stubborn, don't be angry, come to me now.

Why this anger?
Rise, beautiful one, I will not leave you even for a moment.
Embrace me, and give me the sweet nectar (*rasa*) from your lips.
Why are you not granting me the pleasure of making love?
I am waiting.

Listen to the pleas of my heart, let us live in happiness!
I thought you were a great king, so I came.
You are the one who will protect me,
you alone like a husband to me.
I have been waiting for so long, I can't bear it,
Ocean of Compassion!
Please oblige me.
Take your hand and press it on my heavy breast!
Now is the time to show me your skills in love-making!
Let me experience the beauty of your love.
What you are doing does not befit a king.
Please listen to me.

Like the *svarajati*, in performance, the *varṇam* too is punctuated with sequences of abstract dance and the recitation of rhythmic syllables and solfège. The persistence of erotic lyricism and the complex structure of this piece speak not only to the deployment of older idioms but also to the fact that this composition was meant as a "showpiece," a way of staging Serfoji's efficacy as the titular ruler of colonial Tanjore. Its lingering presence—and indeed its canonization as one of the "five great *varṇams*"—in contemporary *devadāsī* communities indexes the importance of these displays of culture within Tanjore's network of hereditary performers.

AFTERLIVES

After Śivājī died in 1855, the Company was prepared to declare the title "raja of Tanjore" extinct and take full control of the region's administration. Śivājī's widow Kāmākṣī Bāī, however, sued for the right to claim the title "Ranee of Tanjore" and for the stipend attached to the position.[81] Her appeal was successful, but either the stipend was severely downsized or its value had decreased beyond measure—in any event, there was less money to run the court and fewer wealthy inhabitants of Tanjore who could employ courtesans. Official performances of dance at the Tanjore court slowly began to fade after the time of Śivājī's widow, Kāmākṣī Bāī in the 1880s. On February 16, 1887, the Tanjore palace celebrated the Golden Jubilee of the accession of Queen Victoria to the throne. In the afternoon, a portrait of the empress, placed in a howdah mounted on an elephant, was processed around the town and through the palace grounds. In the evening a *darbār* was held at the Śivasaudha hall, where the Tanjore Palace Band played the national anthem. Following a brief address by T. Saminada Iyer, one of the members of the Tanjore Jubilee Committee, a "nautch dance" was held, followed by a display of fireworks and the distribution of *attar* (perfume) and *pān* (betel leaf) (Lawson 1887, 175). This account represents one of the last formally documented instances of courtesan dance at the Tanjore palace.

The patronage of Serfoji and Śivājī generated an exuberant but unfortunately short-lived moment of cultural production, a reminder of the unfinished condition of courtly dance forms originating in Tanjore. By way of conclusion, I offer some trajectories following by certain dancers and musicians and their descendants. Nautch dance—salon dance, as I call it—and to a lesser degree gramophone recording and film work, represent the main areas of artistic activity taken up by men and women from hereditary artistic families who migrated to Madras city. The next chapter will examine the aesthetic and political contexts of such work and its connection to social reform and the "dance revival"; I argue that these movements were in large part the result of reactions to the salon culture thriving in Madras city in the early twentieth century.

In the Quartet's direct lineage, only Civāṉantam had sons, Mahātēvaṉ (1832–1904) and Capāpati (1836–1894), who could carry on the artistic traditions of the family. They became reputed *naṭṭuvaṉār*s who trained a number of *devadāsī*s in and around Tanjore.[82] The Quartet's new "suite" and compositions for dance, however, traveled through their wide extended-kinship network, and presumably also through the *naṭṭuvaṉār*s and *devadāsī*s thought to have been their students. In a remarkably short period of time, these compositions became a part of the repertoire of *naṭṭuvaṉār*s and *devadāsī*s throughout the Tamil- and Telugu-speaking regions of the Madras Presidency, and ultimately became the "mainstay" of "nautch" performances in Madras city.

The new opportunities afforded first by "nautch" performances, then the emergence of gramophone and cinema, and then even later by the development of nationalist reinventions of music and dance, led to the gradual movement of *devadāsīs* and *naṭṭuvaṉārs* from Tanjore to Madras city and beyond. Among the early wave of *devadāsīs* who moved to Madras was Tanjore Kamakshi (1810–1890), great-great-grandmother of T. Balasaraswati (1918–1984). Around 1857, Kamakshi moved to Madras from Thanjavur and bought a house on Nattu Pillaiyar Koyil Street in Georgetown, Madras. Among the Quartet's immediate descendants, Poṉṉaiyā's daughter, Ciṉṉakuṭṭi Ammāḷ, married a man named Jagannātha Naṭṭuvaṉār, and also moved there toward the middle of the nineteenth century. Their son was Chennai Nellaiyappa Nattuvanar, whose notebook was mentioned above.

Another *devadāsī* to migrate to Madras was Tanjore Bhavani, a student of Capāpati (1836–1894), son of Civāṉantam of the Quartet. It is not clear when she went to Madras, but she did return to Tanjore years later, and her house there came to be known as *paṭṭaṇattu ammāḷ vīṭu* ("house of the lady from Madras"). She had one daughter, Kuchalambal, one of the last court dancers of Tanjore. Kuchalambal had several biological and adopted daughters including Ranganayaki, Sarasvati, Damayanti, and Dhanalakshmi. Two of her younger daughters, Damayanti and Sarasvati, also danced and lived inside the Tanjore palace. They were the concubines of a palace official whose name is unknown. Damayanti's daughter, Kuchalakumari (b. 1937), was taken to Madras and became an actress. Dhanalakshmi, the youngest daughter of Kuchalambal, also received an offer to act in movies, and she eventually married S. M. Letchumanan Chettiar, a businessman turned film producer and owner of Krishna Pictures in Madras. When Dhanalakshmi came to Madras to act in films, she was accompanied by her niece, Rajayi, daughter of her sister Ranganayaki. The Tamil film director K. Subrahmanyam (1904–1971) approached Rajayi to act in one of his films, and she became the extremely popular film star known as T. R. Rajakumari (1922–1999).

With Tanjore in fiscal decline, Madras city clearly held out a number of opportunities for dancers and musicians who could no longer support themselves according to the systems of patronage that were the hallmark of the Marāṭhā period. Indeed, Avanthi Meduri has presented a convincing argument that Śivājī's death resulted in a "mass migration" of artists from Tanjore to Madras (1996). While the evidence supports the claim that many people did migrate in this manner, it is important to note that a contingent of dancers and musicians remained in Tanjore and nearby districts well into the twentieth century. Neither should we assume that all dancers and musicians who moved to Madras occupied roles similar to the ones they and their families had left behind. Just as the courtesans of Marāṭhā-period Tanjore occupied an ambiguous social position that combined elements of other identities (as concubines, artists, and ritual performers), the variety of labor that women from such families performed in twentieth-century Madras (and, indeed, in India and the world) is equally diverse. Accounting for the afterlives of colonial Tanjore represents one task of the chapters that follow.

CHAPTER TWO

Whatever Happened to the South Indian Nautch? Toward a Cultural History of Salon Dance in Madras

In 2002, while I was conducting ethnographic research on dance traditions in the Godavari Delta in Andhra Pradesh, I met Sheikh Sur Jahan (fig. 2.1), a musician who accompanied a troupe of Telugu-speaking courtesans on the harmonium in the town of Muramanda. He had been playing for dance troupes (*bhogamēḷams* or *mēḷams*) since he was twelve years old, and at nearly seventy he was still a fine musician. Sur Jahan and his family regularly participated in *mēḷam* performances in this region, as both musicians and dancers. But Sur Jahan's female relatives were by no means the only Muslim women in the region who performed dance as part of *devadāsī* troupes. Late nineteenth- and early twentieth-century colonial ethnographies mention Muslim dancing women named as "*turku-sani*s" who performed in famous *mēḷam*s in the Godavari Delta and also had sexual relations with men from any of the "non-polluting" castes like their Hindu counterparts (Hemingway 1907, 58). They also go to great lengths to demonstrate that the community of "dancing girls" in the region consisted of "both Hindu Bogams and Muhammadan Bogams . . . and Muhammadan girls are married to a khanjir or dagger" (Ul-Hassan 1920, 91–92).[1] In the late nineteenth and early twentieth centuries, Muslim rulers such as the Nizams of Hyderabad (Fateh Jang Nawab Mir Mahbub Ali Khan Siddiqi, also known as Asaf Jah VI, for example) also patronized performances by dance *mēḷam*s from the Telugu-speaking regions.[2]

Indeed, figures such as Sur Jahan and the lineage of Muslim *bhogam*s from which he descends are discomfited signs of the secular nature of the dance *mēḷam* in South India. But why do we not hear of the secular "salon performances" by *devadāsī*s in cultural histories of South India? Why are historical representations of dance in South India linked almost exclusively to temples and temple culture? How has the use of the term

2.1 Sheikh Sur Jahan (*right*). Photograph by the author.

"*devadāsī*," full of ritual and religious connotations, eclipsed possibilities of thinking about the nonreligious lives of professional dancing women in this region?

While in many parts of North India, *tawā'if* courtesans in their capacity as entertainers have become part of the cultural and historical imagination of that region, courtesans in South India have for the most part become fossilized into "temple women"—"wives of the god"—and thus ostensibly, it appears that there is no courtesan culture in South India. If salon performances are mentioned at all by historians or dance practitioners, they are cast as symbols of the "degeneration" of dance practice in the region, though ironically this period saw the efflorescence of genres and compositions that form the mainstay of "classical Bharatanāṭyam dance" today.

Though some courtesans in South India have had very important relationships with temples and ritual cultures, and while many South Indian temples supported dancing women who underwent rituals of "dedication" to temple deities, a large number of courtesans did not participate in these religious activities. They professional women dancers who performed in artistic guilds (*mēḷams*), and did not have much, if anything, to do with temples. Even in communities such as those of the Kaveri Delta region in Tamil Nadu where temple dedication was a key marker of status and ritual privilege, normally only one girl in each generation would have such honors. Other girls in the household would simply become nondedicated courtesans who lived in the quasi-matrifocal home and participated in the nonconjugal sexual lifestyles associated with these communities. As for Tamil-speaking women who did undergo dedication rituals at temples, performances in other contexts, such as weddings and salons, also constituted a very significant aspect of their lives as performers in the nineteenth and early twentieth centuries.

The rise of the culture of salon performance in Madras, which as I have argued in the previous chapter, may have instigated the radical shifts in the presentation of dance in nineteenth-century Tanjore, roughly corresponds to the growth of the city itself. The distinctly urban culture of the salon emerged at a time when a number of commercial groups (and more specifically, the *dubash*-brokers employed by the Company) gentrified parts of the city's "Black Town."[3] Although salon performance flourished in the Madras Presidency in the nineteenth century, it became increasingly rare by the third decade of the twentieth century. The disappearance of the salon as a venue for courtesan performance gave rise to publicly funded institutions like the Madras Music Academy (est. 1928) and several other cultural organizations calling themselves *sabhā*s ("assemblies"). A handful of *devadāsī*s performed at these venues until the 1940s, perhaps in a final nod to the culture of the old-style salon, but this too was short-lived. Meanwhile, a small number of *devadāsī*s living in and around places like Madras, Thanjavur, Kumbakonam, and Trichy attempted to continue their performance practices, such as Papanasam Ramatilakam (1919–2000) and Kumbakonam Papammal (fig. 2.2), who performed on makeshift *pandal* stages and in the homes of patrons in Kumbakonam. But by the 1940s, the tide had turned, and the aesthetics and politics of dance were already in the hands of non-*devadāsī* women.

Recovering the history of salon performances of dance in South India is an arduous task. In this chapter I chart one of the fundamental ironies of salon culture in South India, namely, that the moment of its emergence also signaled the beginnings of its demise. I do this by historicizing salon performances through their most representative performance genre, the *jāvaḷi*, a short, usually fast-paced, erotic lyric. Like the culture of salon performance itself, the history of the *jāvaḷi* is unfinished. It has eluded critical historicization and has traveled through salons into the writings of Orientalist scholars, and moved into the cinematic imaginary, only to be neglected as an "inappropriate" dance genre in the contemporary world. Salon dance, as a secular form of entertainment, came to define dance as a specifically urban, cosmopolitan practice, and the *jāvaḷi* travels as a sign of the cultural eclecticism represented by colonial modernity. Bringing together colonial travel accounts, early Tamil and Telugu print material,

2.2 Papanasam Ramatilakam and Kumbakonam Papammal (1933), perhaps at the Kumbakonam Mahamakam Exhibition. Their accompanists, from left to right: Kumbakonam Tambuswami Pillai (*mṛdaṅgam*), Tanjore Ratna Nattuvanar, and Kumbakonam Swaminatha Pillai (clarinet). Photograph courtesy of B. M. Sundaram.

and ethnographic data, this chapter offers the first critical account of salon culture in Madras in the late nineteenth and early twentieth centuries. By focussing exclusively on the religious dimensions of South Indian dance, scholars and practitioners have missed an opportunity to engage with a unique performance style that offers an expanded view of what South Indian dance accomplished in the moment prior to the dance revival and social reform.

EUROPEAN ENGAGEMENTS WITH SALON DANCE

European administrators, missionaries, and visitors encounter *devadāsī*s and their performance practices in a variety of contexts, from temple and wedding processions to the salons of native elites. They almost always appeared as "peripheral (yet riveting) details in the narration of India's erotic landscape" (Taranath 2000, 7). European accounts of *devadāsī*s are heterogeneous and complex and have already been the subject of several studies (Bor 2007; Leucci 2005; Paxton 1999; Spear 2000; and Svejda-Hirsch 1992, among others). As a fundamentally unstable signifier, the South Indian *devadāsī*-courtesan is represented in mercurial ways from the eighteenth to the twentieth centuries. Representations of *devadāsī*s in this period emerge out of alliances between Christian evangelicalism, colonial anthropology, and imperial medicine, all of which are directed toward the moral reformation of women from these communities. Many colonial accounts of *devadāsī*s thus dwell, unsurprisingly, on the morality engendered by their dance. As with representations of sati, dancing by *devadāsī*s is ubiquitously identified—especially in missionary writings—with the civilizational depravity of "the oft-conquered people" of India.[4] By the end of the nineteenth century, mission work had become a highly feminized activity, and some late nineteenth- and early twentieth-century female missionaries such as Amy Charmichael (1867–1951) focused their efforts specifically on communities of *devadāsī*s. In many ways, the rhetorical and other strategies deployed in their attempts to "rehabilitate" *devadāsī*s are echoed in mid-twentieth-century reform activities spearheaded by Indian nationalist elites.[5] Consider the somewhat typical evangelical missionary account from 1853 of the conversion of children born to a Telugu-speaking *devadāsī* through her relationship with a British surgeon:

> It so happened, that there were two children who had come down from Masulipatnam to Madras, whose father, a European surgeon, had died when they were young; leaving them property. But the mother, a Teloogoo woman, who had been a dancing girl, had brought them up in heathenism. After much legal delay, Mr. Tucker was appointed guardian to these children, a girl fourteen years old and a boy, thirteen . . . The girl was perfectly wild and ignorant and it was with difficulty she could be taught to use a spoon instead of her fingers, to sit on a chair instead of on the ground, or to wear European dress. Her notions of religion were of the most debasing character, and her mind was thoroughly imbued with the heathen superstitions she had learnt from her mother . . . Having passed through a preliminary process of breaking in, the character of this girl began rapidly to develop, and greatly to improve. During a residence of two years on the Neilgherries, so great was the change, that she returned to Madras, where she was sent to a boarding school, quite a transformed character . . . The improvement of her character continued after her removal to school; and there was every reason to believe that she had become a truly converted follower

> of our Lord, when in the year of 1848, she was removed by an early and sudden death, at the age of nineteen. (Fox 1853, 126–127)

At stake in these representations is the "character" of *devadāsī*s. As we see in this account, the wild and ignorant daughter of the dancing girl is transformed into an exemplary, civilized native. More than other natives, *devadāsī*s and their children, as representatives of "another kind" of morality, are subject to excessive and unusual forms of scrutiny, sympathy, and objectification.

I wish, however, to shift our focus specifically to colonial representations of the aesthetic practices of *devadāsī*s, noting that most of these accounts refer not to dancing in temples, but to private soirees, "nautch" performances hosted by both colonial and native elites. Imbricated in these discursive constructions of the simultaneous sexual desirability and vulnerability of *devadāsī*s is the *fact* of the patronage of *devadāsī* dance by European elites. European support of salon performances anchored discursive constructions of native female sexuality that enabled Europeans to profit—economically, sensually, and politically—from its exotic, lascivious dimensions. As Anupama Taranath notes, "Metaphorizing Indian, and by extension all racialized sexuality, into the figure of woman . . . was a colonial strategy to encourage comprehension of the unfamiliar, and on a more general level, to partake in various excesses, sexual and otherwise, that India seemed to offer" (2000, 15). As we have already seen in the previous chapter, *devadāsī*s were mobilized as signs of cultural power and authority by native rulers like Serfoji and other landowning elites, especially *zamīndār*s.[6] As *devadāsī*s were coopted into the new economies of the emergent metropolis, their aesthetic practices found new, albeit highly competitive, patronage among native elites and British administrators.

Colonial engagements with cultural forms such as music and dance in South India are documented as early as 1727. That year, South Indian "nautch" dance was introduced into colonial public ceremony, when a *devadāsī mēḷam* accompanied Major John Roach in a procession to mark changes to the Royal Charter in Madras.[7] From at least this time onward, the South Indian salon dance or "nautch" was canonized as *the* most viable expression of elite sociopolitical authority. In some contexts, the space of the salon served to cement relations between Indian elites and Europeans in the sociological theater of colonial Madras. To be sure, women who performed in these contexts were not only objectified sexually by both groups, but were also racialized by Europeans across axes of imperial power. One only has to look, for example, at the "Nautch Dancing Girls" brought to New York to perform in an opera production in 1880, or those brought to perform in P. T. Barnum's shows in 1884, and the subsequent debates on race and citizenship they engendered in America (P. Srinivasan 2003, 2009). Returning to nineteenth- and early twentieth-century Madras, however, *devadāsī* dance was instrumentalized largely in the context of the reception and entertainment of guests by both the old aristocracy and the emergent gentry. Lavish dinner parties were hosted for guests, native and European, in the homes of these elites, in a manner parallel to concurrent developments in Calcutta. Representations of these performances of salon dance as displays of prestige in colonial Madras are found in a number of sources that traverse visual, literary, and anthropological terrain.

Officers of the Company were quick to capture the "nautch" in visual form. A number of commissioned paintings and later photographs of *devadāsī*s circulated through imperial networks, and these visual representations supplemented written accounts of *devadāsī*s beginning in the early eighteenth century. Paintings like the one in figure 2.3 from early nineteenth-century Madras, depict dance *mēḷam*s in great detail, usually showing a single performer, inevitably in a dance position, flanked by a *naṭṭuvaṉār* and other musicians, including drummers (*muṭṭu* or *mṛdaṅgam* players), flutists, violinists, and *tutti* players (men who played the bellows to maintain pitch). With the advent of photography in colonial India, images of "nautch girls" became a staple in collections and albums that journeyed from the colony to the metropolis. *Devadāsī*s in Madras were doubly fascinating because of their legacy as "temple dancers" in the colonial imaginary and their very real presence as "nautch" artists in the colonial city.[8] Like salon performances themselves, photographic representations of *devadāsī*s are undeniably sexually charged. But the sexuality of most of these photographs is subtly crafted. Indeed, many of the subjects of the photographs are carefully posed, often in positions that intentionally appear "dignified," and "respectable" enough, likely to assure audiences at home that upright morality prevailed among British men living or traveling in the colony. Indeed, it is rare to see photos of *devadāsī*s in performance. Figure 2.4, depicting a Telugu *bhogamēḷam* performing an acrobatic dance in 1862, presents somewhat of an exception to the rule. On the one hand, photographic representations serve to reify images of a "traditional" India represented by South Indian "temple dancers" found in missionary and travel writings in the nineteenth century, but on the other hand also create a dissonance. Photos of *devadāsī*s are rarely taken on temple grounds. Rather, they almost always posed in salon or outdoor settings with their *mēḷam*s.

2.3 *Representation of the Dancing Girls on the Coast of Coromandel,* Christopher Green (c. 1745–1805). © The British Library Board (WD 4510).

2.4 "Hindoo Dancing Girls," from *Sketches in India; Taken at Hyderabad and Secunderabad, in the Madras Presidency by Captain Allan N. Scott,* edited by Charles Richard Weld (London: Lovell Reeve, 1862). © The British Library Board (Photo 961[70]).

Written accounts of performances by professional dancing women in colonial India, as Regula Qureshi has observed, "tend to privilege the visual since these authors lacked the familiarity and comprehension to relate to the words [of the songs] or their musical setting" (2006, 316). "First-hand" accounts of nautch performances in Madras city by British authors are extensive. Indeed, these texts could very well form a major study unto themselves. I will now turn briefly, therefore, to some representative examples in which salon performances are described by colonial administrators. The first specimen comes from 1838, and describes a "subscription nautch" (a commissioned performance, negotiated by contract) hosted by V. Juggarow in honor of Englishman A. R. McDonnell at Vepery, a suburb of Madras:

> The European gentlemen were about sixty in number, principally of the civil and military services; and several ladies were present also. The following programme exhibits the entertainment above stairs.
>
> - A set of three Mahomedan dancing women, dancing in a circular form round the hall.
> - A young Hindoo girl, dancing on the sharp edges of swords, which are fixed in a ladder, at the same time cutting pieces of sugar-cane, applied below her feet.
> - A set of eight Hindoo dancing women, each of them holding a string fixed in the ceiling, dancing in different ways, and forming the strings into nets, ropes, &c. at the same time singing and beating time with their feet and hands.
> - A set of three Hindoo dancing girls, dancing in the Carnatic form.
> - A Hindoo dancing girl, dancing in the Hindoo form, to an English tune.—Music with European instruments.
>
> . . . It was said that the value of the jewels on three of the girls, who were dancing together could not have been less than ten thousand pagodas! They were literally covered with brilliants, not excepting their noses, which were positively tortured with precious stones.
>
> The rather alarming exhibition of a young girl dancing on the sharp edges of swords, which formed the second act, was repeated late in the evening; but on the second occasion, she cut limes with her heels, instead of sugar-cane. It appears hardly credible that a delicate little girl should be able to stand on the edge of a sharp sword, and at the same time, by pressing with her heel, cut a lime in two on the same instrument.
>
> Throughout the evening, the European guests, and especially the ladies, experienced the most polite and unremitting attention from the

> native gentlemen who gave the entertainment. A room was laid out with every luxury to gratify the palates of our omnivorous countrymen—wine cooled to a fault; and indeed, nothing omitted which could render the entertainment worthy of the occasion.[9]

This description captures the complexities of European representations of native dancers and their arts. There is certainly a fascination, usually erotic (as we will see more obviously in the example that follows), with any of the visual markers of difference—in this case with the dancers' jewels that subtly evoke an exotic sexuality. But this is immediately juxtaposed with a moral judgment. The observer is simultaneously disturbed by the risks posed to the "delicate little girl" who dances on the edge of swords. These kinds of representations are best understood as metonymic; the elements of any single version parallel those of imperial adventure in the male imagination: the confrontation, rescue, reform, and conquest of natives all live through these tellings.[10]

But this account also reveals the fundamental aesthetic heterogeneity of salon dance itself. The dancers hosted by Juggarow present both "Mohamedan" and "Carnatic" styles of dance, a reference to the presence of North Indian genres and styles alongside South Indian ones. We also see that these courtesans are performing to an English tune and with European musical instruments, and this characteristic persists in a number of descriptions. Finally, the dancers are engaged in acrobatic feats, including chopping lime and sugarcane with their heels while dancing on the blades of swords, and the performance of the dance with "string fixed in the ceiling" (*piṉṉal kōlāṭṭam*) that we will discuss below. The inclusion of these kinds of numbers as innovative modes of entertainment was another pervasive aspect of salon dance: Telugu-speaking *devadāsī*s in the Godavari River delta and in the southern Nellore and Chitoor districts regularly performed dance while standing on the edge of brass plate, for example. In Madras city, Chennai Nellaiyappa Nattuvanar (1859–1905), the grandson of Poṉṉaiyā of the Quartet, choreographed a *varṇam* for his students (sisters named Duraikkannu and Parvati) in Mylapore, in which the dancers tied vegetables to their bodies, and at the end of every rhythmic sequence chopped off one vegetable with a knife (Sundaram 2003, 271). Other *devadāsī*s in the city performed a popular Hindustani piece called *pataṅg uḍāī* ("kite flying") that resembled North Indian courtesan dance (Sankaran 1986, 64). These acrobatic and other novel additions to performance practices allowed *devadāsī*s and *naṭṭuvaṉār*s to thrive in the competitive aesthetic economy of Madras city.

Let us return to Qureshi's notion of the "privileging of the visual" in colonial descriptions of courtesan dance. In 1875, Prince Albert Edward (1841–1910), eldest son of Queen Victoria who would later become King Edward VII, visited Madras. He was treated, in Royapooram, a suburb of Madras, to a performance that he watched, it seems, out of obligation:

> The hall, nearly two hundred yards long, was filled with princes, the Madras staff, and hundreds of ladies. His Royal Highness, who wore his scarlet uniform of field-marshall, was presented with a casket and address when he entered the building. The most enjoyable part of the scene was the stage with the groups of black-haired dancing girls, attired in dresses of white and gold, with shoulder-sashes of yellow and purple and scarlet, and armlets and bracelets of diamonds and all manner of precious stones. In their ears and noses there were rings, which were simply constellations of diamonds. These ladies and their male accompanists with tom-toms, fiddles, and zithers, sang songs and shared in grotesque dances. It was a picture the strange beauty of which could not be eclipsed.
>
> In the nautch dances there are sometimes two or three performers; sometimes, as on this occasion, only one. They are always young, and frequently beautiful. The dancer clashes together the silver bands worn on the feet above the ankles, and raises her arms, jingling the bangles, in alternate movements above her head, to a droning accompaniment from the musicians; now and again she bursts into a twangy song with apparently no distinct air or meaning, and which always ends abruptly. The character of the dance itself is wearyingly changeless, with the exception of an occasional turn which loosens the gauze scarf and reveals for an instant the figure of the still well-clothed chest. There is nothing lively, graceful, or attractive about it. No one cares to see a nautch twice unless the dancers have very pretty faces and very pretty dresses . . .
>
> The Prince of Wales was obliged to yield to native prejudices and witness the nautches; but long before he reached Madras, His Royal Highness, like every one else with the expedition, seemed to have become thoroughly tired of the stupid spectacle.
>
> There are Hindoo nautch girls and Mahomedan nautch girls all over India, and everywhere they seem to awaken the same veneration in the native mind and to receive abundant presents and remuneration for their services. Perhaps the prettiest execution of this evening was the Kolattam, or plait dance, round a maypole, to the air of "Bonnie Dundee," rather differently rendered from the way we are accustomed

> to hear it in Scotland. A dozen girls of splendid physique took part in the dance; they had castanets in their hands, and their dress, bloomer fashion, was of muslin trimmed with long gold fringe and tassels; their slight waists were encircled with belts of solid gold. During this dance the lime-light was thrown with full fervency upon the waltzers, and the little muster of fairlylike costumes and dark but animated faces was one of unparalleled beauty. (G. Wheeler 1876, 176–178)

Because these descriptions relied largely upon the ocular, colonial observers almost never commented on the lyric poetry that was at the heart of *devadāsī* dance. Instead, they view it almost wholly as the skill of displaying the body. Indeed, this writer is disappointed that the dancer's scarf reveals nothing but her "well-clothed chest," and notes that all the dancers had a "splendid physique," but comments that no one really cares to see them unless "the dancers have very pretty faces and very pretty dresses." The Prince of Wales is evidently "tired of the stupid spectacle." Aesthetic judgments on the dance are also central to this descriptive mode: the dance is "grotesque" and there is "nothing lively, graceful, or attractive about it." The one dance the writer singles out is precisely one of the visually "novel" type—the *pin̲n̲al kōlāṭṭam*—a group dance performed with sticks, a genre that was also performed by courtesans at Tanjore.[11]

In one final example dated 1888, General E. F. Burton reminisces about a nautch he attended more than thirty years earlier during a visit to "Bhowany" (presumably the Bhavani River, in the Nilgiris):

> The public bungalow or rest-house at Bhowany . . . was erected many years ago by a civilian of the old school. He lived in native style, as many people did sixty or seventy years ago, and he left his mark behind him, not only by building this house, but also by establishing a corps de ballet, i.e., set of Nautch girls, whose accomplishments actually extended to singing "God save the Queen," . . . and this has been kept up by their descendants, so that in 1852, when I first visited the place, I was greeted by the whole party, bedizened in all their finery, and squalling the National Anthem as fervently as if they understood it, which they did not.

This passage speaks to ways in which dance was mobilized as a sign of the modern. I do not think that these types of compositions served an instrumental function of creating and identifying Anglophone subjects for cultural proselytization in a Macaulayan sense; it would be difficult to simply dismiss this as a case of mimesis. In chapter 4, I will examine the life of these compositions in greater detail, looking at how women in *devadāsī* communities themselves understand such interventions.

European readings of native dance only through its spectacular and ocular dimensions appear to have disturbed some native elites. As early as 1806, a Telugu Brahmin named Partheputt Ragaviah Charry, who was a native informant for Holt Mackenzie's Mysore Survey Project, wrote a booklet entitled "A short account of the dancing girls, treating concisely on the general principles of Dancing and Singing, with the translations of two Hindo songs."[12] This text was an introduction to South Indian "nautch" dancing for his European employers, whom he felt were missing something as they observed the form. While technical aspects of both music and dance in the *mēḷam*s were sometimes formulaic, and thus slightly more accessible to Europeans, the improvisational aspects of courtesan dance, their mode of poetic exegesis through gestural interpretation (*abhinaya*) was not. Ragaviah Charry writes this tract to help Europeans understand this essential dimension of courtesan performance:

> The habitual politeness of English gentlemen ever induces them to accept the attentive invitations of the Natives to partake in the pleasures of a *natch*, or the feats of Dancing Girls: an entertainment common throughout Hindostan, nay India. But I am inclined to think that many of the Gentlemen, and more particularly the Ladies, who are not acquainted with the Poetical part of the Native languages in which the songs are composed, must remain contented with the information of the eye . . . Men are inquisitive in the first instance and that very properly to know the history and character of the objects presented to their view. (1)

As Amanda Weidman has noted, "For anything to be properly available to the European gaze . . . a certain structure or order had to be discernable beneath the surface. To such a gaze, the surface appeared as a kind of mask of insensible repetitions and embellishments" (Weidman 2006, 209). But Ragaviah Charry's work also provides us with some key information on salon performances in Madras at a time when descriptions of these soirees are extremely rare. The document details the performance practices of the dance *mēḷam*s. Toward the end of the text, the author proceeds to describe a typical salon performance in its entirety. The essay includes deliberations on aesthetics (*rasa* theory), the classification and names of hand gestures, and *tāla* (rhythm). The latter half of the essay describes a performance of *devadāsī* dance from beginning to end. It opens with the *naṭṭuvaṉār* reciting the *mēḷaprāpti*, a rhythmic prelude, followed by the *toḍaya maṅgalam* (*jaya jānaki ramaṇa*, described and translated in the text as "a Prayer to Rama"). Next is the "Hymn of Salam," the *salām jati* or *salām-daruvu*, a composition in honor of the Marāṭhā kings of Tanjore. He provides a translation of the following *salam-daruvu* in praise of King Pratāpasiṃha (r. 1740–1763), which is still remembered in courtesan communities in coastal Andhra Pradesh:

> Pratapa Sinha, the valiant in war; You are exclusively endowed with the accomplishments of Music and Poetry, in the abstruse science of Bharata Sasha [*bharata śāstra*], and in the art of Abhinia [*abhinaya*] or counterfeited—you are well versed on all subjects and your mind is liberal and you posses unbounded courage—To you, O Maha Raja, I render Salam. (9)

Following this "bustling and noisy commencement," Ragaviah Charry informs us that the remainder of the performance consists of *abhinaya* in the form of *varṇam*s, *padam*s, and *kīrtana*s, and proceeds to describe the genre that comprised the mainstay of the salon performances, the Telugu *padam*. This is a most significant aspect of Ragaviah Charry's work. He presents two full *padam*s in English translation. These are certainly the earliest translations of the poems of the seventeenth-century composer Kṣetrayya, and are also the first English translations of any of the song-texts associated with dance in South India. Below is Ragaviah Charry's translation of the *padam* "bāgāya nī vagalella" in Āsāvarī *rāga*, in which a woman confronts her lover about his infidelity:

> 'Tis very surprising, O Muvva Gopala, all your gallantries,
>   *'tis exceedingly pretty.*
> To you I give the folded beetle, but you hand it over to that lotus-eyed
>   (a pretty woman) with whom this world laughs at your intrigues.
>   *'Tis very surprising.*
> I waste my intreaties on you; but you love her, whose eyes are beautiful as
>   lotus;
> you freely express a contempt of me, and the circumstance is ridiculed at the
>   houses of those flowerlike framed women of delicate and elegant
>   constitutions.
>   *'Tis very surprising.*
> I'd throw myself into your arms and take an interest in your amusements,

> Oh Muvva Gopala, but you listen to malicious reports and live at
> variance, you hold me in disdain, and esteem her, that female friend.
> *'Tis very surprising.* (10)

This work provides us with a description of salon dance as it was performed in Madras prior to the advent of the Tanjore Quartet's innovations, and this is still more or less the suite remembered by the *kalāvantula* community in contemporary Andhra Pradesh, as we will see in chapter 5.

*DEVADĀSĪ*S AND SALON DANCE IN EARLY TELUGU AND TAMIL PRINT MATERIALS

Some of the earliest texts that describe salon scenes in Madras are in Indian languages—Sanskrit, Telugu, and Tamil. Many of these texts provide us with rich accounts of the lavish lives of modern Indian elites and also furnish details about dance and music practices. Most of these works also point to the always ambiguous social status of women in *devadāsī* communities, who are usually glossed by terms such as *veśyā* (courtesan). It is important to note that these texts are *not* about the idealized "*devadāsī* temple-woman" retrieved by contemporary historians, but rather about the courtesans—professional dancing women. It is also important that the stereotypes embedded in this kind of literature fuel the conscious exclusion of the history of salon performances from the writings of nationalist historians of dance.

Representations of *devadāsī*-courtesans in vernacular literatures of South India thus enable us to trace, with some degree of precision, their persistently ambiguous social and moral status. Beginning as early as the eighteenth century—the period of the Nāyaka overlords—Tamil poets, particularly those connected with *zamīndāri samasthāna*s and other local networks of literary patronage, wrote about *devadāsī*-courtesan characters that are identified as performers at both courtly *darbār*s and in temple *maṇḍapa*s. It is important these texts establish the trope of the lascivious and money-hungry courtesan, a theme that is fully realized in late nineteenth- and early twentieth-century print materials I will discuss later. I briefly turn now to the plot of a new genre patronized by "little kingdoms" in the Tamil-speaking regions of South India. This genre, known as *viṟaliviṭutūtu*, the "poem of the female bard messenger," forms the basis for many of the modern literary representations of women from *devadāsī* communities that emerge at the high points of social reform in the early twentieth century.

Kūḷappa Nāyakaṉ Viṟaliviṭutūtu is a long poem composed by Cupratīpa Kavirāyar in the early eighteenth century, and is dedicated to his patron, Nākama Kūḷappa Nāyakkaṉ, the Nāyaka overlord of Nilakkoṭṭai.[13] It is perhaps the best-known example of the *viṟaliviṭutūtu*, although certainly not the earliest. It also contains all of the narrative tropes and archetypal characters that come to define the genre. The *Kūḷappa Nāyakaṉ Viṟaliviṭutūtu* is also the subject of a brilliant essay by David Shulman (2001) on innovative genres in Nāyaka-period Tamil poetry. The poem is framed as a panegyric, but the plot of the poem itself is about a Brahmin who has an extramarital affair with a dancer whom he meets while she is performing at the temple of Śiva-Cevvantīca at Tiruchirappalli. His wife, hearing of the affair, forces him to leave their house, and he wanders from place to place until he reaches Madurai, where he meets Mataṉāpiṣēkam, a highly accomplished courtesan. Mataṉāpiṣēkam fleeces the Brahmin, who is so overcome with desire that he leaves behind his ritual duties, and eventually loses all his wealth to her. When he is completely broke, the *devadāsī*-courtesan (*tēvaṭiyāḷ*)'s mother, Māṇikkamālai, humiliates and abuses him. She takes the issue up with the local temple officials, who tell the Brahmin that he should forego his relations with courtesans, return to his village, and earn a decent living by using his intellectual skills. The Brahmin then witnesses a grand temple ritual, patronized by the righteous King Kūḷappa Nāyakkaṉ. He decides to approach the king, who, impressed with his poetic skill, appoints him as a court poet. He accumulates wealth in this capacity, and eventually sends a messenger to appease his wife. We are left with the anticipation of their conjugal reunion.

Another *viṟaliviṭutūtu* text comes from the Ramanathapuram *zamīndāri*, and is composed about one hundred years after the *Kūḷappa Nāyakaṉ Viṟaliviṭutūtu*. The *Cētupati Viṟaliviṭutūtu* is a poem by Ciṟiya Caravaṇa Perumāḷ Kavirāyar, a poet at the Ramanathapuram court, and was likely composed sometime between 1845 and 1862. This poem has recently been discussed in Sascha Ebeling's pathfinding new work on nineteenth-century Tamil literature (Ebeling 2010, 144–159), and Ebeling has also critically dated the work (253–255). Here, as in the *Kūḷappa Nāyakaṉ Viṟaliviṭutūtu*, the hero at first loses his wealth to a *tāci* named Māṇikkam in the town of Uttirakosamangai, then again to another *tāci* named Mōkaṉamuttu of Thiruvidaimarudur. This text replicates the plot of the earlier *viṟaliviṭutūtu* poems, and as we will see below, is itself replicated by writers in the twentieth century.

Other nineteenth-century works such as the Sanskrit *Sarvadevavilāsa* ("Sport of All the Gods," likely composed around 1820, extant only in the form of a single paper manuscript) and the Telugu *Cĕnnapurivilāsamu* ("Sports in the City of Chennai," composed by one Nṛsiṃhaśāstri and first printed in 1863) describe private gatherings in homes that cemented social relations among high-ranking men and provide us with some of the earliest documented scenes of salons in South India.[14] In the *Sarvadevavilāsa*, the *dubash*es of Kovur and Manali (localities just outside Madras), merchants, and non-Brahmin temple administrators (*dharmakartā*s) are imaged as regal patrons of learning and the arts, creating the illusion that they were free from any superior authority (Peterson 2001). They hosted lavish assemblies known as *sada*s, both inside and outside temple contexts, and on festivals such as Navarātri, these soirees revolved around the presentation of concerts of music and dance. In the *Sarvadevavilāsa*, many of these men are depicted with their courtesan-mistresses who are described as famous singers and dancers of the time, and are referred to as *gaṇikā*s and *dāsī*s. Thus we have the names of Nārāyaṇī of Kumbhakonam, Maṅgai of Tanjore, and Mīnākṣī of Salem.[15] The last of these figures was a very prominent courtesan of Madras who paid for the Brahmin vocalist, Patnam Subrahmanya Ayyar (1845–1902), to move to the city from Tiruvaiyaru in Tanjore district, so that he could teach her daughters vocal music. He stayed in the city for twelve years in the outhouse of Salem Mīnākṣī, who paid him Rs. 100 a month. It is here that he composed a large number of *jāvaḷi*s, songs in the distinctly modern genre that I will discuss later in this chapter.

The advent of print culture in colonial South India, as Stuart Blackburn has demonstrated, "enabled change, allowing certain texts and forms of information to spread . . . more quickly and widely than was previously possible by speech or writing" (2003, 10). Blackburn concedes that it "is beyond dispute is that print increased literacy, multiplied the copies and widened the distribution of traditional text; it reached new audiences with new types of information and encouraged new literary forms. And through all these innovations, print facilitated public debate on everything from vernacular education to child marriage and nationalism" (12).

As we will see below, the advent of print culture reified extant social and moral ambiguities around *devadāsī*s in the emergent colonial public sphere. However, before we move on to discussing this effect of print culture, it is important to realize that a handful of men and women from the *devadāsī* community mobilized print media to other ends. Some Tamil-speaking *naṭṭuvaṉār*s engaged print culture to write about their dance traditions or to preserve them.[16] We have, for example, the *Naṭaṉāti Vāttiya Rañcaṉam*, a text written by Pasuvandanai Kaṅkaimuttu Piḷḷai (1837–1920), a distant relative of the Tanjore Quartet living in Madurai, in 1898 that preserves a number of compositions meant for courtesan dance (Krishnan 2008, 78–82), including songs in the *kavuttuvam* genre meant for ritual performances in temples.[17] In 1904, Aruṇācala Piḷḷai of Pandanallur (1873–1939), a descendant of the Quartet, published a Telugu work called *Abhinayābjodaya Sulocani*, a theoretical work on gestures and their applications (Aruṇācala Piḷḷai 1907). In 1908, Ulsur Venkatasundarasani, a courtesan who performed at the Mysore court, published a voluminous Sanskrit treatise in Kannada script entitled *Rasikajana Manollāsinī*, which contains theoretical material as well as analyses of compositions meant for courtesan performance from her repertoire (Veṅkaṭasundarāsāni, 1908). She is also the author of another work called *Bharata Kalpalatā Mañjarī* (Veṅkaṭasundarāsāni, n.d.). The emergence of texts such as these forces us to consider the fashioning of the performing arts as knowledge systems that, from the standpoint of these hereditary performers at least, could be integrated within the cultural world of colonial modernity. Finally, in 1911, Ka. Añcukam, a Tamil-speaking *devadāsī* from Kochchikade, Colombo in Sri Lanka, deploys print technology to compose a lengthy text called *Uruttirakaṇikaiyar Katācārattiraṭṭu*, "A Compilation of Stories about Śiva's Courtesans" (Añcukam 1911; Soneji 2010). This remarkable 240-page work represents the author's attempt to locate *devadāsī*s in a timeless distinctiveness, foreground their links to the iconic institution of the temple, and script herself into a civilizational genealogy palatable to reformers and other native Tamil elites. For Añcukam, print afforded possibilities for self-representation in the face of early reform movements in colonial Ceylon (Soneji 2010).

Having noted some of the ways in which *devadāsī*s and their families engage print technology, I want to now shift our attention to presentations of courtesans that come from outside the community and are widely circulated in the form of printed tracts, poems and novels in Tamil, Telugu, and English between roughly 1850 and 1950.[18] All of these literary works (save one, *Tāsikaḷ Mōcavaḷai* [1936], written by Muvalur Ramamirttammal, which I will discuss in chapter 3) are composed by men, and most employ a graphic descriptive mode or satire. As the examples below will demonstrate, the texts combine literary virtuosity with a moralizing discourse that inevitably maligns courtesans and salon culture. The earlier texts among these are precursors of the public "Anti-Nautch" debates that begin with Kandukuri Viresalingam (1848–1919), a Brahmin from Rajahmundry, and then continue in the work of Dr. Muthulakshmi Reddy.

In 1864, Rācaveṭikavi, a resident of Tiruttani, wrote a short text entitled *Gaṇikāguṇapravartana Tārāvali* ("Poem on the Transformation in the

Nature of the Courtesan"). Published in Madras, the work is technically a secular poem centered on a female character (a *laghukāvya*), and is in the subgenre known as *tārāvali* ("row of stars," consisting of verses in the *sīsapadya* meter). The work focuses almost exclusively on depicting the cunning nature of the courtesans (*gaṇikās*) who ensnare "innocent" men into their traps of sexual pleasure, greed, and disease. It juxtaposes graphic descriptions of sexual acts with depictions of the pain of venereal disease that has affected the male protagonist. No doubt, there is a titillating dimension to this literature meant for its elite male consumers. It narrates, in a linear manner, one man's encounters with a courtesan, and consistently oscillates between representations of pleasure and pain. Unlike the other texts we have discussed, *Gaṇikāguṇapravartana Tārāvali* does not dwell on the lure of the aesthetic skills of the courtesan as much as it does on men's vulnerability when they are aroused by the sight of the bodies of available women. Indeed, dance and music are only mentioned once in the text. The courtesans are referred to in Telugu by the terms *veśyā* and *vārakānta* ("one who has a new lover each day") or its variant, *vārakāmini*. The poem opens with an image of a respectable city man who is "born into a good family" and "expresses love toward his wife, embraces her, and kisses her on the cheeks. He meticulously collects all his savings, and thinks about his future." On the next page, we are introduced to the courtesan as a kind of sorceress, conjuring a potion that will ensnare young men:

> How the prostitute keeps her man under her control: she makes a potion. Taking lentils, garlic, the wax which is in the ear of a dog, she mixes it, boils it, and adds the flesh of a crow, the nerve of a scorpion, the root of the tree of heaven, and the flank of a cat which has been butchered on a Sunday. Bringing these together, she prepares an ointment and applies it on the man's legs. Such *veśyā*s should certainly be avoided. (Rācaveṭikavi 1864, 6)

In the following section, the mood shifts dramatically. The text presents explicit images of the same man afflicted by venereal disease after intercourse with the courtesan. This is preceded by a description of the various reasons why men visit courtesans:

> One type of man complains that his wife cannot have children. A second person says that all his friends and relatives have turned against him. A third man says that he is unable to reach self-awareness (*kaivalyapadavi*). A fourth man complains that he is addressed in a dis-

> respectful manner— "Hey!" A fifth one says his body is giving him trouble. A sixth man feels excessive heat all over his body. A seventh is afflicted with various diseases [and so no woman will have relations with him]. An eighth man himself tortures his own body [by masturbating]. These kinds of people want to have relationships with a *vārakāmini*, and she knows this. He dedicates all the gold he possesses to this woman, yet cannot expect anything in return. But he *does* contract a number of diseases from her, leaves her house, and shamefully returns to his own home. Without even a penny to his name, he admonishes himself for having gone to the *vārakānta*'s house. His body becomes warped like a half-moon (*ardhacandra*). But full of lust, he feels the urge again . . . On seeing her, he pulls back the foreskin, and notices a small leakage of blood and urine. He looks down into his hand, but now the line of fortune (*dhanarekhā*) is in *her* hand! The only goal of these women is to attract young men and take away all their money. (20–21)

The poet also preempts any sympathy the reader might feel toward the courtesan. The familiar trope of "rescue" is completely absent in his text. He makes it clear that courtesans are incorrigible and that attempts to engage with them in any way are ultimately futile:

> Even if one is favourable to the *veśyā* and makes a gesture to help her, his attempts will ultimately be transformed into the situations described above. Each and every syllable uttered by the *vārakānta* is soaked in poison (*viṣam*). *Vārakāmini*s are willing to go to any extreme [to get what they want]. (ibid.)

The sexual boldness of the courtesan, titillating as it is, is later transformed into frightful demonic force. The courtesan "swallows" the man and ultimately subjugates him:

> Like water flowing from a tap, they speak obscene words and have cunning eyes . . . She herself pulls out the organ of the man which looks like a plantain (*rambhā-phalam*). She starts to squeeze it, and pulls the foreskin back, and places it in her hole. What should I say about men who resort to the houses of such prostitutes who have the acquisition of wealth as the singular goal of their life? . . . She makes him happy with her love play and finally she shows him a place in the corner of the house where a curtain is drawn, and makes him join her cohort of cooks and servants! This place is the kitchen, where he becomes one in a line

> of several others . . . The man's mind becomes a ball in her hands . . . She seems to blush at the sight of a man, and her face becomes red. But she swallows the man through her eyes. She holds the smoke from incense up to her genitals as if to dry her wet pubic hair. She ties a knot in her petticoat. She applies perfumed substances to her body and looks out for a prospective client . . . Discarding shame (*lajjā*) or honour, with only the thought of intercourse on his mind, without any fear or sense of propriety, this man is prepared to have union even with his own mother! He comes to surrender his money to her. Such men are cunningly "tonsured" (humiliated) by the *vārakāmini*. (34–36)

The courtesan also "emasculates" her partner, by turning him into a cook or servant in her house. This motif appears at least five times throughout the poem, in a move that dwells on the valorization of the economics of "respectable" family life in which gender roles are clearly defined.

Another text is *Vārakānta*, with the English subtitle *The Nautch Girl* (fig. 2.5), a Telugu novel by Raja M. Bhujanga Rau Bahadur, *zamīndār* of Elluru, published in 1904. Bhujanga Rau was a connoisseur of Telugu literature, and in 1928 he coauthored with P. Chenchiah an English-language work called *A History of Telugu Literature*. *Vārakānta* is a complex narrative that focuses on a professional dancing woman named Kanakāṅgi and on her relationship with a married man named Keśava Rāv. The familiar trope of the money-hungry courtesan using black magic is central here as well. Kanakāṅgi and her mother Pāpa con Keśava Rāv into giving up all his money, and eventually take him to court, arguing that even his house should rightfully belong to them. They win the case, since *veśyā*s are dharmically entitled to support from their patrons. A broken man, Keśava Rāv seeks solace in his virtuous wife and friends, and ultimately is consoled by them. In the end, the novel, like the Tamil *viṟaliviṭutūtu* texts discussed above, enforces the triumph of monogamous, conjugal sexuality and valorizes the institution of marriage. In addition to very plainly contrasting the figures of courtesan and wife, the novel also casts professional dancing women as temptresses who lure men into the nets of their deceitful love.

The second chapter of the novel includes a two-page section entitled "The Commencement of the Mejuvāṇi" (*mejuvāṇi prārambhamu*). There the author is clearly conversant with many of the technical dimensions of courtesan performance, but he ultimately foreshadows the tragic end of the narrative with a recurrent moralizing discourse on the dangers of associating with *sāni*s or courtesans. I cite this lengthy passage almost in its entirety because of the great care with which it treats the dance and

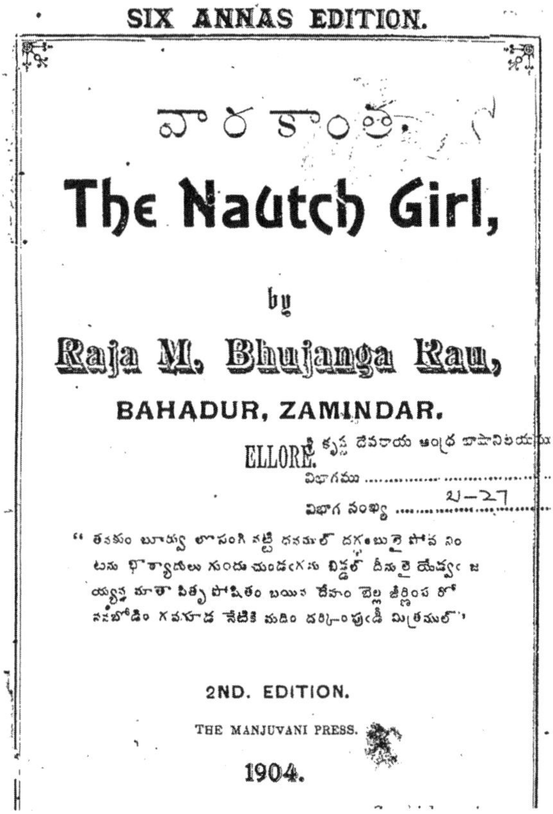
SIX ANNAS EDITION.

వారకాంత.

The Nautch Girl,

by

Raja M. Bhujanga Rau,

BAHADUR, ZAMINDAR.

ELLORE.

" [illegible] "

2ND. EDITION.

THE MANJUVANI PRESS.

1904.

2.5 The cover of *Varakanta: The Nautch Girl* by Raja M. Bhujanga Rau (1904), a Telugu novel that contains long and detailed descriptions of *mejuvāṇi* (salon) performances by Telugu-speaking courtesans. Collection of the author.

music practices of *devadāsī*s in the *mejuvāṇi* (salon) context. It is clear that the author has witnessed a great number of these performances, and his description of the event is remarkably detailed. It mentions specific genres such as *padam* and *pallavi* practiced by Telugu-speaking *devadāsī*s. It also specifically mentions Kanakāṅgi's performance of a *jāvaḷi* during which she repeats lines again and again, affecting several new, improvised interpretations, in a process referred to as *sandhi-viccheda sañcāri* among Telugu courtesans.

> The *maddaḷa* drum resounds. Bangles jingle. Some people come to the dance arena and offer obeisance. Some think, "How fortunate am I to

be here!" Others are quiet. The *śruti* (drone) sounds in at perfect pitch, the musicians tune either instruments in unison, and sit on one side. Then the melodious voices of women are heard. It is like the sound of celestial musicians (*kinnaras*). Then they begin to sing beautifully in chorus. But even the God of Desire hangs his head in shame when the dance begins. The dance is exhibited according to the tenets of Bharata, and to the accompaniment of the bagpipe. Watching the *abhinaya*, you feel the dancer is beckoning you, intoxicating you. With her gorgeous face, she appears exceedingly beautiful. The audience lose themselves in that beauty. Watching the *abhinaya*, one hears exclamations: "Bravo! What is life without dance?" At times she lifts her hands, at times her feet, she whirls, she performs *abhinaya* while reclining. She raises one hand and the other falls. An audience member tries to tie a handkerchief around her. That young girl sings song after song in heavy, difficult *rāgas* (*ghana rāga*). She appears like a play-thing reveling in acts of pleasure. She performs various types of footwork that befit the song she is singing. That young, beautiful girl Kanakāṅgi wears various jewels on her body. Young and old in the audience are bewildered. "Who will be fortunate enough to get close to her?" they think . . . Not this one, not that—she sings all the *padas*, *svaras*, *kṛtis*, and *pallavis*. "Do the *śloka* I taught you, darling" says someone. "Bravo! Bravo!" they cry, as if drowning in the juice of aesthetic pleasure (*ānanda rasa*). She turns her face here and there, and finally the dance with a vase is done and the audience is completely spellbound. She performs . . . *abhinaya* looking at Keśava. [Through her *abhinaya*] she says to him, "You should come at midnight," in a manner smooth as a simile (*upamā*) . . . Kanakāṅgi received accolades for her performances of *abhinaya* in *kṛtis*, *pallavagītis*, and for showing the various positions of love (*sarasas*) . . . Looking in the direction of Keśava Rāv, she performs *abhinaya* to a *javali* entitled *ninne namminānurā* ["I believed in you"]. She expresses that she has so much love toward him, as if she really does. She repeats the words "ninne, mari ninne, ika ninne, ninne." The [implied] meaning of this can easily be understood by anyone . . .

"In this world, *sānis* [courtesans] alone can provide such pleasure. *Sānis* are the only ones who can do this. She sings and dances with a *double entendre*!" they think, until the early hours of the next morning. With the performance of song after song, the *meḷam* finally comes to an end. Uncontrollable urges overcome those men who watched the performance. Most do not have the courage to act upon their urges, even though they feel them deeply. They get up and leave, cursing the fact that the performance has come to an end. (Bhujanga Rau 1904, 19–21)

Much later, just before the promulgation of the Anti-Devadasi Act of 1947, the trope of the excessively erotic and "cunning" courtesan was still present in popular Tamil literature. *Meṭrācai Viṭṭu Nāṭṭipurattukku Oṭṭam Piṭitta Tācikaḷ Taṅkappāṭṭu* ("Songs about the *dāsīs* who left Madras and ran away to the villages," 1943) is a text by K. Kurucāmitās.[19] The poems center around the "*veśyā* whores" (*vēci-muṇṭaikaḷ*) who "pollute" Madras city, and out of fear of being persecuted under the new Devadasi Abolition Bill of 1929 are "running back" to their villages in the Kaveri Delta. The writing style and content continue trends seen in earlier texts such as the *Gaṇikāguṇapravartana Tārāvali.* The focus is on the intensity of the sexual experiences shared by the *dāsī*s and their lovers, but the "innocent young men" are fleeced by the *dāsī*s, wander about Madras like emasculated beggars, and ultimately contract venereal disease. The first section cautions the reader against the evils of the *dāsī*s. The second, using images of the "Madras Surgeon's" pronouncements on venereal disease together with the Devadasi Abolition Bill introduced in 1929, celebrates the cleansing of Madras city from the moral "filth" represented by *devadāsī*s. The language of the songs is harsh, and threats to *devadāsī*s and their potential male partners pervade the work. The text opens, for example, with the following couplet: "Don't believe them, don't believe them, the *dāsī* whores (*tācimuṇṭaikaḷai*). Don't ruin yourself by trusting them, those *veśyā* whores (*vēcimuṇṭaikaḷai*)." *Dāsī*s are vilified as selfish, impure, and diseased women. Kurucāmitās explicitly also contrasts courtesans with "good" married women, and curses the former repeatedly:

> Virtuous married women (*pattiṉikaḷ*) are ruined by these whores.
> Great people lose their honor (*māna*) and abandon their virtuous lives. (1.10)
> It seems there are fights over this slough from the gutter.
> These folks are buying disease, they just don't know any better. (1.13)
> If these "golden" *dāsī*s live in this town,
> I will torture them and make sure they flee. (2.10)
> Let the *dāsī*s and *veśyā*s rot.
> Let the middlemen who earned money rot. (2.12)
> The *dāsī* ran away,
> and now Kāsi [the middleman, pimp] has been pacified. (2.14)
> The age-old filth has disappeared,
> and the people of Madras are elated. (2.15) (Kurucāmitās 1943, 1–3)

These early Tamil and Telugu print materials produced in Madras by men—which include poems, tracts, and novels—thus facilitated new urban representations of *devadāsī*s as worthy targets of moral and aesthetic reform. These literary representations of *devadāsī*s in Madras embodied masculine anxieties about the shifting sexual and moral economy of late nineteenth- and early twentieth-century India. In her work on representations of *devadāsī*s in British and Anglo-Indian novels, Nancy Paxton has noted that unlike their Romantic forbearers, who idealized *devadāsī*s as embodiments of sacred sexuality, the authors of these texts present them as signs of "unresolved conflicts concerning gender, sex, and romantic love" (1999, 86). I would argue that *devadāsī*s represented similar concerns for the authors of the Telugu and Tamil early print materials discussed here. In most of this writing, the culture of the salon is pitted directly against that of the home and conjugal unions. As Charu Gupta has demonstrated in her work on sexuality and the mobilization of communal rhetoric in Hindi-speaking India in this period, economic instabilities, combined with an emergent public discourse of social purity, affected a major reorganization of social space in which courtesans and prostitutes were ultimately "indentified as a malignant sign of the loss of wealth and wasteful expenditure" (2001, 115). Gupta goes on to say that in spite of the displacement of these women through public condemnation (as seen in the examples above from Telugu and Tamil print materials), courtesan culture continued to thrive, but on the margins. The courtesan "was a threat to civilization and at the same time ensured its sanctity by operating outside the norm, hidden from respectability" (122). In South India too, as I will show below in my discussion of the *jāvaḷi* genre, the public condemnation of courtesan performance by native elites existed *alongside* its patronage. Indeed, the high point of the aesthetic innovations of salon culture in South India also ironically coincided with the beginnings of its disappearance. Both sides of the coin were fundamentally shaped by transformations of masculinity in the public sphere (Sinha 1995). On the one hand, the male body needed to be secured from pollution and corruption, strengthened by its commitments to (and control over) the world of monogamous, domesticated female sexuality. On the other hand, economic security and power continued to be expressed through displays of nonconjugal female sexuality that were emblematic of engagements with colonial authority and traditional expressions of sexual virility. Courtesans were ultimately pushed to the cultural margins, overwhelmed by the valorization of monogamy and domesticity in nationalist discourse. As we will see in chapter 3, reinventions of masculinity and citizenship from both within and without the *devadāsī* community led to their disappearance from public culture and rendered hegemonic the authoritarian morality of the patrifocal domicile.

JĀVAḶIS AND SALON PERFORMANCE: ORIGINS AND SOURCES

In 1960, eminent Sanskritist V. Raghavan was asked to write the preface to a volume of Telugu *jāvaḷi* songs. Dr. Raghavan appears frustrated in the preface, unable to crack the historical puzzle of the *jāvaḷi*. He writes: "[C]uriously for a type which has come up in times so near to us, the Jāvaḷi is really obscure in its origins."[20] And Raghavan is not alone—over the past century, the *jāvaḷi* has been contentious in terms of both its origins and its status. Excepting Raghavan and a few others, most contemporary writers and performers dismiss *jāvaḷi*s as degenerate expressions of poetry that are meant to arouse the senses, and nothing more.[21] Unlike the songs of the older Telugu *padam* genre from which they derive their structure and narrative contexts, *jāvaḷi*s are rarely thought of as "highbrow" or "classical" songs. Traditionally associated with *devadāsī*s in colonial Madras and their upper-caste male patrons, *jāvaḷi*s are the quintessential marker of salon performances by courtesans. They unsettle nationalist reinventions of dance as temple-based and purely religious, and perhaps because of this, they are rarely heard in contemporary performances of Bharatanāṭyam dance and Karṇāṭak music. The elusive nature of the *jāvaḷi* mirrors that of salon culture more generally, and so now I shift my focus to retrieving the limited but highly significant, if unfinished, cultural life of this genre.

In form and structure the *jāvaḷi* is basically indistinguishable from the *padam*, except perhaps for its lighter, more playful style. What makes the *jāvaḷi* unique, and what has perhaps contributed to its opacity as a form, is the very context of its performance, the relations that it proposes between dancer and audience. The field of its production is also radically different from that of the *padam*s composed by apotheosized Telugu poets such as Annamayya and Kṣetrayya. While these composers lived and worked at medieval centers of religious pilgrimage and devotion like Tirupati, *jāvaḷi* composers (*jāvaḷikarta*s) worked in the civic heart of the colonial city, employed as Taluk clerks or post office workers. Unabashedly erotic, sometimes sarcastic, and always upbeat, *jāvaḷi*s are also signs of the volatile, sexually charged space of the salon, one that was diametrically opposed to the contained, private sexuality of the conjugal home.

Emerging between the demise of courtly forms of the nineteenth century on the one hand, and India's emergent entertainment industry on the other, the *jāvaḷi* defies existing generic classification. In this section, I argue that it is precisely this "transitional" status of the *jāvaḷi* that has made it an unsolvable riddle for scholars and historians like Raghavan. As texts, jāvaḷis are sites for multiple experiments in syncretism with regard to language and music. They are incorporated into Parsi theater–inspired Tamil plays, sometimes written in a combination of South Indian languages and English, are subject to Orientalist analyses, and even enter films.

For over a century, scholars have grappled with the definition and etymology of the *jāvaḷi*. In 1894, Reverend F. Kittel in his *Kannada-English Dictionary* defined *jāvaḷi* as "a kind of lewd poetry," evidently derived from the Kannada word *jāvala*, which he translates as "common, vulgar, or insignificant." Kittel's definition appears to have been the point of reference for nearly all subsequent attempts to pin down an etymology for the word. Similarly, when it comes to the content of the *jāvaḷi*—namely, exactly how it is different from the *padam*—there is an absolute lack of consensus. The *jāvaḷi* shares the tripartite structure of the *padam*: it contains *pallavī*, *anupallavī*, and *caraṇam*. This threefold unravelling of the poem, literally from the "sprout" (*pallavī*) of the poem to the elaborate *caraṇam* stanzas, enables narrative and aesthetic movement through the text. Like songs in the Telugu *padam* genre, *jāvaḷi*s are usually dedicated to a localized form of Kṛṣṇa. Often the *mudrā* or "signature" of the composer of the *jāvaḷi* is the name of the God. So, for example, the *jāvaḷi*s of Patnam Subrahmanya Ayyar are identifiable through their inclusion of the names "Veṅkaṭeśa" or "Varada-Veṅkaṭeśa." These similarities, combined with the emphasis on eroticism, or *śṛṅgāra*, in both the *padam* and *jāvaḷi*, mark them as nearly indistinguishable.

Two major historical trajectories prevail when it comes to the invention of the *jāvaḷi* as a musical form. The first, perhaps more historically accurate, narrative situates the genesis of the genre at the Mysore court under the patronage of the kings Mummaḍi Kṛṣṇarāja Uḍaiyār III (1799–1868) and Cāmarāja Uḍaiyār IX (1881–1894). Two Kannada paper manuscripts from the time of Kṛṣṇarāja Uḍaiyār that are preserved in the library of the Institute of Kannada Studies at the University of Mysore attest to the fact that the genre was in existence during his reign.[22] Later, under the patronage of both of these kings, the Tanjore Quartet dance master Ciṉṉaiyā, who was employed, among others, by the king, is known to have composed songs that were known as *jāvaḍi*s or *jāvaḷi*s. The other narrative revolves around events at the court of the last king of Travancore, Mahārāja Svāti Tirunāl

(1813–1846). Here, the first *jāvaḷi* is said to have been crafted by the dance master Vaṭivēl of Tanjore (1810–1847, younger brother of Ciṉṉaiyā). On the whole, there appears to be less evidence to support such a claim.[23]

Sources for studying *jāvaḷi*s as literature or as scripts for performance are few and far between. With the exception of the two Kannada paper manuscripts mentioned above, manuscripts of *jāvaḷi*s do not exist in library collections. Notations of *jāvaḷi*s can be found in the personal notebooks of some *naṭṭuvaṉār*s, or dance masters, such the one belonging to Chennai Nellaiyappa Nattuvanar (1859–1905) that I discussed in chapter 1. Other sources include nineteenth- and twentieth-century print materials in Tamil and Telugu, such as the chapbook *Teluṅku Ciṅkāra Jāvaḷi* (Telugu Śṛṅgāra *jāvaḷi*s) published in 1924 (fig. 2.6) and more elaborate

2.6 The cover of *Teluṅku Ciṅkāra Jāvaḷi* (1924). Collection of the author.

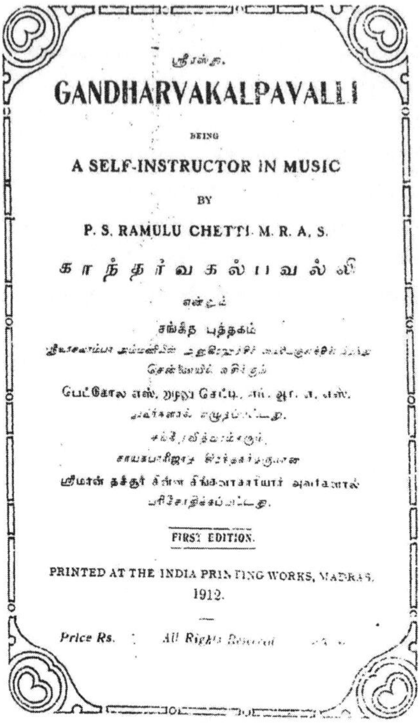
ஸ்ரீரஸ்து.

GANDHARVAKALPAVALLI

BEING

A SELF-INSTRUCTOR IN MUSIC

BY

P. S. RAMULU CHETTI. M. R. A. S.

காந்தர்வகல்பவல்லி

என்னும்

சங்கீத புத்தகம்

பெட்கோல எஸ். ராமுலு செட்டி, எம். ஆர். ஏ. எஸ்.

FIRST EDITION.

PRINTED AT THE INDIA PRINTING WORKS, MADRAS.
1912.

Price Rs. All Rights Reserved

2.7 The cover and frontispiece of the Tamil edition of Ramulu Chetti's *Gāndharvakalpavalli* (1912). Collection of the author.

books on South Indian concert music, such as the treatises of Taccur Singaracharyulu[24] and the *Gāndharvakalpavalli* (fig. 2.7).[25] This last work by P. S. Ramulu Chetti was published in both Telugu and Tamil versions in Madras in 1911–1912. Not much is known about Ramulu Chetti other than the fact that he was a non-Brahmin master of the harmonium, an instrument that was banned by All India Radio in 1930 and much despised by many traditional Brahmin musicians in South India. The large number of compositions in this work that are traditionally associated with *devadāsī* performance points to the fact that he may have been in contact with *devadāsī*s, perhaps even as an accompanist. I shall return to this text later.

The last and perhaps most abundant source of *jāvaḷi*s comes from within the traditional community of *jāvaḷi* performers, the *devadāsī*-courtesans of South India themselves. In both the Tamil- and Telugu-speaking regions—from the northern tip of the Godavari Delta to the Kanyakumari district in the deep south—these women have continued to preserve the texts and performance techniques of *jāvaḷi*s. In the latter half of this section, I will discuss the ways in which contemporary *devadāsīs* talk about and perform texts and techniques traditionally associated with *jāvaḷis* and salons.

Although the *jāvaḷi* is traditionally understood as a Telugu or Kannada genre, between roughly 1880 and 1910 *jāvaḷis* became extremely popular as Tamil *devotional* songs meant for theatrical performance. The new scripting of *jāvaḷi* in religious language indexes the flexibility of the genre and the heterogeneous constitution of artists and audiences who encountered it as a distinctly modern form. These circulated in small inexpensive chapbooks, usually eight–ten pages in length, each of which consisted of a set of songs dedicated to localized Tamil deities. Thus, we have collections of Tamil "*jāvaḷis*" called *Citamparam Naṭarāja Civakāmiyiṉ Pēril Pārsi Ati Aṟputa Jāvaḷi* (1906) dedicated to Śiva-Naṭarāja and his consort at Chidambaram, and *Maturai Cuntarēśvarar Jāvaḷi* (1888) dedicated to Śiva as Sundareśvara at Madurai. Here the *jāvaḷi* as a "popular" genre of literature and music easily fits into the emergent contexts of Tamil theater that consciously presented itself as *innovative* (note the term *ati aṟputa*, "astonishing," in the title above), and linked itself to the Parsi theater.

Most of these songs were composed by non-Brahmin Vēḷāḷars who were involved in the emergent world of Tamil popular drama known as *icai nāṭakam*, or "special" *nāṭakam*, that was shaped by Caṅkaratās Cuvāmikaḷ (1867–1922) between 1887 and 1922. Indeed, many of the chapbooks are written and/or published by members of popular early drama companies in Madras with names such as Chennai Manoranjita Nataka Sabha (Chennai Association for Entertaining Theater). These songs are also part of a new set of performance practices deeply affected by Parsi theater companies that toured the Madras Presidency in this period. As Susan Seizer (2005, 52–54) has convincingly demonstrated, the aesthetics of popular theater in Tamil Nadu emerges out of a peculiar kind of nineteenth-century cultural modernity in which Vēḷāḷars and Tēvars are literally the new dramatis personae, deploying consciously innovative staging, music, and acting technique.

More generally, early South Indian print materials on music also contain large sections called "Pārsī Pāṭṭukaḷ" (Parsi songs), and often *jāvaḷis* are subsumed under this category, which usually contains Hindi and Urdu love songs from Parsi plays such as "āo jī āo" from the play *King Lear*.[26] These songs, which employed North Indian melodies adapted from Hindustāni *rāgas*, gave rise to a catchall genre in South Indian music, called "*pārsī meṭṭu*," or "Parsi tunes." Thus, many *jāvaḷis* are not in known South Indian *rāgas*, but in their printed forms are listed as set to

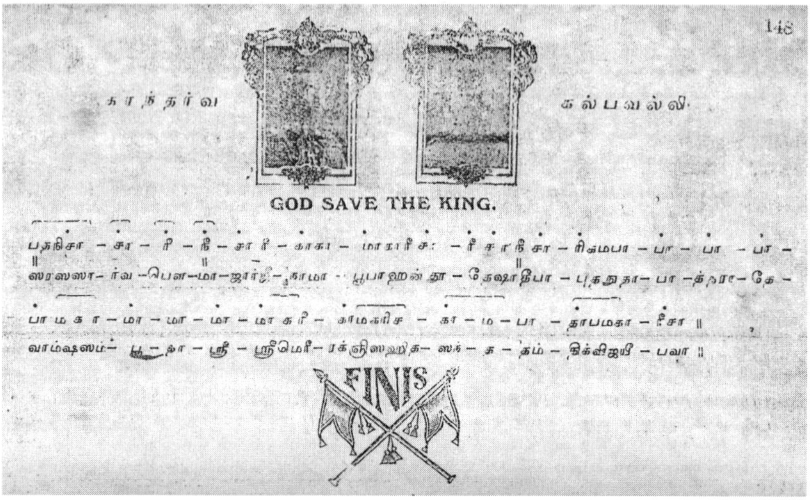

2.8 "God Save the King" in Sanskrit in honor of King George V and his wife Queen Mary from *Gāndharvakalpavalli.*

the *pārsī meṭṭu.* By the 1920s, the terms "*pārsī meṭṭu,*" or "Hindustān *meṭṭu,*" referred to any "odd" tune or song that could not be classified as part of the indigenous South Indian music or dance repertoire. These included *jāvaḷi*s, "gramophone songs," and even popular everyday Tamil song genres such as *naḷaṅku* ("wedding songs") and *oṭam* ("boat songs"). In the *Gāndharvakalpavalli,* the final tune listed under "Pārsī Pāṭṭukaḷ" is a Sanskrit version of "God Save the King" entitled "*sarasa sārvabhauma jārjīnāma bhūpa*" in honor of King George V and his wife Queen Mary, who visited India in 1911 and staged the now infamous Coronation Darbar in Delhi that same year (fig. 2.8).

The forms of cultural hybridity that surround genres like the *jāvaḷi* also include radical experiments with language similar to those we have already seen in Tanjore (in the performance of the *kuṟavañci,* for example). In the *Gāndharvakalpavalli,* we also find a *jāvaḷi* in a mixed-language genre, consisting of four languages—Tamil, Telugu, Kannada, and English. Composed by the Tamil poet Śivarāmayya (c. 1798–1820) from the village of Karur near Trichy, nearly each word in this song alternates between the languages, and clearly, the song is meant for consumption by a cosmopolitan audience.[27]

Jāvaḷi in Four Languages (*caturbhāṣā jāvaḷi*)[28]
Pallavi (refrain):

my dear come [English] *varuvai* [Tamil] *ī veḷa* [Telugu]
Caraṇam (stanza):
ninnujūci cāla [Telugu] *divasa āyite manna* [Kannada] *nī nā manasu impaina* [Telugu]
kālaharaṇamiñca [Telugu] *for me now* [English] *beḷatiṅgaḷu bisallavāyite* [Kannada]
kuḷuku taḷakugaḷa [Telugu] *come* [English] *birāna* [Telugu] *well I shall sing* [English] *Śivarāmuni* [Telugu] *songs* [English]

A translation would read something like this:

My dear, come, come here now! Many days have passed since I have seen you.
O King! Fill my heart with your sweetness. Why do you delay for me now?
Months have passed—it all seems a waste!
With all your charms, come quickly, well I shall sing Śivarāma's songs.

THE PRODUCTION AND PERFORMANCE OF *JĀVAḶIS*

Many prominent *devadāsī*s and *naṭṭuvaṉār*s from Tanjore moved to Madras after the annexation of Tanjore to the British in 1856.[29] Among them was Tanjavur Kamakshi (1810–1890), whom we met toward the end of the previous chapter. Kamakshi supplemented her income as a dancer by giving weekly private recitals of Tamil hymns from the devotional text *Tiruppukaḻ* at the family shrine in the home of a prominent merchant named Rangoon Krishnaswami Mudaliar (Menon 1999, 56). Vina Dhanammal (1867–1939), Kamakshi's granddaughter, was one of the most celebrated female artists of her time, and as Lakshmi Subramanian (2009) has demonstrated in a recent biography, became a symbol of "authentic" Karnatak music on the eve of its reinvention in the mid-twentieth century. Dhanammal became famous for the musical soirees she hosted—"salon performances" in her own home—every Friday from 6:00 to 8:00 in the evening. In addition to these performances amid boughs of jasmine flowers, Dhanammal also performed in the homes of a number of Madras's commercial elite—Tirumalaiya Naidu, T. Sitapati Iyer, Raja Sir Ramaswami Mudaliyar, and A. Rangaswami Iyengar (editor the *Hindu* newspaper), and others.[30] Dhanammal met Dharmapuri Subbaraya Ayyar (c. 1864–1927, fig. 2.9), a clerk in the Taluk office at Hosur, while she was singing at a festival in Tiruvottriyur just outside Madras (Sankaran 1982a, 24). The two shared an intimate relationship, and it was for her and her

2.9 Dharmapuri Subbaraya Ayyar (c. 1864–1927). Photograph courtesy of T. Sankaran.

family that Subbaraya Ayyar, who was also an accomplished musician, composed over thirty *jāvaḷi*s. Several of these make anecdotal references to their sexual relationship.[31] In some senses, this exemplifies the social dynamic that characterizes the creation of most *jāvaḷi*s —composed by upper-caste men, performed by courtesans, and usually symptomatic of an intimate relationship between the two.

This tradition of salon-based performance was also very common in the Telugu-speaking parts of the Madras Presidency from the late eighteenth century onward. Here, troupes of courtesan performers who were known as *kalāvantulu* or *bhogamvāḷḷu* were contracted to perform in the homes of Brahmin and non-Brahmin elites and would receive obligatory fees and gifts called *ŏsagulu* for their performances. In Telugu, these salon performances were called *mejuvāṇi* or *mezuvāṇi*, from the Urdu word *mezbān* or *mezmān*, meaning "landlord, master of the house, host of a feast, a man who entertains guests." But in fact the repertoire they performed was continuous with the repertoire of their Tamil-speaking counterparts. For example, they performed compositions dedicated to Tanjore's Marāṭhā kings, Serfoji and Śivājī, and also *jāvaḷi*s composed by Patnam Subrahmanya Ayyar of Madras, whom I have already discussed.[32]

Literally embodying the aestheticized ideal of the *nāyikā* or heroine of the *padam*s and *jāvaḷi*s, the South Indian dancing woman relied on artful self-representation in the salon context. The bulk of Telugu *jāvaḷi* texts are written from the perspective of the *nāyikā*, and it is not surprising that there is a certain self-consciousness among courtesans today when they talk about these texts. Kotipalli Hymavathi, from a *kalāvantula* community in the village of Muramanda in coastal Andhra Pradesh, told me "*Jāvaḷis* are my favorite songs. I like how the woman talks to the *nāyaka* [hero] in these songs. She can tell him what she really thinks, and there's nothing wrong with that (*emi tappu ledu*)!"

Indeed, the themes of *jāvaḷi*s are sometimes bolder than those of the Telugu *padam*. In one very popular *jāvaḷi* from coastal Andhra Pradesh composed by Neti Subbarayudu Sastri (c. 1880–1950), the heroine admonishes Kṛṣṇa for approaching her on the days of her menstrual period. She says, "*You* made the rules of purity and pollution, and now you want to break them? No way! You'll just have to wait."[33] *Jāvaḷi*s also commonly deploy rhetorical strategies familiar from other *bhakti* contexts, such as those of *nindā-stuti* ("complaint-praise") and, of course, the allegorical uses of sexual imagery. But when we watch a performance of *jāvaḷi*s by courtesans, these ideas clearly recede to the background. The *jāvaḷi* is, like the *ṭhumri* of the North Indian *bāījī* or the *lāvaṇī* of the Maharashtrian *kaḷ āvant*, a dance genre whose primary function is to entertain. As an erotic composition meant specifically to entertain urban audiences, the jāvaḷi drew from the standard poetic and narrative tropes that already existed in the lyrics for courtesan performance. The primary actors in *jāvaḷi* poetry—following earlier Telugu and Tamil *padams*—are the heroine (*nāyikā*), the hero (*nāyaka*), and the heroine's confidante (*sakhī*). As Matthew Allen notes in his discussion of Tamil *padam*s, courtesan poetry employs both direct and indirect rhetorical stances, with the heroine either directly addressing the hero, or speaking to him through her confidante (Allen 1992, 337–339).

The movement through the poetry of a *jāvaḷi*, like that of a *padam*, is cyclical. The performance of *padam*s and *jāvaḷi*s as music for dance is

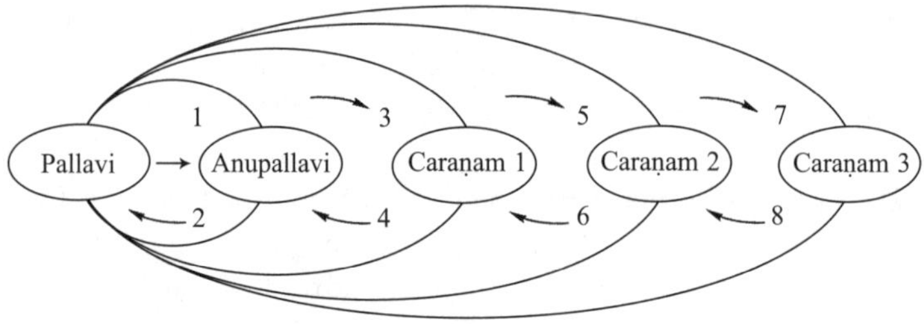

2.10 Movement through the text of a *jāvaḷi* in performance, after Matthew Allen (1992, 288).

itself a lyrical act. The artist renders the text through a movement that returns to a central theme encapsulated in the refrain, or *pallavī* (fig. 2.10). The *anupallavī* and multiple *caraṇam*s have the *pallavī* as their point of reference. Poems meant for performance by *devadāsī*-courtesans are rarely linear "storytelling," but rather cyclical, lyrical texts that suggest emotive landscapes and invoke fleeting visions of erotic and social situations. The cyclical nature of this rendition also allows *jāvaḷi*s to invoke memory and oscillate between past and present.

The *jāvaḷi* that follows was composed for the family of Vina Dhanammal in Madras by Dharmapuri Subbaraya Ayyar in the *rāga* Khamās. In it, the heroine's confidante speaks to the hero, asking him to reunite with the heroine who longs to make love to him:

Pallavī:
nārimaṇi nīkainadira jāracora ma
Crafty lover! This matchless woman is the one for you.
Anupallavī:
dhīra vinarā śrī dharmapurādhipa mā cakkani
Listen, sweet hero of Dharmapuri. *She's the one.*
Caraṇam 1:
boṭi nercina ratipāṭalu saiyāṭale
She has learnt her erotic lessons.
vadhūṭiyu sarisāṭila pāṭiyana kādāṭa mā
No woman can outplay her! *She's the one.*
Caraṇam 2:
mārubalkĕrugani mānini gadarā kāmini
She'll never say no to you, moon-faced one,
tārādhipa nī bhāvakādanare sarasaku
she knows all your lovemaking moods. *She's the one.*

Caraṇam 3:
māravīruni virisaramula korvadhika
She can't suffer Kama's arrows anymore—
rārā saraguṇanu cekorā marukeḷiki mā
come play his games with her. *She's the one.*

In her attempts to entice the hero, the confidante extols the heroine's skills in lovemaking, and these kinds of poetic passages traditionally provide courtesans ample scope for depicting various kinds of sexual union through elaborate metaphors and complex gestural vocabulary. The Telugu-speaking courtesans of the Godavari River delta deployed *rati-mudrās*—a set of over fifty different hand gestures that depicted the positions (*bandhālu*) of lovemaking—in their performances of *jāvaḷis* (fig. 2.11). They also performed another technique known as *nakha-śikhā varṇanam*, "praise [of a woman's body] from the toenails to the crown of the head."

2.11 Maddula Janakamma (b. 1932) demonstrates the use of *rati-mudrās* in the rendering of compositions like *padams* and *jāvaḷis*. Manepalli village, East Godavari district, Andhra Pradesh, 2002. Photograph by the author.

Here, the various parts of a woman's body are compared to images found in the natural world, largely in keeping with lyrical conventions used by Telugu and Sanskrit poets. Variation and improvisation are at the heart of courtesan interpretations of songs like *padams* and *jāvaḷis*; therefore the texts themselves are often open-ended to allow for flexibility in their interpretation through *abhinaya*. In addition to the complex improvisations in *abhinaya*, *jāvaḷis* also provided an occasion for the display of improvised patterns of abstract movement for the body (*aḍavu* or *aḍagulu*) among Telugu-speaking courtesans. At the conclusion of the last line of the *jāvaḷi*, the musicians improvise on the *rāga*, and abstract dance movements are performed to this musical sequence. The clusters of movement end with a tripartite cadence called *muktāyi*. This technique, which almost always follows the rendition of *jāvaḷis* by Telugu-speaking courtesans, is called *gaptu-varusa*, a "string of dance movements," and was an indispensable technique in the performance of *jāvaḷis* in the Godavari Delta region.

JĀVAḶIS AND NEW MEDIA

Another new performance opportunity was presented to professional dancing women in the first decades of the twentieth century, namely, that of gramophone recordings. As Stephen Hughes (2002, 450–451) has noted, recording companies promoted these recordings by emphasizing the "respectability" of the listening experience—that is, enjoying *devadāsī* music without any personal contact with the performer herself. Printed indexes to gramophone recordings with titles like "Gramophone Kīrttaṉāmirtam" contain the texts of several *jāvaḷis* sung by *devadāsīs* such as Tiruchendur Shanmukhavadivu, Tiruvidaimarudur Bhavani, Coimbatore Thayi, and Salem Godavari, all of whom produced top-selling records for company labels such as HMV in the first two decades of the twentieth century (Hughes 2002, 2007; Weidman 2006).[34]

The first women to appear on gramophone recordings made in India were courtesans from Calcutta—Soshi Mukhi, Fani Bala, Saila Bai, and Gauhar Jan (Kinnear 1994). Gauhar Jan, born as Angelina Yeoward, produced some of the most famous recordings of all.[35] In 1910, Gauhar Jan came to Madras for a performance at the Victoria Public Hall, organized by C. Gopala Chetty, a wealthy textile merchant and music connoisseur.[36] By this time, Gauhar Jan was a celebrity, with hundreds of her songs circulating across India from 1903 onward. In Madras, she was hosted by a *devadāsī* named Salem Godavari. Vina Dhanammal organized a catered dinner in honor of Gauhar Jan and taught her a Telugu *kīrtana* by Tyagaraja, which Gauhar Jan recorded a year later (Sampath 2010, 144). By 1912, the texts of Gauhar Jan's recordings of Hindi songs were already circulating in Tamil print, for example, in our *Gāndharvakalpavalli,* where they are found under the heading "Songs by Gauhar Jan of Calcutta" (*kalkattā kōhar jāṉ pāṭṭukaḷ*), but still under the metagenre of Parsi theater songs.[37]

*Devadāsī*s were also in high demand by early Indian cinema. Prominent early film producers and directors such as Lakshmana Chettiyar and K. Subrahmanyam recruited *devadāsī*s to act in their films, some of whom, like M. S. Subbulakshmi, gained iconic status largely because they *left* cinema to pursue more "respectable" professions early in their career. In the context of cinema, we see how the *jāvaḷi* indexes a major cultural transition—from the intimate salons of Madras elites to the artifacts of mass culture. The journey of one *jāvaḷi,* travelling from a traditional community of performers, through the fieldnotes of an Orientalist musicologist, and into a Telugu film, foregrounds the genre's distinctively modern life. An example of this is the *jāvaḷi* "aṃtalone tĕllavāre," which has been attributed by some to Dharmapuri Subbaraya Ayyar. It describes a married woman after a night of illicit lovemaking. She wakes in the bed of Kṛṣṇa, who is "full of desire" (*makkuvato gopāluḍu*), and sings: "In the meanwhile, dawn has come. Ayyo! What can I do?" This composition makes an early appearance in a text by Captain C. P. Day, who wrote his famous work *Music and Musical Instruments of Southern India and the Deccan* in 1891. The text provides the *jāvaḷi* in Western staff notation and indicates that it is in the Śaṅkarābharaṇam *rāga* and Rūpaka *tāla*. Captain Day also notes that this was "perhaps the most popular" of the "*javadi* airs" danced by the nautch girls of the Madras Presidency (fig. 2.12).

2.12 The *jāvaḷi* "aṃtalone tĕllavāre" from C. P. Day's *Music and Musical Instruments of Southern India and the Deccan* (1891).

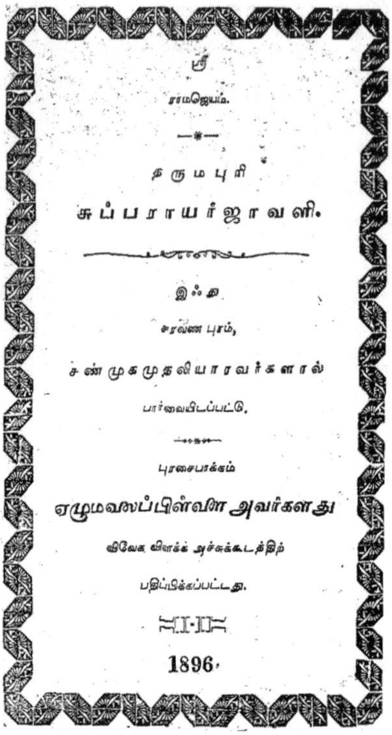
ஸ்ரீ

ராமஜெயம்.

தருமபுரி

சுப்பராயர்ஜாவளி.

இஃது

சரவண புரம்,

சண்முகமுதலியாரவர்களால்

பார்வையிடப்பட்டு,

புரசைபாக்கம்

ஏழுமலைப்பிள்ளை அவர்களது

விவேக விளக்க அச்சுக்கூடத்திற்

பதிப்பிக்கப்பட்டது.

1896.

2.13 The cover of *Tarumapuri Cupparāyar Jāvaḷi* (1896), an anthology of *jāvaḷis* attributed to Dharmapuri Subbaraya Ayyar published during his own lifetime. Collection of the author.

Oddly, the same song also appears as one of the *jāvaḷi*s composed by Dharmapuri Subbaraya Ayyar in a text called *Tarumapuri Cupparāyar Jāvaḷi* (1896), which was published during the composer's own lifetime (fig. 2.13). Here we see it in the *rāga* Behāg. It is highly improbable that Dharmapuri Subbaraya Ayyar composed this song, since it does not contain the characteristic "signature words" (*mukuṭa* or *mudrā*) used by Subbaraya Ayyar, but instead contains the signature "*siṃhabhūpāla*," sometimes associated with the one the last *zamīndārs* of Gadval, in today's Mahbubnagar district of Andhra Pradesh.

The next appearance of this *jāvaḷi* is in the Telugu film *Muddu Bidda* ("Darling Child") directed by K. B. Tilak in the year 1956 (fig. 2.14).[38] In this film, one of the young male protagonists is chastised for watching a performance of dance by the courtesans or *bhogamvāḷḷu*. But the scene

2.14 Stills from the Telugu film *Muddu Bidda* (1956) depicting a performance of the *jāvaḷi* "aṃtalone tĕllavāre" by Krishnajyoti, an actress from a *kalāvantula* background.

that depicts the performance by the *bhogameḷam* seems to celebrate the culture of courtesan dance, leaving the viewer confounded by a spectacle that animates the simultaneous desirability and vilification of the courtesan and her art, an anxiety that is so much a part of reform discourse in this period, which is largely engineered by *smārta* Brahmins, Chettiyars, Mudaliyars, and other elite men. The release of this film also happens to coincide with another intervention—the passing of the Andhra Pradesh state government's amendment to the Madras Anti-Devadasi Act, on August 14th, 1956. The original Madras Devadasi (Prevention of Dedication) Act of 1947 only banned the temple dedication rituals and temple-oriented performances by *devadāsī*s, and so in most parts of South India, especially coastal Andhra Pradesh, salon performances by courtesan troupes continued well into the 1950s. This 1956 amendment criminalized performances by women from hereditary courtesan communities at marriages and other private social events. This film in many ways represents one of the last official nods to the culture of the salon in Telugu-speaking South India. The poignancy of the film sequence is remarkable—the main performer, the actress Krishnajyoti, is from a *kalāvantula* family in the coastal Andhra Pradesh region.[39] The distinctive feature of *jāvaḷi* rendition in that region—the *gaptu-varusa*, or improvised dance sequence, at the end—undeniably marks the technical and aesthetic continuity of *jāvaḷi* rendition in the courtesan community. It is a reminder of the precarious fate of traditional *jāvaḷi* performance. The social reform movement directed toward *devadāsī*s in this period was not so much directed at dancing in temples but instead toward dance performed at private events—or in colonial parlance, the South Indian *nautch*. For the women who were the traditional keepers of these cultural practices, the *jāvaḷi* oddly presented an opportunity in the new world of colonial modernity, but also would come to be seen as morally questionable and would eventually play a role in the criminalization of their lifestyles.

As indices of the transformations of culture—salons, print materials, gramophone recordings, and films—*jāvaḷi*s lived complex and multivalent lives. The various historical, aesthetic, and even affective registers of *jāvaḷi*s can only be understood in the context of a hybrid, cosmopolitan Madras Presidency, in which the new flows of culture involved Telugu poetics, European languages, and performance idioms, as well as an unstable political and sexual economy. The fundamental linguistic, social, and choreographic hybridity of *devadāsī* dance in the nineteenth and early twentieth centuries—expressed exclusively through the culture of salon performance—enabled the development of the *jāvaḷi*, and allowed it to move so quickly and effortlessly through the sites of urban cultural practice and innovation that I have discussed. Lodged as they were in the liminal space between colonial modernity and the emergent nationalist reinvention of South India's arts in the 1930s, it is easy to imagine how *jāvaḷi*s, like the salon lives of *devadāsī*s, slipped through the cracks of historicization and historiography.

CHAPTER THREE

Subterfuges of "Respectable" Citizenship: Marriage and Masculinity in the Discourse of Devadāsī Reform

Given the overwhelming force that stigma exerts over the lives of *devadāsī*s, how is it that the highest political office in the state of Tamil Nadu was, until very recently held by an individual from this community? The iconic politician Muthuvel Karunanidhi is the son of Anjukam Ammaiyar, from a *devadāsī* community in Tirukkuvalai in the Tiruvarur district. Karunanidhi's phenomenal power in contemporary South Indian politics speaks directly to the "success" of *devadāsī* reform in the twentieth century—a distinctly gendered success that did little for women in these communities but allowed men to reinvent themselves as powerful and legitimate members of the modern non-Brahmin body politic. It also speaks to another unfinished thread in the modern history of *devadāsī*s —that of "respectable" citizenship promised, but never fully delivered, to women in *devadāsī* communities by twentieth-century reform. This chapter revisits some dimensions of the famous "anti-*devadāsī*," or "anti-nautch," debates in the Madras Presidency.

The issue of *devadāsī* reform was embedded in larger public debates about women and sexuality in colonial India. In the nineteenth century, women and issues related to sexuality—including sati, widow remarriage, age of consent, among others—were referenced largely in a symptomatic sense, as signs of India's social and moral lack. As we see in Lata Mani's now classic formulation in her work on sati, women were essentially the ground on which larger concerns about tradition and culture were staged (1998); they were neither the objects nor subjects of these debates. As we move into the twentieth century, however, women's involvement in the public sphere, combined with the power of Gandhian nationalism and cultural nationalism more generally, shaped the distinctively modern legal, social, sexual, and political boundaries of the female subject. Much has been written about the construction of the female citizen in modern India as a project based on a politics of exclusion that valorized female chastity, conjugality, and motherhood. As Mrinalini Sinha points out, "The patriarchal anxieties about potentially 'disorderly women,' no less than the imperatives of anticolonial nationalist politics, animated the assertion by century's end of the collective prerogatives of the nation as the final arbiter of social changes for women" (2006, 45). National imaginaries and identities, inflected by class and caste anxieties, undoubtedly hinged upon constructions of gender, and specifically on the control and regulation of female sexuality. Reform projects around *devadāsī*s also represented a persistent, middle-class altruism that was justified through a discourse of moral recuperation. Nonconjugal female sexuality represented a near-irrevocable moral degeneration, and it was in large part the responsibility of middle-class women to reform and neutralize its dangers by way of example.

This chapter also maps the shifting moral economies of colonial modernity that fundamentally could not accommodate the social and aesthetic practices of women from *devadāsī* communities. In the nearly hundred-year-long legal debates about the status of *devadāsī*s within these new economies, it becomes clear that the only option for them is to become "respectable" through marriage. As we saw in chapter 1, the tying of the *poṭṭu* emblem, understood as a marriage to a temple deity, carried economic and social consequences that resonated far beyond the supposedly religiouscontent of the ritual. In this chapter, we will observe the way in which parties on all sides of the abolition debate use religious discourses strategically in order to justify particular economic relationships. Twentieth-century reform movements promised to grant *devadāsī*s full participation as citizens in the emergent nation-state only if they were able to "reform" themselves through marriage. Rites of passage that set certain women apart from conjugal life were progressively invalidated, while the ritual of normative marriage became increasingly fetishized as the panacea for society's ills.

Legal interventions in the Madras Presidency were engineered by Muthulakshmi Reddy, daughter of a Brahmin father and a mother from a *devadāsī* community in Pudukkottai. Reddy was also the first female doctor in the Madras Presidency, and she was responsible for implementing a series of reforms related to women's physical and social health. The explicit purpose of her activities was to criminalize the "dedication" of girls (*poṭṭukkaṭṭutal*). For reformers, the ritual of *poṭṭukkaṭṭutal* enabled prostitution and the abuse of women that resulted from relationships unsanctioned by marriage. *Devadāsī* reform aimed to detach modern India from the archaic and patriarchal sign of temple dedication by instituting a new form of citizenship for *devadāsī* women. Reddy was not alone in charting pathways to conjugal life for *devadāsī*s. The *devadāsī* abolition movement stood at the intersection of Congress party and non-Brahmin politics in Madras, and was strongly supported by both Gandhi and E. V. Ramasami Naicker (also known as Periyar; 1879–1973).

This period of South Indian history essentially witnesses the discursive construction of the *devadāsī* in legal, medical, and religious terms. The process of drafting anti-*devadāsī* legislation and the debates surrounding it have already been well documented (for example, Hubel 2005; Inoue 2005; Jordan 2003 Kannabiran and Kannabiran 2003; Meduri 1996; Srividya Natarajan 1997; A. Srinivasan 1984; Sundara Raj 1993; Vijaisri 2004; Whitehead 1998, 2001). What remains are questions concerning the politics of conjugality and the real effects and successes of this legislation in the modern nation-state. In the first half of this chapter, I retell the story of the Madras Legislative Assembly debates up to 1947 using archival data, including materials that focus on the role of Gandhi and the establishment of rehabilitation centers (*śaraṇālayams*) for *devadāsī*s in the Madras Presidency. I focus on three women with links to the *devadāsī* community—Reddy, Yamini Purnatilakam, and Muvalur Ramamirttammal—who attempted to transform *devadāsī*s into "normative citizen-subjects," to borrow Mrinalini Sinha's term (1999, 207). Each of these women valorized conjugality and went to great efforts to actually oversee marriages for women in *devadāsī* communities. Groups of *devadāsī*s staged what Partha Chatterjee calls "fragmented resistance" (1993, 13) to this totalizing civic and nationalist project, but these voices slipped between the cracks of South Indian politics and could not produce effective or enduring results. Antiabolitionist rhetoric, like abolitionist rhetoric, was couched in the language of nation and religion, the only vocabulary through which *devadāsī*s could speak in the civic sphere.

In the latter half of this chapter, I offer an alternative view of the anti-nautch debates that highlights the tacit tensions of nationalist masculinities in Tamil Nadu, and foregrounds the concerns of men from the *devadāsī* community. In the debates we see the creation and mobilization of new caste identities—"*icai vēḷāḷar*" in the Tamil-speaking regions, and "*sūryabaḷija*" in the Telugu-speaking regions—by male relatives of *devadāsī*s. The reinvention of caste status is borne from reactions to the stigma of precolonial and early colonial caste legacies on the one hand,

and from the social potential inscribed in emergent non-Brahmin politics on the other. New non-Brahmin caste associations headed by men almost universally joined the movement to outlaw professional dancing by women from their communities. *Devadāsī* reform thus engendered serious deliberations on the control of women's sexuality and the restoration of patriliny in these communities, even as women themselves remained largely absent from these debates.

Toward the end of this chapter, I shift the discussion to the post-1947 period. Many *devadāsī*s continued to dance in public despite the official state-endorsed ban on their performances. Court cases from the 1950s–1990s offer perspectives on the deployment of anti-*devadāsī* legislation in independent India, the persistence of *devadāsī* dance after it had been criminalized, and the continuing and unfinished gendered struggles over power and resources within the community.

The key promise of *devadāsī* reform for women—namely, "respectable" citizenship in the emergent nation—was never actualized, primarily because ultimately the movement itself was monopolized by men, and it was transformed into a project for men. It was men's reform *of* women cloaked as reform *for* women that enabled the unusually high prominence of men from the new "icai vēḷāḷar" community in the official mechanisms of the state. It is the reason why an office such as the chief minister of Tamil Nadu—one of the highest political positions in the country—could be occupied by a man from the *devadāsī* community. Women from the same communities, however, remain irrevocably stigmatized and unintegrated.

SCRIPTING *DEVADĀSĪ*S AS PROSTITUTES IN EARLY LEGAL, MEDICAL, AND EDUCATIONAL DISCOURSE

As we have already noted, *devadāsī*s occupied an ambiguous social status in colonial South India right from the time of their presence at the Marāṭhā court in Tanjore. But this ambiguity—which encompassed the uneasiness around their sexuality, their role in the economies of land, and the legitimacy of their profession—was amplified by reform efforts that brought these issues into the public spaces of debate. For almost a hundred years, public deliberations on *devadāsī*s took the form of judicial debates, anthropological inquiry, and medical and legislative interventions; they scripted *devadāsī*s into what Dipesh Chakrabarty has described as a political modernity that depends largely on the historicist discourses and ontological assumptions of Europe (Chakrabarty 2000, 15–16).

In a brilliant essay entitled "A Corporation of Superior Prostitutes: Anglo-Indian Legal Conceptions of Temple Dancing Girls, 1800–1914," Kunal Parker (1998) demonstrates how legal definitions of *devadāsīs* as prostitutes were codified by the High Court of Madras. Most of these early cases revolve around three issues: the scripting of *devadāsīs* as a definite caste in legal terms (the "dancing girl caste"); the legitimacy of adoption in *devadāsī* communities; and the recognition of a "unique custom" of quasi-matrilineal inheritance in the communities. The construction of *devadāsīs* as prostitutes was central to each of these issues. Most of the cases established that *devadāsīs* formed a caste of professional prostitutes; that *devadāsīs*, as per the "custom of their caste," were adopting young girls with the intention of making them into prostitutes; and that "prostitute heirs inherited the property of prostitutes," who were legally constituted as a class of "degraded Hindu women" to whom normative Hindu laws of succession did not apply (1998, 567–570). These early nineteenth-century legal assertions conditioned the moral justifications for the twentieth-century anti-nautch movement. They left enduring impressions on the legal system and continue to be cited in cases related to *devadāsīs* into the twenty-first century.

Women's bodies came under colonial surveillance as sexual contact between native women and colonial men increased. As Philippa Levine notes, these contacts resulted in a complex, racialized stratification of "moral hierarchies" in which nonwhite women could easily be marked as prostitutes who personified the "queer and uncivilized" colony (Levine 2003, 193). Military cantonments and civil spaces were both susceptible to the dangers of native women's sexuality, but potential threats to military efficiency in India due to the spread of venereal disease prompted serious action on the part of the government. The Indian Contagious Diseases Acts, modeled after those implemented in Britain, were passed in 1864 and 1868, largely for the protection of members of the British Army, who were encouraged to have noncommittal sexual relations with native women. In the case of prostitutes, the government expected them to be clean and in good health if they were to service military cantonments.[1]

The implementation of contagious disease legislation was dependent on an Orientalist sociology that was created to map the sexuality of the colonized through technologies of surveillance. Victorian notions of sanitary reform and social hygiene were also influenced by the growing importance of eugenics, and as Judith Whitehead notes, "extramarital sexuality, especially that of women, was dangerous because it could spread disease and degeneration throughout the body politic . . . [and] tendencies toward prostitution could be identified by heredity" (1998, 95). The acts implemented strategies of compulsory registration for women who were sexually active outside the constraints of marriage and incarceration in lock hospitals for women suspected of having venereal disease.[2] In the Madras Presidency, the acts were implemented in a highly systematized manner, and registered prostitutes were required to present themselves at the lock hospitals for regular physical examinations (Hodges 2005).

The presence of *devadāsī*s and deliberations on their status are thus also found in documents related to the regulation of prostitution and venereal disease, which were major issues in both the colony and metropole in the middle of the nineteenth century. Chapter 2 showed how the trope of *devadāsī*s as carriers of sexually transmitted disease was ubiquitous in early Tamil and Telugu print literature in the same period. Yet the conflation of the *devadāsī* lifestyle with prostitution was contested by dancing women themselves. In September 1866, "Davadassee Mungoo of Madras" submitted a petition to the Government of Madras stating that, as a *devadāsī*, she should not be required to register as a prostitute under the Contagious Diseases Act (Levine 2003, 220 n. 134). Much later, in March 1874, a Telugu-speaking *devadāsī* from Bellary petitioned the governor of Madras to delete her young daughter's name from the register of prostitutes being compiled by the police (Inna Reddy 1998, 106–107). Cases such as these prompted a special inquiry into placing *devadāsī*s under medical surveillance. In August 1875, E. G. Balfour, surgeon-general of the Indian Medical Department at Fort St. George, met with administrators (*dharmakartā*s) from a number of temples in Madras city to discuss the health of *devadāsī*s. The temple *dharmakartā*s vehemently denied that *devadāsī*s were infected with venereal disease and told Balfour that health staff should not interfere with *devadāsī*s who were associated with the town temples. *Devadāsī*s with temple affiliations were thus officially exempted from the rigorous forms of medical examination under the Contagious Diseases Act of 1868 (Sundara Raj 1993, 49–50). Three years later, in 1878, the new surgeon general, G. Smith, informed the Government of Madras that *devadāsī*s are a "somewhat dangerous class of prostitutes" who are indeed carriers of venereal disease. As late as 1887, another set of *devadāsī*s from Bellary wrote to the governor-in-council stating that they were being harassed by the collector of Bellary in his attempts to enforce the Contagious Diseases Act. They were later found to be having sexual relations with local sepoys in the army, but no action was taken.

The emergent public education system also registered the growing public disdain toward *devadāsī* women and their children. As early as 1874, debates about allowing girl children of *devadāsī*s into new government and local board schools in the Madras Presidency are initiated because "native feeling is against the admission of these girls." The government decided to "leave the disposal of the question to Local Boards," in an open-ended gesture that would ultimately allow school officials to discriminate against *devadāsī* girls with the sanction of the government. In December 1874 and February 1875, district collectors and the director of Public Instruction submitted reports to the government, in which some officials noted that it "it is monstrous that Government money should be expended in qualifying professional prostitutes for their future career . . . such girls cannot but exercise an evil influence over their companions"[3] As part of the ensuing government debate, other officials argued that only prepubescent girls should be admitted to these schools and that their education should cease after the age of ten. The "native opinion" that instigated these debates is mentioned time and time again. Sir W. Robinson, a prominent official who was firmly against the admission of *devadāsī* girls into the schools, submitted a lengthy document that included excerpts from an essay published in the journal *Indian Native Opinion*:

> Native parents are only too apt to think that educated girls are sure to turn out as wicked girls. This fear, absurd as it may be . . . is by no means unreasonable when the girls are exposed to the danger of mixing with girls of the dancing girl class, who from their earliest years, and long before they are physically fit for prosecuting their infamous trade, are depraved in all manners and dissolute in morals. A girl of this class, even before attaining the age of puberty, is a prostitute.[4]

Just as legal definitions of *devadāsī*s as prostitutes were emerging in the Anglo-Indian legal sphere, the female children of *devadāsī*s were denied access to education in government and local board schools, and they too were inscripted as objects of stigma in public discourse. The constant reference to "native opinion" suggests that stigma was always at stake for dancing women, but the scripting of *devadāsī*s as prostitutes in legal, medical, and educational discourses lent systematic structure to their always marginal position.

THREE WOMEN AND TWENTIETH-CENTURY DEVADĀSĪ REFORM: MUTHULAKSHMI REDDY, YAMINI PURNATILAKAM, AND MUVALUR RAMAMIRTTAMMAL

Anti-nautch discourse cannot be fully understood apart from the discursive and praxical interventions made by three women from the *devadāsī* community. Muthulakshmi Reddy, Yamini Purnatilakam, and Muvalur Ramamirttammal all recognized the local patriarchies at work in keeping *devadāsī* women out of the public spaces of modernity. To be sure, I regard each of these women as radical figures in their own right. Their radicalism, however, was cultivated and sustained through strategic political affiliations—all three were associated with the Congress Party, and Ramamirttammal later rose to prominence in the Self-Respect Movement.[5] One of my goals in this chapter is to question the presumption of "authenticity" on the part of these women simply because they had familial ties to *devadāsī* communities, because, in other words, they were "speaking from within." It is crucial that we understand their initiative as forming one part of larger nationalist political trajectories. In the case of a figure like Yamini Purnatilakam, her public visibility was almost completely dependent on her participation in Congress propaganda. These women also undeniably saw marriage as the only "respectable" option for *devadāsī*s, and all three of them went out of their way to enforce or oversee marriages within the *devadāsī* community. It was, as Janaki Nair puts it, "a symptom of the success of new nationalist patriarchy's 'modernising impulse' that [they] . . . saw the resolution of the 'problem' of the *devadāsī*s within the framework of marriage" (Nair 1996, 166). Reddy's radical first-wave feminism did, to be sure, critique the inequalities of marriage and even questioned the legitimacy of the institution. "Why should [the] marriage of every boy and girl be made compulsory and considered necessary in a land that once advocated lifelong *brahmacharya* [celibacy] and continence for the attainment of intellectual and spiritual greatness?" she asked (Reddy cited in Sreenivas 2008, 80). Even in this critique, however, the ideal of marriage is pitted against that of celibacy; while a "solution" to the inequalities represented by marriage might be celibacy, the solution to the "problem" of nonconjugal relationships can *only* be marriage.

MUTHULAKSHMI REDDY, MARRIAGE, AND THE BIRTH OF ANTI-*DEVADĀSĪ* LEGISLATION IN MADRAS

The well-known anti-nautch debates cannot be severed from the larger discourses on morality, health, and justice in the Madras Presidency outlined above. As we move toward the twentieth century, efforts to curb prostitution altogether come into sharp focus. Concerns over child prostitution in particular, and the well-being of children in general, characterized the shifting concerns of moral debates in the twentieth century. As we shall see below, religion too entered the debates in an unprecedented way. This chapter, therefore, also tells the story of how religion became the dominant category at stake in debates over *devadāsī* lifestyle and its proposed reform. In response to Reddy's 1927 resolution to the Legislative Assembly, different groups mobilized the religious significance of the *devadāsī* in order to make different ideological investments. From Reddy's claim that the *dāsī*s represent "a blot on Hindu civilization" to the Madras Devadasi Association's comparison of the *devadāsī* to "Buddistic [*sic*] Nuns," religious vocabulary charged the debates and often masked the material concerns at stake for the different parties.

Before Reddy's introduced her appeal in 1927, there were movements on several different fronts to address the "*devadāsī* problem" through legislative means. In 1872, the central government proposed measures to check the practice of raising girls for the purpose of prostitution. The major purpose of this legislation was to monitor brothels that housed girls under the age of ten, which was the age of consent at the time. The proposed legislation had, as its ultimate aim, the prevention of kidnappings of very young girls for the purpose of prostitution. The legislation was opposed by some in Madras, where dancing girls were seen as "necessary adjuncts to the Hindu ritual, and also . . . their attendance on private families is customary and necessary on many domestic occasions. That to legislate *with the intention of the gradual extinction of the dancing girl caste* would be viewed with extreme dislike by the great majority of Hindus" (cited in Jordan 2003, 61, emphasis mine). This is perhaps the earliest documented legal deliberation on the potential abolition of *devadāsī*s in the Madras Presidency. The idea for the proposed legislation was dropped in 1873, after a year of debate. The period from 1890 to 1911 saw increasing concerns over the protection of children after the Phulmonee Das case of 1890 in which an eleven-year-old girl died of hemorrhage after being raped by her twenty-five-year-old husband (Sarkar 2001 210–215; Sinha 1995, 138–180). In the Telugu-speaking regions of the Madras Presidency, reformers like Kandukuri Viresalingam (1848–1919) began to write essays, tracts, and dramas that spoke of the exploitation of young girls and ridiculed men who had relations with *devadāsī*s in Godavari delta (Soneji 2004), while figures such as Raghupati Venkataratnam Naidu (1862–1939) solicited "purity pledges" (modeled after those used by Christian organizations in America) from elite South Indian men in which they would promise to refrain from watching or sponsoring performances of "nautch" dancing (Naidu 1901).

In September 1912, banker, industrialist, and legislator Maneckji B. Dadabhoy (1865–1953) proposed legislation in the Imperial Legislative Council to outlaw the adoption of girls by prostitutes (including *devadāsī*s) and criminalize *devadāsī* dedication (again, this included the entire spectrum of women who are "offered, dedicated, or married to a symbol, deity, or shrine or other place of worship," including Dalit women).[6] The year 1912 marks as well the first recorded petition supporting reform signed by men from *devadāsī* communities in the Godavari, Krishna, and Guntur districts that made its way to the colonial legislature (Jordan 2003, 80).

But it is in the 1920s that significant legal interventions directed toward *devadāsīs* occurred in the Madras Presidency, largely through the efforts of Dr. S. Muthulakshmi Reddy (1866–1968). Reddy's mother Chandrammal was related to the family of the dance master Sivarama Nattuvanar (1879–1945) in Pudukkottai.[7] Reddy's father was a *smārta* Brahmin, S. Narayanaswami (Ayyar), who was the principal of the Maharaja's College in Pudukkottai. In Reddy's own words, he was also "a great patron of music, dance and drama . . . in [whose] bungalow entertainments would be held very often for these Vidvans" (Reddy 1964, 5). Reddy was the first female medical graduate in the country, earning her degree from the Madras Medical College in 1912. In April 1914, she married Dr. T. Sundara Reddy, whose family was deeply involved with the Justice Party. In addition to continuing with her medical practice, Reddy was the first female Indian legislator prior to independence, and was also a prominent member of the All India Women's Conference. During her tenure as a member of the Madras Legislative Assembly, Reddy voiced opinions on a number of issues related to gender and sexuality including the age of consent, the suppression of brothels, female education, women in the police, medical aid for women, and of course, the prohibition of *devadāsī* practices.[8] Many scholars have described Reddy's contribution to the first wave of Indian feminism; it is clear that her investment in social purity and eugenics bears important resemblances to the work undertaken by feminists in the metropole in the early twentieth century.

The genealogy of Reddy's interventions in the Madras Legislative Assembly is fairly complex, and this nearly three-decade-long legal and bureaucratic struggle has been well documented by a number of scholars. For our purposes, three stages are significant. First, on November 4, 1927, Reddy "recommends to the Government to undertake legislation to put a stop to the practice of dedication of young girls and young women to Hindu temples for immoral purposes." The recommendation is accepted, and *devadāsīs* immediately organize protests. This 1927 resolution, which urged the government to legislate against *devadāsī* temple dedications, provided a major impetus for the concerted legal effort to criminalize the *devadāsī* lifestyle. Second, in 1930, this resolution was put into action in the form of a bill, entitled "A Bill to Prevent the Dedication of Women to Hindu Temples," which Reddy had proposed to the Legislative Council in 1930. Finally, seventeen years later, Reddy's bill was transformed into an act passed by the government of independent India entitled the Madras Devadasis (Prevention of Dedication) Act of 1947. A significant dimension of Reddy's 1927 and 1930 interventions was the enfranchisement of *devadāsī* lands (*ināms* or *māṉiyams*) in the names of women who would no longer be obliged to perform dance, music, or other tasks in order to lay claim to this land.[9] As we shall see later, this was a contentious proposition for men in *devadāsī* communities.

Reddy's anti-nautch activities were inextricably linked to Congress politics and the Theosophical Society (largely through the mediating figure of Annie Besant), and emergent notions of eugenic health. Annie Besant (1847–1933), was president of both the Theosophical Society (1908) and the Indian National Congress (1917).[10] Besant first wrote about *devadāsīs* in 1919:

> There was a band of pure virgin devotees attached to the ancient Hindu temple. They used to preach religion like other religious teachers to the common people that resort to the temple for daily worship. In those days they were held in high esteem and were very well looked after. They would spend their time in doing religious service to the Gods, and the devotees of the temple, as the word dasi itself signifies. They would follow the procession of gods dressed in the simplest sanyasi garbs and singing pious hymns suitable to the occasion. This is the history and origin of the devadasi class. (cited in Reddy 1927, 5)

No concrete source exists for Besant's claim, and she likely derives her opinions about the "pure virgins" once attached the Hindu temple from the long history of Orientalist romanticizations of *devadāsīs* (Bor 2007). Remarkably, in a document entitled *Why Should the Devadasi Institution in the Hindu Temples Be Abolished?* (1927), Reddy reproduces Besant's narrative as authoritative, adding the following:

> So there are authentic records to prove these Dasi girls were pure virgins spending their time in religious study, meditation and devotional service in the temples akin to the Roman Catholic nuns of the present day. Now-a-days we find to our great sorrow that all their accomplishments such as music and dance are being utilised in the majority of cases to promote their evil and immoral trade and to drag the impru-

dent and unwary youth of the country into immorality and vice and hence the word "dasi" has become one of reproach. (1927, 3)

This narrative of the "fall" of *devadāsīs* from a Hindu golden age—premised on little more than fantasy—has an enduring, systemic presence in the structures of the state and enabled twentieth-century reformers to justify the "rescue" of women from these communities. As Judy Whitehead has noted, these narratives of degeneration "converged with a modernist and eugenicist conception of the nation, articulated most clearly by Dr. Muthulakshmi Reddy" (1998, 102). Reddy's insistence on the location of healthy sexuality squarely within the "respectable" parameters of marriage coincided with male concerns over community honor and pedigree. As Whitehead explains, "In Dr. Reddy's conception of the 'nation,' medical health and moral boundaries become conflated. The future of the nation and the health of the "race" were linked to sexual continence, motherhood, and the hygienic education of young girls and women" (99). Later in this chapter, we shall see how these same issues surfaced among men concerned not so much about race as about caste and class identity.

Women's Devadāsī Associations and Devadāsī Protests

Reddy's 1927 resolution catalyzed an explosion of responses from myriad groups of men and women with their own unique investments in the aesthetic, religious, economic, and sexual practices of dancing women. Her personal archive preserves a number of letters, newspaper clippings, and handbills that document both support of and resistance to Reddy's interventions between 1927 and 1947 (some of these documents, including those cited in this chapter, are reproduced in the appendix to this volume). To be sure, the voices in the archive are eclectic and reflect the complex range of actors who had deep investments in the question of reform. For the most part, however, the archive discloses the undeniably gendered nature of the debate; with a few notable exceptions, almost all of the documents supporting abolition are signed by men, while those opposing the legislation are signed by *devadāsīs*.

In this section, I focus on a small but representative selection of letters of dissent from the archive, composed by *devadāsīs*. The earliest of these protest documents date to 1927, when *devadāsīs* in Madras city first heard of Reddy's proposed resolution. Many of these were disseminated under the aegis of "*devadāsī* associations," which were loosely yet strategically founded on the eve of the legislative debate of the resolution. The early protests came from within Madras city, but very quickly started to pour in as well from individuals and "*devadāsī* associations" spontaneously created all around the Presidency.[11] As Kalpana and Vasanth Kannabiran note, the antiabolitionist stance that was adopted by many *devadāsī*s had its "own radicalism and sensitivity," and it was precisely the "impossibility of fixing the anti-abolitionists within any of the political-ideological frameworks [such as those of Congress nationalism or the non-Brahmin movement] that wiped out their resistance" (2003, 32). This political liminality of *devadāsī* protest is a clear sign of the "unfinished" nature of the entire project of reform. There was, in fact, no real political location from which women could challenge reform discourse, just as there is no real political, social, or aesthetic citizenship that *devadāsī*s can claim in the postreform period.

In 1927 and 1928, the newspaper *Cutēcamittiraṉ*, largely Brahmin and pro-Congress, carried several stories and reports on *devadāsī* protests and rallies, mapping the places where meetings of *devadāsī*s were convened. One of these reports, entitled "The Question of Devadāsīs: A Meeting of the Devadāsīs, Cheyyur," for example, describes a meeting in Cheyyur, just outside of Madras. At the meeting, twenty-five *devadāsī*s unanimously agreed to "severely oppose" Reddy's 1927 resolution and asserted that "the ancient honorable religious practice of tying *poṭṭu* in the temples is not related whatsoever to the mean practice of prostitution. Hence this meeting requests our benevolent Government not to appeal any bill that will put an end to our ancient traditional rights." These women are conscious that Reddy has represented them as "a blot on Hindu civilization," but lament the fact that many non-Hindus also support the proposed legislation. "It is improper that our Muslim and Christian brothers and sisters also support this bill which has been proposed without proper investigation," they write.

*Devadāsī*s criticized the men from their communities who were among Reddy's strongest supporters, indicating their consciousness of the gendered nature of reformist principles that will benefit the men in their communities while leaving them disenfranchised. T. Duraikkannu, secretary of the Madras Devadasi Association, published a small handbill in 1927 in which she accused the men in her community of deception:

> It is certain that the bill to abolish the practice of tying the *poṭṭu* will put an end to the social practices and hereditary rights of our community, and this has created unending worries for us . . . It is unbelievable that prostitution can be eliminated by putting an end to the practice of

> tying the *poṭṭu*. The supporters of this bill can give a lame excuse that a majority of *icaivēḷāḷar*s support this agitation to destroy this practice of tying the *poṭṭu*. *Icaivēḷāḷar*s are none other than the male members of this community, and it is strange that they support this agitation. Let's think about the intention behind this carefully, which is nothing but selfishness. It should be noted that women of this community alone are entitled to inherit entire property and perform funeral rites as well. It is well known that every human being works in his or her selfish interests alone. *The men of this community, who are like axes felling their own community, are responsible for this bill. It is clear that they are doing so with the selfish intention of inheriting property.*[12]

The most well-known protests from *devadāsī*s demonstrate their rhetorical ability to take on the valorized religious identity in order to defend their lifestyles. Such an identity is often assumed even when the women writing such protests were not themselves associated with temples. Several of these voices can be heard in an English document entitled *The Humble Memorial of Devadasis of the Madras Presidency* (1928), addressed to Sir C. P. Ramaswami Iyer, law member, government of Madras, in light of discussions around the prevention of *devadāsī* dedication introduced in the Legislative Assembly by Reddy earlier that year.[13] The memorandum was signed by eight members of the "Madras Devadasi Association," known in Tamil as the Ceṉṉai Uruttirakkaṇikai Caṅkam, whose members included prominent *devadāsī*s of the city including the famous vocalist Bangalore Nagaratnammal (1878–1952).[14] The memorandum clearly deploys religious rhetoric, and this temple past is claimed by women like Nagaratnammal, who had never participated in temple dance. The memorandum references the Śaivāgamas (Sanskrit ritual manuals), the Tamil epic *Maṇimēkalai*, and the hymns of the *nāyaṉārs* (Tamil Śaiva saints). It claims that the *devadāsī* "institution" is "similar to that of Mutts [monasteries] presided by Sanyasis [*sic*] for the propagation of religion" and argues that *devadāsī*s are comparable to "the Buddistic [*sic*] Nuns and the several Roman Catholic Nunneries of the West"[15] The text also contains citations in Sanskrit from the Śaiva temple manual *Kāmikāgama*, and ends with a plea that *devadāsī*s be "reformed" through education: "Give us education, religious, literary, and artistic. Education will dispel ignorance and we will occupy once again the same rank which we held in the national life of the past" (6). The stance that was adopted by the Madras Devadasi Association is complex, and at times contradictory; it too references narratives of degeneration, and is inflected by Theosophical Orientalism. It is indicative of the foreclosure of enunciative possibilities for *devadāsī*s within the framework of nationalist discourse: assuming and even exaggerating their religious identity becomes the only way to be heard, but even this is not enough.

Besides the memorandum issued by the Madras Devadasi Association, other letters of protest in Tamil issued by individuals and smaller groups (with names such as the Tirukkalukunram Devadasi Association) also describe resistance to reform from within the *devadāsī* community. The following letter published in the Tamil newspaper *Cutēcamittiraṉ*, for example, which predates "The Humble Memorial of Devadasis of the Madras Presidency," also invokes a similar religious genealogy for *devadāsī*s, tracing their origins to the figure of Paravaiyār, wife of the Śaiva saint Cuntaramūrtti, and positing *devadāsī* dance as sanctioned by religion. The letter is written by Duraikkannu and Parvati, two *devadāsī*s who held land grants (*māṉiyams*) from the Ekāmbareśvara temple at Kanchipuram:

> *Devadāsī*s, who are also referred to as *uruttirakaṇikayar*, are a community of women who, out of devotion to god, worshipped him and offered themselves to him. They performed service (*toṇṭu*) in his temples and lived as pure and noble souls. It seems that Śrīmati Muttulakṣimi Ammāḷ has proposed a bill to abolish the practice of tying the *poṭṭu* for *devadāsī* women in temples . . . Moreover, the question also arises of whether this bill will completely eliminate prostitution (*vipacāram*, *vyabhacāra*) in India, and whether women practicing prostitution will become "purified" (*cuttacaitayarkaḷāy*) . . . In obedience to the will of the omnipotent Lord, Paravai Nācciyār, the beloved of Cuntaramūrrti Nāyaṉār, was born in this untainted, pure tradition of *devadāsī*s . . . it is improper to attempt to destroy a practice which is traditionally sanctioned by religion and is practiced by a respectable community . . . If the Indian Penal Code cannot abolish prostitution, it is inconceivable how banning the practice of tying the *poṭṭu* will abolish it.[16]

As Avanthi Meduri notes, the *devadāsī*s who composed these protest letters selectively foregrounded "only those devotional and textual aspects of their tradition which would have currency in colonial and national debates" (Meduri 1996, 182). These writings project *devadāsī*s back into an imagined Śaiva world, a distinctly religious, hence respectable, space. Indeed, it is the instability of religion itself that is at the heart of many early twentieth-century reform movements including the anti-nautch movement, and *devadāsī*s strategically placed themselves in a discourse that aligned them with new valorizations of India's religious past. While the anti-nautch movement in Madras sought to criminalize the tying of the *poṭṭu*, understood as a sign of the archaic in the new nation, *devadāsīs* were harnessing the entire Tamil past in an attempt to assert their right to citizenship in the changing moral economy of the emergent nation-state. These women recognized the power and authority of religious language in the context of the new public sphere. Indeed, writing by *devadāsīs* throughout the twentieth century is at once self-directed but outward-turning, reflective yet persuasive. If we think of rhetorical strategy as a social and political act through which individuals access the symbolic resources of culture, as historian Stephen Howard Browne (1999) has suggested, then we might interpret this rhetorical self-fashioning as a narrative strategy to authorize the female subject.

Organizations such as the Madras Devadasi Association caused a considerable stir in the press. One English newspaper report called the protests "extremely revolting," and another labeled the resistance "ignorant opposition engineered by disinterested parties," while Reddy, in a letter to A. R. MacEwen, secretary to the government of Madras, reacts with the following remarks:

> In the first place it is well known that the very word Devadasi has come to mean a prostitute. Therefore I cannot understand how a petition from an Association of such women could be countenanced and further sent out for opinion from others. The fact that one or two devadasis out of hundreds and thousands have made a name in the world of music and dancing does not disprove that 999 out of 1000 are prostitutes and one in a thousand of them the mistress of married men. Exceptions do not make a rule.[17]

Like Gandhi, Reddy discounts the protests of these *devadāsīs*, invoking both the trope of false consciousness and exaggerated accounts of their sexual and aesthetic lives to justify her stance on the issue of reform.

Devadāsīs in Support of Reddy

Reddy unquestionably garnered support for her bill from women in the *devadāsī* community; the cases of Yamini Purnatilakam and Muvalur Ramamirttammal, which I discuss below, offer the most visible examples. In 1928, following the protests by *devadāsīs* such as those described above, Reddy published a small booklet entitled *The Awakening: Demand for Devadasi Legislation*, arguing that the "demand" for this legislation comes from within the community. In it, she presents a number of letters and petitions from *within* the community that support her interventions, and argues that these "memorials and petitions [are] from *reliable* Devadasi associations requesting me to go on with my resolution and bill" (1928, 1). Sensing, perhaps, some of the gendered tensions within the communities over reform issues, she is careful to mention that both men *and* women support her efforts. Rather awkwardly, she states that a number of *devadāsī*s are ready to support her "propaganda work" if they can be "financed," reiterating the Gandhian notion of poverty as a political virtue, and destabilizing the moral economy of the *devadāsī* lifestyle.

> I have also received memorials and petitions from *reliable* Devadasi associations requesting me to go on with my resolution and bill . . . For the information of the public I append below a list of the associations that have supported my proposed bill. I may also mention that many members of the Devadasi community, both men and women, who demand reform have attended the Indian National Social Conference as delegates, have waited upon me and are anxious to undertake propaganda work throughout the Presidency if helped with funds by the enlightened public. The reformed Devadases, *who have preferred a life of poverty to a life of shame and affluence and who are prepared to do propaganda work if financed, do not refute any of my statements which I have made in my speech* and on the other hand they even go so far as to say that I have been very mild in the description of the real state of affairs that obtains in that community. As for the misrepresentations and falsehoods which a few misguided Devadases who are actually in the trade and who are being profited by such a life have been spreading through pamphlets to undo my good work, it is for the enlightened public to judge. (Reddy 1928, 1, emphasis added)

At the end of this document, she provides a long list of *devadāsī* and *icai vēḷāḷar* associations that support her efforts, and also a letter signed by four *devadāsī*s who represent "Kalavantulu and Shengunthar women, Devadasis in Andhra desh and Tamil Nadu." These women support Reddy, referring to themselves as victims of an "evil practice" characterized by "the dangers of life-long serfdom." Their letter speaks of the exploitation of women at the hands of temple trustees and villagers, and also voices concerns about the antiabolition stance developing within the community as a result of the formation of groups such as the Madras Devadasi

Association. They seek Reddy's assistance in ensuring that rites of passage that mark women as *devadāsī*-courtesans be permanently abolished: "We humbly beg to submit that the practice existing in this presidency of dedicating young girls to temples and performing "Gazzela Puza" [*gajjala pūjā*, "worship of the ankle-bells," an important rite for courtesans who danced professionally] is fraught with the greatest danger to the women of this community in particular and to the society in general."

A few years later, Reddy herself spoke at the 1932 Andhradesa Kalavantulu Conference in Rajahmundry and represented *kalāvantula* women as eagerly awaiting the reforms she had in mind:

> I have had the joy of knowing some of the Kalavanthulu women who, having given up their traditional mode of easy and luxurious living have of their own choice taken up to a very simple yet honourable mode of life . . . I have found . . . that they are as good and pure as any woman could be but only custom—wicked custom, has made them otherwise. I found them clean-hearted, earnest and anxious that their children should lead a different life from theirs and be made good, pure and respectable women. (Natarajan 1997, 127)

As we will see in chapter 5, Reddy's claims for the widespread positive response to her intervention leaves out the substantial groups of women who were, suspicious and critical of her project. Reddy and Gandhi both, in turn, refuse to admit the voices of dissenting dancing women into the debate, claiming that such women remain illegitimate until they have forsaken their lifestyle and taken up the bonds of normative conjugality.

Brahmanic Orthodoxy in Defense of Devadāsīs

One of the more interesting defenses of the *devadāsī* lifestyle, however, came from Brahmin men. Upper-caste men provided some of the strongest antiabolition voices in the Madras Legislative Assembly debates from 1927 to 1930. On the one hand, *devadāsīs* were by and large the mistresses of upper-caste elites, including Brahmins, and thus it is not at all surprising that Brahmin men would defend their own rights to this institutionalized form of concubinage by adopting an antiabolition stance. On the other hand, some Brahmins (such as Viresalingam, for example) were instrumental in pointing out the immorality of concubinage. Both positions deployed nationalist rhetoric, but in radically different ways. For the antiabolitionists, concubinage is seen as one aspect of culture under threat of extinction; they are concerned about the state intervening in the private sphere and the loss of a national heritage that results from such interventions. The proabolitionists, on the other hand, see Brahmanical values of purity and conjugality as the vehicle for female citizenship in the nation. Neither position can be described as liberal; rather, each represents a strain of conservatism with its own priorities.

While non-Brahmins in the legislature such as C. N. Muthuranga Mudaliyar and V. I. Muniswami Pillai unanimously supported Reddy's 1927 resolution and actively participated in the debates until 1947, Brahmins associated with the Congress Party such as C. Rajagopalachari and S. Satyamurti took a stance against the anti-nautch movement. Satyamurti (1887–1943), a prominent politician who would later become president of the Indian National Congress in Tamil Nadu and the mayor of Madras, insisted that the artistic practices of *devadāsīs* could be incorporated into the Congress's broader initiatives on national culture.[18] As Anandhi (1991, 740) has shown, however, Satyamurti's agenda has to be read in the wider context of the growth of non-Brahmin assertion, and his own concerns about the preservation of Brahmin authority in temple contexts. During the debates in 1927, Satyamurti mentions his fear that non-Brahmins might eventually demand a bill that would dispense with Brahmin priests (*arcakas*) in temples, and he justifies his pro-*devadāsī* stance as "cultural preservation" in the face of colonial domination. Satyamurti's agenda is critiqued by *devadāsīs* themselves. The November 5, 1927, issue of the newspaper *Tamiḻ Nāṭu* contains a pagelong feature entitled "Should Poṭṭukkaṭṭutal Be Banned?" (*poṭṭukkaṭṭutal oḻiyumā?*) It reports that a meeting of *devadāsīs* in Mayuram concluded that Satyamurti's justification for supporting *devadāsīs* as part of an "ancient Hindu religious tradition" is analogous to supporting the practice of sati on these same grounds.[19]

Satyamurti's justification of *devadāsīs* as living symbols of ancient Hindu society resonates far beyond the legislature and print media. A remarkable handwritten Tamil paper manuscript dated to 1928 entitled *Tācikaḷ Tarmam* ("Dharma of the Dāsīs") by a Śrīvaiṣṇava Brahmin named Koṭṭaiyūr Mahākavi Cēṣacāyi is preserved in the Thanjavur Sarasvati Mahal Library.[20] The author, who lived in Thanjavur, is the creator of several modern Sanskrit works that focus on orthodox Brahmanic religious values.[21] Some of his other Sanskrit works specifically discuss reform issues. In a short text called *Vivāhakāla Vicāraḥ* ("Deliberations on the [Appropriate] Time for Marriage"), for example, he refutes the Child Marriage Restraint Bill of 1929. Unlike Satyamurti's voice, which reverberates through the cosmopolitan technologies of the state, Cēṣacāyi's work remains within orthodox, localized circuits of knowledge. *Tācikaḷ Tarmam* illustrates how non-Brahmin assertion in Madras city was seen as threatening to nonurban orthodox Brahmins as well, and how *devadāsī* abolition indexed this threat in a very real way.

Cēṣacāyi's text opens with a call for men to reject the ideology of atheism, in an indirect reference to Periyar. He continues by claiming that "[s]ome people like the learned Srimati Muthulakshmi Reddy do not show the world the reality about the caste (*jāti*) and rites (*ācāram*) of *veśyā*s. It is necessary, therefore, to demonstrate the truth about *veśyā*s based on traditional understandings." By "traditional understandings" Cēṣacāyi is referring to canonical Sanskrit texts—*dharmaśāstra*s, *purāṇa*s, and the *Kāmasūtra*—which are cited liberally throughout the text.[22] The text is divided into four sections: (1) *vēciyājāti svarūpam* (the types of *veśyā*s, also called "*veśyā*s are not prostitutes"); (2) *avarkaḷin naṭattai* (their behavior); (3) *avarkaḷināl erpaṭum nanmaikaḷ* (what they have accomplished); and (4) *avarkaḷiparri erpaṭṭa prācīna rājīyavaḷakkaṅkaḷ* (perceptions of them under the old kingdoms). Each of these sections posits "*veśyā* sexuality" as central to Hindu (Brahmanic) moral, philosophical, and physical well-being. The passage below dramatizes his anxieties about how reform activities could destabilize "traditional" caste and gender roles:

> In our times, religious and caste-based values are in a degenerate state. Even Brahmins, who are venerated as the superior caste (*uttama-jāti*), have discarded their own religious rites; they behave as they wish, and do not wear the topknot and sacred thread. In the past, when kings and others discarded the laws of caste and religion, great disasters (*anarttam*) occurred. It is worrisome that religious laws (*tarmaṅkaḷ*) relating to both men and women may be altered very soon. I too agree that women should have freedom in some matters, but that freedom should ultimately be focused on making the world a better place.
>
> Practicing a religion means understanding the essential truth (*tattvam*) of that religion and respecting the authority of its leaders. Permitting widows to remarry or making the *caṇḍāla*s equal to the upper-castes is ultimately of no use . . . If we examine all the information [I have presented] and give it serious thought, one simple question remains—what benefit would we accrue by destroying the community of *veśyās* (*vēciyājati aḻippatināl*)? If one looks deeper into the present situation, it becomes clear that the question of the status of this *jāti* is central to [contemporary] political negotiations.

While reformers posited contemporary *devadāsīs* as signs of moral degeneration, Brahmins such as Satyamurti and Cēṣacāyi turned this argument around, positing instead that *devadāsī* abolition, together with other reforms related to sexuality and caste, signals the apocalyptic decline of Hinduism in the twentieth century. Cēṣacāyi's text is limited to the argument about the decline of Hinduism but also clearly upholds the idea of Brahmin privilege over non-Brahmin women's sexuality.

2. YAMINI PURNATILAKAM, GANDHI, AND THE TELUGU *KALĀVANTULU* OF THE MADRAS PRESIDENCY

From the beginning, Reddy's interventions were directed toward both the Tamil- and the Telugu-speaking courtesan communities in the Presidency. The Telugu-speaking communities, dispersed throughout Andhra Pradesh but heavily concentrated in the coastal areas, were known by the terms *bogamvāḷḷu* (or *bhogamvāḷḷu*, "embodiments of enjoyment") or *kalāvantulu* (from the noun *kalāvant*, "artist," which we already encountered in the Tanjore Moḍi records). The *kalāvantula* community (the subject of chapter 5) played a central role in reform debates and mirrored in many ways the developments taking place within Tamil-speaking *devadāsī* communities. In some ways, we can think of the Telugu-speaking parts of the Presidency as the originary site for public debates on *devadāsī* reform, considering that late nineteenth-century elites like Kandukuri Viresalingam and Raghupati Venkataratnam Naidu were directly addressing the *kalāvantula* community in their pleas for reform.

By the second decade of the twentieth century, however, Gandhian nationalism, in particular the ideology of self-governance ("home rule," *swaraj*), shaped some of the most prominent voices of support for reform among Telugu-speaking courtesans, among them Yamini Purnatilakam. As Judy Whitehead points out, "the health of the nation was linked to the goal of *swaraj*, through self-governance over physical, moral, and spiritual aspects of life" (1998, 99). In the 1920s, the "moral health" of the nation was a growing concern; as Anandhi has pointed out, the "politics of respectability" was a cornerstone of Congress nationalism in South India, and these clearly privileged patriarchal norms were deeply embedded in the discourse of its women activists. Gandhi's perspectives on female sexuality influenced the discourse of all three figures we are discussing here: Reddy first met Gandhi in 1927, the same year that she presented her resolution before the Legislative Assembly and later resigned from the Madras legislature to protest Gandhi's arrest in 1930; Ramamirttammal joined

Gandhi's Congress Party in 1921; and Yamini Purnatilakam, the focus of this section, became one of the most prominent women associated with Gandhi in the south.

In 1921, Gandhi made his first visit to Andhra Pradesh, and it was here that Yamini Purnatilakam heard him speak about *devadāsī*s. He met several members of the *devadāsī* community in Kakinada, a stronghold of *kalāvantula* culture. Gandhi later reflects on that moment:

> I had my full say at Rajahmundry on an important matter, and I hope that some Telugu friend will reproduce that speech, translate it, and spread it broadcast among hundreds of our countrymen. It was about ten o'clock last night in Cocanada that dancing girls paid me a visit when I understood the full significance of what they were. I felt like sinking in the earth below . . . I ask you, brothers and sisters, to send me assurance, as early as possible, that there is not a single dancing girl in this part of the land. I charge these sisters who are sitting behind me to go about from place to place, find out every dancing girl, and shame men into shunning the wrong they are doing. (M. K. Gandhi 1942, 174)

Gandhi's visceral reactions to seeing "real" professional dancing women in South India take the shape of a charged plea. He urges women in particular to "find" the dancing girls and rehabilitate them, a challenge taken on by Yamini Purnatilakam as early as two years later.

Gandhi's reactions to *devadāsī*s are remarkably consistent: he felt repulsed by *dāsī*s and also used the familiar trope of false consciousness when it came to *devadāsī* resistance to reform. He refused to listen to *devadāsī* voices: "The opinion of the parties concerned in the immoral traffic cannot count, just as the opinion of keepers of opium dens will not count in favour of their retention, if public opinion is otherwise against them" (M. K. Gandhi 1942, 203). Recent studies such as those by Alter (1994; 1996; 2000), Caplan (1987), Chakrabarty (2002, 51–64), Katrak (1992), Lal (2000), and Patel (2000) have analyzed Gandhi's attitudes toward sexuality in general and female sexuality in particular. As Ketu Katrak remarks,

> Gandhi's involvement of women in his "satyagraha" . . . movement—part of his political strategy for national liberation—did not intend to confuse men's and women's roles; in particular, Gandhi did not challenge patriarchal traditions that opposed women within the home. Furthermore, his specific representations of women and female sexuality . . . promoted . . . a "traditional" ideology wherein female sexuality was le-

> gitimately embodied only in marriage, wifehood, motherhood, domesticity. (Katrak, 1992, 395–396)

Gandhi's commentary on *devadāsīs* continued over the next decade and a half, surfacing in a number of talks he delivered to the Presidency. In an address to a gathering at the Gandhi Ashram in Pudupalayam, Tamil Nadu, on March 21, 1925, Gandhi supported the institutionalization of *devadāsī* reform, suggesting that "domesticating" the women by teaching them handicrafts would somehow solve the "problem" of prostitution. He also suggested that *devadāsīs* are in need of "purification" and offered them the spinning of *khādi* "as a sacrificial practice," a moral penance:

> [W]e must take up the case of these unfortunate women and find them suitable employment . . . The income of these women is large; we cannot promise them the same income in their alternative professions as they are getting from their sinful practice; nor would they require such an income if they lead a reformed life. Spinning may not secure a living for them. They could take to it only as a recreation, as a sacrificial practice. I place it before them only as purification. But other occupations can be found for them which they can easily learn and follow. There is weaving, tailoring, or fancy-work on khaddar. Some Parsi women have taken to fancy weaving. There is also lace-work, embroidery and other handicrafts which can easily yield them an income of three quarters of a rupee to one and a half rupees per day. The Devadasi class being small, it must not be a difficult matter to find five or six handicrafts for them. We require men and women—preferably women who been trained in these handicrafts and lead a pure life—to take up this cause of reformation of their fallen sisters. You may also study and copy the institutions with similar objects working in other places. There should be a specialist to devote his life to the noble work of reclamation. (M. K. Gandhi 1963, 351–352)

Anandhi narrates another incident that occurred in Mayuram in 1927. A number of *devadāsīs*, including Muvalur Ramamirttammal and Dasi Jagannathammal, wanted to make gifts of their ornaments to Gandhi, who would not accept them until the women had proved that they led "a respectable married life." He asked that they wear and display *tālis* or *maṅgalasūtras* (marriage emblems), contrary to their community's social practices, for this, he felt, was the mark of a "respectable Hindu woman" (Anandhi 1997a, 209–210).

The links between Gandhi and the *devadāsī* question became deeply sedimented in the popular consciousness, so much so that in 1934, after all of the major interventions by Reddy and Yamini Purnatilakam had occurred, a young man from the *kalāvantula* community wrote to Gandhi about the persistence of *devadāsī*s in the Telugu-speaking regions. He calls Andhra Pradesh the "heartland of this evil," and refers to *devadāsī*s as the "sister community" of Dalits, arguing that both are in urgent need of "moral elevation." Gandhian "education," a sign here for nationalist patriarchy, he hopes, will be able to accomplish what women such as Reddy and Purnatilakam could not—namely, *respectability for men*, such as himself, from these communities:

> I wanted to write to you long ago. But I was awfully shy. Thank God, I am at last confiding my burden to you.
>
> I come from the devadasi community. My life was socially a torture. Mahatmaji, do you think that there is any other profession worse than that of the dancing girls in the universe? Is it not a blot on India that prostitution should personify in a community?
>
> Andhradesh, I think, is the heart of this evil. Hindu society here engages dancing girls—especially during marriages and festivals of the deity—to sing obscene songs accompanied by obscene gestures before the pious deity, and sets a bad example before the newly-wed couple.
>
> The misery of a whole community consigned to a life of prostitution is great. Young men here are trying to do their best to root out this evil. But they badly need guidance. Won't you kindly take up this matter as equally important and emergent as the Harijan movement? Please have this affair always in a corner of your heart and give it publicity. You have not only the Congress but the whole public opinion at your back. What the Brothels Bill and the I.P.C. could not do, I am confidant a word from your mouth would do.
>
> I am legally and religiously married to a girl of my own community, and I am a father of two daughters. My wife is pious in my eyes as any other Hindu wife. Still society looks down upon us. The sins of our ancestors are wreaking vengeance on us. The stigma of prostitution is attached to us, though both of us are free from the vice.
>
> Harijans and devadasis are the only two communities which are almost in the same degree of depravity. Of course, they will have to

> help themselves to moral elevation. Still a teacher like you would educate them and the society more quickly than they can do it for themselves. These are two sister movements. Please don't forget the sister community in your enthusiasm for the Harijans. (M. K. Gandhi 1942, 205–206)

Yamini Purnatilakam (c. 1890–1950), a middle-aged woman from the *kalāvantula* community, inspired by Gandhi's visit to Kakinada and his stance on the *devadāsī* issue, became a spokesperson for *devadāsī* reform in Andhra Pradesh. Purnatilakam's biography appears to be the most elusive among the three women featured in this chapter. She was not a public figure in the same way as the others, nor did she produce a substantial amount of writing. In addition, the official records related to the rehabilitation centers (*śaraṇālayams*) she founded in the Presidency are nowhere to be found. We do know, however, it was with the backing of the important nationalist figure Darisi Chenchaiah (c. 1890–1960) that Purnatilakam first made herself visible by lecturing on Gandhian philosophy and Telugu literature in the 1920s. In fact, much of the information about her life is available only from Chenchaiah's autobiography published in 1952. She became a key disciple of Gandhi's in the south, and was imprisoned several times for her activities as a member of the Andhra Provincial Congress Committee. In 1921, she also picketed in front of shops that sold foreign cloth, and she urged women to sell their jewels to raise money for Gandhi's Tilak Swaraj Fund (Seshagiri Rao n.d., 216). Her Gandhian connections also brought her into contact with the Theosophical Society in Madras, and it was in this connection that she met Muthulakshmi Reddy.

In 1923, Purnatilakam founded a fortnightly newspaper, *Hindu Yuvati*, which ran for seven years. Also in the same year, she set up an institution in Madras called Hindu Yuvati Saranalayam. Modeled after other vocational institutions for destitute and widowed women, the Yuvati Saranalayam was a "rehabilitation centre" set up for *devadāsīs*. It saw to the "moral, vocational and literary instruction of the inmates to wean them away from their traditional lives . . . the vocational part of the instruction consisted of spinning, weaving, basket-making and gardening" (Kesavanarayana 1976, 222). The institution was financially supported by Chenchaiah and other Madras elites. Purnatilakam's *śaraṇālayam* inspired men from the *kalāvantula* community in Andhra Pradesh to set up similar institutions in Guntur and Narasapur, and this activity was also replicated by *"icai vēḷāḷar"* associations in Tamil-speaking areas like Tanjore, where the first *śaraṇālayam* was set up in 1927. Most of these were short-lived enterprises that were operational for less than a decade.

In 1924, Purnatilakam was instrumental in organizing the first Andhra Provincial Kalavantula Social Reform Conference in Guntur. In his introductory address, conference president C. Anjaneyulu echoed the voices of Gandhi and Purnatilakam. He advocated a return to "a wholesome atmosphere for healthy progress," referring to the *kalāvantula* tradition as a "moral depravity" and to the fact that it was "unmeaning [*sic*] that Hindu civilization should have given recognition to it" (Kesavanarayana 1976, 223). The conference ended with several resolutions, including the organization of an annual meeting to implement the changes necessary to rehabilitate the *kalāvantula* community, the official proposal of an amendment to the section of the penal code dealing with prostitution, an appeal to franchise *inām* lands held by *kalāvantulu*, and the creation of a "marriage board" to initiate *kalāvantula* women into normative sexual roles. In 1925, this board secured marriages for three *kalāvantulu*, K. Sitaramamma, Annapurnamma, and D. Venkatamahalakshamma (225).

Purnatilakam's efforts in mobilizing caste associations would find their fullest expression in the vast numbers of letters and memos sent to Reddy in support of her bill from 1927 to 1929. But Purnatilakam's presence also inspired a number of early grassroots reform activities throughout the Telugu-speaking regions. In May 1926, a new group called the Kalavantula Social Reform Propaganda Committee, encouraged by Purnatilakam, began to visit the homes of *kalāvantula* women in their villages with a view to dissuade them from teaching music and dance to their female children. The vernacular press, the magazine *Krishnapatrika* in particular, highlighted the "successes" of this organization. In Rajahmundry, where there were close to 120 *kalāvantula* households, the reformers could only persuade 25 to give up their hereditary profession. Many families in Rajahmundry refused to let the reformers into their homes, in spite of warnings that they would be violating the newly amended section of the penal code in doing so. The committee also visited Masulipatnam, where forty *kalāvantula* families signed a reform pledge, and at Eluru a woman named K. Manikyamba convinced four young *kalāvantula* women to stop performing dance and promised to get them married (Kesavanarayana 1976, 225). In Vijayawada, twenty-five *kalāvantula* families pledged to have their girl children married, but many others in the town insisted that they would continue their profession "as *sāni*s [*kalāvantulu*], not prostitutes." In the Rayalaseema region, in 1927, members of the committee met with *kalāvantula* families in the towns of Tadpatri (Anantapur district) and Proddatur (Kadapa district), and spoke against the sponsorship of dancing by *kalāvantula* troupes (226). At a meeting of the *kalāvantula* community at the home of a man named Chengal Rao Naidu in Bellary on August 8, 1927, "thirteen ladies came forward with the undertaking that they would marry their girls and gave a written undertaking to that effect"[23]

In a letter to Reddy dated October 10, 1929, G. Nagabhushanam, secretary of the Andhra Desa Kalavantula Reform Association at Pedapulivarru in Guntur district, laments the persistence of dance in the *kalāvantula* community. He requests Reddy to build a clause into her forthcoming abolition bill that would penalize those who teach dance to women in the community as well:

> I must bring to your kind notice that the work of the Kalavantula Reform Society is handicapped at Tenali where there is some re-action. There, there is one teacher of the Kalavantula caste only, by name Raghavaiya, who will be teaching and producing fifteen or twenty nautch girls every year and [this] is this adding numbers to the system of prostitution. As such I wish your bill proposes some punishment to such teachers also, as such a measure appears to be essential in places like Tenali.[24]

These activities continued with a great degree of zeal even into the 1940s. In August 1944, for example, the Brahmo Samaj convened a meeting in Kakinada that was presided over by Pyda Venkatanarayana, a local *zamīndār* who later became the MLA for the town of Kakinada. The meeting was attended by members of the *kalāvantula* community from towns such as Tuni and Pithapuram, and again, members were urged by Venkatanarayana to give up their traditional social and aesthetic practices. In November of the same year, a local reform association in Kakinada staged a protest at the venue of a performance by *kalāvantulu*, and the *mēḷam* of artists was forced to disband. During the Vijayādaśamī festival in 1945, the trustees of a local temple advertised a dance performance by *kalāvantula* women. A local reform body, led by a man named Bhaskara Hemachandra Rao, published circulars that shamed the temple trustees for supporting "nautch parties." This caused a great commotion in Kakinada, and ultimately, the *kalāvantulu* withdrew and did not proceed with the performance (Inna Reddy 1998, 113–114).

Little else is known about the rest of Purnatilakam's life, except that she became disgruntled by the male dominance within various *kalā-*

vantulu reform organizations, specifically the Kalavanthula Samskarana Sanghams in Guntur, Narsapuram, and Secunderabad. No official archives of the Madras Hindu Yuvati Saranalayam exist.

MUVALUR RAMAMIRTTAMMAL AND THE NON-BRAHMIN MOVEMENT

Muvalur Ramamirttammal (1883–1962) was born in the village of Muvalur (Thanjavur district), as a child was sold in adoption to a *dāsī* named Achikkannammal, later schooled in Tamil, Telugu, and Sanskrit, and taught music and dance (Jīvacuntari 2007, 20). Not much is known about her early life other than the fact that she married her music teacher, Suyambu Pillai, before she became active in Congress politics (Anandhi 1991, 741). Ramamirttammal began her career as an activist in the Congress party, and was a member of the Congress Provincial Committee for a couple of years. In 1925, E. V. Ramasami Naicker (Periyar) left the Congress to launch the Self-Respect Movement (Dravida Kazhagam [DK]), and Ramamirttammal followed him in 1927. She became a popular orator, and she also published a number of essays in the Self-Respect journals, *Kuṭi Aracu* and *Tirāviṭanāṭu*. She served a six-month jail sentence for picketing in the Self-Respect anti-Hindi protests in Madras in 1938 (Ramaswamy 1997, 188–189). In 1949, Ramamirttammal left the DK, protesting the seventy-year-old Periyar's marriage to the thirty-year-old woman Manniammai, and joined C. N. Annadurai's Association for the Progress of Dravidians (Dravida Munnetra Kazhagam [(DMK]). She died in 1962.

Several substantial discussions of Ramamirttammal's role in *devadāsī* abolition have already been produced (Anandhi 1991; Geetha 1998; Geetha and Rajadurai 1998; Kannabiran and Kannabiran 2003; Srilata 2003), and Ramamirttammal is best known for her Tamil novel *Tāsikaḷ Mōcavaḷai allatu Matipeṟṟa Maiṉar* ("The *Dasi*sí Web of Deceit, or How the Minor Came to His Senses"), published in 1936, and recently translated by Kannabiran and Kannabiran (2003). The novel provides a fictionalized account of what Ramamirttammal claims to see around her—unscrupulous, money-hungry *devadāsī*s who ensnare young men ("minors") into their deceitful world of pleasure. Ultimately, the *dāsī*s at center of the narrative who initially resist the *devadāsī* abolition movement later embrace it, having lost all their money to the man who was their *māmā* (*lit.* "uncle," pimp). As V. Geetha notes, Self-Respect discourse held that "women who felt 'dedicated' into the profession did not really seem to understand the vicious logic that held them captive . . . The novel [*Tāsikaḷ Mōcavaḷai*] betrays a certain puritanical will to 'cleanse' the diseased devadasi of her powers of seduction and in doing so ends up blaming the victim as much as the victimizer" (1998, 13). While I take seriously the calls of Anandhi and Srilata for a feminist reading of the text that does not reduce it merely to the realm of Self-Respect propaganda, *Tāsikaḷ Mōcavaḷai* does build on well-established literary tropes in writings by elite urban men about deceitful courtesans in the Madras Presidency, as examined in chapter 2. In fact, just six years before *Tāsikaḷ Mōcavaḷai* was published, a satirical set of Tamil songs bearing an unbelievably similar title, *Tācikaḷ Vēcam Maiṉarkaḷ Mōcam* ("Guises of the *Dāsīs*, Deception of the Minor"), written by Muhammata Yūcup in 1930, was already circulating in Madras. Even though the style of this work is somewhat different from that of *Tāsikaḷ Mōcavaḷai*, it is broadly based on the same theme of *devadāsīs* duping "minors" through their arts of seduction.[25]

As the work of V. Geetha (1998), Geetha and Rajadurai (1998), and Srilata (2003) has clearly demonstrated, Periyar's radical ideas about gender and sexual equality were revolutionary in the Indian context. In addition to his critique of the ideal of female chastity, as Geetha notes, "we find Periyar arguing against a sexual ethic which sanctioned and legitimised male promiscuity while reproving of and rendering illegitimate female desire" (1998, 13). Periyar's radical reformulation of marriage itself and his vision of "revolutionary family life" (Hodges 2005b; Sreenivas 2008, 67–93) present a bold and powerful critique of the peculiar intersection of religion, caste, and male sexuality that curtailed Tamil women's subjectivity in late colonial India.

Periyar was a strong supporter of *devadāsī* abolition, and voiced his support of Reddy's proposed 1927 bill in the form of a letter to the secretary of the Madras legislature, which was then published as an essay in 1930 entitled *The Law Prohibiting Poṭṭukkaṭṭu* (*poṭṭukkaṭṭu niruttam cattam*). Periyar also wrote another essay, published just days before the other, entitled *The Devadāsī Abolition Act* (*tēvatāci oḻippu cattam*).[26] In these writings, Periyar takes a radical stance against the *devadāsī* "system." He argues that the lives of *devadāsīs* "are vulgar and artificial to the extreme. They are often responsible for spreading diseases such as gonorrhoea. They must therefore be prevented from pursuing their profession" (Srilata 2003, 185). Periyar interprets the persistence of *devadāsīs* as a concrete sign of the subordination of lower-caste women to the fulfillment of the needs of upper-caste men. But unlike other reformers, including Reddy, Periyar does not advocate marriage as the solution for *devadāsīs*, nor does his discourse valorize chastity (*kaṟpu*) or motherhood for women generally.

However, as Whitehead has pointed out, Periyar's rhetorical "reclamation" of non-Brahmin women's rights ultimately "placed the control over women's sexuality securely within the boundaries of the [male, non-Brahmin] community" (1998, 101). Indeed, the enforcement of patriliny and middle-class morality in their communities by *icai vēḷāḷar* men provides a clear example of how non-Brahmin political assertion enabled the invisibility of contemporary *icai vēḷāḷar* women as a group.

Ramamirttammal herself undeniably saw marriage as the most feasible solution for *devadāsī*s. Even during her early days as a member of the Congress Provincial Committee, convictions about the "respectability" of monogamous conjugality led her to arrange a number of intercaste marriages of consent for *devadāsī*s in Ramnad, Trichy, and Thanjavur districts in 1927. These public events were supported by some *devadāsī*s and vehemently opposed by others. In a letter written to Reddy on the letterhead of the "Third Conference of the Icai Vēḷāḷars of Thanjavur Jillā," dated October 13, 1927, Ramamirttammal tells Reddy that she knows of a number of young *devadāsī*s who have consented to getting married and are eagerly awaiting the opportunity:

> Dear Madam, mother to the young girls of our community!
>
> I have received everything you have sent. I was unable to reply sooner because I was out of town. Please pardon me. [I am writing to you] immediately upon my return [to Muvalur]. Through the *Cutēcamittiraṉ* newspaper, I have come to know what those shameless and dishonorable Chennai *dāsī*s have written. I waited to see how far they would go. Please peruse the enclosed and forward them to [local] newspapers. Copies of these may be sent to the [Justice Party's] *Tirāviṭaṉ* newspaper as well.
>
> I don't have the details as to whether the girls who wanted to marry are minors or majors. If these details are furnished, I will make sure to get their consent [for marriage]. Moreover, I will ask others to write articles as well.
>
> As I am a member of Congress Provincial Committee, I will be in the city on 19–12-27 to attend the meeting scheduled for 20–12-27 in Egmore, Chennai. I will obey your instructions without fail. More when we meet in person.
>
> Ramamirttam Muvalur[27]

In this letter, we see Ramamirttammal not only moving forward with her agenda of "respectable" marriage for *devadāsī*s but also denouncing the attempts of *devadāsīs* who are resisting reform. The letter also points to the deep political connections between Reddy and Ramamirttammal as women participating in public life. While Kannabiran and Kannabiran (2003, 23–24) have rightly pointed to the differences between Ramamirttammal's mobilization of *devadāsī* issues to critique Brahmanical Hinduism and Reddy's view of *devadāsīs* as a "blot on Hindu civilization," it is significant that much of Ramamirttammal's "grassroots" *devadāsī* activism takes place in 1927 (the same year that Reddy's bill was introduced) as she, following Periyar, leaves the Congress Party and joins the nascent Self-Respect Movement. But even then, her early ideas about the importance of marriage for *devadāsīs* resound in her later activities, specifically in the plot of *Tāsikaḷ Mōcavaḷai*.

The connections between Ramamirttammal and marriage run deep in public memory and continue to be invoked through the mechanisms of the state.[28] Around 1990, during his second tenure as chief minister of Tamil Nadu, M. Karunanidhi announced a "marriage scheme for poor women." The project was called "Moovalur Ramamirtham Ammaiyar Memorial Marriage Assistance Scheme" (*mūvālūr rāmāmirttam ammaiyār niṉaivu tirumaṉa utavi tiṭṭam*). The scheme remembers Ramamirttammal as a crusader for marriage, and points to the gendered shortcomings of Dravidian politics in the present. The scheme is part of the larger "social welfare" programs of the Tamil Nadu State Government, and in order to receive assistance from the scheme, a woman must meet the eligibility criteria. The Kanchipuram District Social Welfare Office explains the scheme:

> Objective of the scheme is to help financially poor parents in getting their daughter's marriage and promote the educational status of poor girls. Quantum of assistance Rs. 10,000. Eligibility criteria—the bride must have appeared for 10th Std examination. In the case of ST [scheduled tribes] the bride should have studied upto 5th Std. Annual Income should not exceed Rs. 12,000.
>
> Age: Bride should have completed 20 years of age. Only one daughter in a family is eligible.[29]

The scheme was briefly revoked by Karunanidhi's rival J. Jayalalithaa when she came to power as chief minister of Tamil Nadu in 2002. During the 2006 state elections, Karunanidhi promised to reinstate the scheme if elected—a task he accomplished within a month of taking office as chief minister.[30]

THE BIRTH OF A *JĀTI*: CASTE ASSOCIATIONS AND REFORM POLITICS

Icai vēḷāḷar means "cultivator of music." It is essentially a caste designation created by men associated with dance and music in the early twentieth century. The use of the term *icai vēḷāḷar* can be traced in documents dated to the 1920s, and letters of support for Reddy's bill in the late 1920s often appear on letterhead bearing variations on the name "icai vēḷāḷar caṅkam." Beginning in this period, a number of conferences (*makānāṭus*) were held throughout Tamil Nadu for the consolidation and crystallization of the caste status of men from *devadāsī* communities.[31] These communities were traditionally understood as being mixed-caste, and this liminal caste status was increasingly becoming a concern for men, especially in light of the potential eradication of *devadāsī* culture. The aim of the caste associations was ultimately not only to fix the place of men from *devadāsī* communities within the hierarchy of caste but also to define their role in a larger civilizational genealogy—who were they as a caste group, and what was their hereditary occupation? In this process, *icai vēḷāḷar*s claimed their links to music in a move that provided them with a niche occupation as the hereditary keepers of music traditions that as early as the 1920s were already understood as "respectable." This conscious self-styling also disassociated them from their links to the barber community, and enabled their participation—as "authentic" dance masters from the past—in the emergent urban reinvention of *devadāsī* dance in Madras in the late 1930s. But other caste associations such as the South Indian Sengundar Mahajana Sangam of Coimbatore vehemently denied their associations with the culture of *devadāsī*s, even through many *devadāsī*s did come from the weaver communities of *ceṅkuntar* and *kaikkōḷar*. In 1927, the editor of the *Ceṅkuntamittiraṉ* weekly (a magazine for the *ceṅkuntar* community) announced, for example, that "the brave men and women of Sengundar community should safeguard the caste honour against the *devadāsī*s' attempts to identify themselves with our caste. Unless we wake up, our sacred caste's honour will be even lower than that of the *devadāsī*s" (Anandhi 1991, 747).

In the Telugu-speaking regions of the Presidency, the issue is a little less clear. The term *kalāvantula* (from *kalāvant* or *kalāvantī*, "artist") appears to have been in use quite early. Although it does not appear in early Telugu print materials, it does make it into Thurston's *Castes and Tribes of Southern India* (1909), under the heading "Kalavant." Thurston defines women from this community as "dancers and singers, who, like other dancing-girls, are courtesans. The name occurs only in South Canara, but also in the Telugu country" (Thurston 1909, 3: 47). Caste organizations with names such as the Kalavanthula Samskarana Sangham ("Association for the Reformation of the Kalavantulu") and Andhra Provincial Kalavanthula Conference are found in letters addressed to Reddy supporting abolition, very much like the letters from *icai vēḷāḷar* associations in the Tamil regions.[32] These letters too, like the one addressed to Gandhi quoted above, are always composed by men. Occasionally a few women's signatures do appear, but even this is rare, and it is clear that the documents are wholly engineered by men. Contemporary caste associations in these communities, however, claim for themselves the caste status of "*sūryabaḷ ija*," aligning themselves with the larger agrarian-merchant community known as *baḷija*. *Baḷija*s, of course, deny that their caste is related to the new *sūryabaḷija* or *kalāvantula* caste, much as *vēḷāḷar*s (who were traditionally farmers) deny their relationship with *icai vēḷāḷar*s in the Tamil-speaking regions. It is still unclear when the *kalāvantula* community adopted the caste name *sūryabaḷija*. This name does not appear in early census data or colonial ethnography and hence must have been created sometime in the early twentieth century.

Regardless of when this shift took place, as early as 1906, men from Telugu-speaking *kalāvantula* communities took a stand not to support the professional practices of women in their communities. By refusing to participate in the income-generating performances of the women, *kalāvantula* men were clearly asserting a new patriarchal order that was actualized, in part, through the marriage of their girls in the community. An article in *Krishnapatrika* magazine dated April 15, 1906, for example, mentions that

> . . . in Guntur town the male members of the nautch community met and entered into an agreement not to accompany on violin and *mridangam* [drum] during the nautch performances. They further took a vow to educate their female children and get them married . . . [A] committee was formed to supervise the conduct of the members of the community, and it was empowered to take action against those who violate the agreement by imposing fines up to Rs. 500. (V. Ramakrishna 1983, 143, n. 46)

As Priyadarshini Vijaisri has pointed out, by 1929, caste associations within the *kalāvantula* community focused exclusively on charting the progress and restoring the honor of its men (2004, 184). In a letter to Reddy, the secretary of the Guntur Kalavanthula Vidya Sangam makes it clear that his organization is committed to "helping the poor boys of the community with schooling" (ibid.). Kalāvantula caste associations continue to exist, particularly in the coastal areas, where the *kalāvantula* population is high. Over the course of my ethnography in Duvva village (West Godavari district), for example, I met the leaders of the local Kalavantula Sangam, Saride Seshagiri Rao, and Saride Narasimha Rao. In the postreform period, small rural organizations such as these seek to regulate outsiders' representation of and accessibility to *kalāvantula* women in the region and also to provide political platforms to men from the community.

BARBERS, MUSICIANS, DANCE MASTERS: *ICAI VĒḶĀḶAR* MEN IN SUPPORT OF MUTHULAKSHMI REDDY

The birth of the *"icai vēḷāḷar" jāti* in the 1920s signaled a reinvention of masculinity within *devadāsī* communities in the Tamil-speaking regions. It also gave a fixed and uniform identity to an otherwise heterogeneous social group.[33] Before the political mobilization of these communities in the 1920s, men who were relatives of *devadāsī*s identified themselves using a range of caste names and occupational titles. The most broad and far-reaching of these was *mēḷakkārar* ("one who plays in the *mēḷam*"), which functioned as an umbrella term for the various subgroups that made up the community. The subgroups existed within a hierarchy, with men who were dance masters (*naṭṭuvaṉār*s) for *devadāsī*s or professional ritual musicians who played the oboelike *nāgasvaram* (also known as *nāyaṉam*) and its accompanying drum (*tavil*) at the top. Members of these groups often identified themselves with *vēḷāḷa*s, *piḷḷai*s, and *mutali*s in early colonial census reports and ethnographies, were generally associated with urban temples of Śiva and Viṣṇu, and also performed at marriages for Brahmins and others of the upper castes. They were considered the repositories of "high" music and dance traditions. Toward the bottom of the hierarchy were men who were barbers by day but also performed as semiprofessional *nāgasvaram* or *tavil* musicians.

In Tanjavur district alone we can see the enormous complexity of *jāti* identities and titles claimed by men in these communities. In and around Tanjavur, the "barber-musicians," as they were called in the 1901 census, were divided into Tamil- and Telugu-speaking groups. The Tamil-speaking barber-musicians were known as *ampaṭṭaṉ* ("barber," from the Sanskrit *ambaṣṭha*), *nāpitaṉ* ("barber," *napita*), or *parikāri* ("remover," *parihārin*).

These communities performed music for lower, non-Brahmin patrons and also at temples dedicated to village deities. In Tanjavur, men from this community who were "full-time" *nāgasvaram* and *tavil* players often distinguished themselves with the title *maruttuvar* (meaning "practitioner of medicine," a common epithet for "barber"). They also used the term *pajantiri* ("musician") to identify themselves. Among the Telugu-speaking barber-musicians in Tamil Nadu, the surnames *nāyuḍu* and *reḍḍi* were very common. They usually claimed superior status to the Tamil-speaking barber-musicians, but were still considered much lower than "professional" *nāgasvaram* artists and *naṭṭuvaṉār*s, who were employed by larger temples and patronized by elites during marriage functions.[34]

Generally, the term *periyamēḷam* ("large band," referring to the use of the large *tavil* drum) was reserved for troupes of these professional *nāgasvaram* artists, but not without exception. Barber-musicians are known to have joined professional troupes in Tanjore and later in Madras when large numbers of these men migrated to the urban center in the late nineteenth and early twentieth centuries. By contrast, the men who accompanied *devadāsī* performance as *naṭṭuvaṉār*s and musicians practiced a highly specialized function. This retinue of dancers and musicians was sometimes known by the term *ciṉṉamēḷam* ("small band," referring to the small drum. the *muṭṭu*, which accompanied *devadāsī* performance). Occupational "slippage" was less common in these cases, and for the most part, these men were able to maintain a social distance from the lowest rungs of their own communities, namely, men who were barbers and amateur musicians (Srinivasan 1984, 223). The reinvention of these communities as the *icai vēḷāḷar jāti* in the 1920s reified these social hierarchies within the communities on the one hand, but also enabled some mobility between the categories. That barbers could now officially claim the same *jāti* status as professional *nāgasvaram* players and *naṭṭuvaṉār*s certainly created tensions within the community, even as it was clear that the new *jāti* identity would ultimately endow *all* of these groups with respectability and political agency in the nation-state.

These new forms of respectability relied upon the enforcement of conservative, patrilineal attitudes toward women that were traditionally held by men in the community—such as *nāgasvaram* and *tavil* players—who were *not* associated with the quasi-matrifocal households of *devadāsī*s. As Amrit Srinivasan notes,

> Authority, both private and public, and professional monopolies remained entirely in the hands of men. In the *nagasvaram* tradition, to

> teach women any art as a professional interest was seen as a "waste" and a "loss" since she would take the knowledge and secrets out of the house when she married . . . Significantly, however, women did not go entirely unacknowledged . . . they especially contributed to the art tradition as wives and mothers . . . It is significant that marriage with the undedicated women of the *chinnamelam* took place frequently whereas their own women were rarely given to the *chinnamelam* men. Indirectly this acknowledged the pre-eminence of the *chinnamelam* women in the eyes of the outside world whereas the men were dishonoured by being dependent on and dealing with women. (A. Srinivasan 1984, 217–218)

The status of men who were associated with the *ciṉṉamēḷam* or *devadāsī* performance practices was contentious at best, and often a source of embarrassment. Though among *nāgasvaram* players the potential dominance of women as artists was kept under control through the structures of patriliny, this was not the case for men within *devadāsī* households who were usually economically dependent on their mothers and sisters. According to Srinivasan, men who lived or worked as part of the *devadāsī* community perpetually felt a deep "need to develop a 'closed' patrifocal tradition for themselves within the *chinnamelam*, independent of their illustrious womenfolk" (A. Srinivasan 1984, 201). These tensions are clearly dramatized in the course of the anti-nautch debates. As we shall see below, it is these men who fight proactively for abolition and the complete restoration of patriliny in *devadāsī* communities.

Reddy's 1927 resolution, and in fact all subsequent reform efforts, were almost unanimously supported by men from *devadāsī* communities. On November 19, 1927, P. Shanmuganantha, vice-president of the Tanjore District Esai Vellalar Sangam, wrote Reddy in 1927 to congratulate her on the passing of the resolution in the Legislative Assembly.[35] In the letter, he calls Reddy the "ornament" of the colonial government and informs her about the Southern India Yuvathi Saranalayam that he has founded in Tanjore for "the promotion of the welfare of the community and for the total abolition of unchastity." He honors Reddy because she has "evinced such a real and abiding interest in the elevation of this community in India." As in the letter to Gandhi by the young man from the *kalāvantula* community quoted above, the concerns here are threefold: the enforcement of chastity for women in the community, community building and solidarity across the Madras Presidency, and citizenship and the restoration of "respectable" status within the structures of the nation-state.

Men from *devadāsī* communities not only rallied support for reform but also repudiated the protests from organizations such as the Madras Devadasi Association. A letter printed on the letterhead of the Kadalur (Tanjore District) Icai Vēḷāḷa Caṅkam, for example, dramatizes the anger and frustrations of men from *devadāsī* communities who reacted immediately to *devadāsī* protest documents such as *The Humble Memorial of Devadasis of the Madras Presidency*. The letter opens with a deification of Reddy: "Unable to tolerate the atrocities committed by women of this community, the merciful Lord bade the goddess Mahālakṣmī herself to incarnate as Dr. Muthulakshmi to redeem these women and ensure they live a respectable life." The tone of the writing becomes increasingly vicious, and mocks the *devadāsī*s who mounted resisted to abolition:

> Having heard of our support to this bill, some in the Ceṉṉai Uruttirakaṇikaiyar Caṅkam have opposed this bill and have described us as "selfish" individuals who have clamped down like an axe on our own clan. In this way, they have revealed their greatness! It is pathetic to know that their intention is to wear the *poṭṭu* under the pretext of serving the god only to satisfy the sexual lust of the so-called aristocratic devotees of the temple.

The letter continues with insulting advice to the *devadāsī*s who do not affirm the politics of reform:

> [W]e suggest that in the first place you oppose and reject the bill. Thereafter, you can compile a list of the dignitaries who visit your homes [for sex], and after their death, construct a temple with their images installed. Since it is important to worship these images, you may want to stage a protest demanding allocation of funds collected through land tax for this project over the next ten years. We wish you success in securing these funds from the government. By the way, we return to you the two epithets— "selfish people" and "harmful traitors of the clan"—that you have conferred upon us because of our support of this bill.
>
> May you delight in stringing these epithets to both sides of the emblem of prostitution (*poṭṭu*) worn by your women, just as married women string beads to both sides of their *tāli*.[36]

This passage clearly illustrates the public recovery of conservative attitudes toward women that were held by segments of this community. The final blow comes with the cynical call for *devadāsī*s to embrace marriage.

The text insults *devadāsīs* by calling the *poṭṭu* an "emblem of prostitution" (*vipacāra*) and juxtaposing this with the "respectable" *tāli* worn by married women. Discourses of shame and stigma for women were perpetuated from within the community as well, and ultimately, marriage within the community for *devadāsī* women, like the promises of respectability, remained unattainable and unfinished.

In 1927, Reddy first proposed an amendment to the Madras Hindu Religious Endowments Act of 1926 that would give hereditary "*inām* lands" (largely the tax-free *māṉiyam* lands that some *devadāsīs* received for their affiliations with temples) over to *devadāsīs* without any further obligation on the part of the women. In cases where *devadāsīs* received a portion of the revenue from the land (cultivated land, for example), they would continue to receive this for the span of their lifetime, after which it would be received by the temple authorities. This was passed as "Act V of 1929." In some cases, the promise of the Act V of 1929 to enfranchise lands to *devadāsīs* caused considerable uproar. Men who either legitimately held a portion of the *inām* lands or who wanted to lay claim to a portion of the lands could not have them enfranchised since the amendment only applied to women. In the Telugu-speaking regions, because most women were not dedicated to temple deities, the issue became even more unclear and contentious. In a case from the "Sree Venkateswara Swami and Sree Visweswara Swamy temple" in Vadapalle (East Godavari district) dated November 1929, temple trustees object to the enfranchisement of temple lands to professional dancing women who performed on occasion at that temple. The trustees argued that "there has never been any custom or practice of dedicating young girls for service in Hindu temples in this district and hence the Hindu Religious Endowments Act does not apply to them." They explained that that "portions [of the *inām* lands] are enjoyed by men for the service of fiddling, etc., done by them in connection with the dancing service by nautch parties in temples. The men enjoy portions of the Inam as registered holders." Moreover, they claimed "the service by a nautch party consists of Nayakaram [leading the troupe], Fiddling, Drum, Sruti-talam, and natyam, of which the first four are to be rendered by men and the inams enjoyed by men cannot be enfranchised [according to the new amendment].[37]

Reddy also received a number of letters from men who challenged her decision to enfranchise land only in the name of women from these communities.[38] The Devadasi and Kalavantula Samskaranam Association of Bezwada Taluk, for example, expressed its concern over the gendered implications of the enfranchisement of the *ināms*:

> The Hindu Religious Endowment Amendment Act 5 of 1929 which was brought into being, in compliance with our constant requests through your honour's endless efforts to effect a congenial atmosphere in our Sangham and to facilitate a thorough upliftment of the same, is likely to be foiled in its express purpose by the circular recently sent round by the Inam Commissioner . . . It has been the constant custom of the males as well as the females of this association to hold the Inam lands granted to them in lieu of the services in the temples which they jointly, with strict mutual aid, turned out, without fail. Accordingly both the sexes had the equal rights in the Inam lands. But on observing the recent circular of the Honourable Inam Commissioner to enfranchise only those lands which are directly in the possession and enjoyment of the *females only*, all of us turned pessimistic over the future success in the reform of the said association.[39]

As we shall see toward the end of this chapter, men from *devadāsī* communities continued to vie for *inām* lands well into the twenty-first century.

NON-BRAHMIN PUBLICS AND THE RESTORATION OF PATRILINY

The future of men in the *devadāsī* community could only be imagined through the forging of strategic political alliances and the creation of new, modern, non-Brahmin publics. As Amrit Srinivasan shows, the gradual disappearance of the "*mēḷakkārar*" and "*dāsī*" categories from official census statistics in the twentieth century points to "the first stage of their absorption into broader political communities organised around new, shared identities of non-Brahmin, Backward, or Dravidian status" (A. Srinivasan 1984, 112). Non-Brahmin assertion in the Tamil- and Telugu-speaking regions radically transformed the political landscape. As M. S. S. Pandian notes, it forged "a new public which brought together the realm of the everyday and the politics of inferiorized identities" (2007, 211). I do not need to rehearse the complex genealogies of non-Brahmin politics here, but I would like to point out that by the time Periyar formed the Self-Respect Movement (*cuya mariyātai iyakkam*) in 1925, a great deal of social ferment had begun in the *devadāsī* community.

Non-Brahmin assertion in Tamil Nadu, animated in large part by the Self-Respect Movement, allowed men from *devadāsī* backgrounds to participate in political spaces. Styled "*icai vēḷāḷar*s," they now claimed the caste status of *vēḷāḷar*s, and participated in a radical regional politics that permanently transformed the public sphere in Tamil Nadu.[40] Men from the *devadāsī* community were pivotal figures in Dravidian party politics in the middle of the twentieth century. In the early 1930s, immediately following the debates around the 1927 bill, some men such as the poet V. Ramalingam Pillai (1888–1972) supported the Congress presence in the Madras Presidency (Irschick 1986, 215), but things changed drastically with the emergence of the Dravida Kazhagam (Association of Dravidians [DK]) in 1944.

Five years later, C. N. Annadurai (1909–1969) split from the DK and formed his own party, the Dravida Munnetra Kazhagam (Association for the Progress of Dravidians [DMK]). Annadurai was born to a *devadāsī* named Bangaru Ammal, whose family had links to the Varadarāja Perumāḷ temple in Kanchipuram. He attended Pachaiyappa's College in Madras and graduated with a master's degree in economics and politics. In 1935, he joined the Justice Party, and then later broke with the DK, as noted above. In 1967, he became the first non-Congress chief minister of Tamil Nadu. Annadurai was also the earliest figure to communicate Tamil political propaganda through the medium of cinema, and he scripted three major Tamil films. By the late 1940s, *icai vēḷāḷar* men moved into the realm of cinema, at a time when women from these communities were becoming less visible as heroines, largely due to the increasing dominance of Brahmin women in the field.

Throughout his political career, Annadurai's morality was questioned because of his *devadāsī* parentage (Price 1999, 162), but at the same time, his eloquent oratory and often misogynistic public persona appealed to a new generation. As Geetha and Rajadurai point out,

> Annadurai was erudite, intelligent and had a way with words, and his inexorably gendered discourse, which, even when it spoke of women's freedom, objectified them as creatures of beauty and desire, proved alluring and therefore curiously educative. Drawn to his wonderful rhetoric, part prurient, but always well-informed, an entire generation of youth came to be schooled in politics, history and culture. (1998, 511)

Annadurai represents one of the earliest successes of the restoration of patriliny in *devadāsī* communities. His rise to political stardom *despite* his *devadāsī* origins signals successful incorporation of the *icai vēḷāḷar jāti*—as a "modern" caste group with normative gender roles—into the public sphere. Annadurai's successor is Muthuvel Karunanidhi (b. 1924), former chief minister of Tamil Nadu, with whom I began this chapter.

Karunanidhi's successes in the 1971, 1989, 1996, and 2006 Tamil Nadu state elections as well as his persistence as a cultural icon parallel the steady disappearance of *icai vēḷāḷar* women from the public life of modern India.[41]

Karunanidhi's iconic status is reified by some of the contemporary *icai vēḷāḷar* caste associations in Tamil Nadu. For example, the Talaimai Icai Vēḷāḷar Caṅkam (Association for Leadership among Icai Vēḷāḷars) is an organization based in Chennai. The organization institutes awards and certificates bearing the image of Karunanidhi, and also publishes a monthly Tamil-language journal, *Icai Vēḷāḷar Muracu* (Victory Drum of the *Icai Vēḷāḷars*, fig. 3.1). The journal emphasizes the social, cultural, and political achievements of members of the *icai vēḷāḷar* caste and devotes a sizeable portion of each issue to matrimonial advertisements. The organization is clearly aligned politically with the DMK, and Karunanidhi's image figures prominently in nearly every issue. The same organization also publishes another magazine, *Apūrva Rākam* (Unparalleled *Rāga*), focused on achievements in the fields of music (and marginally dance). Unlike *Icai Vēḷāḷar Muracu*, *Apūrva Rākam* does not claim to be exclusively for members of the *icai vēḷāḷar* community. It carries articles on "mainstream," upper-caste musical events and performers, but juxtaposes these with notices about performances by *icai vēḷāḷar* artists.

Recently, the web domain Isaivelalar.com has been claimed by a group called Isaivellaler Murpokku Nalasangam (Association of Progressive Icai Vēḷāḷars). The description of the organization on the website begins as follows:

> Isaivellaler Murpokku Nalasangam, a nonpolitical association for the development of our community, was started in the year 1999.
>
> We the members of the Isaivellaler Community have launched this organization with a view to uniting our community and facilitate Horoscope exchange, Educational and Career development within the community circle. Needless to say, we also aim to rejuvenate those hoary art forms that used to be the mainstay of our community. Our first ambition was why we Isaivelalers had not made any effort earlier to unite ourselves through "Internet" and [have] our collective voice heard.
>
> With this in view we present to you "Isaivellaler.com," our Isaivellaler Murpokku Nalasangam site. We want this site to bring about unity in our community. Every Isaivellaler can contribute to our site. We want your contributions also to develop our community. After all, this is your community site and you are responsible for its success.[42]

3.1 Cover of a recent issue of the magazine *Icai Vēḷāḷar Muracu* (Victory Drum of the Icai Vēḷāḷars).

Unlike the "Talaimai Icai Vēḷāḷar Caṅkam," this organization does not explicitly claim any political allegiances, allowing its members, who include some of the most prominent percussionists in South Indian music today, to slip, if they desire, into the AIADMK-BJP political matrix led by Karunanidhi's rival Jayalalithaa that is supported by most Brahmin musicians in contemporary Chennai. The website also claims that this relatively new organization has a "Women's Wing," although it is perhaps too early to trace any effects that such a collective will have in the community.

POSTSCRIPT: *DEVADĀSĪ*S IN THE CONTEMPORARY LEGAL SYSTEM

On December 5, 1947, twenty years after Reddy's initial resolution of 1927 and four months after independence, the government of India passed the Madras Devadasis (Prevention of Dedication) Act. The act retained much of the language of Reddy's bill of 1927, and focused almost exclusively on the criminalization of *poṭṭukkaṭṭu* rituals (the full text of the act is reproduced as appendix 2). I now shift our discussion to the post-1947 period, a period that has remained uncharted in modern studies of *devadāsī* reform in South India. I pursue two questions here: (1) how effective was the Madras Devadasis Act in supporting legal claims against women from Tamil- and Telugu-speaking *devadāsī* communities? and (2) how do material contestations over inheritance (built into anti-*devadāsī* legislation) continue to be invoked in the contemporary Indian legal system by men from the community? The act, as I have mentioned, specifically criminalized *poṭṭukkaṭṭutal*, yet only a minority of dancing women underwent the dedication rituals described in the legislation. It therefore became difficult to identify who could be subject to prosecution and who was safe from the threat of legal action. If anything, reading the history of the implementation of the act reveals the instability of the category of *devadāsī* identity, since women in Tamil- and Telugu-speaking communities could effectively dodge the law simply by denying that they had ever been dedicated. Thwarted efforts to use the act to prosecute *devadāsī* women led the Andhra Pradesh state government to make an important amendment in 1956 that identified public dancing itself as the transgression, a move that rendered *devadāsī*s more visible and, therefore, more susceptible to discipline. Ironically, men from *devadāsī* communities increasingly *affirm* their relationships to deceased dedicated women in order to claim the right to inherit the property that had historically been left to the next generation of women. While the act made no stipulation in this regard, such men clearly seized the financial opportunity afforded by social reform, which, as I have shown, sought to normalize the gender dynamics in *devadāsī* communities by valorizing conjugality and, consequently, the structure of patriliny.

Attempts to Prosecute *Devadāsīs* under the Anti-Devadasi Act

Devadāsīs continued to dance in public despite the official state-endorsed ban on their performances. The Madras Devadasis (Prevention of Dedication) Act of 1947 is itself a vague document that focuses squarely on the ritual- and temple-based roles of *devadāsīs*. The two examples of legal cases from the 1950s discussed below demonstrate how the parameters of the act were insufficient to prosecute women who continued to dance at weddings and other private celebrations. In the second case, men from within *devadāsī* communities were among those who attempted to take legal action against women who were thought to be violating the act.

In 1950, three years after the passing of the Madras Devadasis (Prevention of Dedication) Act, a case was brought before the Madras High Court, perhaps one of the first that attempted to deploy the act. Eight Telugu-speaking *kalāvantulu* and six of their musicians "took part in a melam or nautch in celebration of the marriage of the first accused, along the streets of Mukkamala." The first accused was a man named Saride Narayana, who was married on June 17, 1948, in the village of Mukkamala in East Godavari district. The group of dancers who performed included two girls below the age of sixteen. The court ultimately ruled that the troupe was in fact *not* violating the terms of the act of 1947 because the performance was not by women who were dedicated to temple deities, nor did it take place in a temple.

The debate in this case involves two distinct sections of the act (3.1 and 3.2), which according to the judges are unclear, or as they put it, "very inartistically worded." These sections of the act attempt to define the legal parameters by which a woman is considered a *devadāsī*, and, by extension, the circumstances and customs that would render a woman from a dancing community "incapable of entering into a valid marriage." In this case, the deliberations revolve around the *precise* definition of the "dedication" ceremony. If the accused were involved in a ceremony of dedication, then their dance could be construed as unlawful by the parameters of the act:

> It is conceded that the petitioners herein have not taken part or abetted the performance of any ceremony or act for dedicating a woman as a devadasi in which case they would have violated S.3 (1) . . . Both the sub-sections of S.3 can relate to a case of ultimate dedication either by actual dedication to a temple or by doing and performing acts that would be in substitution of dedication to a temple. It seems to us therefore that accused 2 to 9 cannot be held guilty of having committed an offence under S.4.(1) in merely taking part in a dance in celebration of the marriage of accused 1. (*All India Reporter* Vol. 37, Madras Section, 615–617)

The second case, as I mentioned above, involves a man from a *devadāsī* community taking action against dancing women. This case also highlights the difficulties involved with demarcating appropriate and inappropriate venues for dance by *kalāvantula* women after the institution of the act. What kind of image or apparatus has to be present in order for it to be considered equivalent to a temple? On April 13, 1949, K. Satyanarayana, owner of Sri Venkateswara Motor Service Co. in Gudivada, erected a *pandal* in front of his office in order to celebrate the festival of Rāma Navamī. In the *pandal,* he placed a lithograph of the deities Rāma, Lakṣmaṇa, and Sītā. Two unmarried dancers from the *kalāvantula* community, aged twenty and thirty, were contracted to perform dance at the *pandal* from 9:00 P.M. to 12:00 A.M., along with three musicians who played the drum, harmonium, and clarinet.

Five months later, on September 13 of the same year, a "spirited" individual, P. Venkateswara Rao, the secretary of the Town Kalavantula Sanskarana Sangam of Gudivada, filed a case against K. Satyanarayana and the performers, claiming that they had violated sections 3 and 4 of the Madras Devadasis (Prevention of Dedication) Act. The case was acquitted by the Court of the Additional First Class Magistrate during a hearing at Bandar (in Krishna district). Venkateswara Rao was not satisfied and pursued the matter. A petition by Venkateswara Rao appealing the acquittal was brought to the High Court at Madras on December 8, 1950.

At the Madras hearing, the key issue was whether or not the *pandal* and the lithographs it temporarily enshrined could be construed as a "temple," thereby violating the prohibition on dancing in temples contained in the act. The section 3 (3) of the act under question reads as follows:

> Dancing by a woman, with or without *kumbharathy,* in the precincts of any temple or other religious institution, or in any procession of a

> Hindu deity, idol or object of worship installed in any such temple or institution or at any festival or ceremony held in respect of such deity, idol or object of worship, is hereby declared unlawful.

The judge upheld that the dance performance could not be construed as illegal because Satyanarayana's *pandal* was *not* a temple. The case was dismissed, much to the disappointment of the men of the Kalavantula Sanskarana Sangam of Gudivada (*The Madras Law Journal* 1 [1951]: 234–236).

Stigma, Suspicion, Proving, "Passing"

I end this chapter with a discussion that brings us to the present. From the 1950s onward, *devadāsī*s appear with some frequency in a range of court cases, the majority of which turn on questions of inheritance. There is a remarkable continuity between legal rhetoric used in such cases in the 1950s and the contemporary period. The contemporary legal system inevitably views women from the *devadāsī* community with suspicion; they are consistently asked to prove either that they are "legitimate" *devadāsī*s if they are seeking to claim a share of inheritance (by providing deeds, photographs, and birth registers), or that they are legally married if they want to step outside the legal category of "*devadāsī*" or the "dancing girl community." Even as this book is being composed, men are usurping *devadāsī inām*s under the pretext that inheritance in these communities was "traditionally" passed on to both male and female children. In what follows, I briefly examine some of these issues, illustrating them with a selection of cases that were presented before the Chennai (Madras) High Court, Andhra High Court, and Supreme Court, from 1953 to the present.[43] In this chapter I am only able to skim the surface of the vast number of contemporary court cases involving *devadāsī*s, and it is my hope that others will pursue this very fertile ground for research on *devadāsī*s in the near future.

In *Saraswathi Ammal vs. Jagadambal and Another* (Supreme Court of India, 1953), a *devadāsī* named Saraswathi Ammal, the only "dedicated" girl among three sisters, claims that as a *devadāsī* she should, unlike her married sisters, rightfully claim the properties owned by her mother Thangathammal, who received the properties from the Saranatha Perumal temple in Tanjore. A number of *devadāsī*s are brought in as witnesses to prove that inheritance in *dāsī* communities does in fact pass from mother to daughter on the basis of "custom." In a somewhat dramatic turn, however, Saraswathi's appeal is dismissed; the judges look to Mitakshara law for direction, concluding that "it is inconceivable that when the sages laid down the principle of preference concerning unmarried daughters they would have intended to include a prostitute within the ambit of that text." This case marks the incremental ways in which *devadāsī*s were left out of new models of economy and family in the postreform period. In this process, which Mytheli Sreenivas characterizes as "the discursive alignment of conjugality and capital," (2008, 45) *devadāsī*s and other nonconjugal female subjects are inevitably at a loss.

In several other cases, women from *devadāsī* communities attempt to claim fixed deposits or land held by their deceased partners, but almost always fail to succeed in their claims by virtue of being concubines and not legitimate wives of the deceased. A remarkable illustration of the state's enforcement of patrifocal family structures is *Dalavayi Nagarajamma vs. State Bank of India and Others* (Andhra High Court, 1961). Dalavayi Ramaswami was married to a woman referred to only as "Mrs. Dalavayi Ramaswami," but had a relationship with a woman named Nagarajamma, from the *kalāvantula* community at Markapur (Prakasam district). An *inām* record from the Markapur temple is strategically produced by the defense counsel, and Nagarajamma, now legally cast as a concubine, is denied any access to Ramaswami's fixed deposit held by the State Bank of India, and her appeal is dismissed:

> [T]here can be little doubt that the appellant belongs to the Kalavanthula community and was treated prior to her becoming the mistress of Ramaswami as a *devadasi*. Exhibit B-11 establishes that she was one of the *inamdar*s of the devadasi *inam* in Markapur temple. The evidence on record and the surrounding circumstances clearly establish that the appellant was not lawfully married to Ramaswami but went to him as his concubine and lived in that status till his death.

The legal interventions made possible by the act also extended to formal interrogations of the social and sexual identities of women suspected of being from *devadāsī* backgrounds. Disclosing women's "suspected" *devadāsī* backgrounds is a key element of many contemporary legal cases involving inheritance. In a fascinating case from 1992, *Kumari Baghyavathi vs. Smt. Lakshmikanthammal* (Chennai High Court), the children of the junior and senior widows of one Srinivasulu Naidu are vying for his properties. One of the key questions upon which the issue of inheritance hinges is the marital status of the junior widow, Rajalakshmi Ammal. As the case proceeds, counsel strategically reveals that Rajalakshmi belonged to the "Balija Naidu" *devadāsī* community, and thus her marriage to Srinivasulu Naidu, which she claimed took place in 1947 at the Parthasarathi temple in Triplicane, Madras, "cannot be a valid marriage by reason of her caste."

In *Nayudu Venkataranga Rao and Another vs. Ramadasu Satyavathi and Others* (Andhra High Court, 2001), we see another dispute of inheritance in which a *kalāvantula* woman attempts to claim a greater share of her adoptive mother's inheritance. Ramadasu Satyavathi launches an appeal against a 1979 settlement in which she was denied what she considered a fair share in the property of her deceased mother, Nayudu Ranganayaki. In attempting to prove her status as the adopted daughter of Ranganayaki, Satyavathi provides details about her premarital career, notably that she had danced in her adoptive mother's *mēḷam*.[44] Satyavathi further claims that in 1979, she was blackmailed by the defendant Venkataranga Rao into signing blank papers in which she had mistakenly given him a full share of her mother's inheritance. The inheritance itself consisted of land, gold ornaments, and a number of silk saris. Moreover, she claimed, Venkataranga Rao and others had in fact murdered Ranganayaki, and threatened Satyavathi herself on several occasions. This was not the first of Satyavathi's appeals; she had appeared in court not only in 1979 when Ranganayaki died, but also in 1985. After a long and drawn-out hearing, the judge dismissed Ranganayaki's appeal when the defense counsel successfully proved that Ranganayaki was not the victim of "fraud or misrepresentation by the defendants" and that she was still legally bound by the terms of the 1979 settlement.

Rajam, Murugabai, Ramasubramanian, Gomathinayakagam, Muniaswami, and Vijayalakshmi vs. Chidambaravadivu and Others (Chennai High Court, 2002) is an appeal brought before the High Court to contest a ruling made by the District Munsif Court (subcourt) at Tuticorin. The subcourt judge ruled that a woman named Rajam (a *devadāsī*), was in fact not legally married to the late Muthukrishna Pillai, and therefore her five children are not heirs to his property. The judgment makes reference to the Anti-Devadasi Act of 1947, stating that prior to the passing of the act, women from *devadāsī* communities were "incapable of entering into a valid marriage." Since Rajam claimed that the "alleged" marriage took place in 1938, the judge ruled that the marriage was invalid in any case. Rajam and her children appeal this decision on the grounds that the marriage was "proved not only by long cohabitation but also by documentary evidence on record." The documentary evidence was in the form of a "training school" application, a ration card, a photograph, and family pension records in which Pillai was the beneficiary, all owned by Rajam and her children. The case was eventually dismissed, and the decision of the subcourt was upheld because Rajam belonged to the *devadāsī* community and it was "proven" despite the evidence, that she lived as a concubine outside the domicile set up by Muthukrishna Pillai, his wife Vellammal, and their family. Given Rajam's *devadāsī* status, the court also questioned whether her children were fathered by Muthukrishna Pillai:

> [A]ssuming, for the sake of argument, the children were born to Muthukrishna Pillai, they were not living as husband and wife. Hence we fully concur with the court below that there was no marriage at all.

Taken together, these cases, and large numbers of others that exist in the legal structures of contemporary India, complicate our notions of *devadāsī* reform. Indeed, they mark it as a clearly unfinished project of modernity. Beyond that, they also demonstrate that the conjugal ideal is incessantly upheld in the nation's multiple imaginaries and that citizenship—in its legal totality—seems to be unattainable for many *devadāsī*s. The cases examined here show one way in which the past lingers through the present in the lives of women from *devadāsī* communities. Of course, the interruptions, unevenness, and incompleteness that characterized reform live not only through the troubling postcolonial politics of the legal system, but also through the lives of real women who continue to occupy the suspended subjectivities engendered by reform. Conversations with these women shape the remainder of this book.

CHAPTER FOUR

Historical Traces and Unfinished Subjectivity: Remembering Devadāsī Dance at Viralimalai

In contemporary Tamil Nadu, the town of Viralimalai has a reputation. It is located along the Trichy-Madurai national highway and over the past fifty or sixty years has acquired the status of a "red-light" town whose sex workers are particularly favored by lorry drivers. Official reports on sex work claim that Viralimalai has high rates of prostitution because of its links with *devadāsī* culture.[1] For example, a recent study entitled *Trafficking in Women and Children in India* (2005) claims:

> Viralimalai, which is located in Pudukottai, Tamil Nadu, is one of the most vulnerable areas for trafficking of women and children for CSE [commercial sexual exploitation]. As the story goes, it began with *potttukattuthal*, a version of the *devadasi* system, in which the girl is "dedicated" to god, and thereafter becomes the chattel of the "godmen" and their hangers-on. Though the *pottukattuthal* system does not exist anymore, it has been replaced by exploitation of girls, reminiscent of the exploitative system that existed earlier under the *devadasi* cult. (Nair and Sen 2005, 616)

The high numbers of brothels in Viralimalai are certainly anomalous for a town its size; but in representations like the one above, Viralimalai's *devadāsī*s are implicated in historical representations that exaggerate their rather marginal presence in the town. Not only is sex work "blamed" on

Research for this chapter was funded by a grant from Fonds québécois de la recherche sur la société et la culture (FQRSC), 2005–2008. I would also like to thank Hari Krishnan, B. M. Sundaram, H. H. Meena Vijayaranga R. Tondaiman, and Archana Venkatesan for their help and valuable suggestions.

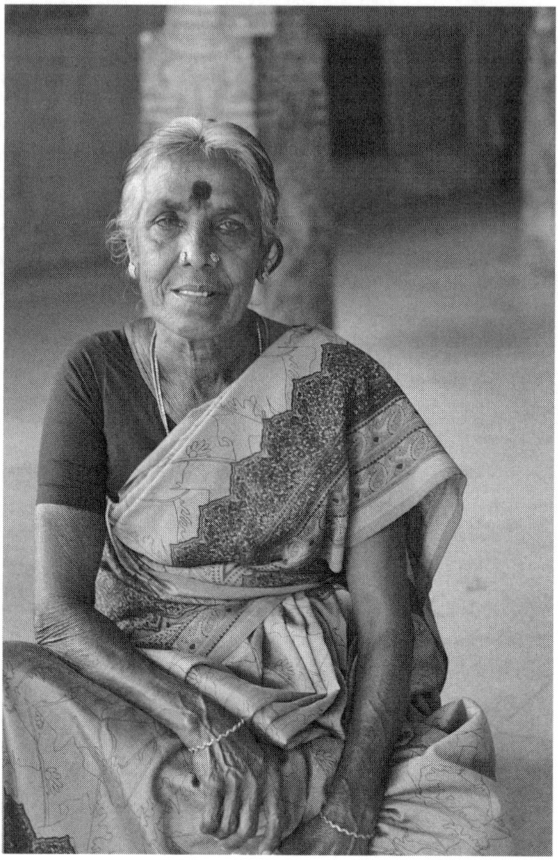

4.1 R. Muttukkannammal (b. 1929). Photo by Cylla von Tiedemann.

the handful of *devadāsī* families in Viralimalai, but *devadāsī*s are targeted for rescue efforts that univocally cast them as victims of a "system."

This chapter is about R. Muttukkannammal (b. 1929; fig. 4.1), the last woman to have *poṭṭukkaṭṭutal* performed at the Viralimalai temple. Over my years of work with Muttukkannammal, my project increasingly moved in the direction of documenting her dance repertoire. This direction came from her. Every evening, Muttukkannammal would take me to a performance atop her roof, a private theater of virtuosity, a place of hope and possibility. It was during these performances that Muttukkannammal recalled, through performance, the most rare and precious compositions in her repertoire. As a living sign of Viralimalai's past, Muttukkannammal's "rooftop" performances force us to reconsider the loose ends of the anti-nautch movement and the horizons of modernity and citizenship it promised for women in *devadāsī* communities. As we have seen in chapter 3, although the anti-nautch movement identified the situation of *devadāsī*s in larger worlds of patriarchal servitude, it was ultimately a nationalist project that failed to make citizenship available to these women in the context of the emergent state. Critical scholarship around the anti-nautch debate dwells on the interface between caste, nation, law, and sexuality that led to the disenfranchisement of *devadāsī*s. But what happens to *devadāsī*s who live through social reform, and bear the marks of failed citizenship and the stigma of sexual reform? What opportunities for self-representation and articulation are available to them? This chapter focuses on aesthetic practices and cultural memory in a *devadāsī* community—issues systemically excluded from scholarly discussions of *devadāsī* history in modern South India. I argue that aesthetic practices—dance and music, in particular—are fully inflected with all the gendered, social, political, historical, and aesthetic resonances available to an individual.

This chapter consciously marks the difference between "aestheticizing" the *devadāsī*s as subjects and attending closely and seriously to the role that aesthetics plays in their lives. To speak to Muttukkannammal involves acknowledging and respecting her status as a virtuosic artist. In this chapter, I examine the ways in which dance repertoire—and the process of recalling that repertoire—enables a doubled reading of *devadāsī* history. On the one hand, it allows for the retrieval of historical traces (musical compositions, texts, movements) that survive only in evanescent, embodied forms and that cannot be accessed through material archives. On the other hand, the act of recalling the past (and the persistence of dance itself) magnifies the liminal social identity of the performer. Located between the demise of colonial courtly culture and the emergent industry of "classical" dance in the twentieth century, Muttukkannammal's performance practices, like her social location, elude obvious categories. It is impossible, and perhaps even unproductive, to detach the pieces of repertoire from the network of personal associations Muttukkanammal illuminates when she performs them. As she begins to speak, she also begins to gesture, to use *abhinaya*, eventually dancing entire compositions. Muttukkannammal's articulations of the past emerge from historical fragments that permeate and linger in the corporeal memory. In these spontaneous recollections, the dance moves beyond the moment of its performance, connecting with other layers of embodied memory, accessing the fullness of history. The act of performance ignites an affective resonance between the flashes of quotidian memory—about her *naṭṭuvaṉār* father, about the royal rituals of the Pudukkottai palace with which her family was associated, and the social stigma she confronts today, for example—and the traces of an aesthetic history represented by her repertoire. If the art of the *devadāsī* is in part an art of commentary, of glossing lyrics with gestural interpretations that change as they are repeated in time, then Muttukkannammal's private performances constitute enactive interpretations of what she has already experienced during "official" performances before audiences. The historical world of nineteenth-century Pudukkottai, the worlds of play and performance, and Muttukkannammal's own subjectivity unfold together; this kind of performative recollection creates a narrative that is simultaneously in dialogue with both the past and the present.

GENEALOGIES: VIRALIMALAI, PUDUKKOTTAI, AND TIRUGOKARNAM

The town of Viralimalai lies at the base of a magnificent hilltop temple, which rests at the top of a great staircase. The primary image (*mūlavar*) in the temple is called Caṇmukanātacuvāmi, and represents six-faced Murukaṉ flanked by his consorts, Valli and Tēvaceṉā. Though the temple is not among the six famous pilgrimage centers or "houses" of Murukaṉ (*āṟuppaṭai vīṭu*), it is intimately associated with Murukaṉ *bhakti*, especially the life of the fifteenth-century saint Aruṇakirinātar, author of several popular Tamil poems including *Tiruppukaḻ* and *Kantar Aṉupūti* (Clothey 1978; 1996; 2006, 199–211).[2] A shrine to the saint is found closer to the base of the hill. The temple has a structure common to other hilltop temples such as Swamimalai in Thanjavur district. It consists of three *maṇḍapa*s, on two different levels: the Candana Koṭṭam on the lower level, and the Navarāttiri and Caṇmukamūrtti *maṇḍapa*s on the top of the hill. The primary image of Murukaṉ is found in the Caṇmukamūrtti *maṇḍapa*, which contains only one circumambulatory passageway (*prākāram*), housing the processional icons (*utsava mūrtis*).[3]

Muttukkannammal, whose family was one of the main reasons why local pilgrims flocked to Viralimalai on festival occasions, is now rebuked and insulted when she visits the temple; she is a reminder, to temple priests and administrators, of the "shame" associated with the town.

Although the early history of Viralimalai is unclear, the temple has traditionally been associated with the military and administrative chiefs appointed by the Nāyakas known as *pāḷaiyakkārar*. The present temple structure evidences Nāyaka-style renovations, and the *pāḷaiyakkārar* Vāḍi Lakkayyā Nāyaka was largely responsible for these renovations in the sixteenth century. It later came under the control of the Marungapuri *zamīndāri*, and then in the eighteenth century, the "little kingdom" of Pudukkottai ruled by the Tondaiman *rājā*s, who provided military aid to the British and the Nawab of Arcot in their battle against Haidar Ali, Tippu Sultan, and several local *pāḷaiyakkārar* chieftans (Dirks 1993, 165). An acknowledgment of the definitively modern colonial-*pāḷaiyakkārar* heritage of Viralimalai survives in a number of oral narratives that circulate in the town today. In the popular imagination *pāḷaiyakkārar*s are associated with the unusual custom of presenting a cigar as a food offering (*naivedya*) to the god. The popular story of the cigar offering, as narrated by a priest at the temple, is as follows:

> The minister of a *pāḷaiyakkārar* chief named Kaṟuppamuttu Piḷḷai visited the Viralimalai temple every Friday. On one occasion, because of heavy rains, the river Mamundi, which separated Kaṟuppamuttu's home from the temple, had become impassable. Stranded on the bank, Kaṟuppamuttu was left without food and, more importantly for him, his most beloved cigars (*curuṭṭu kāḷañci*). Murukaṉ, seeing his devotee in such a condition, appeared to him in a human form holding a cigar and matches in his hand, and led Kaṟuppamuttu safely to the temple. From that day onward, Kaṟuppamuttu decreed that cigars be offered to the Lord at Viralimalai along with the food offerings (*naivedyam*) on a daily basis. ("Swaminathan," personal communication, December 28, 2005)

From at least the time of Rājā Vijaya Raghunātha Rāya Toṇḍaimān (r. 1807–1825), Viralimalai has been home to a number of lineages of professional dancers and *naṭṭuvaṉār*s. These artists also maintained contacts with the Tirugokarnam temple in Pudukkottai dedicated to Śiva and the goddess Bṛhadāmbāḷ, the clan deities of the Tondaiman kings. In fact, it is productive to think of Viralimalai-Pudukkottai-Tirugokarnam as a kind of aesthetic circuit for *devadāsī*s and *naṭṭuvaṉār*s. *Devadāsī*s who had their *poṭṭukkaṭṭutal* performed at the Viralimalai temple were also called *araṇmaṉai māṇikkam* ("rubies of the palace"), referring to the prominent role they played in the cultural life of the Pudukkottai palace, especially on occasions such as Vijayādaśamī. As a rule they received tax-free land grants (*māṉiyams*) from the temple, which were administered by the Pudukkottai *samasthānam*.[4] As we shall see, Tanjore also plays a significant part in this circuit; a large amount of repertoire performed at these sites came from Tanjore, via *naṭṭuvaṉār*s who trained under Tanjore masters or were brought to Pudukkottai from Tanjore. The Viralimalai

4.2 Sivarama Nattuvanar (1879–1945). Image from the Government Museum, Pudukkottai. Photograph by Cylla von Tiedemann.

devadāsī tradition, though "headquartered" at the temple, clearly extends far beyond it. This arrangement demonstrates how even at sites where *devadāsī*s had minimal ritual tasks to perform, their artistic and personal lives were inextricably linked to knowledge systems produced, reified, and transmitted in courtly contexts.

The genealogies of the *devadāsī*s and *naṭṭuvaṉār*s who served at the Pudukkottai *darbār* are difficult to trace with any degree of accuracy. However, we do know that one of the most popular *naṭṭuvaṉār* families was that of Sivarama Nattuvanar (fig. 4.2, 1879–1945), whose earliest traceable ancestors were two brothers named Ramasvami (1768–1836) and Malaikkoluntu, who served during the reign of Rājā Vijaya Raghunātha Rāya

Toṇḍaimān.[5] Sivarama Nattuvanar was the great-great-grandson of Malaikkoluntu, and served during the reign of Martanda Bhairava Tondaiman (r. 1886–1928). Martanda Bhairava Tondaiman, the English-educated king of Pudukkottai, was an enigmatic figure who was the hero in several compositions meant for *devadāsī* performance.[6] Joanne Waghorne has produced an excellent study of Martanda Bhairava's cosmopolitanism and his unstable political location as the last of the great Tondaiman rulers of Pudukkottai. Among the several important *devadāsī* performers at the court was Tirugokarnam Muttuvelammal (1884–1942; fig. 4.3), a disciple of Sivarama Nattuvanar. She became the primary courtesan of Vijaya Raghunatha Pallavarayar, regent and son of Ramachandra Tondaiman, who granted her a

4.3 Tirugokarnam Muttuvelammal (1884–1942), court dancer at Pudukkottai and student of Sivarama Nattuvanar. Photo courtesy B. M. Sundaram.

4.4 Arunachala Nattuvanar (1874–1952). Photo courtesy B. M. Sundaram.

palatial home (Sundaram 2003, 129–131). Two of Sivarama Nattuvanar's daughters, Ranganayaki and Sayimata Siva Brindadevi (fig. 4.6 below), were also trained in music and dance.[7] His son, Ulaganatha Pillai, was a violinist and *naṭṭuvaṉār* whose daughter Abhirami and granddaughter Gayatri continue to teach and perform dance in Pudukkottai.

Another contemporary of Sivarama Nattuvanar was Arunachala Nattuvanar (1874–1952; fig. 4.4), who trained almost all the *devadāsī*s who doubled as dancers at the Tirugokarnam temple and the Pudukkottai *darbār* in the early twentieth century. Arunachala Nattuvanar married a woman named Kamalam, and their daughter Gangai Ammal (1922–1994), who was among his star pupils, performed regularly at the *darbār* functions held by the Pudukkottai royal family.

DEVADĀSĪ REFORM IN PUDUKKOTTAI STATE

Devadāsī reform in Pudukkottai began long before the anti-nautch debates were launched in Madras. The precarious political status of *devadāsī*s overlapped with the moment when dance culture was at its height in the Pudukkottai *darbār*, namely, during the rule of Ramachandra Tondaiman (1829–1886), and his successor, his adopted grandson Martanda Bhairava Tondaiman (1875–1928; fig. 4.5). In 1878, the newly appointed diwan of Pudukkottai, A. Sashiah Sastri, ushered in a series of "reforms" to palace life.[8] Sashiah Sastri was a Tamil *smārta* Brahmin who was brought to Pudukkottai after a long tenure as diwan of Travancore state. One of his top priorities was to rid the palace of its resident "dancing girls" who were seen as visible signs of the king's excessive sensual indulgences.[9] Following Sashiah Sastri's reforms, temporary troupes of *devadāsī*s were brought into the palace from the Tirugokarnam temple to participate in palace celebrations (Waghorne 1994, 217). Although little is known about the effects of this initial exodus of *devadāsī*s from the *darbār*, we can assume that this removed all *devadāsī*s who were permanently living in concubinage at the palace, since only "contracted" dancers from Tirugokarnam, Viralimalai, and Tanjore are known to have performed at the *darbār* since then.

Twelve years earlier, Dr. S. Muthulakshmi Reddy (fig. 4.6) was born to a woman named Chandrammal, who was related to the family of Sivarama Nattuvanar in Pudukkottai, and a *smārta* Brahmin, S. Narayanaswami. Ironically, as Sivarama Nattuvanar and his *devadāsī* students were composing and performing compositions in praise of Martanda Bhairava Tondaiman in Pudukkottai, Reddy was drafting the bill in Madras that would remove them from public life altogether. As we already know from chapter 3, Reddy's Bill to Prevent the Dedication of Women to Hindu Temples (Madras Act No. 5 of 1929) was passed in 1929. By the late 1920s, associations consisting of men from the *devadāsī* community such as the Mutturaja Mahajana Sangam in nearby Trichy began a public "clean up" campaign in towns such as Viralimalai, owing in large part to Reddy's Bill. Caste associations made up of men from the *devadāsī* community such as the Isai Velalar Sangam in Kudalur (Tanjore district) wrote letters that mocked *devadāsī* resistance to the proposed bill, and urged other men from the community to support it.[10]

Though questions of immorality and the *rājā*'s "vices" were part of Sashiah Sastri's early *darbār* reforms in the late nineteenth century, the status of *devadāsī*s in the state was formally debated in the Pudukkotah

4.5 Martanda Bhairava Tondaiman (1875–1928). A portrait made in 1914 by Venkatarayalu Raju, currently in the Pudukkottai palace. Photograph by Cylla von Tiedemann.

Legislative Council on January 8, 1931, following the acceptance of Reddy's bill by the Madras Legislative Assembly in 1929.[11] Martanda Bhairava Tondaiman died in 1928, and that same year, Raja Rajagopala Tondaiman, still a minor, was declared ruler by Colonel Crosthwaite, agent to the Governor General.[12] During the debates at the Pudukkotah Legislative Council in 1931, one speaker of the council, P. G. Nallasivam Chettiar, suggested that the state wait until Rajagopala matured to decide whether he should be entertained with dance:

> These *devadasis* are intended to expound Bharata Sastra which is a special feature of this country . . . Among all the respects shown to

the Ruler of the State *Chinna Melam* is the most important and so the question should be deferred for consideration till after His Highness the Rajah becomes major and takes up the reins of administration. (MRP [Subfile 11], 571)

Over the course of the daylong deliberations, it became clear that the majority of council members supported the resolution to abolish the service of *devadāsīs* in the state. At the end of the day, twenty-seven members voted for abolition and five against, and the resolution was carried.[13] Reddy expressed a special interest in the reform debates, for Pudukkottai was her birthplace, and the passing of the resolution was a victory in light of

4.6 Dr. S. Muthulakshmi Reddy (*right*) with her niece Sayimata Siva Brindadevi, daughter of Sivarama Nattuvanar, c. 1960. Photo courtesy of Dr. B. M. Sundaram.

her bill. A few months later, an anonymous article entitled "The Abolition of Devadasi Service in Pudukotta Temples" appeared in *Stri Dharma*, the magazine of the All-India Women's Association edited by Reddy. The article, which reads more like an advertisement and appears to be written by Reddy herself, extols the Pudukkottai court as a progressive establishment, and laments the fact that such reforms had not yet been systemically implemented in Madras:

> Even though agitation for this urgent moral reform has been set on foot in British India by Indian reformers from the year 1886, still British India has not tackled this question as effectively as the Indian States. Therefore it is a matter of just pride and joy that Mysore, Travancore, Cochin and Pudukotta are far ahead of British India in this particular legislation. Our readers may know that a similar Act has been passed by the Madras Legislative Council as an amendment to the Hindu Religious Endowment Act, but it is very regrettable that even in the city temples, service by the Devadasi maids is allowed to go on owing partly to the non-interference policy of the Government, and partly to the ignorance of the mass and the apathy of the so-called educated class amongst us. (Anon. 1931, 457–458)

But as Muttukkannammal's own story below demonstrates, until approximately 1950, the effects of the Pudukkottai legislation remained ambiguous at best. *Devadāsīs*—including those from Viralimalai—continued to perform extensively at the *darbār* and during festivals at temples administered by the Pudukkottai Devasthanam Committee throughout the reign of Martanda Bhairava Tondaiman and his successor Raja Rajagopala Tondaiman, who died in 1947. *Devadāsīs* danced in *maṇḍapa*s and other public spaces of temples (such as Viralimalai) until the late 1950s. The persistence of the dance despite the legal interventions by the anti-nautch lobby suggests the failures of this project and also the emblematic need to mobilize dance as a display of cultural patronage by elites in rural, early postcolonial South India.

DANCE AT VIRALIMALAI IN THE EARLY TWENTIETH CENTURY

Muttukkannammal's father, Ramachandra Nattuvanar (1890–1988; fig. 4.7), comes from a family that has held hereditary rights in the Vira-

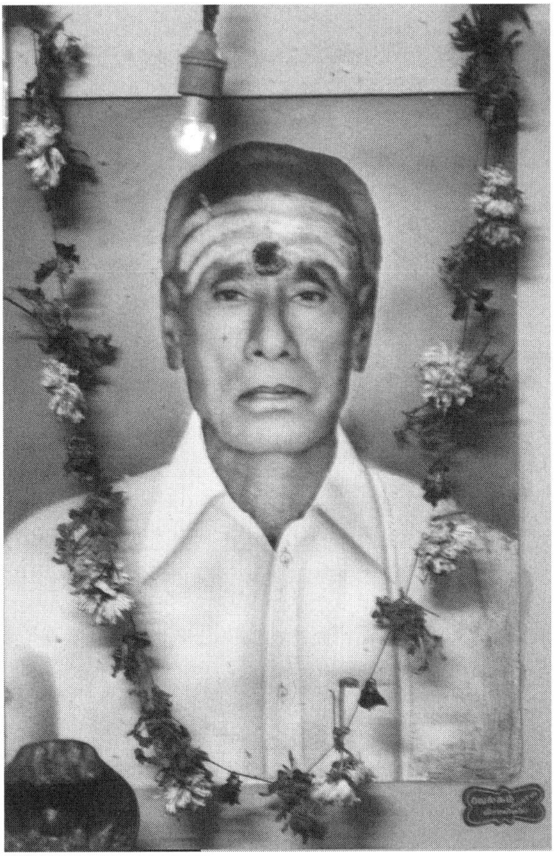

4.7 Photograph of Ramachandra Nattuvanar (1890–1988), housed in the family shrine of R. Muttukkannammal, Viralimalai. Photo by Cylla von Tiedemann.

limalai temple for at least three generations. His grandmother Ammakunjammal and mother Nagammal were both *devadāsīs* who had *poṭṭukaṭṭutal* performed at the temple. Nagammal and her sister Ammani (1861–1908) were students of Pandanallur Kumarasvami Nattuvanar of Tanjore, and Nagammal was also his companion for some time.[14] Ramachandra Nattuvanar was the only son of Nagammal, who also had three daughters. He was initially trained in dance by his aunt Ammani, who presumably taught him the dance repertoire related to the Viralimalai temple and the Pudukkottai palace. She also taught him the *Virālimalai Kuṟavañci* that was performed annually by *devadāsīs* in the Viralimalai temple on Śivarātri, which I will discuss briefly below.[15] Later he was sent to her teacher, Kumarasvami Nattuvanar, to be trained in the technique and repertoire of the Tanjore court.

Ramachandra Nattuvanar quickly became a competent dance master and was soon the most popular and respected *naṭṭuvaṉār* in Viralimalai.[16] In addition to performances at the Pudukkottai *darbār*, his students were regularly invited to the *zamīndāri* estates of Marungapuri (Trichy district), Kolumam (Coimbatore district), and Settur (near Srivilliputtur). In his twenties, he married a woman named Kamalammal from the village of Unnaiyur. They had nine children, three daughters (Muttukkannammal, Pattammal, and Kunjammal) who were trained in dance, and six sons (Picchai, Periyasami, Rattinam, Meyappan, Sankaran, and Nagarajan). Of these, Muttukkannammal was the last woman to have *poṭṭukkaṭṭutal* performed at the temple.

The practice of dedicating one daughter at the Viralimalai temple had been in place in this family for several generations, largely because this ensured that *māṉiyam*s provided by the temple remained within the family. In Ramachandra Nattuvanar's household, the succession of inheritance continued through both male and female offspring, in a style typical of the loose matriliny of many *devadāsī* households. Male offspring were entitled to inheritance if they accompanied dancers in an official capacity as musician or *naṭṭuvaṉār*, whereas only women who had undergone *poṭṭukkaṭṭutal* received *māṉiyam* from the temple. According to Muttukkannammal, the family did not use the term *tāci* or *tēvaṭiyāḷ* to refer to "dedicated" women, but rather used the term *aṭaku* (meaning "pledged"), a reference to the fact that in every generation, one woman was to be dedicated or "pledged" to the Viralimalai temple.

Ramachandra Nattuvanar led the main *tācimēḷam* or *devadāsī* troupe at Viralimalai, which normally included a *mṛdaṅgam* or *muṭṭu* drummer, a clarinet player, a bellows player to maintain the *śruti* or pitch (fig. 4.8), and Ramachandra Nattuvanar himself, who would sing and keep the rhythm on a small pair of cymbals (*tāḷam*).[17] Occasionally, Ramachandra Nattuvanar and his troupe would collaborate with other *tēcimēḷam*s from Tirugokarnam and present either the Tanjore-style courtly dance (*catirkkaccēri*) or the *Virālimalai Kuṟavañci* on makeshift *pandal*s or in the homes of *zamīndār*s or other local elites.

By the time Muttukkannammal was born, the anti-nautch movement had reached its high point in Tamil- and Telugu-speaking parts of South India. In order to assure the continuation of *māṉiyam* grants, *devadāsī* families rushed to have their daughters dedicated, and Muttukkannammal's family did the same. In 1936, at the age of seven, she had *poṭṭukkaṭṭutal*

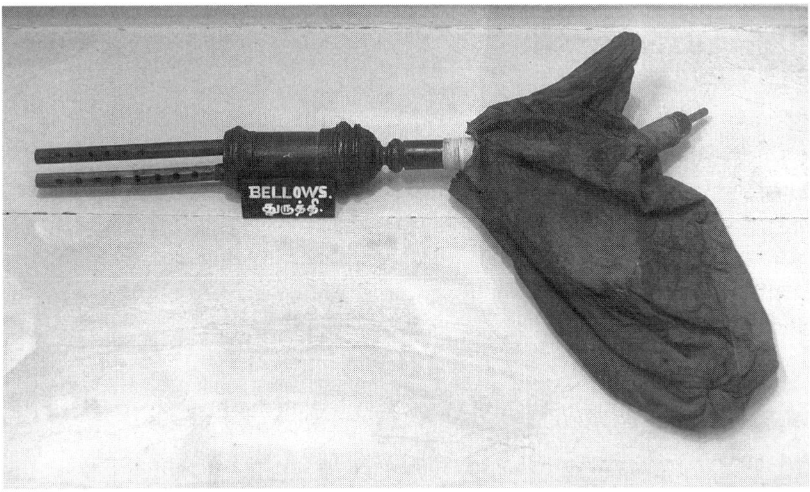

4.8 Bellows (*tutti*) exclusively used to accompany *devadāsī* dance in the Pudukkottai region. Currently housed in the Government Museum, Pudukkottai. Photograph by Cylla von Tiedemann.

performed in the temple of Caṇmukanātacuvāmi, the localized form of Murukaṉ who presides over Viralimalai hill. In 1931, two years after Muttukkannammal was born, the Pudukkottai *darbār* passed an order that would downsize activities in all temples administered by the Devasthanam Committee to accommodate only the "essentials of worship" (Ayyar 1940, 909). The tax-free land grants or *māṉiyams* that *devadāsīs* and other temple servants received at Viralimalai gradually began to disappear and over the next few years ceased completely. Muttukannammal also took on a partner in the mid-1940s, and her daughter Kannamani and sons Rajendran and Kamalanathan were born from this relationship. By this time, when Muttukkannammal's performance career should have been at its peak, the temple staff was facing severe economic difficulties. Muttukkannammal remembers:

> There was no interest in the dance. But we felt we had to keep it up, even though we were getting almost nothing from the temple. Besides, what else could I do? Singing and dancing were the only things I was taught to do. I couldn't just leave, and I used to think in those days, "Why should I leave? This is *my* temple!" After 1947, we faced real problems. Ayya [her father, Ramachandra Nattuvanar] had 20 acres of land as *māṉiyam*, and so did his mother, Nagammal. First he sold all the dry land because he wanted to keep the more valuable land for us,

> but then he eventually had to sell everything. By that time our savings had also been used up.[18]

Economic disenfranchisement was perhaps the most palpable effect of reform legislation for *devadāsīs* in Viralimalai. Muttukkannammal's partner eventually moved away, and Ramachandra Nattuvanar also passed away. By that time, she was able to survive because of the meager earnings of her son who continued to live with her and his sister. As the following section explains, however, another significant loss involved the disappearance of an audience capable of engaging with her work.

MUTTUKANNAMMAL'S DANCE REPERTOIRE

When Muttukkannammal performed at the Viralimalai temple during the period 1937–1955, there was outright disinterest in her dance. For the most part, temple administrators, priests, and audiences thought of the dance as perfunctory, a residual performance of the past that had very little relevance, or was of little interest to anyone. What exactly did Muttukkannammal perform in Viralimalai from the early to mid-twentieth century, and how are traces of this past sustained through Muttukkannammal's own acts of remembrance?

Muttukkannammal's vast dance repertoire can be divided into three categories: the courtly Tanjore-style concert dance repertoire, called *catirkkaccēri*, which also included songs in praise of Martanda Bhairava Tondaiman of Pudukkottai, compositions meant to be performed as part of daily and/or festival events at the Viralimalai temple, and "popular" dances such as the *mōṭi* and *noṭṭusvaram*, which I will discuss in detail below.

Muttukkannammal's Catirkkaccēri

As was the case among most nineteenth- and twentieth-century *devadāsīs*, the majority of Muttukkannammal's performances of dance were at the request of private patrons. She was regularly invited to perform at the Ayyampalayam *zamīndāri* (Dindigul district), and also performed on an outdoor platform during the annual festival at the Māriyammaṉ temple in the village of Pollachi (Coimbatore district). Muttukkannammal referred to these concerts as *catirkkaccēri*, a term likely derived from the Urdu words *ṣadr* or *ṣadar* ("seat in an assembly") and *kaćahrī* ("office," "court"), respectively, indexing the very public, courtly contexts of *devadāsī* dance.[19]

In addition, every Friday, Muttukkannammal performed a concert repertoire in the Candana Koṭṭam, a pavilion on the premises of the Viralimalai temple. This was a residual practice from the time when Muttukkannammal's family possessed *māṉyiam* rights in the temple. Muttukkannammal told me that she herself decided to keep up this practice until the late 1950s, in spite of the fact that she was not receiving money for it—otherwise, she claimed, she "would forget everything."

Muttukkannammal's *catirkkaccēri* reflects the developments at the nineteenth-century Tanjore court discussed in chapter 1. In fact, many of the compositions are in praise of the Tanjore Marāṭhā kings and include texts in Hindi and Western music. The standard Tanjore genres—*alārippu, jatisvaram, śabdam, varṇam, padam,* and *tillānā*—are all present. This repertoire likely comes from her father Ramachandra Nattuvanar's training under Kumarasvami Nattuvanar of Tanjore. Compositions in her repertoire—such as a *jatisvaram* in the *rāga* Bhairavī, and a Telugu *varṇam* ("manavi") in the *rāga* Śaṅkarābharaṇam—are attributed to Poṉṉaiyā (1804–1864) of the Tanjore Quartet, discussed at length in chapter1. Another example of the courtly repertoire is the *śabdam*, also called *salāmu* (fig. 4.9), a genre that combines praises of King Śivājī II in Telugu with rhythmic syllables (*coṟkaṭṭu*). This is a piece that Muttukkannammal is only too happy to perform, for it was apparently a "signature" piece that her father taught all his *devadāsī* students. To my knowledge, this piece does not appear in any of manuscripts or notebooks from Tanjore or Madras, and thus seems to have survived only through oral transmission. The text ends with the Telugu word *bhaḷi* or *bhaḷira* ("bravo!"), and the Urdu word *salām* ("salutations"), capturing the cosmopolitan spirit of colonial Tanjore:

> Scion of the Bhosala clan, protector of the people,
> I have always believed that there is no ruler equal to you.
> Residing in the city of Tanjore, you are the most opulent, wealthy king.
> Śivājī Mahārāja! *Salām* to you!
> [*bhosala kula soma budhajana viśrama*
> *nīku sāṭi dora nīvani ninne nĕra nammi nānu* |
> *tañjapurini vĕlasina śrīmantuḍu nīvera*
> *śivoji mahārājendra bhaḷira melu salāmu re* ||
> tā-tā-tā-dhi, taka-tā-tā-tā-dhi
> tā-tā-dhi, taka-tā-dhi, dhalāṅgutakatadhiṅgiṇatom |||]

The courtly repertoire that Muttukkannammal inherited from her father also included a number of compositions in praise of the kings of Puduk-

4.9 Muttukkannammal performs a gesture depicting the city of Tanjore in the *abhinaya* (gestural portions) of the *śabdam*, or *salāmu*. Photo by author.

kottai, especially Martanda Bhairava Tondaiman. Some of these included pieces like *maṅgalam*, a song used to herald the king in the *rāga* Sindhubhairavī, but others are clearly more reminiscent of the "novel" kinds of compositions we have already encountered in chapter 2. These included *kōlāṭṭam* (the "stick dance") performed by groups of women as public entertainment. At Viralimalai and Tirugokarnam, the texts for the songs recited while *kōlāṭṭam* was performed bore the names of the Pudukkottai kings. By the time Muttukkannammal was performing in public in the 1930s, the "nautch" repertoire had become incredibly pervasive as a systematized set of practices that inevitably included a combination of the compositions from cosmopolitan Tanjore and a number of novel pieces, including *jāvaḷis*, *kōlāṭṭam*, Hindustānī dances, and various acrobatic numbers. Later in this chapter, I will shift my focus to two striking compositions from Muttukkannammal's repertoire, *mōṭi* and *noṭṭusvaram*.

Temple-Related Repertoire

> Why should I lie to you? When I was ready to dance in the temple, nobody cared. See, I was dancing at a time when the temple administrators looked down on *tāci* women. You can see how they look at me even today when we go into the temple. Now even my brother, the *maddaḷam* [drum] player, has to sell peacock-feather fans [to pilgrims] at the base of the temple hill. We are always under pressure because we don't have any money. When nobody else cared to support dancing in the temples,

> why should we continue? I was so angry about that. But that didn't mean I stopped dancing. You know, when great people would invite me to perform for them in their houses—like in Ayyampalayam—*that* was when I loved to dance. They really appreciated what I was doing. They enjoyed my dance, they liked Ayya's *naṭṭuvāṅkam* [the way he recited rhythmic syllables], not like those people in the temple today!

In December 2005, Muttukkannammal took me up the hill at Viralimalai into the main shrine of the temple. She said, "Today I want to show you what we did here in the temple." We went into the Navarāttiri *maṇḍapa*, and there she showed me two dance pieces and sang three songs that she would perform in the temple every evening until the early 1960s. Like her weekly Friday concerts in the Candana Koṭṭam *maṇḍapa*, Muttukkannammal kept up the performance of some evening performances as part of the daily (*nityapūjā*) rituals. As Ramachandra Nattuvanar got older in the 1960s, she decided to stop daily performances. Until then, her performances were limited to the evening rituals—the *cāyaraṭcai pūcai* performed around 6:00 P.M. and the *palliyaṟai cēvai* performed around 9:00 P.M. She describes the *cāyaraṭcai* rituals as follows:

> I would come to the temple wearing a *maṭisār* (a nine-yard sari, worn in the ritually pure Brahmin manner). After the *dīpārādhanā*, I would come forward and improvise some movements (*aṭavukaḷ*) while Ayya would recite "*tā tai-tai tatta tā, tai-tai tatta tā,*" and I would just dance some steps, whatever came to mind. After this the *kuṭam* (potlamp, *kumbhadīpa*) would be given to me, and I would quickly perform the *ārati*. Then, my father and I would leave, and nobody would even look at us.

During the *palliyaṟai cēvai*, Muttukkannammal sang at the threshold of the *palliyaṟai*, or bedchamber, of the temple. She remembers,

> After the waving of lamps (*dīpārādhanā*), I would stand at the doorstep of the *palliyaṟai* and just sing a *viruttam* (Tamil verse) *ūñjal* (swing song), and *lāli* (lullaby). There would be no musical accompaniment and no dance or *abhinaya*.

The Tamil verse (*viruttam*) Muttukkannammal sang described the god Murukaṉ and his consort Valli, seated in full splendor on a swing. The swing song (*ūñjal*) that would follow was a popular song often sung at the time of Tamil Brahmin weddings.[20] These genres of repertoire appear to have been consistent among women who served ritual functions in temples in both the Tamil- and Telugu-speaking regions. Saskia Kersenboom's (1987, 1991) work on the Tiruttaṇi tradition of *devadāsī* music and dance describes a similar set of genres performed inside the temple on a daily basis.

Another major event for the *devadāsī* and *naṭṭuvaṉār* community at the Viralimalai temple was the annual performance of the *Virālimalai Kuṟavañci* staged on a makeshift *pandal* at the temple on the night of Śivarātri. This *kuṟavañci* text was composed by the poet Muttupaḻaṉi Kavirāyar at the behest of Cuppiramaṇiya Mutaliyār, a minister during the reign of King Vijaya Raghunatha Raya Tondaiman (r. 1807–1825). In the typical format of a *kuṟavañci* drama like the *Carapēntira Pūpāla Kuṟavañci* discussed in chapter 1, the plot revolves around a royal woman named Rājamōkiṉi who is lovesick, and her confidante, Curatavalli. The latter half of the text introduces the fortune-telling woman from the Kuṟa tribe (*kuṟatti*) and her bird-catcher husband, Ciṅkaṉ. The fortune-teller diagnoses Rājamōkiṉi's illness and predicts that she will soon be united with her love, the minister Cuppiramaṇiya Mutaliyār. There is of course a double entendre in the name Cuppiramaṇiya, which could also refer to the god Murukaṉ of the Viralimalai temple. Overseeing the annual performance was one of Ramachandra Nattuvanar's major responsibilities. Muttukkannammal could only perform in the *kuṟavañci* drama a few times in her youth, and she would inevitably play the role of the *kuṟatti* fortune-teller. She remembers: "This was the time when so many people would come to watch us. You know, everyone wanted to go to Trichy to watch the cinema back then, and so we felt satisfied as artists when people came in such numbers to watch. After all, the *kuṟavañci* was entertaining!" The performance of the *kuṟavañci* at Viralimalai, however, also disappeared in the 1960s.

TRACES: *MŌṬI* AND *NOṬṬUSVARAM*

One evening in 2004, Muttukkannammal took me to her rooftop. There, in the relative quiet of the night, she asked me to videotape her performance of two specific forms of dance—*mōṭi* and *noṭṭusvaram*. Of the hundred or so hours of performance I have witnessed by Muttukkannammal over the span of four years, the *mōṭi* and *noṭṭusvaram* were perhaps the most striking. For Muttukkannammal too, these pieces resonate in a way that others do not. As she prepares to perform them, a smile comes to her face, and she inevitably begins to talk about the past. But these pieces are neither part of the temple repertoire of Viralimalai, nor are they part of the courtly Tanjore-style *catirkkaccēri*. Both of these pieces bear traces of the hybrid cultural history of *devadāsī*s and their aesthetic practices. It is the hybridity, the suspended location of these pieces, that draws Muttukkannammal to them time and time again. They are both pieces that were "favorites," or "crowd pleasers" when Muttukkannammal performed them in front of audiences in places like Viralimalai, Ayyampalayam, and Settur. For Muttukkannammal, these dances signify a gesture toward citizenship, a public acknowledgment and appreciation of her art, a place for her in the public sphere that is virtually impossible for her to inhabit today. These two pieces are the *noṭṭusvaram* ("note" song), based on Irish marching-band tunes, and *mōṭi* or *mōṭi-eṭukkiṟatu*, a hybrid Hindi-Tamil "drinking song" mentioned in early colonial sources and outlawed by Serfoji's court.

Mōṭi

In 1933, when R. S. Shelvankar was working on the earliest study of Moḍi language records of the Tanjore palace, he noted in passing that one of the bundles contained a unique set of injunctions that were to be followed by court *naṭṭuvaṉār*s (Shelvankar 1933, 15). The Moḍi document he was referring to is from the rule of Serfoji II. This document, which lists a number of restrictions on performers at the court, also includes a prohibition on the *mōṭi* dance:

> In the event that a *dāsī* is unable to walk due to weakness, she may ride in the *ḍolī* (palanquin) if she is granted such permission by the court (*sarkār*). Without the permission of the court, *puṅgī* (the snake charmer's pipe) should not be played, nor should the *moḍi* dance be performed.[21]

Though the *mōṭi* dance has been mentioned by at least one contemporary historian (Seetha 1981, 115), the exact nature of this dance has remained ambiguous. From the Moḍi document above, we can gather that it is a dance that was prohibited by the Tanjore *darbār* in 1820 and that it was accompanied by the playing of the snake charmer's pipe.

Another crucial clue to the *mōṭi* dance can be accessed through colonial ethnography. In 1867, John Shortt, an anthropologist, wrote an essay entitled "The Bayadère; or, Dancing Girls of Southern India," which was read before a meeting of the Anthropological Society of London. After the usual deliberations on the morality of the "Thassees" (*dāsīs*), he presents the reader with a very detailed description of the styles of dance performed by these women. Of these, some are recognizable: "kencheenee nateum" (*kañcanī nāṭyam*) is the *kiñjin naṭaṉam* or Hindustani dance performed at the Tanjore *darbār* referred to in chapter 1; and "colla auteum" (*kōlāṭṭam*) is the popular dance with sticks that was a very common group dance among *devadāsīs*. In addition to these dances, Shortt also mentions a dance called "modiyedoocooroothoo" (*mōṭi-eṭukkiṟatu*), which is the *mōṭi* dance mentioned in the Tanjore records. He goes on to provide an extensive description:

> Modiyedoocooroothoo.— In this dance the word "modi" is a term used to designate a craft or enchantment practiced by a conjuror, who places or hides money or other valuables in a certain place, and often in the presence of his opponent, with the view of testing his ability, and challenges him to remove it, which the opponent endeavours to do by playing on a pipe termed "makedi," and if he is not equally skilled, he is struck to the ground in a mysterious manner, sick and ill, frequently bleeding from the nose and mouth profusely. The dance is in imitation of this by the girl playing on a "makedi," dancing at the same time and throwing herself on the ground—the right leg is stretched out at full length, forming a perfect angle with her body on one side; on the other, the left leg doubled under the knee, is stretched out in like manner on the opposite side, producing a most singular appearance, and as if there were no joint in the hips. (Shortt 1867, 190)

In Shortt's description we see the emergence of details about *mōṭi* that have hitherto remained hidden: (1) the dance is about two figures, one male and one female, and both play pipes, (2) it references the notion of "enchantment," or magic, and (3) the dance involves a kind of competition in which one of the figures loses control of herself. Here, it is useful to think about the semiotic range of the term *mōṭi*. According to the *Tamil Lexicon*, the terms *mōṭi*, *mōṭiyeṭu-*, and *makiṭi* all have the same doubled meaning. It defines the verb *mōṭiyeṭu* as "to discover and remove the articles of witchcraft buried in the ground belonging to a person with a view to cause him harm" (*Tamil Lexicon*, 3384).

Muttukkannammal's *mōṭi* dance is a hybrid piece, performed in two languages, Tamil and Hindi, and in many ways its content matches the description provided by John Shortt in 1867. The *mōṭi* dance at Viralimalai was performed by two women, one dressed as a male (*āmpḷai vēcam*) and the other as a female (*pompḷai vēcam*). The first half of the song is in Tamil, sung to the Punnāgavarāḷī *rāga*, traditionally associated with snakes. The man casts a spell on the woman, a snake charmer, by hiding her snake. The woman then "removes" the *mōṭi* magic by invoking the goddesses Caṇḍī and Cāmuṇḍī from Kochi and Bengal. Meanwhile, during this long process, the man has fallen asleep and awakes to find that his magic has been removed. He confronts the snake charmer woman, who admits to removing his *mōṭi* magic. The text of the Tamil portion is as follows:

MALE: Hey, look now, I have cast *mōṭi*.
FEMALE: Hey, look now, I have removed the *mōṭi*.
Mothers Caṇḍī and Cāmuṇḍī, come from the Kocci-Malayāḷa and Vaṅgāḷa countries, crossing the Māmuṇḍī River!
I have believed in you, worshipped you!
MALE: Where is the *mōṭi* I had cast?
Who has challenged the *mōṭi* I had cast?
FEMALE: I challenged the *mōṭi* you had cast!
[*To the audience*] Sir! I have taken away the *mōṭi* he has cast!

The dance then switches into "Hindustānī" mode, becoming a kind of romantic drinking song in which the woman pulls her sari over her head (*ghūṅghaṭ*) like a North Indian woman, and performs the rest of the piece in this manner.[22] The man makes advances toward the woman, who resists by singing *dūr haṭ jā re, maiṁ to nāhī ek māne* ("Go away, I won't believe it even once!"). He takes her to a garden near a river where he has set up a bed (*nadī kināre bāgh lagāyā, palaṅg lāyā*), and offers her a glass of toddy (*ek pyālā le madhu kā*, "take just one glass of this liquor"), which she accepts. As she becomes intoxicated, he splashes some water into her eyes as another spell. Temporarily blinded, she begins to stagger about the riverbank, and asks the audience for help. Eventually the man comes to wipe her eyes and expresses his love for her. The second *mōṭi*, it turns out, was a love spell. The piece ends with the couple walking away hand in hand. The Hindi text runs as follows:

FEMALE: Go away, I won't believe it even once!
MALE: I've set up a garden on the riverside, brought five hundred thousand coins, and a bed!

FEMALE: My mother calls, I won't believe it even once.
MALE: Take just one glass of liquor, come on, take a swig!

A far cry from the poetry of longing and pleasure that characterized formal presentations of solo courtly dance, one can see how a figure like Serfoji II might have prohibited this presentation in his *darbār*. On the other hand, this composition has a tremendous popular value because of its linear narrative context and its thematic focus on magic, drinking, and seduction, and was an ideal addition to the "nautch" repertoire as it developed in colonial Madras.

Noṭṭusvaram

In chapter 1 of this book, I mentioned the presence of Western music at the Tanjore *darbār*. The accession of King Serfoji II (1798–1832) to the throne in 1798 and the total subordination of Tanjore to British authority the very next year resulted in a dynamic revisioning of the art of kingship, even as Tanjore's economy was incrementally yet determinately exhausted. Serfoji instituted the Tanjore Palace Band as a permanent fixture at the Marāṭhā *darbār*. The systemic presence of music at the Tanjore *darbār* enabled bold cultural experiments with music; on one hand it brought a number of Western musical instruments (such as the violin and clarinet) and Western melodic forms into South Indian concert music, on the other hand it produced markedly distinct forms and practices that stood outside the "canonical" courtly genres of performance. As we have noted in chapter 1, the Brahmin composer Muttusvāmi Dīkṣitar (1775–1835), who lived during the rule of Serfoji II, composed over forty songs based on Western melodies, and these are generally known as *noṭṭusvara sāhitya*s (the word *noṭṭu* here referring to the English word "note").

The Government Oriental Manuscripts Library at the University of Madras houses a Telugu paper manuscript entitled *Jātisvara Sāhityamulu* [D/2536]. The word *jāti* here refers to *jātivāḷḷu*, a common designation for Europeans in Telugu,[23] and hence the title of the manuscript could be translated as "Words, Lyrics [*sāhityamulu*] for European Songs." The work is attributed to one Kuppayya Śeṣayya of Chittoor and the colophon states that it was given to Charles Philip Brown in the month of Caitra (April–May), 1833, during the lifetime of Muttusvāmi Dīkṣitar. The manuscript provides both Sanskrit and Telugu songs, and all of the Sanskrit songs bear the *mudrā* or "signature," *guruguha*, used by Dīkṣitar. The intriguing aspect of the manuscript that sets it apart from other compilations of Dīkṣitar's songs is that almost each folio begins with the name of the corresponding Western tune that Dīkṣitar adapted for the creation of these pieces. In the manuscript, these songs appear as follows:

rāmacandram rājīvākṣam	Here is a health to all good lasses
pītavarṇam bhaje bhairavam	Taza-ba-Taza
sakala suravinuta śaṃbho	Quick March
kāñcīśam ekāmram	Country dance
subrahmaṇyam surasevyam	British Grenadiers
śakti sahita gaṇapatim	Voulez vous danser [very good song]
vara śiva bālam	Castilian Maid [Moore]
kamalāsana vandita	—
santāna saubhāgyalakṣmī	—
cintaya cinta śrī	—
śauri vidhinute	O whistle and I will come to you my lad
jagadīśa guruguha	Lord Macdonald's Reel
varamaṅgala tanu	Marlbrook
śrīraṅga hari kṛpāmaya	Moll Rowe
rāja śrī veṅkaṭarāya bhūpāluni	March

The kinds of cultural and generic experiments that we see with music also affect the culture of dance. As noted in chapter 1, in 1848, the court dancers at the Tanjore court danced to "God Save the King." Each of the *noṭṭusvara sāhitya*s by Dīkṣitar is set to the *rāga* Śaṅkarābharaṇam, which corresponds roughly to the C-major scale in Western music. Śaṅkarābharaṇam was also a key *rāga* deployed by the dance masters known as the Tanjore Quartet (1802–1864), who reworked the dance repertoire in the nineteenth century. The Quartet, thought to have been disciples of Dīkṣitar, composed at least eight major compositions in the Śaṅkarābharaṇam *rāga*. The aural semblance between Śaṅkarābharaṇam and the popular Western-major scale enabled a number of slippages and cross-fertilizations.

Muttukkannammal's repertoire includes a song that she calls *noṭṭusvaram* or simply *noṭṭu*. Like the songs by Dīkṣitar mentioned in the *Jātisvara Sāhityamulu* manuscript, it also has its origins in popular Western tunes. "The Rakes of Mallow" is a well-known Irish drinking song that was first printed around 1733 in London, and this is Muttukkannammal's *noṭṭusvaram*. The term "rake" (a shortened form of "rakehell") refers to a wandering man who lives a life of debauchery, and Mallow is the administrative capital of County Cork in Ireland. Dīkṣitar also composed a song based on "The Rakes of Mallow" dedicated to the goddess Mīnākṣī

4.10 Muttukkannammal performs the colonial military-style "*salām*" gesture that concludes each phase of movement in the *noṭṭusvaram*. Photo by author.

of Madurai.[24] Muttukkannammal's version of "The Rakes of Mallow" involves only *svaras* (solfa syllables)—*ga ga ga ri ga pa ma ma ga*. The dance for the *noṭṭusvaram* itself consists of footwork characteristic of many European folk dances, and the imperial context of the dance can clearly be seen in the military-style *salām* gesture that concludes each phrase of movement (fig. 4.10).

According to Muttukkannammal, her *noṭṭusvaram* was performed at the Pudukkottai *darbār* for Martanda Bhairava Tondaiman. Muttukkannammal jokes that apparently it was a composition that Maharaja Martanda Bhairava was very fond of, on account of his Australian wife, Molly Fink, whom he married in August of 1915. From November 1915 to April 1916, the raja and his new wife lived in Pudukkottai and are said to have visited the Viralimalai temple on at least two occasions. Muttukkannammal told me that at this time, according to her father, dances such as the *noṭṭusvaram* and folk genres such as *kummi* and *kōlāṭṭam* bearing his name would have been performed.[25] Whether or not Martanda Bhairava understood or appreciated it, several dance compositions were created in his honor, likely by Sivarama Nattuvanar.

The *devadāsī*s of Viralimalai and Tirugokarnam were the inheritors of performance practices that stood at the brink of an incipient cultural modernity. This kind of experimentation inserted *devadāsī*s into a new field of cultural forms and attitudes that staged, in a bold and discernable manner, the transfigurative capacities of colonial modernity. But for *devadāsī*s the horizons of this modernity were bleak. The embeddedness of the colonial modern in aesthetic forms coincided with public challenges to the social legitimacy of *devadāsī* identity. Cultural forms such as *noṭṭusvaram* carried the potential for the emergence of the citizen-subject of modernity. This opportunity could only be seized by middle-class women who mobilized the flexibility and "modernity" of these forms by reworking them to nationalist ends, and not by *devadāsī*s, who were framed by the state as archaic emblems of a degenerate, embarrassing past. For Muttukkannammal, postcolonial modernity represents a necessary yet insufficient condition.

THE UNFINISHED AS A CONDITION OF DEVADĀSĪ SELFHOOD

Muttukkannammal's experiences suggest a mode of engagement with modernity and with the world at large that was directed by priorities other than those singled out by middle- class nationalists in the twentieth century. Dances such as *mōṭi* and *noṭṭusvaram*, artifacts of the colonial modern, have perhaps always been "homeless": they stood outside the canon of the hereditary courtly repertoire (*catirkkaccēri*) of the prereform period, and were not "classical" or religious enough to be integrated into the postreform-period reinvented Bharatanāṭyam of the urban middle class. These forms, which appear as empty rituals with no audience, meaning, or context today, have a relevance to Muttukkannammal's sense of self; they are emblems of memory that are, to borrow Homi Bhabha's words, "produced in the act of social survival" (1994, 247). They are harnessed and iterated by Muttukkannammal for no one other than herself:

> I have been singing these songs to myself since I stopped dancing in my thirties. Sometimes I think, "Why do I bother?" It might seem like

> I have lost everything, and these songs may not be important for other people, for you, but they are—and always will be—a part of me. So I keep singing.

I want to conclude by suggesting that mnemonic iteration through the act of performance is effective for *devadāsīs* at the level of individual identity. Here I am not referring to the ways in which contemporary cultural theorists speak of "collective memory," but rather invoking a theory of "individual remembering" that recognizes the value of the individual's ability to make sense of her life. This "individual remembering," commented upon most recently by historian Anna Green, subverts the idea that memory must compose a past that is "publicly acceptable" (2004, 36). I suggest that at the individual level, memory augments the conscious self's ability to contest and critique cultural scripts and thus affirms self-worth and personal identity. Thick description and emotional intensity characterize these movements through the remembered landscape. These embodied memories are an invaluable source for the historian—they provide us with affective insights into *devadāsī* culture that cannot be found in the archive or texts.

As I was leaving the Viralimalai temple with Muttukkannammal one night, a monkey happened to cross our path. This reminded her of the wild peacocks, associated with Murukaṉ, which used to gather in great numbers atop the hill at Viralimalai. Inhabitants of Viralimalai saw the peacocks as auspicious omens signaling the god's presence in the town. Muttukannammal voiced an elegy:

> When the Maharaja of Pudukkottai was gone, the peacocks left with him. Now even his house has been made into a government building! That's why you don't see any more peacocks at Viralimalai. That's why you don't see *catirkkaccēri* anymore. That's why my land is gone, and I'm like this. But this isn't how it used to be.

CHAPTER FIVE

Performing Untenable Pasts: Aesthetics and Selfhood in Coastal Andhra Pradesh

"Memory can be spiteful." The town of Peddapuram is known for the exceptionally high numbers of prostitutes who inhabit its streets. Many of them are *kalāvantulu*. In February 2002, I went to the red-light areas of Peddapuram and met Jakkula Radha, considered an elder among local women. Today Radha sells *bīḍīs* (tendu-leaf cigarettes), candy, and other confectionary at a small stall outside her home. Radha was initially reluctant to talk about her past, but once I mentioned that I had heard she used to perform the *varṇam* in the *rāga* Bhairavi, Radha immediately perked up. But she insisted on continuing our conversation elsewhere. I helped her into my rented Ambassador car and started to back out of the lane on which her house was located. Four young men rushed out from nearby houses, and started yelling "*muṇḍālu muṇḍālu*" ("whores! whores!") at us, throwing small stones at our car. That day Radha wept for about half an hour, and said, "People can be spiteful . . . so can memory."

The women in Peddapuram's red-light areas stand at the intersections of a number of very public discourses on health, development, and trafficking. In a provocative essay on sex work in Peddapuram, entitled "Night Claims the Godavari" (2008), writer Kiran Desai presents one side of this very complex culture of sexual commerce. Desai interviewed a number of women from *kalāvantula* backgrounds who manage brothels and refer to themselves as "class" girls, coveted sex workers who cater largely to affluent men. She paints a vivid picture of the trafficking and abuse of women that is rampant in the brothels of towns like Peddapuram and Kakinada. Desai also notes that HIV infection rates in Andhra Pradesh's East Godavari district are 25 percent higher than in other parts of the state. Undoubtedly a number of *kalāvantula* women are commercial sex workers in places like Peddapuram, but Desai's straightforward presentation of the lives of contemporary *kalāvantula* women ignores the tremendous heterogeneity of their experiences. On the one hand, her essay resonates with the totalizing ideology of first-wave and radical feminist discourse on prostitution that, in the manner of nineteenth-century social purity movements, conceives of all sex work as abuse, and casts all sex workers as victims (Bell 1994, 130). In India, these kinds of representations have been critiqued by feminists who work on issues of sexuality, law, and citizenship such as Ratna Kapur (2005, 95–136; 2010). On the other hand, it presupposes that all *kalāvantula* women have become the "victims" of brothel-style sex work. The experiences of *kalāvantula* women in the postreform period, however, are diverse: today some are involved in sex work; others are married; and the older generation of women invariably dwell on their very peculiar social, civic, and aesthetic marginality. This chapter examines a specific set of experiences that are hinged to the past in palpable and affective ways. My interest is in the unfinished dimensions of *kalāvantula* lives, the ways in which some women in these communities—especially those who lived through social reform—fashion distinct identities based on the past that run alongside the cell phones and flat-screen TVs proudly displayed by a younger generation of *kalāvantula* sex workers as signs of their engagements with the flows of advanced global capitalism.

In this chapter, I examine the persistent yet invisible performance practices of a section of the *kalāvantula* community that has witnessed the drastic social and political transformations of their communities we have discussed in chapter 3. Their narrations of selfhood and identity emerge through encounters with their dance and music repertoire, which they are careful to preserve "behind closed doors" in the relative privacy of their homes. These iterations of repertoire that take place with some regularity among *kalāvantula* families are also the sites that produce personal and collective imaginations; identity lives through mnemonic bodily practices. Outside the *kalāvantula* community, the notion of "courtesan dance repertoire" is usually read (and subsequently dismissed) by urban elites as a vestige of feudal history, a sign of the "backward" past that cannot and should not be accommodated in India's present and future. For some women in courtesan communities today, however, the repertoire is used as a mode of telling; it is mobilized to consolidate an identity they can live with.

What is articulated by women in the Godavari delta is, I think, an alternate mode of being, an identity that uses the past in order to establish a relationship with themselves in the present. In Foucauldian terms, this constitutes an "ethics" of selfhood. Deliberations on the devalued nature of their cultural practices, their experiences of nonconjugal sexuality and institutionalized concubinage, and their willingness to engage with issues of self-representation are instrumentalized to this end. As Nikolas Rose (1996, 24) points out, Foucault's notion of the *relations* that individuals establish with themselves is central to critical psychocultural constructions and representations of selfhood. *Kalāvantula* women evince an ethical awareness about their own marginality; they dwell on their location within the binary of social centers and peripheries. In inviting women in coastal Andhra Pradesh to tell and perform their own narratives, I write about courtesan identity without subsuming it under preexisting categories, allowing complex and even contradictory subjectivities to emerge and coexist with the archival and other historical constructions of these communities observed in the rest of this book. This chapter stages some of the complex questions of what it means to be a *devadāsī* in contemporary South India.

SOCIAL FAILURES AND UNTENABLE CONCUBINAGE

In late nineteenth- and early twentieth-century coastal Andhra Pradesh, the public presence of *kalāvantula* women was visible in the form of *bhogameḷam*s ("bands" or "troupes" of *bhogamvāḷḷu* or *kalāvantulu* women). These troupes were, in a sense, professional guilds made up of several women, most of whom were trained in music and dance by one community elder, who would usually be the troupe leader. The "troupe leaders," called *nāyakurālu*s, directed the troupe in the sense of procuring and negotiating performance contracts, and also by playing the *tāḷam* or cymbals during the performance. For the most part, male dance masters (*naṭṭuvaṉār*s) did not accompany courtesans in this region as they did in the Tamil-speaking regions. The term *meḷam*, in fact, is also used in a verbal sense. *Kalāvantula* dance was also called *meḷam*, and "doing *meḷam*" is how many *kalāvantulu* refer to the practice of their art. Unlike in many parts of Tamil Nadu, after the Madras Devadasis (Prevention of Dedication) Act of 1947 was passed, salon performances of *bhogameḷam*s continued in coastal Andhra Pradesh, as these did not seem to interfere with the prohibition on "temple dancing" as described by the act. However, on August 14, 1956, the government carried out a final amendment to the act that outlawed dancing at marriages and other private social events as well.

Each and every one of the women I met in the Godavari delta expressed the opinion that social reform had failed. Even those who were extremely sympathetic to the values represented by the discourses of social purity were disappointed with the fact that "whatever happened over the last hundred years did not bear any fruit (*phalamu*) for us." Today "*devadāsī*" and "*kalāvant*" are undeniably unstable social categories. They are pervaded by historical fissures, lived trauma, and a complex and problematic relationship with hegemonic, state-endorsed understandings of gender justice. Most women in the *kalāvantula* communities of coastal Andhra Pradesh speak about themselves as *distinct* from middle-class women, even as they see their female children and grandchildren move, sometimes very painfully and at great personal loss, into that social category. Many of these women are critical of both the system of institutionalized concubinage represented by their past, and the conjugal lifestyle represented by middle-class women.

Women in *kalāvantula* communities commonly identified the men with whom they had relationships using the term *uṃcukunnāru* ("one who takes care [of you]"), clearly indicating the power dynamic implied by the system of institutionalized concubinage. As mistresses or concubines, the women were sometimes referred to as *abhimāna strīlu* ("affectionate or desirable women").[1] Almost all of the women I met who lived through the period of social reform, and even a number of relatively younger women, spoke at great length about their male partners. Some women like Subbulakshmi, in her early sixties, who lives in a suburb of Rajahmundry, valorized concubinage; she understands, however, that her situation is exceptional. She lives together with her partner and his wife in their home as a kind of "second wife" and has a relatively comfortable life:

> I live with my man in his house. He is a *caudari* ("village headman"). This may seem strange to you, but his wife and I live together, and he thinks of me as a second wife. This is hard in a town like Rajahmundry, where everyone knows everything and gossip is rampant. But what do I have to lose? He looks after me. I am better off than most other *kalāvantulu* whose men have left them out of a feeling of shame. I am also better off than those married women who live like servants in their husband's house.

Subbulakshmi defends concubinage through a critique of the power relations she understands to be embedded in marriage. Kotipalli Hymavathi, relatively younger than most of the women I worked with, has no more contact with her partner. She does, however, have a daughter who is married and has young children of her own. Hymavathi, by contrast, is adamant in stressing that the "old system" of concubinage cannot be sustained today and ultimately works against women in the *kalāvantula* community. She evinces an acute awareness of the patriarchal servitude implied in concubinage:

> Look, a woman is "kept" (*bandha*) by man as his mistress. Say she has four daughters and two sons through this relationship. If he leaves her—for whatever reason—how can she support the children or herself?

Similarly, Saride Varahalu, living in Duvva village in West Godavari district, explains that sometimes, as in the case of her family, concubinage was "arranged," in a manner parallel to upper- and middle-caste wedding alliances. She narrates how her father had chosen appropriate partners for her and her sisters, and that each of these men came from different class backgrounds:

> Let me give you the example of my own family. We all had relations with men, but all of our men were from different communities [all from elite class backgrounds]. My man was a *saukār*, a *komaṭi* (a businessman). Anusuya had a Brahmin, Seshachalam had a *kamma* (an influential agricultural community) man, and Maithili had a *vĕlama dŏralu* (a wealthy landlord).

But she continues in a defiant tone, "Where are these men today? Do you see them around? We are left to fend for ourselves. Look at Anusuya [her eight-four-year-old sister]. She has children who can't stand her. She is virtually blind, and so frail, but no one looks after her except us." Duggirala Satyavati from Mandapeta town (East Godavari district) expresses a similar frustration: "I used to play harmonium and do 'record' dance [dance to popular film songs]. My mother used to do all these *padam*s, *jāvaḷi*s, and other things. We're *veśyā*s. Nobody cares about us. I could have sex with ten men, but not a single one will look after me when I need it. So why should I care about them? Men are all like that. But then, we also have to live, don't we?" Many of the women interviewed in this chapter had only one partner over the course of their lives, while others had several. As a result of the public stigma attached to concubinage in the postreform period, many such men abandoned their *kalāvantula* partners in the mid-twentieth century. Others died long before the women themselves.

While some contemporary *kalāvantulu* critique the notion of concubinage, they also adamantly defend the nonconjugal aspects of their lifestyles; they very clearly distinguish their lifestyles from those of middle-class "householders." These distinctions are upheld through linguistic markers. *Kalāvantulu* deploy the term *saṃsāri* (from the word *saṃsāra*, "worldly existence") to refer to householders (*gṛhasthin*s, that is, ordinary married couples and their extended families) and the term *sāni* (from *svāminī*, female leader, "respected lady") to refer to themselves. This clear distinction between the contemporary middle-class "householder" and the courtesan, or *sāni*, was iterated by nearly all the *kalāvantula* women I worked with. The marked separation of social spheres was enforced, I was told, by the difference in terms used for life cycle rituals. According to Maddula Venkataratnam of Tatipaka village, "*kalāvantulu* do not use the word *pĕḷḷi* [marriage], and householders do not use the word *kannĕrikam* ["initiation of a virgin," i.e., dedication]."

A brief discussion concerning rituals of "dedication" among contemporary *kalāvantulu* would be useful here. Dedication ceremonies, usually performed at home, were often accompanied by the simultaneous commencement of training in music and dance. The *kannĕrikam* was usually a "sword marriage" (*katti kalyāṇam* or *khaḍga vivāha*), as discussed in chapter 1. Kotipalli Hymavathi recounts her own *kannĕrikam*:

> I started to learn dance at the age of seven. At the age of eleven, I had *gajjapūjā* ["worship of the ankle bells"] and *kannĕrikam* performed. During the *gajjapūjā*, my *gurugāru*, my mother, tied my ankle bells for the first time. For just over two years, I performed in the *meḷam* headed by my sister Satyavathi. Let me tell you about this *kannĕrikam*. *Kannĕrikam* refers to the transformation of an ordinary girl into a *sāni* when she attains maturity. We celebrate a puberty ritual (*peddamānuṣi paṇḍugalu*) for seven full days. On the last day, the girl is made into a *sāni* by tying a *kaṅkaṇam* [the thread tied around the wrist at the commencement of a marriage] to a knife (*katti*) in the morning. This is done by an elder woman of the family, usually the girl's aunt. Then a great feast is prepared for lunch, and all the guests are fed goatmeat in celebration of the event. Sometimes the girl's partner is selected at this point, and he pays a brideprice. If not, the girl will forge a relationship with a man at a later stage.

Kannĕrikam ceremonies—including the *gajjapūjā* in which *kalāvantulu* would formally take on the identity of a public performer—were held in conjunction with puberty rituals, which were also common among householding women. As in the Tamil-speaking regions, there also appears to have been a much less prevalent tradition of dedicating girls to temple deities in coastal Andhra Pradesh. The late Saride Manikyam, whom I met in the village of Kapileswarapuram, was one of the last women to have been dedicated at the Madanagopālasvāmi temple in Ballipadu. She provides an account of this rather rare occurrence:

> There are four of us who had *kannĕ rikam* performed in the temple. My sister and I were brought to Ballipadu together with my cousins Mutyam and Anusuya. I was trained in vocal music by Rudrabhatla Ramamurti, and in dance by my grandmother, Dasari Mahalakshmi, for a period of four years, from age five to nine. I was nine years old when I performed my *gajjapūjā* [ceremony of worshipping the ankle-bells, a kind of debut performance]. Subsequently, I had a dedication ceremony performed. The *kaṅkaṇam* was tied by a priest from the temple. From that day onward, after the *alaṅkāra* (adorning of the deity) and *bālabhogam* (midmorning meal), I would perform the daily ritual of the *pañca-hārati* (waving five lamps in front of the deity), while singing the song "jaya maṅgalam, mahotsava maṅgalam" . . . Every Friday, at the time of the evening *abhiṣeka*, I would perform a selection of *alarimpu, pallavi, svarajati, varṇam, padam, jāvaḷi,* and *kīrtana.*

Manikyam's case is a rarity. The majority of *kannĕrikam* rituals were performed at home and therefore rarely included the recitation of *mantra* or the presence of a priest. Saride Varahalu of Duvva was adamant about stressing that this was a domestic rite of passage in *kalāvantula* communities, while at the same time commenting on the potential exploitation of women that *kannĕrikam* rituals can engender today:

> Yes, we are *vesyas* (*memu vesyalamu*). We had *kannĕrikam* performed only in the house (*iṇṭilonĕ cestunnāru*). They would tie the *kaṅkaṇam* to a knife and this would replace the ritual of marriage for the girl . . . Whatever this meant in the past, today it has become a selfish ritual. The girl is given over to any man who can pay 1,000 or 2,000 rupees. I have seen this happen with other girls in our community. Our situation was different; I was with that *komaṭi* man for so many years. I feel terrible when I see what happens to our girls nowadays.

These accounts present the self-consciousness with which *kalāvantulu* who lived through social reform see its awkward and unresolved consequences in their lives and in the lives of younger women in their communities. The fact that some of these perspectives are contradictory and varied speaks to the individual complexities of living as a woman in these communities today. As we shall see later in this chapter, *kalāvantula* women seize this ambivalence in their self-representation, and deploy it to narrate, valorize, and critique their circumstances.

REFORM, LOSS, IMPOVERISHMENT

In chapter 3, I outlined how anti-nautch discourse unfolded in the political and administrative center of South India. In many ways, the public deliberations on *devadāsī* sexuality engendered by reform debates stigmatized women even further in local communities; it marked them in new ways as figures of ridicule and sexual objectification. The stigma attached to maintaining concubines forced "respectable" men to withdraw support from their mistresses, and these women and their female children very easily slipped into the contiguous world of brothel-style prostitution.

Stories of disenfranchisement and loss are told and retold within *devadāsī* communities throughout South India. These tellings stand at the crossroads of history and experience, and highlight the problematic consequences of reform debates. Some women live with the burdens of reform extreme stigma being a major dimension of this burden on a daily basis.

The loss of land held by women with links to temples provides us with the most obvious and concrete narratives of *devadāsī* disenfranchisement. As we have already seen, despite Muthulakshmi Reddy's concerted efforts in 1930 to enfranchise land grants (*mānyālu* in Telugu) in the names of their female holders, very rarely did women benefit from Reddy's reform; land grants were usually usurped through legislation by men in the community or by temple officials (*dharmakartā*s). In the case of women in coastal Andhra Pradesh with temple affiliations, such as Saride Manikyam and her sister Anusuya, the material loss represented by the usurping of their land by temple authorities was traumatic. Manikyam, who held *mānyālu* rights at the Madanagopālasvāmi temple in Ballipadu village, remembers:

> I remember, about fifty years ago. Suddenly the temple staff was dismantled. I had nowhere to go. I was miserable. We appealed to have the lands enfranchised in our names, but fought a losing battle in the courts. The case eventually reached the high court, but with no results. Finally, I moved to Duvva [another nearby village]. Then, eventually I moved from there to Kapileswarapuram.

Manikyam owned over twenty acres of land as well as over one hundred *kāsulu* of gold (one *kāsu* equals roughly eight to ten grams). In 1948, her family was no longer entitled to *patrārthamu* (land ownership) from the temple in a private decision made by the temple authorities. As Manikyam mentioned, she attempted to win back her rights over the land through litigation but was unsuccessful. When she and her sister Anusuya moved to Duvva (about six kilometers away), they formed a *meḷam* (dance troupe). They continued to tour rural Andhra Pradesh, performing *mejuvāṇi* (concert repertoire as entertainment) in the homes of patrons, particularly during weddings. They would occasionally perform court repertoire at the Ballipadu temple in the context of the *ūregiṃpu* (temple processions) but only after the temple had obtained permission from the district authorities.

Devadāsī disenfranchisement thus materializes through the cumulative effects of social marginalization, legal intervention, misapplication of the law, and aesthetic loss. The late Saride Seshachalam, who was on the brink of beginning her performing career at the time of the reforms, remembers: "All we did was sign a bond promising to stop even our private (home) performances after the act came. I know I could have become a great 'class artist.' But now look at me. I have nothing but one room in this small house to my name." Kotipalli Hymavathi described how as performance opportunities for *bhogameḷams* decreased, they would live frugally from performance to performance, borrowing cash from moneylenders:

> My mother is Kotipalli Manikyam. There would be very large gaps between performances by her *meḷam* when we were younger. We would live by borrowing money throughout the year, and clear the debt when we received payment after a performance. But we would have to use some of this borrowed money to have jewelry made for the performances. As the troupe leader (*nāyakurālu*) my mother had to divide the money as follows: fifteen rupees for the orchestra, ten rupees for the *meḷam* artists, five rupees (half a share) for child-artists, and thirty rupees for the *nāyakurālu*, who was a "class artist" [English]. It was a very difficult time for us. We simply could not perform in public and so we had no money.

Kola Somasundaram from Muramanda village (East Godavari district), who used to have her own *meḷam* (she was a *nāyakurālu* [troupe leader]), remembers the threat of prosecution, and how she would pray for the success and protection of her *meḷam* in light of efforts by the police to monitor and raid *meḷam* performances. The sponsorship of performances by courtesans after the passing of the Anti-Devadasi Act in 1947 was carefully monitored by local police in small towns and villages in coastal Andhra Pradesh. This appears to have been a way for corrupt police officers to make some extra money and simultaneously humiliate *kalāvantula* women:

> When the act came, I secretly took bookings for *meḷam*. If I was caught, I was arrested by the police. This happened a few times. They took me to the station, and called me all sorts of names, too.
>
> I didn't know what to do—should I leave *meḷam* behind or not? I remember, in those days, Vināyaka Chaturthi [festival dedicated to the god Gaṇeśa] was very important. The *gajja* (ankle bells), *tāḷa* (hand cymbals), *maddaḷa* (*mṛdaṅgam*, double-headed barrel drum), harmonium, and *pīṭha-karra* (wooden board and stick used to keep rhythm) were all placed in front of Lord Gaṇapati. All the *sāni*s (*kalāvantulu*) from one neighbourhood (*basti*) would gather at one woman's home. We broke coconuts, performed *pūjā*, and danced for Gaṇapati to ensure that we had success in the future and, more importantly, to ensure that there would be no breaks or halts in our performances.

In chapter 3, I spoke at some length about the "rehabilitation centers," *śaraṇālayam*s, that were established throughout the Tamil- and Telugu-speaking regions. Painful memories of these institutions survive in the contemporary *kalāvantula* community. A seventy-one-year-old woman from Tanuku (West Godavari district), who did not want to be identified by name, remembers:

> My mother's sister was taken to the *śaraṇālayam* at Narasapur. I was too young to remember that day, but my mother told me they forced her into going there. They told her what she should wear, how she should speak, everything. After that, nobody in our family wanted to make their daughters into *sāni*s. We were so scared. It was difficult for us to survive.

In roughly the late 1960s, as hands-on reform activities in *devadāsī* communities (such as those described in chapter 3) subsided, evangelical Christian missionary groups from North America took up the cause of rescuing the "fallen *devadāsī*s" of coastal Andhra Pradesh. By the early twenty-first century, large numbers of women in the *kalāvantulu* community had converted to Christianity, because this promised them a stable monthly income as members of the new rehabilitation programs of these missions.[2] At the same time, caste associations headed by men in the *kalāvantula* community enforced the radical seclusion of women in their homes. A year before she passed away, Saride Anusuya told me:

> We did what we did with sincerity. But after us, these younger ones do business [*vṛtti*]. Our children get angry with us and say, "Hey, get in the house!" My son doesn't let me go out. If I do, he threatens to beat me. "Hey you!" he says, "We don't want to get a name like you." They allow the boys to study, but the girls can't even leave the house! They tell us to call ourselves *sūryabaḷija*, if anyone asks.

The term *sūryabaḷija*, as I noted in chapter 3, was the twentieth-century caste identity crafted by men in the Telugu-speaking courtesan community in order to distance themselves from the stigma attached to terms like *kalāvantulu* and *bhogam*.[3]

Twentieth-century reform discourse, coupled with the emergence of "classical" dance as a pastime for "respectable" women, had significant effects in rural communities where *kalāvantula* women lived as neighbors of middle-class families. Kotipalli Hymavathi, for example, speaks of the ways in which virtuosity was no longer associated with *kalāvantula* performance practices; it had now become identified with the "Bharatanāṭyam" that was presented on urban stages, or in movies, or later on television. What men "expected" aesthetically from women in *kalāvantula* communities changed in the span of one generation. Hymavathi explains:

> By the 1960s, people in our community began to abandon their profession; everyone left everything behind. Because I only danced for a few years, I couldn't learn too many of those dances [*padam*s, *jāvaḷi*s] or even "record" dances [dances to film songs]. Instead, I performed what people wanted to see—a snake dance, peacock dance, and other acrobatic dances. Sometimes, as a teenager, men would ask me to perform summersaults and throw money at me. Eventually I started to wonder about the past, about what my elders used to do. So I went to them and learned these dances [*padam*s, *jāvaḷi*s]. We all perform them together today. But today most *sāni*s are afraid to come out and talk about their past because of their fears that their children will lose respectability (*paruvu*). When these problems came [because of reform], some women formed *bhajan maṇḍali*s, and sang [devotional songs] for a living. Others focused on making the lives of their children better, and getting

them married so they could avoid this stigma. Some of our women went to places like Peddapuram and started doing business (*vṛtti*). Others are just left with nobody to look after them, and with no options.

The *kalāvantula* body and *kalāvantula* expressivity are scripted in a manner that is personally and aesthetically offensive. By the middle and certainly toward the end of the twentieth century, owing to reform debates, *kalāvantulu* had been conflated with *jogatis* (Dalit women dedicated to the goddess Yellamma) in the popular imagination, especially among a younger generation of men who had not witnessed *mejuvāṇi* performances as they existed in the 1940s and 1950s.

Hymavathi also remembers that some young men would come to the *meḷam* performances led by her sister after having seen the dances of *jogatis* at funerals and expect the same from them. She explains how the requests for songs that subtly equated the identities of *kalāvantulu* with brothel prostitutes became frequent. To illustrate, she sang the following song:

You've done so much, you've ruined my house, you whore.
I'm shocked by all this—you really get around, here and there, you whore.

The context for this song is actually a quarrel between two women who are fighting for the love of the same man. However, the invocation of the language of stigma (the words *laṃja*, *daṃga*, and *muṇḍa*—all synonyms for "whore") serves a reflexive function when the *kalāvantulu* are made to perform the composition. It also forces them to enact the role of "whores" while singing lyrics that explicitly insult such women. The song continues,

You've caught [the Brahmin] by the tuft of hair on his head
and you're swinging on it, playing on it, swinging on it, playing on it . . . [4]

The sexual overtones of the song are clear. As Hymavathi explained, "They enjoyed seeing us talk about each other in that way." Most of these men were businessmen from the city, tax collectors, and ministers. Undoubtedly, we see a new kind of publicization of *kalāvantula* women's sexual availability in the postsocial reform period.

As the performing arts—music and dance in particular—became "classicized" through state interventions in the twentieth century, opportunities for *kalāvantulu* to teach their art to women outside the community for money were rare. According to the late Maddula Venkataratnam from Tatipaka village (West Godavari district), the few women who tried to start dance schools in their villages had to obtain a certificate from the police and hang the certificate in a visible spot outside their homes. The certificate legitimized their status as bone fide dance teachers and made public the fact that they were not bringing young girls into their homes for "other purposes." In the 1930s, there was a movement to create a "regional" dance form for Andhra Pradesh, much like the newly created "Bharatanāṭyam," which had become both a national symbol intimately connected with regional (Tamil) cultural identity (O'Shea 2007; 2008). Nationalists and elite philanthropists in Andhra Pradesh accorded a parallel status to a reworked version of the *smārta* Brahmin male dance tradition from Kuchipudi village, and not to the dance of the *kalāvantulu* (Soneji 2004). From 1940 onward, girls came in large numbers to study from the traditional gurus of Kuchipudi village, but the *bhogameḷam* art of Andhra Pradesh was not refashioned or reconstituted by the upper classes until the 1970s. In 1972, Nataraja Ramakrishna, a dance teacher in Hyderabad, held an *abhinaya sadas* (gathering of traditional *abhinaya* artists) and brought many *kalāvantulu* together in Hyderabad for the first time since the passing of the Anti-Devadasi Act. He urged the women to come forth to teach his students. He aided many of them financially, including Saride Manikyam. Together with many *kalāvantulu*, he created a syllabus for teaching the art of the costal Andhra Pradesh *bhogameḷam* tradition, which he christened "Āndhra Nāṭyam," modeled, so some degree, after the name selectively foregrounded for the reinvented, middle-class version of the *devadāsī* art from further south, "Bharatanāṭyam." From 1993 to 1995, Swapnasundari, one of the nation's most famous dancers, embarked on a project that contested Nataraja Ramakrishna's codification of *kalāvantula* performance art. She studied dance and music repertoire under several *kalāvantulu* in coastal Andhra Pradesh, including Maddula Lakshminarayana, Maddula Venkataratnam, Kola Subrahmanyam, a number of women in Muramanda, and the Saride family at Ballipadu, and named her version "Vilāsini Nāṭyam."[5] These two reclamations of *kalāvantula* art circulate as "middle-class" versions of dance in Hyderabad and New Delhi, while *kalāvantula* women themselves are, for the most, considered "unsuitable" to appear on urban stages.[6]

SITES OF PERFORMANCE AND REPERTOIRE

kalāvantulu aṇṭe kalanu poṣiñcevāḷḷu
[*Kalāvantulu* refers to those who protect their art.]
—Kotipalli Hymavathi

The performance practices of *kalāvantulu* in coastal Andhra Pradesh are diverse, and many are the same as those found in Tamil-speaking courtesan communities. The Telugu language occupies *the* central place of courtesan performance traditions throughout South India, a fact obscured by the regional chauvinism of many contemporary Tamil cultural historians and dance practitioners.

Nineteenth- and early twentieth-century courtesan performance must be drawn out of these parochial historicizations and understood as pivoting around a common vocabulary of practices that undeniably included those developed in colonial Tanjore. This vocabulary permeates all sites of courtesan performance, from salon-style soirees to dancing in temple processions to the nightlong dramatic performances known as *pārijātam*. Each of these types of performances draws upon the interpretation of lyric poetry in techniques already discussed in previous chapters.

Courtly/Salon Repertoire (Mejuvāṇi)

The courtly repertoire of the Godavari River delta, which was replicated in salon performances as well, is incredibly rich. In addition to a number of compositions from Tanjore, it includes several compositions and genres that are exclusive to this region or are long-forgotten in Tanjore and Tamil-speaking South India. The concert repertoire is reckoned by a number of names: *kacceri-āṭa* or *kacceri*, which we have already encountered in the Tamil-speaking regions; *karṇāṭakam* (referring to its "southern" or Tanjorean origins, parallel to the term "Karṇāṭak music"); *keḷika* ("play"); *meḷam* ("troupe or band"); and perhaps most commonly, *mejuvāṇi*, from the Urdu word *mezbān* or *mezmān*, meaning "landlord, master of the house, host of a feast, a man who entertains guests." The movement vocabulary of the dance itself is parallel to that found in Tanjore and the Tamil-speaking regions. The "steps" of abstract movement (*aḍavu-sāmu*), for example, are numerous and complex, and remarkably similar to those from Tanjore.

Kalāvantula performances typically open with a *salām-daruvu*, or song of salutation, usually addressed to one of the Tanjore kings (usually

Pratāpasiṃha, Tuḷajā II, Serfoji II, or Śivājī II). These are short and fast-paced compositions that describe the splendor of the king, often focusing on his physical attributes. Sometimes it would end with an erotic verse in which the heroine would inevitably request the king to fulfil her desires. This would be followed by a short piece of abstract or nonrepresentational dance, the *pallavi*, similar to the *jatisvaram* of Tanjore but performed to the accompaniment of one simple line of music.[7]

The rest of the evening's performance would be dedicated to the interpretation of lyrics, largely in the *varṇam*, *padam*, and *jāvaḷi* genres. The interpretation of *varṇam*s and *padam*s was usually performed at a leisurely pace with the dancer seated on the ground. The *varṇam* was a centerpiece in these performances as it was in Tanjore. In coastal Andhra Pradesh, however, there were no bursts of abstract dance that would punctuate the text. So instead of dancing to the solfège passages, *kalāvantulu* would sing them, while keeping time (*tāḷam*) with their hands. The absence of these rhythmic interludes did not take away, however, from the understanding of *varṇam* as a virtuosic form. At some point in the late nineteenth or early twentieth century, courtesan performers in this region canonized five *varṇam*s as "great *varṇam*s" (*peddaidu varṇālu*), which were taught and performed by all serious artists. According to Kotipalli Satyavathi of Muramanda, the ability to "handle" all five of these compositions was the sign of a great performer. The five *varṇam*s included three compositions attributed to the Quartet (one in *rāga* Bhairavi dedicated to Serfoji II, which we saw in translation in chapter 1; one in *rāga* Toḍi dedicated to Śivājī II, and one in *rāga* Ānandabhairavi dedicated to Kṛṣṇarāja Uḍaiyār, king of Mysore). Not only did these compositions travel from Tanjore into these areas, but they remained iconic markers of virtuosity as they were in Tanjore. Some early, pre-Quartet *varṇam*s that had disappeared from Tanjore and the Tamil-speaking regions were also performed regularly in coastal Andhra Pradesh until the middle of the twentieth century.[8] In addition to these Tanjore *varṇam*s, a number of other "local" *varṇam*s were also performed in this region.[9] The mainstay of *mejuvāṇi*, however, was the performance of Telugu *padam*s and *jāvaḷi*s.

As already noted in chapters 1 and 2, lyrical interpretation characterized courtesan performance in the nineteenth and early twentieth centuries. The *kalāvantulu* of coastal Andhra Pradesh handled a vast and diverse repertoire of *padam*s and *jāvaḷi*s, many of which were composed in these regions, and hence are unknown among Tamil-speaking courtesans.[10] I will return to the function of these pieces in contemporary *kalāvantula* communities in a moment, but first I would like to turn to an example of a *padam* typical of the Godavari delta region. The following *padam*, "ĕnduki tŏndara" in the *rāga* Ānandabhairavi, is dedicated to Ānanda Gajapati Mahārāju (1850–1897), *zamīndār* of Vizianagaram. The maharaja was a key figure in early South Indian nationalist politics and simultaneously was a great patron of music and courtesan dance (Rama Rao, 1985). This *padam* comes from the repertoire of Saride Seshachalam in the village of Duvva, West Godavari district. The *nāyikā*, or heroine, of the poem is married, but her lover can't wait to be intimate with her. He shows up at her husband's house, and she has to convince him to leave, with the promise that she will satisfy him (and herself) later:

Why are you in such a hurry, beautiful one?
Be patient, I will come to you soon.
    Why are you in such a hurry?
You placed your hand on my breast,
and spoke such lovely words.
You placed your hands all over my body
and spoke such lovely words.
But if the eye of my husband happens
to fall upon us, we'll be in trouble!
    Why are you in such a hurry?
It's time for me to serve my husband his meal,
but I will return soon.
You are a connoisseur of enjoyment,
like the old King Bhoja
and the god of desire.
Come back soon, and make love to me!
Salutations to you, Ānanda Gajapati Mahārāja!
    Why are you in such a hurry?

In 1915, observers were already commenting on what they understood as the "degeneration" of courtly styles of dance in the Godavari delta. That year, Devulapalli Vīrarāghavamūrti Śāstri, a Brahmin connoisseur of the arts, published a Telugu-language book entitled *Abhinaya Svayambodhini* ("Teach Yourself Abhinaya"), a codification of courtly repertoire that includes five *svarajatis*, seventeen *varṇams*, and eighty-four *padams* (attributed to Kṣetrayya). For each song, he provides the lyrics together with suggestions on how to perform the *abhinaya* for each word. This text contains the five "great *varṇams*" and a number of other early compositions from Tanjore that are not found elsewhere. In the preface to this lengthy pedagogical treatise he writes about the failing standards of performances practices in the courtesan (*veśyā*) community:

> [*Śāstras* like] *Bharatārṇava* and *Abhinayadarpaṇa* have become rare.[11] This art is to be practiced by women. But women cannot read these texts and therefore cannot acquire knowledge (*vidya*) about the art. I have written this text in Telugu to facilitate learning for *veśyā strī*s and other women who wish to learn this art; they need not look elsewhere. One can learn the art with the help of this book. This *abhinaya śāstra* has been composed in a simple style for them; [they can acquire proficiency in *abhinaya*] without the help of the numerous Sanskrit works. With this book in hand, a woman can become a master of the art. The ladies who want to acquire this knowledge (*vidya*) need not spend any money.
>
> Another reason I have taken up the task of writing this work now, is that this art has devolved into a grave state (*bahu hīna daśāku vaccasunnadi*) and everyone knows this. One reason [for its degeneration] is that the art is kept secret (*gūḍha*). Some *veśyā*s learn a little bit of *abhinaya* and spend all their time repeating [what little they know]. They don't learn the *śāstra*, which speaks of the varieties of *nāyaka* and *nāyikā* (hero and heroine). Without any experience of how to manipulate the hands, eyes, et cetera, in their ignorance (*ajñānam*), they move their hands here and there and say they have mastered *abhinaya*. They perform before large assemblies, believing that they are master performers. If somebody in the audience raises a question about the *śāstra*s, these women [can't respond and] have to leave the assembly [out of sheer embarrassment]. They are not equipped with the knowledge to be able to answer such questions. Therefore [it is my wish that] this tradition of *abhinaya*, which exists in a deteriorated state, should improve. (Śāstri 1915, i–ii)

As we have already seen in chapters 1 and 2, salon performances have always been characterized by hybrid and novel presentations. By the middle of the twentieth century, *mejuvāṇi* performances in coastal Andhra Pradesh included the performance of film songs alongside *padam*s and *jāvaḷi*s. The term "record dance" gained popularity both within and outside the *kalāvantula* community. While many women revel in their performances of these dances, for which they became justly famous (fig. 5.1), other women see the "intrusion" of film songs as the beginning of the end of *kalāvantula* performance practices. According to Nayudu Chilakamma from Mandapeta village, "When the older people used to do *meḷam*, it was good. But then younger ones started to dance for money [given to the

5.1 Subbulakshmi performs the song "gopāla nīku from the Telugu film *Jivitam* (1950) as part of a salon (*mejuvāṇi*) performance in Muramanda, Andhra Pradesh. Photo by author.

performer when she danced a song on request], and they also did "record" dance. Older women such as my sisters wouldn't allow these women to dance in their *meḷam* if they wanted to perform record dance." The ambivalence with which women from courtesan communities regard the culture of cinema in India is something I have already touched on, but suffice to say that cinema represented a world of lost opportunities for women who considered themselves "professional performing artists," while at the same time, it too was marked by a profound stigma that many women, such as Chilakamma's sisters, wanted to avoid at all costs.

Temple Processions (Ūregiṃpu) *and Wedding Performances* (Kañca)

A great majority of *kalāvantula* women in coastal Andhra Pradesh did not undergo temple dedications. As we have already seen, from the seventeenth century onward, many courtesans were not "dedicated" at temples; they may have been marked by rights of passage such as "sword marriage" (*katti kalyāṇam*) discussed in chapter 1, or may have simply been coopted into the courtesan lifestyle without any such rituals. In the Godavari River delta, most women underwent the *kannĕrikam* ritual that marked them as courtesans. It is true, however, that *some* women were dedicated to temple deities in this region. Elsewhere I have written in detail about the ritual duties and repertoire of the Madanagopālasvāmi temple at Ballipadu in the East Godavari district, for example, where compositions such as *maṅgalahārati pāṭulu* (auspicious songs to accompany the ritual waving of lamps), *lāli-pāṭulu* and *jola-pāṭulu* (lullabies), *hĕccarikalu* ("warning" songs sung as part of the *baliharaṇa* rituals to propitiate the *aṣṭadikpāla*s, guardian deities of the eight directions), and others were performed regularly (Soneji 2004). But these kinds of ritual performances represented the exception rather than the rule when it came to courtesan performance in the nineteenth and early twentieth centuries.

By contrast, temples regularly hired *bhogameḷam*s to perform at temple festivals. Sometimes this was specifically to perform a concert of courtly compositions on makeshift stages (*pandal*s) set up for the occasion; at other times, it was to dance with the image of the deity as it was taken on procession around the village streets. This was called *ūregiṃpu meḷam* ("processional band") or *tiruvīdhi grāmotsavam* ("village celebration of a procession on the streets surrounding temple"). The processional performances consisted of a random selection of songs and dances taken from the *kacceri* or concert repertoire, most of which would be performed when the deity would periodically stop for "breaks" en route. These *ūregiṃpu meḷam*s represented some of the most "public" of performances by courtesans.

Until recently, the presence of a *bhogameḷam* was an important marker of a high-society wedding in the Godavari delta. Most of the women in the Godavari delta referred to this as *kañca*, after the *kañcamu*, "metal platters" given to them by the hosts at this time. In the Tamil-speaking regions, these performances were called *kalyāṇakkaccēri*, a term that is rarely used in the Godavari delta. The *kalāvantulu* would not only dance *padam*s, *jāvaḷi*s, and other erotic compositions at weddings but would also be involved in providing blessings to the bride. By tying the black beads (*nallapūsa*) of the bride's *maṅgalasūtra*, or wedding necklace, the *kalāvantula* woman would shower auspicious blessings on the bride. The courtesan's liminal status as neither wedded nor widowed enabled her to stand at social thresholds. The following, in the words of Kotipalli Rajahamsa of Muramanda, is a brief description of a typical *kañca* ritual:

> After the wedding ritual, large amounts of *kuṃkum*, fruits, sweets, and a silk shawl (*paṭṭu śālva*) would be placed on large platters (*kañcamu*). People carry the platters, and we follow them, doing *meḷam* [i.e., singing and dancing] in procession to the bride's new home. When we finally reach the house, the bride and groom are seated on a cot. The hosts will ask the *nāyakurālu* [troupe leader] to take one of the platters, and will also give her a large sum of money and several sets of new clothes. Then the *mejuvāṇi* [performance of dance and music as entertainment for the guests] begins.

At the groom's home, a full-length performance is given by the *kalāvantulu*, and this was a great source of income for *bhogameḷam*s in this region. Often, troupes would be booked a year in advance for such performances, and all negotiations would be performed by the *nāyakurālu*, the woman who led the troupe.

Dramatic Performance (Āṭa-Bhāgavatam)

A unique aspect of the repertoire of many courtesans in the Godavari River delta was known variously as *kalāpam*, *āṭa-bhāgavatam*, or *veṣa-katha* (Soneji 2004).[12] This genre consisted of two types of performance, *Bhāmākalāpam* and *Gollakalāpam*. Like the *kuṟavañci* dramas performed in the Tanjore region, these were nightlong, dramatic performances about archetypal female characters, Satyabhāmā, the consort of Kṛṣṇa, and Gollabhāmā, a highly intelligent milkmaid from the shepherd (*golla*) caste. From both a literary and performance perspective, these dramas were embedded in a larger theatrical ecology that involved the public performance of dramas by male and female troupes, spanning a range of caste backgrounds, from *smārta* Brahmins to Dalits.[13] In the context of courtesan performance, the *Bhāmākalāpam*, known in *kalāvantula* communities as *pārijātam*, revolves around the separation of Satyabhāmā and Kṛṣṇa after a quarrel, and is told from the standpoint of Satyabhāmā. Like the lovesick heroine of the *kuṟavañci* dramas, Satyabhāmā is depicted in varied states of desire and anguish, described in the language of lyric poetry. Satyabhāmā passes through phases of longing poetically represented by sections of the drama including *manmatha-upālambhana* (rebuking the god of desire, Manmatha or Kāma), *candra-upālambhana* (admonishing the moon), *vāyu-upālambhana* (reprimanding the breeze), and *mūrccha-avasthā* (a state of fainting or swooning). The drama ends when Satyabhāmā's confidante Mādhavi carries a letter to Kṛṣṇa, and he finally returns to her. The *Gollakalāpam*, by contrast, represents one of the only elements in the courtesan repertoire that does not focus on eroticism and the poetics of longing. Instead, it consists of a dialogue between a clever girl from the shepherd community and an arrogant Brahmin scholar. The character of the girl is represented in a manner similar to that of fortune-telling woman of the Kuṟa tribe in the Tamil *kuṟavañci* dramas. The various episodes in the drama are structured around songs that address a range of issues including indigenous understandings of conception and fetal development. At the end of the drama, the shepherd girl successfully defeats the Brahmin in intellectual debate, a move that appears to critique both caste and gender roles.[14]

These performances borrowed technique and other conventions from courtly repertoire and were performed on temporary, makeshift open-air structures (*pandals*), usually set up inside the pavilions of temples. These types of open, public performances helped generate income for the temple. The *āṭa-bhāgavatam* or *pārijātam* was a form of "popular" entertainment that attracted audiences from around the Godavari delta to temples such as the Satyanārāyaṇasvāmi temple in Annavaram. Figure 5.2 shows the *meḷam* of Annabhatula Buli Venkataratnam (from Mummidivaram, East Godavari district) preparing for a performance of *Gollakalāpam*, circa 1950. *Āṭa-bhāgavatam* texts were composed by or commissioned from upper-caste (usually Brahmin) poets by the *kalāvantulu*.[15] In many cases, these men taught the meaning of the poetry to the woman and made suggestions as to how it should be interpreted through *abhinaya*. These men

5.2 The *meḷam* of late Annabhatula Buli Venkataratnam (Mummidivaram, East Godavari district), c. 1950. Photo courtesy the Sunil Kothari Dance Collection.

were referred to respectfully as gurus (*gurugāru*). Most *kalāvantula āṭa-bhāgavatam* texts are divided into smaller sections or episodes called *paṭ-ṭu* ("acts"). Often, a full evening would be dedicated to the performance of only one or two *paṭṭus* of the full text, which would be performed over a span of many nights.[16]

NIGHTS OF NOSTALGIA: PERFORMANCE AND AUTOBIOGRAPHICAL REMEMBERING

In February 2002, Saride Maithili introduced me to the mnemonic culture of the *kalāvantulu* by singing *jāvaḷis*. She had gathered a *meḷam* inside her own house. It was around 11:30 P.M., early for a night of remembering. Spontaneously, her nephew picked up a drum (*mṛdaṅgam*) and a violin player from a few houses down was called in. Maithili began to sing a song of salutation (*salām-daruvu*) dedicated to King Serfoji II of Tanjore, and performed an interpretation of the text through gesture (*abhinaya*). Like Muttukkannammal's "rooftop" performances discussed in chapter 4, Maithili, her family, and a number of other *kalāvantula* families regularly engage in evening "sessions" of music and dance performed only for each other. These distinctly private performances take place behind closed doors, usually in the late hours of the night. In a sense, *kalāvantulu* performance culture has gone "underground"—it has found itself living inside the homes of *kalāvantula* women. Today there is no audience beyond the walls of their homes, but this is not a criterion for these mnemonic practices. The *meḷams* have become part of women's interior worlds—they have moved from the realm of public spectacle into the realm of nostalgia and memory.

In an engaging essay entitled "Autobiographical Remembering as Cultural Practice: Understanding the Interplay between Memory, Self and Culture," Qi Wang and Jens Brockmeier have pointed to the narrow focus on collective and institutional forms of remembering in scholarly work on memory. They shift their emphasis instead to the significance and efficacy of "self-memory." They argue that "autobiographical memory, self-construction and narrative exhibit a developmental dynamic in which they mutually . . . confirm each other" (2002, 58). Autobiographical telling, as Kamala Visweswaran notes, "is not a mere reflection of self, but another entry point into history, of community refracted through the self" (1994, 137). In the case of contemporary *kalāvantulu*, performance is a mode of inhabiting a personal past, a "cultural genre of remembering" (47). My presence as an observer of these ordinarily "closed doors" events added another dimension: that of "telling." The performance of the repertoire was now supplemented by the recollection of explicitly autobiographical narratives interspersed throughout the performance. Their self-presentation to outsiders—however rare it might be—involves the strategic elaboration of historical and social positions.

I first became conscious of the relationship between performance and autobiographical remembering through an event coordinated by Kotipalli Hymavathi of Muramanda, who eventually became a central figure in my work and travels throughout the Godavari delta. A few weeks after our initial meeting, Hymavathi invited four women to her house to meet me—Kotipalli Somasundaram, Kotipalli Rajahamsa, Eluru Lakshakasulu, and K. Krishnaveni—who all used to dance in Hymavathi's grandmother's *meḷam*. All of them were trained by Hymavathi's grandmother Kotipalli Subbayi, and all lived in the village of Muramanda like Hymavathi. Some had also performed in her mother Kotipalli Manikyam's *meḷam*. Our conversations began rather informally around 9:00 P.M. About an hour into our conversation, Hymavathi asked Kotipalli Somasundaram, the seniormost woman in the group, to tell me about *jāvaḷi*s. Hymavathi hummed the first line of a *jāvaḷi* in the *rāga* Maṇiraṅgu, *sarasuḍa nīve nāku gati* ("Beautiful lover, you are my destiny"). Somasundaram corrected some of her words, and started to sing the whole song. All of a sudden the rest of the women joined in, and soon they were all sitting in a line and performing *abhinaya*, with slight variations, to this *jāvaḷi*. Somasundaram told me later that she "saw her *meḷam*" that night, and as the night went on, she performed more *abhinaya*, and her performances were laced with autobiographical recollections. After the first *jāvaḷi*, she began her narrative:

> My mother was a *veśyā* (*mā amma vesyā*). In my family, one of my sisters was married, and the rest of us became *sāni*s. My elder sister was a *nāyakurālu* for about five years, and after that, I took on this role. I was a *nāyakurālu* for almost thirty years.

The *jāvaḷi* over, we began to talk about the *pallavi* genre. Somasundaram and a couple of the other women let out a chuckle when I asked if Somasundaram could dance one. "Are you kidding?" she replied, "I'm too old for that kind of thing, but I know Hymavathi remembers a couple of *pallavi*s from our repertoire." Hymavathi, considerably younger than Somasundaram, moved the small table and chairs that were in the way, tightly wrapped her sari around her waist, and started to dance a *pallavi* as Somasundaram and the others sang. When the *pallavi* ended, Hymavathi sat down, and Somasundaram continued.

> But then we faced a lot of problems because of the reforms, and all of a sudden, it seemed, everything came to standstill. My guru was Kotipalli Subbayi, the grandmother of your friend Hymavathi! I have five children through one man, and my third child, a daughter, became a *sāni*. I live with my youngest daughter. I had my *gajjapūjā* [worship of the ankle bells] performed when I was eleven, under the guidance of my guru. As a *nāyakurālu*, I did all the "management" [in English]. I took bookings for performances, brought all the dancers together, and after the performance, I collected payment from the host and distributed it to all the artists in our *meḷam*. Those days were different.

Hymavathi interrupted. "Akka, remember those *aṣṭapadī*s?" Hymavathi had seen Somasundaram perform *aṣṭapadī* poems from the *Gītagovinda* in Sanskrit, and this had apparently left a deep impression on her. The poems of the twelfth-century *Gītagovinda*, like the *pārijātam* dramas, were taught only to highly accomplished courtesan performers in this region by male Brahmin connoisseurs with whom they often shared intimate relationships. Trying her best to remember, Somasundaram began singing and performing *abhinaya* to the first two lines of the twelfth *aṣṭapadī* of the *Gītagovinda*:

> atha tāṃ gantumaśaktāṃ ciramanuraktāṃ latāgṛhe dṛṣṭvā
> taccaritam govinde manasijamande sakhī prāha ||
>
> paśyati diśi diśi . . .

Unable to remember the rest of the song without her notebook, Somasundaram stopped. Tears streaming into the lower rim of her glasses, she continued.

> This is really hard to remember, you know. Nobody wants to hear these songs anymore. These songs were in sweet Telugu or Sanskrit. These were great things. It all makes me very sad. They've stopped our dances (*mā ḍānsulu āpesāru*). Look at the state of dance today. Look at cinema dance today. Hymavathi has a TV, she knows—the people in the movies don't even wear clothes! That kind of dance gets so much respect, but they've stopped our dances. *That* is shameful.

Here we see the affective potential of remembering and the oscillation between past and present embodied in these performances of memory. Performance enables a movement between "what was" and "what is"; Somasundaram is conscious of the fact that her art has been stripped of its value as capital today. The aesthetics of *devadāsī* dance is simply not viable in the age of TV, she notes. Her antagonism toward popular cultural forms hinges on the irony of their acceptance, their "respectability" in the face of the social and aesthetic marginalization of her own cultural practices. The retrieval of the past into the present appears disorienting at one level for Somasundaram ("Why have our dances been banned, when this is allowed to continue?"), but at another level, it resists attempts to erase or deny the past. This kind of commemorative nostalgia serves as a mode of suspending the past in a way that makes it available and affective for the shaping of a contemporary selfhood.

Later in February 2002, Kotipalli Hymavathi held a *mejuvāṇi-meḷam* at her home in Muramanda village. This *meḷam* was organized so I could record some *jāvaḷi*s that I had not yet seen. Hymavathi spent some time in her bedroom, now transformed into a greenroom. She applied a variety of makeup, and started to mix sandalwood powder with water in a small bowl. She also took some jasmine flowers that I assumed were meant to ornament her hair, and plucked the buds, and put them on a small plate. I was a bit confused, believing that Hymavathi was going to use these in some way as part of her makeup. When I asked her about the sandalwood paste and flowers, she simply replied "Just wait, you'll see."

The *mejuvāṇi* performance began. I was caught up in trying to write down the words to the *jāvaḷi*s I had not heard or seen previously. As soon as Hymavathi's sister finished her *jāvaḷi*, Hymavathi brought out the bowl of sandalwood paste and plate of flowers. She placed a footstool in the middle of the room, and asked my research assistant Rangamani to sit down on it. Hymavathi started to sing the following song in the *rāga* Jhuñjhūṭi, applying the sandalpaste to Rangamani's arms and gently showering her with the jasmine buds:

> Great Lover! I'm smearing this fragrant sandalpaste on your body!
> *Leave your doubts behind, my beloved, and come!*
> Don't you have any love for me? Come to look after my needs, come!
> *Leave your doubts behind.*
> We can live like a pair of lovebirds in our love nest, come!
> *Leave your doubts behind.*
> Let's go for a spin in your motor car!

Leave your doubts behind.
We can make a boat of jasmine flowers and sleep in it!
Leave your doubts behind

Composed in the early twentieth century by an unknown author, this song, "mandāra gandham idi," became one of the staple compositions of salon performances. The performer would request the host to be seated, then would proceed to anoint his arms with sandalwood paste, while interpreting the text of the song, effectively seducing him, in very close contact, with her *abhinaya*. Hymavathi sat down with me after her performance, as the musician and next performer decided on their next piece. My assistant and I asked her about the lyrics of this song, and we started to write them down. As I was writing, Hymavathi engaged in what I think of as "reflective nostalgia."

> You know, I have performed this only once or twice for a real man! Now those days of *zamīndār*s are gone. When this song was composed, things were different. You know there is that line "moṭaru kārumida . . ." That was a time when it was very hard to see a motor car. Only *zamīndār*s had those. Other than the wives of *zamīndār*s, only we *kalāvantulu* could ride in those motor cars! Imagine if there were still *zamīndār*s! Today we would still be riding in motor cars! We could have been part of that.

Hymavathi's reflections and longing are part of an imaginary in which *kalāvantula* women were integrated into a new, distinctly "modern" economy, represented by the motor car in the song. Her idealized longing for this past—removed from many of the historical realities of the nineteenth century—nevertheless reflects a nostalgia for an ideal audience and patronage, both of which are impossible for *kalāvantula* women today.

REMEMBERING AN EROTIC SELF

> We have many desires!
> —Maddula Venkataratnam

There is little doubt that *devadāsī* performance articulates female desire that is constructed in the male gaze. The audiences for courtesan performance largely consist of men, some of whom have sexual relations with the performers as well. But limiting the expressive possibilities of performance solely to the effects of the male gaze curtails any potential for the expression of female desire, *jouissance*, moments of resilience among peripheral subjects such as courtesans. As Amelia Maciszewski reminds us in her work with courtesans in North India,

> the woman evoking such [patriarchally constructed] imagery in her performance is exercising creative agency by virtue of using the music, text, and a particular context to elaborate her very own realization of the materials at hand . . . She is both an object of the (male) gaze and purveyor of her own artistic (and professional) gaze—thus simultaneously subsuming her individual identity into the extant artistic form and deploying her creative agency within it. (1998, 88)

I suggest that for some women—and under certain conditions—the visceral, somatic, and material pleasures of performance resonate at a deeply intimate level. My concern here is not with recovering a notion of courtesan agency in the past—in the salons of the Madras Presidency, for example. Instead, I am interested in the mobilization of performance practices as modes of telling in the expression of contemporary *devadāsī* identity. This identity undeniably has aesthetics as its telos, and not religion, as we have seen elsewhere. *Kalāvantula* women in the Godavari delta express an ownership of the idea of the marginal; they articulate an awareness of the socioaesthetics of their past. If we are to envision feminist ethnography, following Chantal Mouffe, as a project of documenting shifting subjectivites that are affected, transformed, and subverted by a range of articulatory practices (1992, 373), then memory-work with *devadāsī*s presents a productive site for such a project.

The freedom to display or discuss sexuality is one way in which contemporary *kalāvantulu* construct themselves in opposition to married women. Again, while it is clear that the foregrounding of female sexuality is meant to titillate the male spectator in performance, our perspective is transformed when we think of performances as primarily mnemonic acts without audiences. In this context, *kalāvantulu* deploy the aestheticized sexuality of the repertoire to articulate a vision of their own sexuality that stands in opposition to that of middle-class, "respectable" women. The affective resonances of the repertoire, made manifest through the inflection and style of courtesan performance, enable women to imagine the past in a manner that has significant personal meaning.

In early March 2002, I met Maddula Venkataratnam (fig. 5.3) at a *mejuvāṇi* session arranged in the village of Manepalli. Venkataratnam

5.3 The author with Maddula Venkataratnam (*center*), Kotipalli Hymavathi, and a number of other *kalāvantula* women in the village of Tatipaka, West Godavari district, in 2002.

was one of the most well-known performing artists of her time. She was born in the village of Tatipaka, where she studied dance under a famous *nāyakurālu*, Maddula Shiromani, and had her *gajjapūjā* performed at the age of nine. She was also a respected performer of *āṭa-bhāgavatam*—both *Bhāmākalāpam* and *Gollakalāpam*—which she studied under Gaddam Subbarayudu Sastri. That day, it was clear that she was the most important figure among those who had gathered for this *mejuvāṇi*. After performing a short *pallavi* in the *rāga* Ānandabhairavi, Venkataratnam began the first major piece. She sat down and began to sing the following *padam* in the *rāga* Mohana, attributed to Kṣetrayya. In this piece, the heroine mocks her lover Kṛṣṇa for not being able to satisfy her sexually. It is a rare example of the explicit expression of a woman's own sexual desire. The refrain (*pallavī*) of the *padam* is as follows:

> If only one round of lovemaking makes you so tired,
> what [kind of love] is this?
> Come, fulfill my desires,
> our Kṛṣṇa-Muvvagopāla!

Venkataratnam performed the *pallavī* alone for close to half an hour. In her performance, Venkataratnam sang the words *makkuva dīrcara* ("Come, fulfill my desires") over fifty times, and provided a new hand gesture to depict sexual union each time. Later she explained these gestures, known as *rati-mudrās*, using terms like *samarati* ("man on top"), *uparati* ("woman on top," also *viparītarati*), and *nāgabandhamu* ("bodies coiled in the serpent position"). Her performance of the whole *padam* lasted more than an hour, at the end of which she decided to take a break. As we sipped tea, she began to talk about sexuality in highly aestheticized terms. She talked me through *nakha-śikhā varṇana*, a metaphoric description of the female body from the toenails to the crown of the head. "Only we *kalāvantulu* can sing and dance like this. I'm still alive, so you've come to see me and hear these songs. If I die, who will come? What will happen to these songs?" Venkataratnam wondered.

A week later, I visited her in own home in the village of Tatipaka. The first question she asked was, "Did you like the *padam* that day?" "Of course, I learned so much," I replied. "Did you see the *rati-mudrās*? I was about twenty years old when Ramamurtigaru [a local Brahmin scholar] told me about them and taught me them with their Sanskrit names. You know, when we perform these things, we *feel* different." She continued,

> There is something about these songs that make you understand your experience (*anubhavam*) of life. We have many desires, just like anyone else! Sometimes those desires are fulfilled, sometimes not. I have fallen in love, too, but maybe not in the same way as those married women. My experience is important, too, just like the *nāyikā* in that *padam*. She has desires that she wants fulfilled.

As Amelia Maciszewski has demonstrated, the *nāyikās* reflect, on the one hand, an abstract, situated, and sexualized subjectivity, and on the other, a distinct corporeality, an affective state and social positioning that "may be internalized, enacted, and appropriated by [courtesan] performers" (1998, 93). More important, Venkataratnam foregrounds the connections between her experience of pleasure in the form of romantic or sexual love and pleasure in the performance of the *padam*.

Another discussion of the erotic took place during a *meḷam* held in the home of Saride Maithili in Duvva village (West Godavari district). Maithili, in her mid-fifties, is a very strong-headed woman, who takes great pride in the very candid and bold personality she has cultivated. As the preparations for the performance were taking place, I asked Maithili if she had children. "For a long time," she replied, "I didn't want them." She explained that many *kalāvantulu* did not want children, especially those who were actively involved in performing dance and music in public. They employed indigenous forms of contraception. The standard way of expressing this was *pillalni puṭṭanivva ledu* ("I did not let children be born") and usually involved the insertion of homemade pessaries into the vagina near the cervix. That night, Maithili performed a *jāvaḷi* that opened up a set of related questions. At around 11:30 P.M., Saride Maithili sang this *jāvaḷi*, "cĕragu māseyemi setura" in the *rāga* Kalyāṇi, composed by Neti Subbarayudu Sastri, a Brahmin composer from the coastal Andhra Pradesh region:

It's that time of the month, what can I do?
I can't even come close to you!
You useless god! You create obstacles to intercourse
For three straight days!
It's that time of the month.
Even on our first night, we did not make love,
though I was revelling in thoughts of union.
It's that time of the month.
Poor Lord of Naupuri with a gentle heart,
Don't harbor any worries,
In another three days
I'll give you much satisfaction!
It's that time of month.[17]

In this *jāvaḷi*, Kṛṣṇa has come to a woman asking her to make love to him. The heroine is menstruating and exposes the hypocrisy of the situation—the very god who has made the rules of purity and pollution now wishes to break them at will. The woman resists and teasingly tells him that he will have to wait until after her period of impurity is over. This *jāvaḷi* bears a striking semblance to a Kṣetrayya *padam*, "cĕragu māsiyunnānu," in the *rāga* Begaḍā, likely composed nearly three centuries earlier. In the *padam*, however, it is the heroine who has come to Kṛṣṇa for sex. Kṛṣṇa is apprehensive about touching her in her polluted state, and she implores him to let go of the "false taboos" (*tappu*) that society places on menstruation:

It's true, I have my period,
but don't let that stop you.
No rules apply
to another man's wife.

I beg you to come close,
but you always have second thoughts.

All those codes were written
by men who don't know how to love.
When I come at you, wanting you,
why do you back off?
    You don't have to touch my whole body.
just bend over and kiss.
No rules apply.

What if I take off my sari
and crush your chest with my breasts?
I'll be careful, except with my lips.
Here is some betel, take it
with your teeth. No one's here.
I'm watching.
No rules apply.

You don't seem to know yourself.
Why follow these false taboos?
Haven't you heard that women like it now?
It's not like everyday.
You'll never forget today's joy.
No rules apply. (Narayana Rao and Shulman 2002, 336–337)

Maithili explained to me that night, as did many other *kalāvantulu* over the course of my fieldwork, that they did not observe menstrual pollution. The obvious reason for the lack of menstrual taboo in courtesan communities, I thought to myself, has to do with giving men access to women's sexuality when they desire it. But that night, in the context of the mnemonic appearance of this issue through Maithili's performance, it was given a commentary. After she sang the *jāvaḷi*, Maithili was quick to add that the morality encoded in this song only applies to *saṃsāri*s (householders) and not to women such as herself. "But who among the *saṃsāri*s will talk about such things? They would be ashamed, no?" she asked. "See, we can do some things they can't, but, you know that they have some comforts we cannot have. Wait, I should say comforts we can *no longer* have." Although it is not possible to go into an elaborate analysis of the performance conventions deployed in the representation of this *jāvaḷi*, one salient point should be noted. In the depiction of the *pallavi* or refrain of the song ("cĕragu māseyemi setura"), Maithili holds the *pallu* or end of her sari, as if to confront the *fact* of menstruation, represented by the soiled clothing. This is not some kind of a stylized, abstract, or displaced representation. It is a way of *marking difference*—the courtesan woman *can* and *will* confront this fact and elaborate upon it in public, whereas according to Maithili, the *saṃsāri*s will not. "*They* can't talk about it, but *we* can" she noted.

I am conscious of the dangers in positing statements such as these as radical. While I take *kalāvantula* critiques of middle-class morality seriously, I am also conscious of the fact that *kalāvantula* women were themselves dependent upon the world of men in ways that implicated them in larger, systemic forms of discrimination and potential exploitation. In a recent work, Rajeswari Sunder Rajan has noted that in scholarly works that focus on courtesan and prostitute sexuality,

> [these women] are exhorted to serve primarily as adversaries or critics of a "society" whose representatives are (all) men and "respectable" women. What such a representation fails to acknowledge is that prostitutes are necessarily and complexly *connected* both to patriarchy and to women as a class, in ways that cannot be only antagonistic and would in fact include dependence and emulation—an acknowledgement that complicates our view of them as consistently subversive agents as much as it does the view of them as invariant "victims" . . . (2003, 130)

How then, are we to understand the critiques offered by the *kalāvantula* women above? Sunder Rajan's observation that courtesans and prostitutes inhabit social locations that are dependent upon both men and "respectable" women adds a degree of complexity to the staging of identities in the manner we see among *kalāvantulu*. While *kalāvantulu* no doubt offer critiques of middle-class women's situations, they also critically reflect on their own situations. Their performative, material iterations of gender roles and difference, in the Butlerean sense, cannot be reduced to antagonism. To dismiss the complexities of their self-awareness would be to deny women's resilience under patriarchy, to close our eyes to how *individual* women can represent themselves in ways that unsettle our notions of power and pleasure in an unfinished past that lives in the present.

ON THE EFFICACY OF INDIVIDUAL REMEMBERING

The world of individual remembering and performance, however, is not a hermetic one; it is not an example of the anthropological romance represented by the idea of "insular purity." It is unfinished, characteristically open, and in contact with social, economic, and cultural developments on the "outside." Women in contemporary *kalāvantula* communities reflect on loss and aesthetics in a manner that takes, for example, the success of "classical" Indian dance, cinema dance, and other elite cultural practices into account; these provide the foil for their own experiences. Their narrations reveal an acute awareness of their social location outside the middle class and enable them to mark their fractured identities within a historically determinate framework.

Such acts of memory also serve the dual functions of conferring positive self-worth and allowing *kalāvantula* women to retain and express, albeit to each other, elements of their identities that they can no longer display in public. In this chapter, I have not sought to establish or critique "truth claims" expressed by the women in these communities or to provide answers to the problems I have staged. Rather, I have tried to bring focus to the processes and concerns around *kalāvantula* identity and self-representation in their postreform world. While official and national histories want to remember these women as *devadāsī*s in order to authorize religious, moral, and aesthetic justifications for the reinvented "classical" arts, many women in these communities deploy their experiences of "being an artist" to imagine a different subjectivity for themselves, one that stands apart from middle-class morals of citizenship. In a recent essay, Margaret Meibohm suggests that the core questions of identity formation, "Who am I?" and "What do I do?" can be partially addressed through the additional queries of "Where have I come from?" and "Who have I been?" (2002, 61) For *kalāvantulu* in Andhra Pradesh today, the answers to *these* questions can only come from behind closed doors, from what we might call "deep memory"—a process that "remakes the self" and reconstructs identity from fragments of remembrance, knowledge, and experience.

CODA

Gesturing to Devadāsī Pasts in Today's Chennai

Much of this book has been concerned with the city of Chennai (formerly Madras), whether the emphasis has fallen on legislative action, the incipient industries of musical and cinematic recording, or the network of salons that formerly covered the city. Even the communities of courtesans living in rural areas considered in the last two chapters must be understood, to some degree, in relation to this nearby metropolis, from which the legal and aesthetic rules that affect them have emanated over the last century. With a population of over 4.5 million, Chennai is one of South Asia's largest cities. Chennai has also been a major site for performative constructions of Indian and particularly Hindu heritage, a place where the gestures of every dancer seem loaded with political significance. Bharatanāṭyam, certainly one of India's most cherished cultural exports, was created in Madras, and this city continues to be considered the capital of "Indian classical dance." The practice and politics of Bharatanāṭyam in today's Chennai make palpable both realist and utopian visions of class, nation, religion, and aesthetics. The invention of South Indian "heritage" is both *told* and *seen* through Bharatanāṭyam. Indeed, embodied heritage, represented by Karṇāṭak music and Bharatanāṭyam dance, is at the heart of South India's urban, middle-class aspirations. In cities like Chennai, dance powerfully mediates the tensions between strangeness and familiarity, tradition and modernity, past and present.

One evening in December 2008, I arrived at an auditorium in Thyagaraya Nagar, Chennai, to attend a dance performance sponsored by the Nungambakkam Cultural Academy Trust, one of the many cultural organizations (*sabhās*) that host the city's annual music and dance events. As I entered through a temporary archway proudly advertising the name of the organization and its corporate supporters, I was greeted by a large table set up by the Thamizhnadu Brahmin Association (THAMBRAAS). A young girl seated behind the table presented guests with a complimentary copy of *Thambraas* magazine and asked them whether they were already a members of the organization. Tickets for the event began at 250 rupees, and the VIP tickets were just over 500 rupees. The dancer performed a "modern" Bharatanāṭyam *varṇam*, one that had been composed just in the past few years by a noted Chennai-based Brahmin composer. Her *varṇam* was about the epic heroine Sītā. It narrated, in an episodic manner similar to that seen in mythological films and television serials, the virtues of Indian womanhood, stressing in particular Sītā's chaste and self-effacing character, interpreted as her power, *śakti*. The performance lasted approximately an hour and a half. Afterward, the dancer was greeted by a number of her friends and family members. The dancer, as it turns out, was an "NRI" Tamil Brahmin, visiting her hometown of Chennai for the music and dance season. This was her last show of the "season" before catching a flight back to California where, with the support of her engineer husband, she runs a dance school that admits over one hundred students.

This anecdote illustrates many aspects of the transnational middle-class morality and cultural economy in which Bharatanāṭyam lives as an art form today. It dramatizes, for example, the ways in which the Tamil Brahmin middle class valorizes bourgeois constructions of art that are clearly rooted in an ethos of orthodox, domestic roles for women. Moreover, organizations like THAMBRAAS nurture Brahmin custodianship over the arts in public culture; they mobilize ideological connections between Brahmin heritage, the arts as cultural capital, and radical assertions of Hindutva in Tamil Nadu (see, for example, Fuller 2001; Hancock 1999; Pandian 2000, 2007).

Brahmin propriety over Bharatanāṭyam has resulted in a reorientation of the aesthetic parameters of dance. These symbolic and somatic shifts have been documented at length by scholars such as Allen (1997), Gaston (1996), Srividya Natarajan (1997), O'Shea (2007), and Meduri (1996). Religious and mythological themes—such as the interpretation of epic narratives seen in the example above—are key elements that self-consciously mark modern Bharatanāṭyam as distinct from courtesan dance. As Matthew Allen has noted, figures like Rukmini Arundale made no qualms about the repopulation of the dance world by Brahmins (Allen 1997), and certainly as M. S. S. Pandian has eloquently pointed out, Brahmin power in the material and cultural domain has been a signpost of Tamil modernity since the nineteenth century (Pandian 2007, 67–76). Today, Brahmin virtuosity in the arts is read as a sign of moral and cultural eminence. It has given rise to an aesthetic standard for dance that draws heavily from cinema, particularly religious cinema, and is, to be sure, highly innovative. "Brahmin taste," to borrow to Kristen Rudisill's term, is universalized through Chennai's global, neoliberal economy. Young Americans and Europeans, for example, flock to Chennai's music and dance season alongside "NRIs" and locals to participate in a moral and aesthetic "tradition" molded by an upper-caste consumer gaze.

Brahmin custodianship of the performing arts, however, does not completely disparage the figure of the *devadāsī*. Today, some of Chennai's cultural elites—for the most part Brahmins associated with dance and music—have attempted to recuperate histories of certain *devadāsī*s whom they consider central to their enterprises of cultural production in the twentieth and twenty-first centuries. The art world in modern Chennai thus commemorates a handful of twentieth-century *devadāsī* artists. These women have been strategically coopted into the scripts of cultural history precisely because they demonstrate "exceptional" qualities for women "of their background." These carefully selected *devadāsī* artists, appropriated and authorized by the world of Chennai's elites as representatives of tradition and heritage in the nationalist imagination, have come to occupy places in the history of arts that other *devadāsī*s could not. As Indira Peterson and I have argued elsewhere, the nationalist reinvention of the arts cannot be read as *the* totalizing project of cultural modernity in South India (Peterson and Soneji 2008); however, the language of nationalist cultural modernity was clearly the only viable medium through which these "exceptional" *devadāsī*s were able to craft and stage their subjectivities. Thus, photographs of the dancer T. Balasaraswati (1918–1984) have made it into most coffee table books about "Indian classical dance," tagged with captions like "Queen of Abhinaya," even though modern performers of Bharatanāṭyam usually mock her dancing as sloppy and unfinished. The vocalist M. S. Subbulakshmi (1916–2004) married prominent Brahmin T. Sadasivam and rose to the cultural front ranks as a domestic icon for Karṇāṭak music in its new twentieth-century form (Weidman 2006, 112–114, 123–128, 145–149). Bangalore Nagarathnam (1878–1952) built a memorial (*samādhi*) for the poet-saint Tyāgarāja in 1925, and thus is remembered as an exceptionally pious devotee of the poet-saint himself. Mylapore Gauri Ammal (1892–1971) is commemorated as the first teacher of Rukmini Arundale and was "attached" to the Kapālīśvara temple in Mylapore, the preeminent site of *smārta* Brahmin cultural nostalgia in the heart of the city. These token gestures toward the *devadāsī* community in the cultural life of modern Chennai are always accompanied by narrative maneuvres—

what Maciszewski (2007, 132–133) has called "mainstream gossip" about courtesans—that reify Brahmin claims over *devadāsī* performance practices. Mainstream gossip about these iconic *devadāsī*s includes, for example, stories that T. Balasaraswati did not want to teach her art or that Rukmini Arundale had to pay for the penniless Gauri's funeral expenses. The strategic deployment of these narratives, whether they are true or not, allow middle-class practitioners to step into this history almost as "rescuers" who repopulate the degenerate arts world and revivify a lost cultural heritage.

Similarly, spaces associated with dance in the city, from the halls of corporate-sponsored cultural organizations (*sabhā*s) to Kalakshetra, the state-sponsored arts institution established by Rukmini Arundale in 1936, belong to the realm of neotraditional public memory. Visitors to these sites encounter the nation and its modernity through gender- and caste-inflected sociomoral discourses encoded in the performances they present. Bharatanāṭyam, as recollected in public memory, celebrates the marriage of capitalism and heritage that is at the core of South India's neoliberal metropolis, described eloquently by Mary Hancock in her new work *The Politics of Heritage from Madras to Chennai* (2008). Sites such as Chennai's *sabhā* halls and Kalakshetra (true *"lieux de memoire,"* to return to Pierre Nora) are preservative in nature: they seek to memorialize authenticating traditions. For the urban elite, there simply are no more "real" *devadāsī*s in the city, and thus the commemoration of a few "acceptable" *devadāsī* women becomes a viable, and certainly profitable, enterprise in the neoliberal economy of urban South India. Ultimately this renewed urban nostalgia about *devadāsī*s only reifies middle-class Brahmin claims to the retrieval and stewardship of *devadāsī* dance and music in the twentieth century. It disseminates historical, moral, and aesthetic pronouncements about *devadāsī* communities in a new cultural market, and inevitably dwells on the perceived successes of *devadāsī* reform. The lingering, undesirable differentness of stigma, however, systemically excludes *devadāsī*s from participating in these larger metropolitan and global flows of culture.

"Saraswati" (b. 1931), who did not wish to be named in this study, lives in the shadow of *devadāsī* reform in today's Chennai. She had *poṭṭukaṭṭutal* performed at the Veṅkaṭeśa Perumāḷ temple in Tanjore in the year 1940 and, like most *devadāsī*s, did not have any ritual obligations in the temple, nor did she ever learn a ritual dance repertoire. Instead, she was trained in the courtly dance traditions of Tanjore by a well-known *naṭṭuvaṉār* in the city. She stopped dancing in public in 1953, six years after the anti-*devadāsī* legislation had been passed, and attempted to focus on becoming a professional vocalist. But Saraswati did not join the emergent film industry, nor did she succeed as a concert vocalist or gramophone artist. Neither did she marry or "adjust" to a domestic lifestyle; she had a relationship with a man and had children, and moved to Chennai. Living in Tondiarpet (a suburb of Chennai) with her children, she went back to dance, and tried to teach to non-*devadāsī* girls in the city. But this, too, was a futile effort. Urban elites were reluctant to send their daughters to *devadāsī*s for training in dance at a time when hereditary male *naṭṭuvaṉār*s received continuous pedagogical opportunities from middle-class practitioners of Bharatanāṭyam. Today, Saraswati has only one student, a young non-Brahmin woman who holds a master's degree in dance from the University of Madras but who like Saraswati has understood that it is near-impossible for a woman of her caste and class background to succeed as a professional dancer in today's Chennai.

Saraswati's story returns to the question of the unfinished nature of *devadāsī* subjectivity in modern South India. How can we characterize her relation to public culture? Even though Saraswati lives in the same city as India's most successful Bharatanāṭyam dancers, she must assume a different temporal position; as a non-Brahmin woman from a *devadāsī* background, she remains suspended in a vestigial, twentieth-century modernity and cannot integrate into the present economies of South Indian culture. Thus, while the *devadāsī* as "icon" becomes the object of a peculiar kind of nostalgia among the middle class, actual women from the *devadāsī* community such as Saraswati live on cultural and social borderlands. Saraswati stands completely outside of what she still considers *her* occupation, yet watches on her TV as Bharatanāṭyam dance morphs into the global commodity that it has become in the twenty-first century. For her, as for many of the women discussed in this book, fragments of the repertoire of nineteenth-century Tanjore, the politics and consequences of social reform, and the real marks of stigma press against each another, causing frictions that arrest the possibility of a socially viable selfhood in contemporary South India.

APPENDIX ONE

Selected Documents from the Files of Muthulakshmi Reddy

1. LETTER (*IN ENGLISH*)[1]

I feel highly thankful to you for your letter of reply to my message of congratulation.

I now want to respectfully inform you that we have started recently a new institution styled "Southern India Yuvathi Saranalayam." This institution is intended for the benefit and upkeep of much of the members of Deva Dhasi Community who at the present moment find themselves helpless if they should abandon their present profession, who all the same dislike a continuance of their profession and who will stop it if they should find the where with all for their future maintenance.

Of course, there may be a number of persons who are well-placed and above want and sufficiently able to live without the assistance such as to be rendered by the above said institution.

In order to efficiently carry on the work it is very necessary that there should be established schools and institutions besides various associations and representative bodies all over the presidency for the promotion of the welfare of the community and for the total abolition of unchastity.

It is also necessary that Government nominates able representation of our community to the local Boards and Municipal Councils so that they man voice forth the grievances and have them redressed.

From your high and noble place, Madam, you have rendered yeoman service for the welfare of this community.

We are also contemplating to hold a conference to concert effective measures for the attainment of our aims.

I am troubling you with the above details only with a view to keep you informed of the activities of the Sangam here and elsewhere so that you may push forth the suitable legislation in the Council and I beg of you to give us a generous corner in your heart and render us every possible help that lies in your hands for our uplift and institute such measures as would make our aspiration to have its fulfilment.

I beg to assure you, Madam, on this happy occasion of your success, of our deep and sincere loyalty and gratitude to the Government of which you are so distinguished an ornament and which has of late evinced such a real and abiding interest in the elevation of this community in India. We are willing and obedient to render any assistance in the said direction.

Begging to be excused for the trouble and very obediently yours.

P. Shanmugananantha

Vice-President of the Tanjore Dt. Esai Vellalar Sangam

2. HANDBILL (*IN TAMIL*)[2]

A Repudiation of the Rutrakaṇikai Caṅkam of Ceṉṉai by the Icaivēḷāḷar Caṅkam of Kudalur, Tanjore district

. . . Unable to tolerate the atrocities committed by women of this community, the merciful Lord bade the goddess Mahālakṣmī herself to incarnate herself as Dr. Muthulakshmi to redeem these women and ensure they live a respectable life . . . Having heard of our support to this bill, some in the Ceṉṉai Uruttirakaṇikaiyar Caṅkam have opposed this bill and have described us as "selfish" individuals who have clamped down like an axe on our own clan. In this way, they have revealed their greatness! It is pathetic to know that their intention is to wear the *poṭṭu* under the pretext of serving the god only to satisfy the sexual lust of the so-called aristocratic devotees of the temple. This great "religious" secret is now exposed. It is the traditional practice to honor the 63 *nāyaṉār*s and 12 *āḻvār*s by installing their images in the temples. For some unknown reason, we have assumed that such great men are not seen in these advanced days of *kaliyuga*. It is now clear that the great men who visit the houses of the *rudragaṇikā*s, "beloved to the Lord," are none other than the great servants of god. Therefore, we have come forward to deliver some good news. It is as follows:

You seem to have the support of some members of the Legislative Assembly and the public to oppose the bill proposed by Dr. Muthulakshmi. Hence we suggest that in the first place you oppose and reject the bill.

Thereafter, you can compile a list the dignitaries who visit your homes [for sex], and after their death, construct a temple with their images installed. Since it is important to worship these images, you may want to stage a protest demanding allocation of funds collected through land tax for this project over the next ten years. We wish you success in securing these funds from the government.

By the way, we return to you the two epithets—"selfish people" and "harmful traitors of the clan"—that you have conferred upon us because of our support of this bill.

May you delight in stringing these two names to both sides of the emblem of prostitution (*poṭṭu*) worn by your women, just as married women string beads to both sides of their *tāli*.

Members of the Icaivēḷāḷar Caṅkam, Kudalur, Tanjore district

3. NEWSPAPER REPORT (IN TAMIL)[3]

The Question of *Devadāsīs*: A Meeting of the *Devadāsī*s, Cheyyur

The meeting of the *devadāsī*s of the Devasthanams of temples in Chinglepet district including the Kantasvāmi temple, Valmīkanāta temple, and Nīlamāṇikkasvāmi temple took place in the outer *maṇḍapa* of the Cheyyur Kantasvāmi temple. All the *devadāsī*s and men assembled in large members, and the association was formed. Smt. Sharada Ammal and Smt. Doraisani Ammal of Ceyyur were unanimously elected as president and secretary, respectively. Twenty-five people were registered as members of this association.

Following speeches by Smt. Sharada Ammal, Smt. Doraisani Ammal, Smt. Sundarambal, and Smt. Balambal about the importance of unity among *devadāsī*s, their progress, and the bill of Dr. Muthulakshmi Ammal, the following resolutions were proposed and passed unanimously:

1. This meeting severely opposes the resolution brought by Smt. Muthulakshmi Ammal in Chennai Legislative Assembly.
2. The ancient honorable religious practice of tying *poṭṭu* in the temples is not related whatsoever to the mean practice of prostitution. Hence this meeting requests our benevolent Government not to appeal any bill that will put an end to our ancient traditional rights.
3. This meeting vehemently condemns speaking and writing in a base manner about a respectable community, comparing them with dis-

honorable prostitutes, in the context of forging a bill to eradicate prostitution.

4. Individuals will naturally object to any law which goes against their religion, social practices, and rights. It is improper that our Muslim and Christian brothers and sisters also support this bill which has been proposed without proper investigation. The secretary records that the meeting regrets the support of Muslims and Christians for this bill.

4. HANDBILL (IN TAMIL)

Ceṉṉai Uruttirakaṇikaiyar Caṅkam
Printed by V. Nayak & Co. Printers, Madras, 1927[4]

It is certain that the bill to abolish the practice of tying the *poṭṭu* will put an end to the social practices and hereditary rights of our community, and this has created unending worries for us. The intention of this bill is not clear, and likewise it is not clear as to how many sisters of our community support this bill. We have the right to insist that it is improper for an individual to arrive at a conclusion about the practices of a particular community based on the opinion of selfish general public, without obtaining the permission of that community, however. Likewise it is neither appealing to law nor to god, to either support this opinion or seek the government's help in this regard. Though not justifiable by law, will this be effective in fulfilling your intentions and usher in the desired results? It is not so. It is proper to venture into any action only after studying its ability to yield the desired results. It is unbelievable that prostitution can be eliminated by putting an end to the practice of tying the *poṭṭu*. The supporters of this bill give the lame excuse that a majority of *icaivēḷāḷars* support this agitation to destroy this practice of tying the *poṭṭu*. *Icaivēḷāḷar*s are none other than the male members of this community, and it is strange that they support this agitation. Let us think carefully about the intention behind this, which is nothing but selfishness. It should be noted that women of this community alone are entitled to inherit property and perform funeral rites as well. It is well known that every human being works in his or her selfish interests alone. The men of this community, who are like axes felling their own community, are responsible for this bill. It is clear that they are doing so with the selfish intention to inherit properties.

The members of this association whole-heartedly and unanimously reject and oppose this bill which will put an end to our ancient rights and properties. This is being conveyed to Dr. Muthulakshmi Ammal, members of the Legislative Assembly, and other sympathizers.

5. NEWSPAPER CLIPPING, EXCERPT (IN TAMIL)

Cutēcamittiraṉ[5]

*Devadāsī*s, who are also referred to as *uruttirakaṇikayar*, are a community of women who, out of devotion to god, worshipped him and offered themselves to him. They performed service (*toṇṭu*) in his temples and lived as pure and noble souls. It seems that Śrīmati Muthulakshmi Ammāḷ has proposed a bill to abolish the practice of tying the *poṭṭu* for *devadāsī* women in temples. We learn from newspapers that some of the brothers and sisters in our province support this bill with much sympathy.

. . . The implementation of such a bill will surely affect the age-old traditions and practices that have been followed by *devadāsī*s with the purest of intentions. Moreover, the question also arises of whether this bill will completely eliminate prostitution (*vipacāram*, *vyabhacāra*) in India, and whether women practicing prostitution will become "purified" (*cuttacaitayarkaḷāy*).

. . . In obedience to the will of the omnipotent Lord, Paravai Nāçciyār, the beloved of Cuntaramūrrti Nāyaṉār, was born in this untainted, pure tradition of *devadāsī*s . . . No survey is known to have been conducted to find out whether prostitution was conducted in a huge level by prostitutes or by *devadāsī*s who belonged to a noble clan that gave birth to Tamil scholars such as Pūṅkōtai.

. . . An objection also arises whether to call all *devadāsī*s prostitutes or call all prostitutes *devadāsī*s . . . It is indeed just to enact any legislation to prevent women from turning into prostitutes. At the same time, it is improper to attempt to destroy a practice that is traditionally sanctioned by religion and is practiced by a respectable community . . . If the Indian Penal Code cannot abolish prostitution, it is inconceivable how banning the practice of tying the *poṭṭu* will abolish prostitution . . . We shall write in detail, at the appropriate time, about the high status and dignity of our community.

Sincerely,
Duraikkannu
Parvati
Servants of Ceṉṉai Śrī
Ēkāmparēsvarar

6. HANDBILL (IN ENGLISH)

The Awakening: Demand for Devadasi Legislation
by Muthulakshmi Reddy (Madras Printing Co., 1928)

We humbly beg to submit that the practice existing in this presidency of dedicating young girls to temples and performing "Gazzela Puza" [*gajjala pūjā*, "worship of the ankle-bells," an important rite-of-passage for courtesans who danced professionally] is fraught with the greatest danger to the women of this community in particular and to the society in general.

Whatever might have been the reasons for this practice in ancient times, it is now an established fact, we are sorry to confess, that the Devadasis are forced to lead an immoral life.

We are initiated at a time when we could not for ourselves discriminate the consequences of our future life and some of us are recruited from other classes for this life of ignominy. It has been our unfortunate lot to be spited by all and we bitterly experience the pangs of our miserable existence. We endure the difficulties in silence and can only curse the custom and the women who have victimised us.

The primary reason for the dedication is the holding of imams by our community for the enjoyment of which we have to perform service in temples. When the women grow old in the service, the trustees and villagers are dissatisfied with them, and to satisfy their demand, young girls are brought up for the service. We need not emphasise the necessary evils attending this practice, having ourselves been victims thereof.

We submit that this is the duty of the well-wishers of society and especially the Government to help us in our efforts of reformation and regeneration. The only remedy to root out the evil and help us is to enfranchise the service imams and grant *pattas* to the present holders.

We beg to draw your immediate attention to the necessity of protecting the minor girls of this community, who are daily subjected to the danger of life-long serfdom. It is our earnest desire that the innocent creatures should be saved from the clutches of people who want to make a living out of the immoral life of the girls.

We are members of the respective Associations organised for the reform and betterment of our community in Andhra and Tamil Nadu. We have already submitted memorials and petitions to the Government to help us to eradicate the evil. If any opposition is raised, it is only engineered by interested parties and we pray that is may not been taken heed of.

Finally we submit that the institution of Devadasis was a subject of condemnation by the poets and sages of India and we have the highest authority to state that there is not even one religious text to sanction this evil practice. We humbly beg to request that you will be graciously pleased to support all measures like the one of Dr. Muthulakshmi Reddy conducive to the reformation of Devadasis for which act of kindness we shall as in duty bound ever pray.

We beg to remain,
PADMAVATI AMMAL
SARADAMBA
RANGANAYAKI AMMAL
BHADRAYAMMA

7. LETTER (IN ENGLISH)

An Open Letter to Sir C. P. Ramaswami Aiyar Avgl. and Doctor Muthulakshmamma Reddi Garoo[6]

Most Honoured Sir & Madam,
The undersigned is the daughter of a respectable devadasi of the original cult here in Bangalore City. Owing to bad Karma she took her birth in the said community and was given training in Arts such as Singing and Abhinaya Shastra as is customary with her profession. She has had good grounding in Arts and won rewards in the Mysore Palace, Sringeri Mutt and such-like places. Though she is middle-aged, she has stopped going for singing parties, being quite disgusted with the deplorable state the Devadasi Institution has reduced itself to.

Without knowing that there are some genuine women in the profession and though there are Shastraic authorities to say that the services to be performed by Devadasees form part and parcel of the worship of God in Hindu temples and that Singing and Dancing in the presence of the Deity are also prescribed, some members of the Madras Legislative Council especially Muthulakshmammal and some Congress Leaders have been condemning the profession wholesale. They have also been carrying on propaganda work to do away with Devadasi system under misapprehension that the morality of the Hindu Society would be improved thereby.

Admitting that there are some black sheep in the family, the moral aspect of the question will not be solved by simply doing away with dedication of girls to temples. There will be ever so many spinsters who are not married, and that is all. No healthy social conditions can be founded on inequality and injustice. Any system that approves and encourages one law for men and another for women in matters of morality, even if it has a "reformative and restraining effect" on women, is in reality only increasing the evils it hopes to check. By simply passing some enactment with regard to the dedication of girls to temples, it is impossible to clear our cities of prostitutes, until men cease to consort with them: for, without male chastity, female chastity is impossible.

If the Government and Congress Leaders want to do away with the so-called black spot in the Hindu Society out of sentimentality, there is no objection for the same.

Devadasees are spoken of as fallen sisters and are said to be helpless victims of a tyrannical pseudo religious custom. If the Govt. and the Congress Leaders really want to introduce reform in the Devadasi system and wean them from the path of wretchedness they should establish at different centres, Rescue Homes, such as Yuvathi Saranalaya at Madras, advise the leading and rich Devadasees to render some help to their community people as the undersigned has been doing in her own humble way (Vide Report on Sree Ramarpana Dhanam), educate their children (male and female) by classifying them as belonging to the Suppressed and Depressed classes and by providing them with liberal scholarships, discourage fostering of children, and encourage marriages amongst them, give some appointments such as nurses in hospitals and Singing mistresses at schools to their community people and amend their law of inheritance.

The humble suggestion of the undersigned is that by introducing such reforms within, the object of the Govt. and the Congress Leaders will be gained and not by any enactment which reduces the status of Devadasees to a more miserable condition by simply doing away with Dedication of girls to temples.

She begs to remain, Most Honoured Sir & Madam,

Your Obedient Servant,
B. Varalakshamma
Bangalore City,
Dated 30th Jan. 1928

APPENDIX TWO

The Madras Devadasis (Prevention of Dedication) Act of 1947

An act to prevent the dedication of women as devadasis in the Province of Madras

(Public [A] Section, Ministry of Home Affairs [1947])

Whereas the practice still prevails in certain parts of the Province of Madras of dedicating women as "*devadasis*" to Hindu deities, idols, objects of worship, temples and other religious institutions;

AND WHEREAS such practice, however ancient and pure in its origin, leads many of the women so dedicated to a life of prostitution;

AND WHEREAS it is necessary to put an end to the practice;

It is hereby enacted as follows:

1. (1) This Act may be called the *Madras Devadasi (Prevention of Dedication) Act*, 1947.
   (2) It extends to the whole of the Province of Madras
2. In this Act, unless there is anything repugnant in the subject of context –
   (a) "dedication" means the performance of any ceremony, by whatever name called, by which a woman is dedicated to the service of a Hindu deity, idol, object of worship, temple or other religious institution, and includes *'pottukattu'*, *'gajje puja'*, *'mudri'* and dancing by *'kumbhaharathy'*;
   (b) "*devadasi*" means any woman so dedicated;
   (c) "woman" means female of any age.
3. (1) The dedication of a woman as a *devadasi*, whether before or after the commencement of this Act and whether she has consented to such dedication or not, is hereby declared unlawful and void; and

any woman so dedicated shall not thereby be deemed to have become incapable of entering into a valid marriage.

Nothing contained in this sub-section shall be deemed to affect the operation of Section 44-A of the Madras Hindu Religious Endowments Act, 1926, or the rights to which a *devadasi* is entitled under that section.

(2) Any custom or usage prevailing in any Hindu community such as the Bogum, Kalavanthula, Sani, Nagavasulu, Devadasi and Kurmapulu, that a woman of that community who gives or takes part in any *melam* (nautch) dancing or music performance in the course of any procession or otherwise is thereby regarded as having adopted a life of prostitution and becomes incapable of entering into a valid marriage, and the performance of any ceremony or act in accordance with any such custom or usage, whether before or after the commencement of this Act whether the woman concerned has consented to such performance or not, are hereby declared unlawful and void.

(3) Dancing by a woman, with or without *kumbhaharathy*, in the precincts of any temple or other religious institution, or in any procession of a Hindu deity, idol or object of worship installed in any such temple or institution or at any festival or ceremony held in respect of such a deity, idol or object of worship, is hereby declared unlawful.

4. (1) Any person having attained the age of sixteen years who after the commencement of this Act performs, permits, take part in, or bets the performance of any ceremony or act for dedicating a woman as a *devadasi* or any ceremony or act of the nature referred to in Section 3, subsection (2); shall be punishable with simple imprisonment for a term which may extend to six months, or with a fine which may extend to five hundred rupees or both.

Explanation: The person referred to in this section shall include the woman in respect of whom such ceremony or act is performed.

(2) Any person having attained the age of sixteen years who dances in contravention of the provisions of Section 3, subsection (3), or who abets dancing in contravention of the said provisions, shall be punishable with simple imprisonment for a term which may extend to six months, or with a fine which may extend to five hundred rupees or both.

5. No court inferior to that of a Presidency Magistrate or a Magistrate of the First Class shall inquire into or try any offence punishable under Section 4.

NOTES

INTRODUCTION

1. As early as 1870, the Madras High Court was citing the writings of missionary Abbe Dubois to prove "beyond historical doubt" that a *devadāsī* of the "Soobramania Swamy Pagoda of Triporoor [Tirupporur]" had adopted girl children for the sake of bringing them up as prostitutes, *Madras High Court Reports, Exparte Padmavati* (1870): 416. In 1901, Edgar Thurston (1855–1935) was appointed as the superintendant of ethnography for the Madras presidency. Thurston's own background was a medical one, and he had, as Nicholas Dirks mentions, a love for anthropometry, which he felt could be useful for the state in helping to identify persons belonging to "criminal tribes" (2000, 165). In 1909, Thurston published his well-known work *Castes and Tribes of Southern India* in seven volumes. The study was produced with the aid of K. Rangachari, a lecturer in botany at Presidency College in Madras. The entry entitled "Dēva-Dāsi" in *Castes and Tribes* runs for twenty-eight pages and is a work that brings census reports and earlier anthropological studies into conversation with a number of legal cases involving *devadāsī*s brought before the Madras High Court from 1876—to 1900. Like the anthropological works he cites, Thurston also conflates the *devadāsī*s of the Tamil- and Telugu-speaking regions with Dalit women known as *basavi*s, and several pages are dedicated to "*basavi*s-as-*devadāsī*s" (Thurston and Rangachari 1909, 2: 133–138). But the style of the work makes it appear both comprehensive and systematic, and perhaps for this reason, it is cited in almost all subsequent writing in English on the subject of *devadāsī*s. Thurston continues to be invoked as authoritative by anthropologists writing about *devadāsī*s in the late twentieth century. Amrit Srinivasan, for example, calls Thurston's work "one of the most exhaustive, descriptive accounts extant on the subject of the period predating the ban on temple dedication" (1984 87). Even though later writings draw extensively from it as if it were a primary source, other than a very brief description of *dāsī*s from the *kaikkōḷar* or weaver community, there is in fact almost nothing original in it. It is representative of what Said has called the "citationary" nature of Orientalism, a selective accumulation of knowledge that results in the "restorative citation of antecedent authority" (Said 1978, 176). Another important point

here is the emphasis that Thurston places on *devadāsīs* in Anglo-Indian courts. The last nine pages of his work are citations from court cases that address issues around rights of inheritance, but also the sale and adoption of girls by *devadāsīs* and temple dedications. Thurston deliberately chooses those passages from the law reports that give the reader a sense of the "customs" of *devadāsīs*, and in doing so he creates accessible, intelligible, and definitive knowledge about these communities—a knowledge drawn from the Anglo-Indian legal system itself. The enduring power of this knowledge can be seen in the fact that Madras High Court cases involving *devadāsīs* that postdate the publication of *Castes and Tribes* cite Thurston as the authority on the legal and cultural practices within the community. For example, in *Bera Chandramma (Wife of Lachanna) v. Chandram Naganna* (April 19, 1923), Thurston's text is used to establish equal rights of inheritance between men and women in *devadāsī* communities.

2. Scholarly literature on Dalit *jogatis* is extensive, and ranges from popular writings such as those by figures like William Dalrymple to scholarly dissertations. Sustained academic discussions on the subject include those by Assayag (1990), Bradford (1983), Epp (1992, 1995, 1997), Evans (1998), Ramberg (2006), and Vijaisri (2004).

3. Traditions of dedicating girls to the goddess Yellammā or her guardian Poṭurāju are found in and around the Nizamabad district in the Telangana region. For details, see Chakrapani (1992); Chandra Mowli (1992); and Misra and Koteswara Rao (2002). Chandra Mowli notes that in the popular imagination, *jogatis* are often confused with mid-caste courtesans known as *kalāvantulu* ("women artists"), who are the subject of this book (1992, 5).

4. On the Gaṅgamma tradition of *mātammas*, see Handelman (1995), Flueckiger (2007), and Flueckiger's forthcoming book, *When the World Becomes Female: The Gangamma Goddess Tradition of South India.* The word *mātamma* comes from Mātaṅgi, a female deity understood in rural South India as the sister of Yellammā-Reṇukā-Māriyammaṉ. The tradition of dedicating girls to local goddesses (*kirāmatēvi*) in northern Tamil Nadu is relatively understudied. The only work on this subject is de Bruin (2007). De Bruin calls these women "rural Devadāsīs" in order to differentiate them from women who performed music and dance in (urban and semiurban) temples dedicated to Śiva and Viṣṇu. In November 2007, a thirteen-year-old Scheduled Caste girl was dedicated to a village deity in Thirukkovilur, Villupuram district. An article in the *Hindu* newspaper entitled "Minor girl made 'Devadasi'" noted that the girl's father, the temple priest, and two others were arrested following the incident (anon. 2007).

5. In the Marathi-speaking regions of the Karnataka-Maharashtra border, young Dalit men who came to be known as *vāghyās* ("tigers") were dedicated to local deities such as Khaṇḍobā and Mhālsā through a "sword marriage," and dedicated girls were known as *muraḷīs*. For details, see Vijaisri (2004, 109–110) and data from *Tribes and Castes of Bombay* by R. E. Enthoven (1922, 70–72). The most comprehensive discussion of Khaṇḍobā rituals and ritual actors (including *vāghyās* and *muraḷīs*) is provided by Sontheimer (1997). For details on *jogappas* (transgendered men who are dedicated to the goddess Yellammā), see Bradford (1983), Ramberg (2006), and Reddy (2006, 67–72).

6. Several journalists have reported on these recent innovations to *jogati* reform. See, for example, Shiva Kumar (2009).

7. The full text of the Andhra Pradesh Devadasis (Prohibition of Dedication) Act of 1988 is found in various online sources, including at http://www.lawsofindia.org/statelaw/2693/TheAndhraPradeshDevadasisProhibitionofDedicatedAct1988.html.

8. Dalrymple's essay "Serving the Goddess: The Dangerous Life of a Sacred Sex Worker" first appeared in the *New Yorker*, August 4, 2008 (Dalrymple 2008a). A slightly different version of this piece was subsequently published as "The Daughters of Yellamma" in *AIDS Sutra: Untold Stories from India*, edited by Negar Akhavi (Dalrymple 2008b). The book was published in collaboration with Avahan, the India AIDS initiative of the Bill and Melinda Gates Foundation.

9. Chinmayee Manjunath's article, "Reluctant Inheritors of a Tainted Legacy?" appeared in *Tehelka* on July 17, 2004 (Manjunath 2004).

10. I would like to draw particular attention to the work of ethnomusicologist Amelia Maciszewski (1998, 2006, 2007), whose ongoing work with *tawā'if*s in North India closely parallels the ethnographic component of my project. The courtesans who are the subject of Maciszewski's research face many of the same problems as women from the Tamil- and Telugu-speaking *devadāsī* communities, and Maciszewski's insights are instructive for those interested in the issue of the displacement of hereditary performers in modern South India.

11. As I have demonstrated elsewhere (Soneji 2010), narratives about temple women pervade the precolonial South Indian literary imagination. For example, in Tamil contexts, we have the figures Paravaiyār, Māṇikkanācciyār, and Koṇṭiyammāḷ, all temple women associated with the Tyāgarāja temple at Tiruvarur. The narrative of Māṇikkanācciyār, which appears in the obscure seventeenth-century text *Tiyākarājalīlaikaḷ*, was also likely the inspiration for J. W. Goethe's 1797 German poem "Der Gott und die Bajadere: Indische Legende" (Peterson 2000). On the North Main Street (*vaṭakku vīti*) immediately outlying the Tiruvarur temple complex, there is a small shrine dedicated to Māṇikkanācciyār as a goddess in which she is represented with four arms and worshipped on occasion by the priests of the Tyāgarāja temple. There are also *sthala purāṇa* trans narratives involving temple women such as that of Poṉṉaṉaiyār of Tiruppuvanam (narrated in the *Tiruviḷaiyāṭaṟppurāṇam*) or that of an unnamed woman at the Saurirājaperumāḷ temple in Tirukkannapuram. Similarly in Telugu-speaking South India, figures such as the temple servant turned goddess Māṇikyāmbā of Draksharamam, and the *sthala purāṇa*s trans of the Kŏppeśvara temple at Palivela and the Ācaṇṭeśvara at Achanta tell of miracles related to female temple servants, "*devadāsī*s." The point I wish to make here, however, is that the processes by which these literary figures are identified with living communities of professional dancing women must be understood as clearly modern.

12. I am certainly not the first to have conducted ethnography among *devadāsī*-courtesans in South India. Two major scholarly works—one unpublished and the other published, by Amrit Srinivasan (1984) and Saskia Kersenboom (1987)—contain ethnographic work that has been invaluable for dozens of scholars who have subsequently written about *devadāsī*s, myself included. But I concede that their ethnographies are driven by a focus on the temple, by a predetermined telos, which has left us with key questions around the nonreligious lives of the women they studied. The ethnographic dimensions of this book are not the result of an attempt to recover the subject of the

"temple dancer" and in this sense, the starting point of my work differs considerably from that of both Srinivasan and Kersenboom.

13. A brilliant discussion of the enduring "postcolonial tragedy of victimisation" is found in Ratna Kapur's *Erotic Justice: Law and the New Politics of Postcolonialism* (2005, 95–136).

14. Kanakambujam became famous for singing and performing *harikathā* at Chettiyar weddings all over Madras Presidency. She eventually amassed a large amount of money through her performances and built a palatial home called Kanaka Vilas just across from the Bṛhadambāḷ temple in Pudukkottai. To be sure, *harikathā* provided opportunities for many other women of *devadāsī* backgrounds as well. Women such as Thiruvidaimarudur Rajambal (1893–1933) and Chidambaram Jnanambal (1889–1984) preceded Kanakambujam. Some—such as Trissoor Rukmini and Premavati (dates unknown)—used *harikathā* as a "stepping stone" to enter the world of cinema (Sundaram 2001, 47–50).

15. The Balamani Drama Company also enabled women to watch Tamil drama performances by allotting separate ticketed spaces to women audiences. It is also significant that Balamani's company was not the only all-women's company. Many others were performing contemporaneously (such as the Kannamani Company and Danuvambal Company), but in the case of the Balamani Company, there is some specific information available about the background of its female performers.

CHAPTER ONE

1. This is excerpted from an anonymous article entitled "Tanjore" that appeared in the October 27, 1894, edition of *All the Year Round*, a British literary magazine founded by Charles Dickens. The author dedicates nearly half of his essay to a discussion of "Nautch girls" in the city of Tanjore. It mentions that these dancing women underwent a "symbolical marriage rite with dagger" (*katti kalyāṇam*), which I will discuss in detail below. The importance and visibility of professional dancing women at Tanjore even after the kingdom's complete annexation by the British in 1856 is stressed time and time again in travel writings and histories of British conquest in India. In *A Familiar History of British India* (1858), for example, J. H. Stocqueler writes, "Perhaps in no part of India had the old Hindoo institutions been preserved with greater purity. Every village possessed its temple, with a lofty gateway of massive structure, and an establishment of Brahmins, musicians, and Nautch girls, whose province it was to dance before the idols on festive occasions. It was the very centre of bigotry" (96). Indeed, in the nineteenth century, few writers spoke of Tanjore without reference to its dancers.

2. Olafsson's memoirs refer to *devadāsīs* as *pagóga sírke* (perhaps from the Tamil *cirukki*, "girl"), and *naṭṭuvaṉārs* as *baldor*, from the Portuguese *bailador*, which is related to the well-known term *bayadère*, often used in various European contexts to refer to South Indian *devadāsīs*. See volume 2 of *The life of the Icelander Jon Olafsson, traveller to India written by himself about 1661 A.D. with a continuation by another hand up to his death in 1679*, translated from the Icelandic edition of Sigfus Blondal by Bertha S. Phillpotts (London: Hakluyt Society, 1931), 122–123.

3. Although some scholars have posited a theory of mass migration of performing artists out of Tanjore after its annexation to the British empire in 1856 (Kersenboom 1987, 59; Meduri 1996), I have not seen any evidence of this in the Moḍi documents. Rather, dance and music repertoire from Tanjore traveled to courts as far away as Bobbili, Vizianagaram, Pithapuram, Gadval, Venkatagiri, Mysore, Travancore, Ramanathapuram, and other places with the regular flows of artists from these regions to Tanjore and back throughout the nineteenth and twentieth centuries. Courtly repertoire, we must also remember, also travels through noncourtly patronage, as we see in the salons of colonial Madras. Rather than positing a single moment for the dissemination of these practices, I prefer to think of this as an ongoing process that spanned almost half a century.

4. The one notable exception is an unpublished Ph.D. dissertation from the University of Hyderabad by V.S. Radhika entitled "Development of Sadir in the Court of King Serfoji II (1798–1832) of Tanjore" (1996).

5. Leslie Orr has recently commented on the problematic construction of the "transhistorical *devadāsī*" in scholarly works from the nineteenth and twentieth centuries. As she notes, "the *devadāsīs*' role has been interpreted almost entirely with reference to abstract, overarching conceptions such *śakti* or auspiciousness . . . This approach obscures historical and regional variations in the activities and circumstances of [these] women, effaces the individuality of temple women, and conceals change" (2000, 10).

6. Rāmabhadrāmba, a highly learned courtesan and consort of King Raghunātha Nāyaka (r. 1600–1634), composed a Sanskrit literary masterpiece called *Raghunāthābhyudaya*, valorizing the deeds of the king and linking him explicitly to god by positing his royal career as a reenactment of Rāma's life (for details, see Hiebert 1988). Raṅgājamma was the author of two dramas in the Telugu literary genre known as *yakṣagāna*: *Uṣāpariṇayamu*, describing the love and eventual marriage of the demon Bāṇāsura's daughter Uṣā with Kṛṣṇa's grandson Aniruddha; and *Mannārudāsa Vilāsamu*, celebrating the marriage of King Vijayarāghava Nāyaka and the courtesan Kāntimati.

7. For example, the Telugu literary work *Rājagopāla Vilāsamu* by Ceṅgalvakāḷakavi composed during the reign of Vijayarāghava names several courtesans who dance, sing, and play instruments at the court (Seetha 1981, 52–57; Kusuma Bai 2000, 128–150). A serious study of dance at the Tanjore Nāyaka court is yet to be written.

8. This period is ubiquitously discussed as one of "degeneracy" by early twentieth-century writers. K. R. Subramanian (1928), for example, states that the "isolated Tanjore Raj had no function or mission in the nineteenth century. It had fallen under effete and helpless rulers who fell easy victims to the might and diplomacy of the Nawab and the Company" (73).

9. The Tanjore Moḍi records are written using a unique vocabulary of "Tanjore Marathi" (Tulpule 1973), which includes loan words from Tamil and Telugu. Dates are also reckoned using Muslim Suhura-sana and hegira eras, the Hindu cycle of Bṛhaspati, or the Christian Gregorian calendar.

10. These do not include the very small collection held in Denmark at the National Archives and the National Museum in Copenhagen, and the Maritime Museum in

Elsinore. These records, most of which relate to Tranquebar, were brought to Denmark when Tranquebar was sold to the East India Company in 1845. Sixty-two of these documents have been meticulously edited and translated by Strandberg (1983).

11. This set is referenced in this chapter as TSML, while the published Tamil translations of the Tamil University set are indicated as TU. The numeric indicators refer first to the bundle number, followed by the subbundle number and folio number (where applicable).

12. Statements about sati are also found in the *Strīdharmapaddhati*, a Sanskrit compendium of orthodox *dhārmic* prescriptions for women written by the court scholar Tryambakayajvan during the rule of Śāhajī (Leslie 1989). The text was likely commissioned by his dowager queen mother Dīpāmbā, who is herself the subject of a hagiography in the Sanskrit text *Dīpāmbāmāhātyam* (N. Srinivasan 1984).

13. Venkataramaiya cites a document dated 1912 in which Hīrā and Komaḷam, two "dancing girls" are included on a list of residents of Maṅgala Vilāsam who continued to receive a pension from the palace (1984, 331).

14. The fine was 1 *cakram* and 2 *paṇams*. Moḍi record dated 1825, Tamil University (*hereafter* TU), 1–263. According to Rajayyan (1969, 55), 1 Tanjore *cakram* was equal to roughly 2.5 to 3 Company rupees.

15. Sayajirao Gaekwad III (1863–1939) belonged to the Marāṭhā Gāyakavāḍa dynasty, which historically had associations with both the Peśvās and the Bhosale dynasty. Sayajirao ascended the throne at Baroda in 1875 by selection of the British government. In 1880, he married a woman named Rani Chimnabai (1864–1884), the daughter of a Marāṭhā noble from Tanjore. As part of her dowry, two *naṭṭuvaṉārs*, one *devadāsī*, one *muttu* drummer, and a *nāgasvaram* and *tavil* player were sent to Baroda. The *naṭṭuvaṉārs* were Kannusvami Nattuvanar (1864–1923), who was the grandson of Civāṉantam of the Quartet, and Kuppusvami Nattuvanar (1843–1914). The *devadāsī* was Gauri (1871–1950). Later, the *naṭṭuvaṉār* Appāsvāmi (1862–1935) and the dancer Kantimati (1872–1953) were also brought to Baroda.

16. In the Moḍi records, the variation *kaḷāvantiṇī* is used most often.

17. The romance between the Muslim *kalāvantīṇ* Mastānī and Peśvā Bājīrāv I became one of the most controversial events of the period, and sparked protest among the Citpāvan or Koṅkaṇastha Brahmins who were the family priests or *purohitas* for the Peśvā rulers (Kadam 1998, 70–73).

18. Veṅkaṭ Narsī was from Karnataka and is known to have performed at the court of Peśvā Bājīrāv II for at least seventeen years after he ascended the throne in 1796. The names of some of her accompanists, such as the vocalist Bhikobā and the female drummer Gaṅgā Pakhvājī, are preserved in the Peśvā Daftar (Kadam 1998). For a three-night-long performance in 1802, she was paid Rs. 26, 000 (Shirgaonkar 1995, 65–66; 2010).

19. The name Hīrā ("diamond" in Hindi) appears in a couple of Moḍi documents from the rule of Serfoji II. One Hīrā was a *dāsī* who had her *poṭṭu* tied at the Kāśi Viśvanātha temple at Orattanadu (Muktambalpuram) (TSML, 9/13, 1819).

20. Variations on *śūlā* are found in Tamil (*cūḷai*) and Konkani and Tulu (*sūḷe*). The term is also commonplace in modern Kannada.

21. Moḍi record, dated 1847, Thanjavur Sarasvati Mahal Library, Thanjavur (*hereafter* TSML), 548.

22. Moḍi record, dated 1847, TSML 104–104.

23. Tanjore "Saraswati" (born 1931), for example, had her *poṭṭukkaṭṭu* ceremony performed at the Prasanna Veṅkaṭeśa Perumāḷ temple in 1940. She was trained in dance by Chinnaiya Nattuvanar (1876–1956) and Picchaiya Nattuvanar (1880–1945). She currently lives outside Chennai, and we shall discuss her in greater detail later.

24. Moḍi record, 1882, TSML, 817–6/19.

25. Moḍi record, TSML 123C/11.

26. Moḍi record, TSML 2C-17/3.

27. Moḍi record, dated 1802, TSML, 104C.

28. The *Bṛhadīśvaramāhātmyam* is a thirty-chapter text in Sanskrit about various Cōḻa, Cēra, Pāṇṭiya, and Vikrama kings who patronize, renovate, and worship at the Bṛhadīśvara temple in Tanjore as well as several other important Śaiva temples in the region. It was translated into Marathi as *Tañjapurī Mahātmya* by a court poet named Śeṣakavi during the rule of King Amarasiṃha. It was then translated into Tamil during Serfoji's rule. Another Sanskrit text, the *Tañjāpurīmāhātmyam*, is about the Vaiṣṇava temples in and around Tanjore city. Each of these texts has been edited and published by the Sarasvati Mahal Library.

29. The Quartet also composed a number of *kīrtana*s (devotional songs) on Bṛhadīśvara and Bṛhannāyaki.

30. Civakkoḻuntu Tēcikar was born in the town of Kottaiyur in Sivagangai district and worked in Serfoji's experimental hospital, Dhanvantari Mahal. He was eventually appointed Tamil *pandit* at the College of Fort St. George in Madras. Another text, the *Devendra Koravañji* in Marathi, is attributed to Serfoji himself. In this unique work, the Kuṟa woman narrates her travels in the form of a geography of the modern world (Peterson 2008a).

31. The *kuṟavañci* as a literary genre has been the focus of several important scholarly studies, including those by Buck (2005), Muilwijk (1996), and Peterson (1998a, 2008a, forthcoming). Peterson's approach emphasizes the performative nature of the genre, and she is currently preparing a book-length study on the subject that addresses many of the *kuṟavañci* texts danced by eighteenth- and nineteenth-century *devadāsī*s in the Kaveri river delta.

32. The first of these rehearsals took place two days before *aṣṭakkoṭi* and was known as *ciṉṉa ottikai*. The second took place the following day and was known as *periya ottikai*; it was performed as a dress rehearsal in costume. Both took place in the shrine of Bṛhannāyakī (K. P. Kittappa Pillai, personal communication; Kalyanasuntaravalli 1958).

33. Moḍi record, dated 1801, TSML, 201C-10/987.

34. Moḍi record, TSML, 622-C/36.

35. The available Moḍi records mention the names of "departments" that specialized in music and dance. The "Huzūr Nāṭyaśālā" is one of these, as is the "Saṅgīt Vidyādhik" (music department). We know the names of individuals associated with these departments, but very little else can be said about their location, operating budget, etc.

36. Moḍi record, dated 1845, TSML 90–40/1.

37. A number of *yakṣagāna* texts (Telugu and multilingual ones) are created during

the rule of Śāhajī right through the rule of Śivājī II. Indira Peterson's work on the court dramas (2004a, 2004b, forthcoming) illuminates the complexities of these dramas and the social, religious, and political agendas they engendered.

38. Historically, the Marāṭhā kings patronized these devotional dramas in five villages—Melattur, Saliyamangalam, Tepperumanallur, Uttukkadu, and Sulamangalam. Today, *bhāgavata mēḷa* only survives in three villages: Melattur, Saliyamangalam, and Tepperumanallur. Most writing on *bhāgavata mēḷa* provides only a vague sense of its history and performance practices, and most works inevitably focus on the village of Melattur (for example, Arudra 1986c; Krishna Iyer 1966, 1969; Natarajan 1990; I. Raman 1999; Ranganathan 1982). Critical academic writing on the topic is virtually absent. A brief article by Clifford Jones in the *Journal of Asian Studies* (1963) provides a cursory overview of the form, while a more substantial recent essay has been written by Japanese ethnomusicologist Takako Inoue (2008). It is significant that the *bhāgavata mēḷa* referred to in the Modi records is not limited to the repertoire performed in Melattur, Saliyamangalam, and Tepperumanallur today. A vast number of *bhāgavata mēḷa* plays appear to have been enacted at the court, and although these exist in manuscript form, they do not survive in performance today.

39. Moḍi record, TSML, 22/24.

40. Moḍi record, dated 1814, TSML, 184C/21.

41. Moḍi record, dated 1811, TSML, 123C.

42. The manuscripts are N2464 and T2803, which have been edited by R. Vivekanandagopal and published by the library under the title *Thanjavur Marathi Lavani Songs: Tañjāvūr Marāṭhī Lāvaṇī Vāṅmaya* (1998).

43. For more on *gondhaḷa* traditions in Maharashtra, see Dhere (1988).

44. The texts of some traditional *gondhaḷa* songs from Tanjore have been published by the Sarasvati Mahal Library. See Bhima Rao (1990).

45. Moḍi record, dated 1819, TSML, 503.

46. Moḍi record, dated 1829, TU, 165C-32.

47. Moḍi record, dated 1837, TSML, 1–133.

48. One writer, in 1935 notes that "'Kinjin' corresponds to the 'tillana' in the Southern dramatic tradition; and it is said of Sitarama Bhagavatar of Soolamangalam, an expert in feminine dance and a consummate master of the art of revelation in concealment, that hundreds of professional dancing girls would hasten to witness his renderings to learn therefrom" (Ramachandran 1935, 3). Another Brahmin performer of *bhāgavata mēḷa* plays was popularly known as "Kinjin" Kodandarama Ayyar, and by the twentieth century, the term *kiñjin* also came to refer to a kind of marionette puppet theater, in which the marionettes were invariably dressed as North Indian dancers. This type of performance, known as *kiñjin bommalāṭṭam*, was presented regularly at the Mangala Gana Sabha in Kumbhakonam well into the twentieth century.

49. Moḍi record, TSML, 2–6/46.

50. For more on the tradition of males performing courtesan dance at the Tanjore court, see Krishnan (2009).

51. Moḍi record, dated 1844, TU, 4–263.

52. This painting was the subject of a short essay by archaeologist and historian R. Nagaswamy entitled "Thanjavur Natya on Canvas" (1989). However, Nagaswamy

only understood this as a representation of North Indian cultural practices at the court, and not as a sign of the court's hybrid cultural practices.

53. Moḍi record, dated 1770, TU, 8–9.

54. Muttusvāmi Dīkṣitar and his brother Bālusvāmi were patronized by Venkatakrishna Mudaliyar, an agent-*dubash* for the East India Company. Venkatakrishna Mudaliyar (d. 1817) and his father, Muddukrishna Mudaliyar (d. 1792) were both *dubash*es of George Pigot (1719–1777), governor of Fort St. George (Madras) in 1755–1763 and 1775–1777. Venkatakrishna Mudaliyar is also mentioned in the *Sarvadevavilāsa*, will I discuss in chapter 2. They were the *zamīndār*s of Manali, a small suburb of Madras near Tiruvottriyur. Venkatakrishna Mudaliyar would often take the two brothers to Fort St. George to listen to the Company's marching bands. According to one narrative, this is how Bālusvāmi learned the violin, which subsequently became the major melodic accompaniment for Karṇāṭak vocal music (Weidman 2006, 29–30).

55. Consider the following anecdote about Rukmini Arundale (1904–1986), one of the key figures who enabled the repopulation of *devadāsī* dance by middle-class women. In her search for the present-day "remnants" of a classical performance heritage, Arundale traveled to Tanjore where she saw one of the last performances of the *Carapēntira Pūpāla Kuṟavañci* by *devadāsī*s at the Bṛhadīśvara temple. She dismissed the performance as artless and low, as it was written in praise of a *mortal*, not a *god*. She vowed to recapture the former "glory" of the *kuṟavañci* and later choreographed the *Tirukkuṟṟāla Kuṟavañci*, which was dedicated to the god Śiva but only existed in textual form. She had the text tuned, and presented this in Madras in 1944.

56. Ciṉṉaiyā moved to the Mysore court at the invitation of Kṛṣṇarāja Uḍaiyār III (r. 1811–1868), and in 1834, the brothers were invited to perform at the court of Svāti Tirunāl (1813–1846), king of Travancore. Impressed by Vaṭivēl's mastery of music in general and the violin in particular, Svāti Tirunāl appointed him as one of the resident musicians of his court. He also gifted Vaṭivēl with an ivory violin marked with the date "1834" (currently in the house on West Main Street) and an ivory box filled with jewels inscribed with an image of the Travancore palace (currently held by descendants in Chennai). Ciṉṉaiyā and Vaṭivēl lived in Mysore and Travancore, respectively, for the entire duration of their later careers, and the critical aesthetic innovations they had earlier made at Tanjore traveled into these regions by the middle of the nineteenth century.

57. Rāmu Naṭṭuvaṉār served in Pratāpasiṃha's court and was the guru of Muddupaḷani, a courtesan who wrote the Telugu text *Rādhikā Sāntvanamu*. His descendants Vaṭivēlu Naṭṭuvaṉār (c. 1870–1930) and his brother Ciṉṉaiyā Naṭṭuvaṉār (1876–1956) were the last dance -masters in this family. Vocalist M. Thyagarajan (d. 2007) was the last musician in this family. Veṅkaṭakiruṣṇa Naṭṭuvaṉār served in the court of Serfoji II, and his descendant Pañcāpakēca Naṭṭuvaṉār (1842–1902) coauthored a Tamil work called *Apiṉaya Navanītam* ("Clarified Essence of Abhinaya") in 1886 (Krishnan 2008). Their lineage continued with Kuppaiya Pillai (1887–1981) and his family, who established the dance academy Rajarajeswari Bharata Natya Kala Mandir in Mumbai in the 1940s.

58. Strategic colonial deployments of "nautch" in Madras date back to 1727, as we shall see in the next chapter. My point here is that "salon" style performances and the mobilization of *devadāsī* dance to express power relations between colonial admin-

istrators and natives existed in Madras city even before the time of Serfoji II and the Quartet. It is not a stretch, therefore, to conceive of "Tanjore court dance" (as it evolved at the hands of the Quartet, for example) as created specifically for a new culture of colonial, salon-style presentation.

59. The manuscripts were discovered by B. M. Sundaram in the home of Chokkalingam Pillai (1892–1972), son of Svaminatha Nattuvanar, a descendent of the Quartet, in Thiruthuraipoondi. Most of the horoscope or *jātakam* manuscripts were written by a man named Govindaraja Pillai, an astrologer-cousin of Svaminatha Nattuvanar, but many such as those of Gopala Nattuvanar, appear to be early nineteenth-century texts. An example of the full text of one of these birth *jātakams*, that of Vaṭivēlu (of the Quartet), reads as follows:

> Birth Horoscope of Vaṭivēlu, with Blessings of Long Life
> In the auspicious Pramodūta year, the month of Puraṭṭāci, on the morning of Monday the 24th morning at 21–22 [these are *nāḻikai*, 2 ½ *nāḻikai*s make one hour, counted from the moment of sunrise] of sunrise hour 11–8, under the star *tiruvōṇam*, at the auspicious moment of 8.12 in the morning, Centilvēl alias Vaṭivēlu, the youngest son of Cuppirāya Naṭṭuvaṉār of the Tanjavur fort was born. With the star *tiruvōṇam*, the powerful effects of the moon (*candra-mahādaśā*) will last for another 3 years, 5 months 2 days. The end of *candra-daśā* will be on 10–3-1814.

60. The family was led by Makātēva Naṭṭuvaṉār (1734–1791), and his two brothers Kaṅkaimuttu (1737–1798) and Irāmaliṅkam (dates unknown). Tuḷajā II granted Cupparāya Naṭṭuvaṉār five units (*veḷis*) of wet land and the house (Sundaram 1997, 31). In 1917, Abraham Pandither, in his encyclopedic work on South Indian music, *Karunamirtha Sagaram*, also mentions Cupparāya Naṭṭuvaṉār:

> Subbaraya Nattuvanar. Proficient in Bharata Sangeeta Sahityam. His Varnams and Keertanams are in praise of Tulajaji maharajah and the deity. He was presented by the Maharajah with a palanquin and other paraphernalia, with land, jewels and with the residence known as Nattuvan Chavadi. (Pandither 1917, 179)

61. Moḍi record, dated 1780, TSML, 545–12. The full text of this Moḍi document reads as follows:

> parvāṅgī hujūr: mahārāja tuḷajarāje sāheb kaḷāvanta subarāyapaikī vilāyatīce kaḷāvantiṇī va naṭhamūṭhagāra dikhiḷa—hujūr sīmaṅgīyāce saṇā badala hājīr jāhale tyāsapoṭagī daṇḍaka pramāṇe roja 9 phaḷam pramāṇe hājīra jāhale terike pāsuna simagī paurṇimā tāgāyī roja dar-roja deṇe

62. TU 4–263, 1844.

63. The available Moḍi records themselves surprisingly contain no references to the brothers, with the exception of one letter signed in Tamil by "Civāṉanta Naṭṭuvaṉ." Unfortunately this document exists in two versions—one which identifies Civāṉanta Naṭṭuvaṉ as the son of Cupparāyaṉ, and another as the son of Paramāṉanta Naṭṭuvaṉ.

64. Sundaram (2002b) also notes that two other untitled manuscripts at Sarasvati Mahal (B11618 and B11605C) also contain *varṇams* and *svarajatis* attributed to the Quartet.

65. The "fact" of this standardization of courtly performance can only be documented through oral narratives. For this reason, even the *content* of this suite is contested. For example, in some accounts, another genre, *jāvaḷi*, which we discuss in detail in the next chapter, is included in the suite, and the *śloka* is not.

66. The descendants of the Quartet survive in several lineages located across contemporary Tamil Nadu. While one small branch of the family continues to live in the ancestral home on West Main Street, and others are settled in Chennai, a great number also live in Pandanallur village, Ammachatram, and Thiruthuraipoondi. My main source for oral narratives about the Quartet was the late K. P. Kittappa Pillai (1919–1999), a fifth-generation descendant of the Quartet who taught dance and also was responsible in the 1950s for publishing the earliest notated versions of the Quartet's compositions.

67. Some of these compositions include a number of *svarajatis* dedicated to figures such as Pāṇṭitturai Tēvar (1867–1911), the *zamīndār* of Palavanattam (Ramanathapuram district), which are actually the compositions of Vadivelu Nattuvanar II (1869–1914), the grandson of Civāṉantam of the Quartet.

68. Unlike his contemporaries Tyāgarāja (1767–1847) and Śyāma Śāstri (1762–1827), Dīkṣitar is remembered for his interactions with the *devadāsī* and *naṭṭuvaṉār* community, and this forms an important part of biographical sources about Dīkṣitar. One of his main disciples was "Śuddhamaddaḷam" Tampiyappaṉ, son of Gurumūrti Naṭṭuvaṉār (1760–1802), who, like the Quartet's father, was also invited to Tanjavur by King Tulaja II (Sundaram 1997, 32; 2002a, 173). According to P. R. Thilagam (b. 1926), the last descendant of the *koṇṭi-paramparā devadāsīs* of the Tiruvārūr temple, one of her ancestors Kamalamuttu had the Telugu song *"nī sāṭi daivamandu"* (Śrīrañjani *rāga*) composed for her by Dīkṣitar, who was also her music guru (P. R. Thilagam, personal communication, January 1999). There is also a set of nine Telugu *kīrtanas* (devotional songs) said to be composed by the brothers as a tribute to their *guru*, Dīkṣitar. These were edited and published by K. Ponnaiya Pillai in 1940 in a book of notations entitled *Tañcai Peruvuṭayaṉ Pericai*. For details on Dīkṣitar's life, see Dīkṣitulu (1904); for notes on his musical style, particularly his emphasis on "place," see Peterson (1986) and Te Nijenhuis and Gupta (1987).

69. We know that both of these women were historical figures. Mīnākṣī of Mannargudi was the great-grandmother of the famous contemporary *tavil* (drum) percussionist Mannargudi Rajagopala Pillai, and Pudukkottai Ammāḷu lived from 1835 to 1886 (Sundaram 2003, 243–247).

70. References to the performance of Kṣetrayya's *padams* appear in a variety of nineteenth- and early twentieth-century print materials that discuss dance by courtesans. A very early English essay by P. Ragaviah Charry, published in 1801 (the period of Serfoji II) that we will discuss in detail in chapter 3 notes that Kṣetrayya's *padams* were central to courtesan performance in Madras at the turn of the century. It also provides the first-ever English translation of two *padams*. *Abhinaya Svayambodhini* (1915), a Telugu work by Vīrarāghava Śāstri, contains a large number of Kṣetrayya *padams* with instructions for how to perform *abhinaya* for each.

71. The focus on the continued patronage of drama and linear narrative, as Indira Peterson notes, indexes the early Marāṭhā interest "in the power of *emplotment* in action, the actual enactment of texts and narratives through gesture, mime and dance

[and thus in] the representational power and dialogism of *drama in performance*, a quality unavailable in other literary forms" (2004, 6).

72. Śāhajī's *padams* on Śiva-Tyāgarāja have been edited by N. Visvanathan (1980). The court poet Vāsudeva Kavi produced a vast number of Sanskrit and Tamil *padas* on Śāhajī and other local landowners. These have been edited by N. Srinivasan (1999, 2006). The *śabda*s and *salām-daruvu*s (salutation songs) by Kāśināthayya and Nāraṇa Kavi have been edited by N. Visvanathan (1985).

73. Śāhajī's court was marked by a proliferation of dramas, some of which were among the earliest multilingual literature produced under Marāṭhā patronage. Indira Peterson has written extensively about the production of drama at the Tanjore court (Peterson 1998a, 2004a, 2004b, forthcoming). The *Śaṅkara-kālī-naṭana-saṃvāda-nāṭaka*, for example, describes a dance contest between Bhadrakālī and Śiva of Tiruvenkadu (Śvetāraṇya), and is written in Marathi, Telugu, Tamil, and Sanskrit. The *Pañcabhāṣā-vilāsa*, as Peterson has noted, is "not only a multilingual play, but a play *about* multilingualism" (Peterson, forthcoming). Composed in Tamil, Telugu, Marathi, Hindi, and Sanskrit, it aestheticizes language in an eighteenth-century "response to the pleasures and burdens of polyglossia" (20). Other major dramatic works produced under Śāhajī's patronage include *Gaṅgā-kāverī-saṃvāda-nāṭaka* (The argument between Gaṅgā and Kāverī) and *Satidāna Śūramu*, recently discussed by Narayana Rao and Shulman (2002, 354ţ380). Of particular note for our purposes is the text known as *Śaṅkara Pallaki Seva Prabandhamu*, which describes the daily palanquin service (*pallaki sevā*) of Śiva as Tyāgarāja that was performed in the Tiruvarur temple. Excerpts from this text were apparently sung by *devadāsī*s in that temple at the time of certain festivals, and their tunes were notated for posterity by musicologist P. Sambamoorthy in 1955. A Telugu text specifically meant for *bhāgavata mēḷa* performance, *Sītā Kalyāṇamu*, is also attributed to Śāhajī (Visvanathan and Srinivasan 1993).

74. The *Śāhavilāsa Gītam* consists of *aṣṭapadī*s that are parallel in form and content to those in the *Gītagovinda*. The text has been edited by S. Ramanathan (1985).

75. The word *koravañji* is used in the Telugu literary work *Raghunāthanāyakābhyudayamu* (1.499), produced in Nāyaka-period Tanjore. However, the earliest extant *kuṟavañci* text in Tamil appears to be the *Tiyākēcar Kuṟavañci*, dedicated to Śiva at Tiruvarur. It is almost universally believed that this text was composed during the reign of Śāhajī because of the king's devotion to Śiva-Tyāgarāja, and because his name is mentioned in one of the benedictory verses of the text. In addition, the only *kuṟavañci* text in Sanskrit, the *Mohinīvilāsa Kuravañji Nāṭakam* attributed to a court poet named Kavi Saptaṛṣi, was also composed during Śāhajī's reign. This text has been edited by N. Srinivasan (1985).

76. During the rule of Serfoji I, the court composer Girirāja Kavi, who also served during Śāhajī's rule, composed a number of erotic *padas*, perhaps meant for dance (Seetha 1981, 87). Two important *yakṣagāna* texts, the Telugu *Śivakāmasundari Pariṇaya Nāṭakamu* (Seetha 1971; Peterson 2004a) and the Sanskrit *Rājarañjana Vidyā Vilāsa Nāṭaka* (Seetha 1981, 92–94) were also written during his reign. During the reign of Veṅkojī II, son and successor of Tuḷajā I, *yakṣagāna* dramas continued to proliferate. We also hear of a court dancer, Muddumaṅgā, receiving special honors from Veṅkojī II (Seetha 1981, 96).

77. Pratāpasiṃha's court is also significant because of the presence of Muddupaḷani, a courtesan and poet of great accomplishment. Muddupaḷani is the author of *Rādhikā Sāntvanamu* ("Appeasing Rādhā") that describes the passion between Kṛṣṇa and his young new wife Iḷādevī. For details on Muddupaḷani, see Tharu and Lalitha (1993) and Narayana Rao and Shulman (2002, 396–399).

78. An extended discussion of Vīrabhadrayya is found in Sundaram (2002b 24–35). Court musicians composed a number of virtuosic pieces for vocal music performances in this period as well. The *varṇam* genre was also likely crystallized in this period. A figure named Govindasāmayya (eighteenth century, dates unknown) and Paccimiriyam Ādiyappayya (c. 1750–1820), are generally understood as the "fathers" of the complex *varṇam* genre. Ādiyappayya was a contemporary of Vīrabhadrayya (ibid., 28–29). The *varṇam* has been a part of the dance repertoire almost since the inception of the genre, and Govindasāmayya's *varṇams* are still remembered among Telugu-speaking courtesans in the Godavari delta region.

79. The *svarajati* in Huseni *rāga* is rewritten a number of times. One early version is addressed to King Pratāpasiṃha, attributed to Poṉṉaiyā of the Quartet, beginning with the words "e mandayānarā," while another is dedicated to the god Viṣṇu as Varadarāja attributed to Melattur Veṅkaṭarāma Śāstri (1743–1809), a *bhāgavata mēḷa* dance master. Yet another version exists in Marathi, dedicated to Śivājī II (beginning with the words "e mājhā velhāḷā gehālāgi"), and the author of this piece is unknown. Many of these versions are preserved in manuscripts such as *Varṇa Svara Jati* in the Sarasvati Mahal Library (Sundaram 2002b), or in the notebooks of nineteenth-century dance masters such as that of Nellaiyappa Nattuvanar (1859–1905), whom we will encounter in the next chapter. In the early twentieth century, this *svarajati* was also translated into Tamil. Three of the four extant versions are still performed by contemporary urban middle-class Bharatanāṭyam dancers, and have been published with musical notation (Kittappa 1961, 1999).

80. The Tamil version of this *varṇam*, "mōhamāṉa eṉmītil," has been the subject of a major study by Saskia Kersenboom (1995). While oral tradition (and subsequently Kersenboom herself) attributes this version to the Quartet, it is anomalous for two reasons. It is the only composition on this deity attributed to the brothers, and it does not appear in any of the manuscript materials at the Sarasvati Mahal Library in which we find other compositions by the Quartet. For these reasons, like many of the other Tamil compositions attributed to the Quartet, it is safe to say that it was actually composed by one of their later descendants, likely K. Ponnaiya Pillai (1888–1945).

81. A document from 1860 entitled *Native Petition to the Imperial Parliament for the Restitution of the Raj of Tanjore and the Restoration of the Property Confiscated by the Madras Government* contains a very dramatic description of how the colonial government seized palace property as part of the "annexation":

> Besides the sequestration of the elephants, camels, horses, cattle, and carriages, sent up to Madras for sale, posts, pans, and such like culinary utensils were sold off within the palace, in which the Ranees were at the time residing; the doors of private apartments were broken open, and valuable property together with the garments of the ladies carried away; the playthings of the children . . . have been

claimed by the East India Company as "State property"; nothing being too great or too small to escape the rapacity of the marauding inquisitors; or as Her Majesty's Attorney general described it "the universal drag net of the all-grasping Company"; but all and everything, valuable or invaluable, was pounced upon indiscriminately." (1860, 11)

82. Mahātēvaṉ is known to have taught dance to men of the royal Marāṭhā household (Krishnan 2009), and introduced the use of the clarinet in performances of dance by *devadāsī*s (Sundaram 1997, 34). The descendants of the family who continued to live in Tanjore and Pandanallur village ensured that the annual performance of *Carapēntira Pūpāla Kuṟavañci* was kept up until the 1940s.

CHAPTER TWO

1. The patronage of *devadāsī* troupes by Muslims is also found in *Qanoon-e-Islam, or the Customs of the Moosulmans of India* (Shureef and Herklots 1832, lxxxii). This account notes that *mēḷam*s are generally invited to perform at weddings, and mentions the *nutwa* (*naṭṭuvaṉār*) who leads the troupe. Professional dancers in Tanjore also performed in Muslim homes, particularly at the time of marriages. A mid-nineteenth-century painting from Tanjore currently held at the Victoria and Albert Museum (2006AV2428–01) depicts a Muslim marriage procession led by dancers performing in the "Hindustānī" style. The participation of Tanjore's *devadāsī*s in Muslim weddings is also confirmed by musicologist B. M. Sundaram:

> "In Tanjore, there were some *devadāsī* dancers who used to give regular performances in the homes of Muslims, whenever marriages take place there. When someone in those Muslim families died, it was a custom for the *devadāsī* who danced in these homes to gift a goat for the [funerary] meal . . . It shows a mutual respect, a mutual affinity." (Sundaram, personal communication)

2. The dancer "Rangapushpa" Chitra of Tenali district, for example, performed frequently at the Nizam's darbar. The title "Rangapushpa" was given to her by the Nizam in the early twentieth century. She also often performed with tambourines and ribbons, dressed in tights, in a manner consistent with the "Parsi dance" performances described in the introduction. For details on Rangapushpa Chitra, see Ramakrishna (1995, 157).

3. The Mutaliyār *dubash* family of Manali, just outside Madras, maintained connections with the Tanjore court. For more on these connections, see Neild (1977); for details on *dubash*es and culture in colonial Madras, see Hancock (2008), Mukund (2005), Neild-Basu (1984), and Waghorne (2004). For a discussion of the patronage of music by *dubash*es and other commercial elites, see the recent work of Lakshmi Subramanian (2006, 2009).

4. The term "oft-conquered people" is used by missionary Caroline Atwater Mason in her discussion of *devadāsī* immorality (1902, 103–105).

5. Amy Charmichael was the author of a book published in 1912 entitled *Lotus Buds* (a reference to the innocence of young *devadāsī* girls) strewn with photos of girl infants. Charmichael founded the Dohnavur Fellowship, and her work was admired by

a number of British feminists including Katherine Mayo, author of the controversial *Mother India* (1927). Nancy Cho (2009) offers a somewhat celebratory reading of Carmichael that does not problematize her representations of systemic child sexual abuse in colonial India, an issue that was by no means limited to girls in *devadāsī* communities, but rather was very common, largely because of traditions of child marriage among all castes (see, for example, Sarkar 2001, 240).

6. *Devadāsī*s were regularly hired by a number of *zamīndāri* courts (*samasthānams*) in the Madras Presidency. In chapter 4, I explore *devadāsī* performance in the context of Pudukkottai, one of the major "princely states" in Madras. In the nineteenth century, *devadāsī*s also performed at the *samasthānam* courts in Ramanathapuram, Sivaganga, Ettayapuram, Ayyampalayam, Settur, Marungapuri, Ukkadai, and Palavanattam in the Tamil-speaking regions, and Karvetinagaram, Kalahasti, Pithapuram, Tuni, Nuzvid, Bobbili, Vizianagaram, Jayapuram, Venkatagiri, Vanaparti, Gadval, and Kollapuram in the Telugu-speaking regions.

7. The Mayor's Court at Madras was reorganized on this occasion, consisting of a mayor and nine aldermen with the power to make decisions on all civil court cases among English inhabitants. The procession included Major John Roach on horseback, followed by foot soldiers playing drums, trumpets, and other instruments, and a troupe of "dancing girls with country music" (T. Wheeler 1878, 133).

8. Unfortunately, critical analysis of photographic representations of professional dancers from colonial South India is severely lacking, despite the great abundance of photos available in archival sources. With the exception of one essay by Joachim Bautze (2006), which is largely descriptive and very brief, and an unpublished work by Sujatha Meegama (2004) dealing with photographic representations of dancers from Ceylon, almost no scholarly writing exists on this subject. More recently, Saloni Mathur's work, which interrogates issues around gender and the visual archive, has included a short but critical analysis of representations of "nautch girls" in photographs from North India (2007, 109–132).

9. *Herald*, February 7, 1838 cited in the *Asiatic Journal and Monthly Register* 26 (May–August 1838): 149–150.

10. British observers' incredulity at the native ability to endure pain and the resonances of such observations in colonial anthropology is the focus of Nicholas Dirks's (1997) brilliant essay "The Policing of Tradition: Colonialism and the Anthropology of Southern India."

11. A sort of "instruction manual" for *pinnal kōlāṭṭam* at Tanjore exists in the form of a Marathi manuscript entitled *Dorā Dharūṇa Gopha Veṇi Paddhati* (Krishnaswamy Mahadik Rao, 2005). The performance of *pinnal kōlāṭṭam* by *devadāsī*s is also mentioned in some detail by Dr. John Shortt in his anthropological essay "The Bayadère; or, Dancing Girls of Southern India" (1867–1869, 190–191).

12. Ragaviah Charry was a "native informant" for Holt Mackenzie's Mysore Survey Project. Holt Mackenzie (1787–1876) is best remembered for drafting a memorandum on land revenue in Northern India that became the template for the revenue systems that were implemented by the British in northern and central India. In addition, Mackenzie was also president of the Council of the College of Fort William in Calcutta. Ragaviah Charry, whose dates are unknown, was educated in mission schools and at the College

of Fort William. A number of manuscripts attributed to him are preserved at the British Library in London. These include his polemics against Thomas Newnham's essay entitled "The Character and Capacity of the Asiaticks" published in 1802. Ragaviah resisted Christian critiques of Hinduism as a religion of "horrid" practices and beliefs. In one of his works, he advocates the formation of a literary association in Madras whose aim would be to facilitate dialogue between natives and Europeans.

13. Cupratīpa Kavirāyar was one of the Tamil teachers of the Jesuit missionary Costanzo Giuseppe Beschi (1680–1747), who is credited with authoring Tamil texts such as the *Tēmpāvaṇi*, an epic poem about Saint Joseph, in addition to other works on Tamil grammar and polemical works against the Lutherans.

14. Here, for example, is an excerpt from the "Veśyā Prakaraṇam" chapter of the *Cĕnnapurivilāsamu* that describes the courtesans' quarters in Madras:

> There are many girls with pleasant eyes and full breasts who have been taught rhythms like *jhampa-tāla* [a ten-beat rhythm cycle] by dance-masters (*nāṭya bharatācāryas*). In Sūryam Paśyalpuri there are plenty of *veśyā*s on the street called *nŏḍakāl vīdhi*. They have beautiful teeth, *kuṃkuma* marking on their foreheads, and their faces shine bright as blue lilies. As they perform the beautiful *lāsya* dance, their graceful gait appears like that of swans. Like lotuses swaying from side to side, they enact a play (*līlā*) of *abhinaya*. They are born of the secret desire of Rati and Kāma. In that *nŏḍakāl vīdhi*, live the women who are victorious over Kāma himself (*smara jaya strīlu*). They exhibit beautiful bodily movements and other alluring traits. They do not appear to be worried about anything. Their attractive features hunt down young men, and they wait, keeping their doors open. Such *veśyā*s live on that street. The sweet ambrosia of their music (*gānāmṛta*) showers down like flowers falling from the branches of a beautiful tree. Those who witness their performances are knowledgeable in the art of *lāsya*. This assembly of connoisseurs adds lustre to the art of the *veśyā*s. On this street, live these *veśyā*s who are like the mantric powers of illusion wielded by Kāma. (Nṛsiṃhaśāstri 1864, 63–64)

15. These names are mentioned in *Sarvadevavilāsa*, 5.21–26.

16. In 1876, a man (presumably a *naṭṭuvaṉār*) named Arapatta Nāvalar published a Tamil text called *Paratacāsttiram* ("Bharata Śāstra"), which mentions the performance of the pot-lamp ritual (*maṅkaḷa kumpa tīpam*) of the *devadāsī*s and talks about the performance of *nāgasvaram* in temples, but also speaks about the complexity of rhythmic theory and the technical dimensions of drumming for court dance (Arapatta Nāvalar, 1876). Similarly, some patrons of dance, such as Sarvajña Kumāra Gopālakṛṣṇa Yācendra, the *zamīndār* of Venkatagiri in Andhra Pradesh, wrote works such as *Sabhā Rañjani* (1890), about aesthetic theory as it related to the performance of poetry, music and dance in courtly contexts.

17. As Krishnan (2008, 77–78) points out, predating the *Naṭaṉāti Vāttiya Rancaṉam*, are two Tamil texts, *Apiṉayacāracampuṭa* and *Apiṉaya Navanītam*, collaborations between a Brahmin connoisseur, Chetlur Narayana Ayyankar, and Panchapakesha Nattuvanar (1842–1902), a descendant of Veṅkaṭakiruṣṇa Naṭṭuvaṉār who served at the Tanjore court during the reign of Serfoji.

18. Over and above the few works I have mentioned in this essay, a number of others in Tamil also exist. A very early example, a Tamil drama titled *Tēvatāci* ("Devadāsī"), was composed in the early nineteenth century by a poet named Paracurāma Kavirāyar, and then translated in 1868 into French by Louis Jacolliot under the title *La Devadassi, Bayadere* (Zvelebil 1998). Other literary works about *devadāsī*-courtesans in Madras include *Mattāppucuntaram allatu Tācikaḷiṉ Ceykai* ("The Beauty of Fireworks, or The Deeds of the Dāsīs," 1916) by Kiruṣṇacāmi Ayyar, *Taṉapālaṉ allatu Tācikaḷiṉ Māyāvañcaka Cūḻccikaḷ* ("Dhanapalan, or the Devious Crimes of the Dāsīs," 1931) by Kōvintacāmi Piḷḷai, and the play *Tācikaḷum Tācikantaṟkaḷum* ("Dāsīs and the Dāsīs' Lovers," 1947) by E. Cokkaliṅkam Piḷḷai. This type of writing also includes works in English, such as *The Days of a Dancing Girl; or, The Inner Life of India Unveiled: A Book of Revelations in the Life of the Rich and Religious in India as seen through the Private Life of an Indian Prostitute* by R. Balasundara Mudali (1913) and the essay *Pen-Pictures of the Dancing Girl*, by M. S. Mani in 1926. Many of these works also resonated deeply with Victorian writing in English on concubines and professional performing artists in colonial India. For an example of such writing, see *The Romance of a Nautch Girl: A Novel* by Mrs. Frank Penny (1898); for an analysis, see Paxton (1999).

19. K. Kurucāmitās was a fairly prolific writer who composed several such poems. He published his own work from 1943 to 1945, and it spans a range of subjects, from murders in the Presidency, to cattle markets in the suburbs of Kumbhakonam, to the British victory over Tunisia during World War I. Another significant work is *Kumpakōṇam Kaikkāṭṭi Marattēruvil Naṭanta Rāmacāmi Kolaiccintu* ("Collection of Songs about the Murder Committed by Rāmacāmi in Kumbhakonam," 1943), which describes the case of Rāmacāmi from Kumbhakonam who murdered a prostitute named Sītālaṭcumi for jilting him.

20. This was for a volume of *jāvaḷi*s edited by T. Brinda (1912–1996), granddaughter of Vina Dhanammal (1867–1939), one of the most prominent courtesans in colonial Madras. The volume, dedicated to the memory of Dhanammal, consists of thirty *jāvaḷi*s with *svara* notation, many of which were composed during Dhanammal's lifetime. See Brinda (1960).

21. Studies on the *jāvaḷi* as a genre are few and far between. Except for the studies by Arudra (1986a, 1986b), Chennakeshaviah (1974), Sastri (1974), Satyanarayana Rao (1964), and a few others, most writing on *jāvaḷi*s consists of short introductions to compilations of *jāvaḷi*s meant for performers (see, for example, Brinda 1960; Kittappa 1979; Kuppuswamy and Hariharan 1996; and Parthasarathi and Parthasarathi 1980). The essays by Arudra (1986a, 1986b) and also by Sankaran (1982a, 1982b) contain some invaluable biographical information about *jāvaḷi* composers.

22. MSS KB 240/2, Kannada Adhyayana Samsthe (Institute of Kannada Studies), Mysore. For more on Kannada *jāvaḷi*s and the Mysore court, see Sastri (1974) and Pranesh (2003). *Jāvaḷi*s continued to be popular in the Kannada-speaking regions until the middle of the twentieth century. Poets such as Hullāhalli Rāmannā (1854–1918) were among the most famous *jāvaḷikarta*s from this region (Chennakeshavaiah 1974; Sastri 1974). To be sure, hundreds of *jāvaḷi*s exist in Kannada, and these were performed by courtesans at the Mysore court and at privately sponsored performances inside

homes. In the recent past, late nineteenth- and early twentieth-century courtesans such as Mugur Jejamma, Mysore Sundaramma, and Nangangud Nagaratamma performed *jāvaḷi*s on a regular basis in and around Mysore and Bengaluru.

23. This is an oral tradition that has been maintained by the descendants of the Quartet. They claim that a single *jāvaḷi*, "iṭu sāhasamulu elarā" in Saindhavi *rāga*, is the earliest song in this genre, and was composed at the Travancore court. There are no records to substantiate this claim, although we do know that Vaṭivēlu did indeed teach dance at the Travancore court, and in the year 1834 was gifted by the Mahārāja Svāti Tirunāl with an ivory violin and an ivory box full of jewels. Both of these artifacts are in the possession of the descendants of the Quartet who live in Thanjavur and Chennai.

24. Tacchur Singaracharyulu (1834–1892) and his brother Chinna Singaracharyulu wrote seven treatises on music that were commissioned by Nālvaḍi Kṛṣṇarāja Uḍaiyār. These included *Gāyakapārijātam* (1882), *Gāyakalocana* (1884), *Saṅgīta Kalānidhi* (1889), *Gāyaka Siddhānjanam* (part 1, 1890; part 2, 1905), *Gānendu Śekharam* (1912), and *Svaramañjari* (1914). All were published in Madras. Singaracharyulu also organized annual "salon style" concerts on the festival of Rāmanavamī near his house in Georgetown.

25. The *Gāndharvakalpavalli* has an English subtitle, "A Self-Instructor in Music." Many such "teach yourself" books on music and dance were composed in the early twentieth century. Another important example related to dance is *Abhinaya Svayambodhini* ("Teach Yourself Abhinaya," 1915) by Devulapalli Vīrarāghavamūrti Śāstri. In the preface to this work, the author talks about the instrumentality of the book: "To make it easy for *vesyā strīs* and other women who wish to learn this art, I have written this text in Telugu, so they need not look elsewhere. One can [now] learn the art with the help of this book." This text has also been discussed in Krishnan (2008).

26. Agha Mohammad Shah (1879–1935), later known as Agha Hashr Kashmiri, wrote an Urdu adaptation of *King Lear* for Parsi theater entitled *Safed Khūn* ("White Blood," 1906). This combined Urdu prose and poetry with Hindustāni music. For details, see A. Kapur (2006). Also see *The Parsi Theatre: Its Origins and Development* by Somnath Gupt (translated and edited by Kathryn Hansen, 2005).

27. Karur Śivarāmayya also composed the *jāvaḷi* "O My Lovely Lalanā" (Kharaharapriya *rāga*) in a mix of English and Telugu, which also appears in the *Gāndharvakalpavalli*. Śivarāmayya lived most of his life in Karur, near Trichy. One of his descendants was the famous violinist Papa Venkataramayya (1901–1972).

28. Rāga: Kāmbodhi; Tāla: Ādi; Composer: Karur Śivarāmayya (c. 1798–1820).

29. A great number of *naṭṭuvaṉār*s moved to Madras throughout the nineteenth century, including Pattnam Muttusvami Nattuvanar (1781–1846) who was originally from Tiruvarur. A number of women who lived in Madras and its suburbs performed regularly at festivals hosted by local temples: Chennai Andal (1871–1919) performed on the premises on the Cennamallikeśvara temple; Mylapore Duraikannammal (1864–1952) performed at the Kapālīśvara temple; and Tiruvallikkeni Krishna (1804–1855) and Nila (1830–1891) performed at the Triplicane Parthasārathi temple.

30. Musicologist T. Sankaran has also written a short essay on Surisetti Ramaniah Chettiar, an important patron and connoisseur of music and dance in Madras city in the early part of the twentieth century. He hosted a monthlong Rāmanavamī festival in his home every year, where the city's top musicians and dancers would gather for salon

performances. Dhanammal and even her granddaughter T. Balasaraswati performed here (Sankaran 1984b).

31. For example, in the *jāvaḷi* in Paras *rāga*, "smara sundarāṅguni sari ĕvvare," the heroine notes that as she plays her *vīṇā*, her lover encourages her by exclaiming "*śābāś* (bravo)!" In a biographical essay on Subbaraya Ayyar, T. Sankaran, a descendant of Dhanammal, notes that another *jāvaḷi* in Jhañjhūṭi *rāga*, "prāṇa sakhuḍiṭu," also refers to the relationship between Ayyar and Dhanammal. He writes: "Some time before his death, he had left Madras, promising Dhanammal that he would return soon. But circumstances beyond his control detained him at Dharmapuri . . . When he came back, on learning that Dhanammal was going through hard times, instead of the usual paltry monetary help, he gifted to her this priceless javali" (Sankaran 1982a, 25). For more on Dhanammal, see L. Subramanian (2009) and Knight (2010).

32. Having noted the continuities between dance and aesthetics throughout the colonial Madras Presidency, it is significant that a number of *jāvaḷi*s were composed in the late nineteenth and early twentieth centuries exclusively for professional dancing women in the coastal Andhra Pradesh region. These include the *jāvaḷi*s of Neti Subbarayudu Sastri. Another example of a localized *jāvaḷi* tradition comes from the village of Ballipadu in the West Godavari district, where courtesans who had connections with the festival worship of Kṛṣṇa at the Madanagopālasvāmi temple sang a number of *jāvaḷi*s composed for this purpose. During my fieldwork with Saride Anusuya (1910–2005), who was dedicated to this temple, I recorded one such *jāvaḷi*, "idi nyāyamā sāmi" in Jhañjhūṭi *rāga*, which made specific reference to the temple at Ballipadu, and it was clearly used in this highly localized context.

33. This is the *jāvaḷi* in Kalyāṇi rāga "cĕragu māse emi seturā" by Neti Subbraya Sastri that I discuss in detail in chapter 5.

34. The story of Coimbatore Thayi is particularly interesting. Her lineage can be traced to a *devadāsī* named Visalakshi in the village of Avinasi in the Kongu region. Visalakshi had two daughters, Shanmukattammal and Venkatammal, both of whom settled in Coimbatore city. In 1872, Venkatammal gave birth to a daughter whom she named Palanikunjaram, nicknamed "Thayi." Thayi had her formal debut in dance (*araṅkēṟṟam*) at the age of eleven, and continued to perform dance till she was nineteen, when she shifted her focus to vocal music performances. She purchased a house on Nattu Pillaiyar Koyil Street in Georgetown, Madras, and moved there around 1892. In Madras, she received further training in music from Tiruvottriyur Tyagayyar (1845–1917) and Dharmapuri Subbaraya Ayyar. Coimbatore Thayi was also the inspiration for a somewhat unique European experiment in music: Maurice Delage (1879–1961), an amateur French composer, came to India in 1912. Delage wanted to access music from all over the country, and so began to purchase gramophone records, including ones produced in Madras (Pasler 2000, 102). As Jann Pasler has observed, Delage's interest in India was rooted in his "own essentially Western preoccupations," namely, his obsession with modernist aesthetics. Delage was attracted to the techniques of Indian music largely with an eye to mine them for a "future-oriented" modernism in European music (ibid., 102). His stay in India resulted in two major musical works, *Quatre poèmes hindous* (Four Hindu Poems, 1912–1913), inspired largely by North Indian music, and *Ragamalika* (Garland of Ragas, 1912–1922), a virtual recreation of a single recording

by Coimbatore Thayi. *Ragamalika* is based on Thayi's recording of Tamil devotional hymns called *Aruṭpā* or *Tiruvaruṭpā* by the saint Irāmaliṅka Aṭikaḷār (1823–1874). Thayi died on August 17, 1917.

35. Gauhar Jan and her mother converted to Islam in 1881 and changed their names to Gauhar Jan and Badi Malka Jan, respectively. Both mother and daughter were trained in music and dance and eventually became renowned courtesan-artists. Badi Malka Jan received the patronage of Wajid Ali Shah (1822–1887). who was exiled from Awadh to Matiaburj outside Calcutta following the annexation of Awadh to the British in 1856. At Wajid Ali's relocated court, Gauhar Jan learnt Kathak dance under Bindadin Maharaj (1830–1918), and studied music with respected teachers such as Kale Khan of Patiala. For an excellent discussion of Eurasian women as *tawā'if*s and recording artists, see Sachdeva-Jha (2009). Details about Gauhar Van are also found in a recent biography (Sampath 2010).

36. This was not Gauhar Jan's only visit to South India. Toward the end of her life, in 1928, she was invited to the Mysore court of Nālvaḍi Kṛṣṇarāja Uḍaiyār (r. 1902–1940). She was appointed as a palace musician, and died of pneumonia at the Krishnarajendra Hospital in 1930 at the age of fifty-seven.

37. Three of Gauhar Jan's songs are listed with South Indian *svara* (solfa) notation in both the Tamil and Telugu editions of P. S. Ramulu Chetti's *Gāndharvakalpavalli* (1912).

38. The music for this film was by Pendyala Nageshwara Rao (1924–1984), and the lyrics were by the poet and historian Arudra (1925–1998), who also likely wrote two of the *caraṇam*s in this version of "aṃtalone tĕllavāre." In the film, the *jāvaḷi* was sung by playback singer P. Susheela (b. 1935).

39. The scene with the dance sequence is notable for a number of reasons. While the main dancer is played by a woman from the *kalāvantula* community, the woman playing the troupe leader (*nāyakurālu*) is Surabhi Kamalabai (1913–1977), a woman born into a community of Telugu drama artists and the first woman to act in a Telugu film (she played the role of Līlāvati in the 1931 Telugu film *Bhakta Prahlada*). The *nāyakurālu* is also supplemented by a Brahmin dance-master from the all-male *kūcipūḍi* village tradition. The film was made at a time when *kūcipūḍi* was being reinvented as an urban, "classical" dance form in Madras, and thus the idea of Brahmin men as teachers (and thus custodians) of courtesan dance was ubiquitous (Soneji 2004, 166–170).

CHAPTER THREE

1. A large body of scholarly writing exists on the topic of the Indian Contagious Diseases Acts and Victorian perspectives on prostitution in India. Particularly noteworthy are works that address the fascinating figure of British feminist Josephine Butler (1828–1906) and the "white woman's burden." See, for example, Burton (1994, 127–169) and Wallace (1998).

2. Lock hospitals were scattered throughout the colonies and the metropole. They were sites where "the contrapuntal forces of colonial social hygiene and military discipline were brought to bear on the diseased bodies of women inmates" (Hodges 2005a, 381). For details on the conditions of lock hospital inmates in the empire, see Levine (2003, 70–80).

3. *Report on Public Instruction in the Madras Presidency for 1875–76*, 203.

4. Madras Government Order 271, June 6, 1877, no. 3–4, cited in Anantha Raman (1996), 36.

5. Having noted the institutional and political frameworks through which these women were given voice, I also take seriously Kalpana Kannabiran's observation that there is an ambivalence in Reddy's position: "While on the one hand she consciously sets herself apart from the community whose cause she espouses (and in doing this she is in a sense reiterating a distinction that already exists and is based on class and political power), on the other hand the sheer range of issues she raises, some of them explicitly feminist, sets her apart from the class she identifies with and the people and institutions she shares power with" (1995, 65).

6. An extensive discussion of Dadabhoy's interventions is found in Jordan (2003, 75–86).

7. It is significant that scholars often gloss Reddy as "the daughter of a *devadāsī*" or simply as a *devadāsī* herself. To be sure, Reddy did not grow up in a courtesan household, and her early academic progress can be attributed to her influential Brahmin father, who brought her to Madras and ensured that she was admitted into the medical college. Although in Reddy's own account (1964, 1–11) it appears that her mother and father were actually married, this may have not been the case.

8. S. Anandhi is currently completing a major work dealing with the life of Muthulakshmi Reddy.

9. The topic of land tenure and *devadāsī*s in colonial South India is a complex one, but this is also terrain that has already been covered by a number of scholars. For a general overview on nineteenth-century South Indian systems of land tenure, particularly with reference to temple and courtly *inām*s, see Appadurai (1981); Dirks (1993, 2001) and Good (2004). For details on *devadāsī*s and *inām* lands, see Kannabiran (1995); J. Nair (1994); Parker (1998); Ramachendrier (1892); A. Srinivasan (1984).

10. As Michelle Elizabeth Tusan (2003) has shown, Reddy was also a close associate of Margaret Cousins (1878–1954), a radical Irish feminist who came to India at the invitation of Annie Besant. Cousins was instrumental in appointing Reddy and Malati Patwardhan as the two Indian general editors of the journal *Stri Dharma*, started in 1918 by British feminists.

11. Meetings of "*devadāsī* associations" were held, for example, in Kanchipuram, Madhurantakam, Tiruchendur, and as far south as the Tirunelveli district.

12. T. Duraikkannu, handbill, dated 1927, the Muthulakshmi Reddi Papers (*hereafter* MRP), Nehru Memorial Museum and Library, New Delhi, subject file 11, (part II), 72, emphasis added.

13. On November 5, 1927, the Madras Devadasi Association resolved to "unanimously and emphatically" protest Reddy's resolution. This statement was typed and sent as a letter to C. P. Ramaswami Iyer and to the governor's office. On November 10, 1927, Iyer responded with a request that the association draft a full memo outlining the grievances of its members. By the next day, on November 11, 1927, the memorandum had already been composed and sent to Iyer's residence. The memorandum has also been discussed at length in works by Jordan (2003), Kannabiran and Kannabiran (2003), Meduri (1996), Srividya Natarajan (1997), and others.

14. Bangalore Nagaratnammal is a significant figure in the context of *devadāsīs* and texts in colonial South India. She was responsible for publishing *Rādhikā Sāntvanamu* ("Appeasing Rādhā"), an erotic text attributed to a courtesan named Muddupaḷani who lived during the reign of King Pratāpasiṃha (r. 1739–1763) at the Tanjavur Marāṭhā court. Considered a masterpiece of Telugu literature, Nagaratnammal had the text published in Madras in 1910, and this sparked considerable debate about *devadāsīs* in the public sphere. Police seized copies of the book in 1911, and its publishers were charged with violating obscenity laws. An official ban on the book was imposed in 1927, and lifted only twenty years later. For more on Nagaratnammal, see Tharu and Lalitha (1993), Jackson (1994), and Sriram (2007).

15. Madras Devadasi Assocation, memorandum entitled "The Humble Memorial of Devadasis of the Madras Presidency," 2. MRP, subject file 11 (part II), 283–287.

16. MRP, subject file 12 (part II), 90–91. A longer excerpt from this letter is reproduced in appendix 1.

17. Muthulakshmi Reddy to A. R. MacEwen, MRP, subject file 11 (part II), 282.

18. Satyamurti's conservatism surfaced in a number of important debates around sexuality, marriage, and family in the Madras Legislative Assembly. S. Anandhi's insightful essay "Sexuality and Nation" (1997) describes Satyamurti's protests against the Child Marriage Restraint Act (the purpose of which was to outlaw child marriage) and the Hindu Marriage Dissolution Bill (granting the legal right of divorce to Hindus).

19. *Tamiḻ Nāṭu*, November 5, 1927, in MRP, subject file 12 (part II), p. 11.

20. This is cataloged as manuscript 6523B. This manuscript is believed to be in the author's own handwriting. Another (presumably later) copy of this same work exists in the library, under the title *Vēciyā Tarmam* (6523A), but this copy omits many portions found in the original work. I am presently completing an essay about *Tācikaḷ Tarmam*, which will include translations of large portions of the text.

21. Cēṣacāyi Ayyaṅkār's other Sanskrit works also housed in the Sarasvati Mahal Library include *Puruṣārthakalpalatā* ("Compendium on the Four Aims of Man"), *Ṛgveda Viṣayaḥ* ("On the Ṛgveda"), *Gāyatrī Japakāla Kartavyam* ("Duty of the Timely Recitation of the Gāyatrī Mantra"), and *Rāmāyaṇa Nāṭakaḥ* ("Drama based on the Rāmāyaṇa").

22. The Sanskrit sources he cites in his discussions of *veśyā*s include *Smṛticandrikā*, *Nāradasmṛti*, and *Śukranīti* (Dharmaśāstric texts), the *Skandapurāṇa* and *Viṣṇupurāṇa*, and even the Sanskrit plays *Mṛcchakaṭikam* and *Vikramorvaśīyam*, whose heroines are understood as "ideal" courtesans because, Cēṣacāyi claims, they were monogamous (*ekacāriṇī*).

23. This is found in an English newspaper clipping entitled "Kalavanthulus in Conference," dated August 15, 1927, MRP, subject file 11 (part II), 66.

24. G. Nagabhushanam to Reddy dated October 10, 1929, MRP, subject file 11 (part II), 373.

25. We have already seen examples of this type of writing. Yūcup *Tācikaḷ Vēcam Maiṉarkaḷ Mōcam* includes passages such as the following:

> Friends, think carefully about the behavior of these *dāsī*s. Let me tell you about them. They are born as female demons, born for the sake of money. They will

profess love to anyone right from God to the lowest class, as long as he has money. If you have money they will welcome you; if not, they'll abuse you like you are a pariah (6) . . . It is said that earlier Brahmā had created these ladies to work as slaves (*aṭimai toḻiḷ*). But in reality, they have the *poṭṭu* tied, and just swindle money from everyone. Do these ladies who have deviated from the righteous path and become prostitutes (*viḷai mātar*), do these bloody women need to justify their existence based on *śāstra*? (7)

26. Both of these essays were published in the Self-Respect Movement's Tamil weekly *Kuṭi Aracu* ("The Republic"), on March 23 and March 30, 1930, respectively. Discussions of these texts and other writing by women of the Self-Respect Movement are found in Srilata (2003).

27. Muvalur Ramamirttamal to Reddy, dated October 13, 1927, MRP, subject file 11 (part III), 461.

28. A recent Tamil feature film, *Periyar* (2006), directed by Gnana Rajasekharan and partially funded by the Tamil Nadu State Government, contains an interesting scene featuring Muvalar Ramamirttammal. The scene opens with a *devadāsī* dancing in a temple *maṇḍapa* before a large image of the god Śiva-Naṭarāja. The song she sings is about her oppression, couched in the metaphoric language of *bhakti*. Suddenly, Ramamirttammal bursts onto the *maṇḍapa* accompanied by a young man who has come forth to marry the *devadāsī*. Periyar too arrives, and after a lengthy debate with the audience gathered at the *maṇḍapa* about the oppressive nature of *devadāsī* culture, Periyar marries the couple right there and then. The film was funded by the Tamil Nadu State Government through a grant of 95 lakh rupees, and Karunanidhi presided over a major function to celebrate the film's 100 day in theaters on August 8, 2007. These kinds of popular depictions of Ramamirttammal inevitably frame the "normalizing" of non-Brahmin women's sexuality as one of the key features of non-Brahmin respectability, a position that is certainly maintained in the contemporary *icai vēḷāḷar* community.

29. The scheme was briefly advertised by the Kanchipuram district website in 2006 immediately following Karunanidhi's victory in the elections that year, but later removed. http://kanchi.nic.in/social.htm.

30. The scheme was officially relaunched on Karunanidhi's eighty-third birthday, less than a month after he was reelected. http://www.hindu.com/2006/06/03/stories/2006060314550100.htm.

31. Amrit Srinivasan notes that one of these meetings took place "around 1948" in Kuttalam. Although this particular meeting might have adopted a motion to publically use only the name *icai vēḷāḷar*, it is clear that the term was being used in an official capacity over two decades earlier. A thorough historicization of this process is severely lacking and offers tremendous scope for future research.

32. In his autobiography, nationalist reformer D. Chenchaiah claims that the name "Kalavantula Samskarana Sangam" was first created by a man named M. Venkata Rao, the first president of that organization, sometime in the late 1920s (Cĕṃcayya 1952, 178).

In her 1928 essay entitled *The Awakening Demand for Devadasi Legislation*, Reddy provides a list of the *devadāsī* associations that support her actions. Many of these are *kalāvantula* organizations in the Telugu-speaking regions, including the Devadasi Association of Tenali Taluq, Repalle Taluq Female Devadasi Sangam, Anantapur District Kalavanthulu Reformation Society, Anantapur Distrcit Kalavanthulu Reformation Society (Tadpatri), Kalavanthulu Social Reform Association of Guntur, Kalavanthulu Association of Bapatla, Kalavanthulu Sevasangam of Amalapuram, and the Andhradesa Devadasis' Sangha Sanskarana Sabha of Tirupati.

33. The most systematic studies of the complexities of *jāti* issues in these communities are found in A. Srinivasan (1984, 75–167) and Terada (1992, 174–243).

34. In the Tanjavur district, life-cycle rituals were overseen by a man from the community who was given the title *rāyar*. The *rāyar* was a key officiant during marriage and funeral ceremonies. He cemented social relations in the community and often mediated between the subgroups within the community.

35. MRP, subject file 11 (part III), 482–485. The full text of this letter is reproduced in Appendix 1.

36. MRP, subject file 11 (part III), 442–443. The full text of this letter is reproduced in Appendix 1.

37. Court case involving Sree Venkateswara Swami and Sree Visweswara Swamy temple in Vadapalle (East Godavari district), dated November 1929, MRP, subject file 11 (part II), 259–260.

38. In some cases it was unclear whether *devadāsī*s were entitled to the *inām* lands or to a portion of the revenue generated from it. In many of these cases, *devadāsī*s petitioned *inām* commissioners to reexamine their original land tenure deeds. An example of this is found in Muthulakshmi Reddy's files (MRP, subject file 11 [part II], 275–276). Two women, Dharanikota Sambrajjam and Kalava Sarasiruham, "in possession of the Kumbaharathi inams" at the "Sree Venkateswara Someswara Kudaleswaraswami temple" situated at Sekur in the Guntur District, asked the Guntur commissioner to reexamine the original land deeds to ascertain that they in fact were the rightful owners of the land.

39. MRP, subject file 11 (part II), 239.

40. To be sure, the informal alignment between sons of *devadāsī*s and *naṭṭuvaṉār*s with *vēḷāḷa*s and *mutaliyār*s goes much further back, as illustrated by a British anthropologist writing in 1871. However, it is significant that anti-nautch debates formalized and politicized these identifications.

> The greater part of the singers now-a-days belong to the anomalous class called nattuvan, the sons of dancing girls, knowing nothing of their fathers and, therefore, of the caste to which they should belong. Formerly they were rigorously shut out of the Hindu body politic, yet as their mothers, they were not despised or treated as outcastes. They were the property of the God, bound to his service, entitled to a share in his offerings. They grew up as musicians, as lighters of lamps, as stewards and general servants in the pagodas. In modern times the English law has made a vast difference in their condition. If the mother be well-to-do and can give her son a good education, she tacks the caste title "Moodelliar" after his name and sends him away from the place of his birth to a district where his antecedents are not known. In his new position none can deny that he is a Vellala. If he becomes rich

> none would wish to refuse him the privilege. Choosing the daughter of some poor Vellala who finds it prudent to ask no questions, he marries into his assumed caste. The issue of the marriage are as good as Vellalas as those who came in the train of Agastya. In this way the sons of the temple women are constantly absorbed. Formerly such things could not be done. The Nattuvan found himself an outsider, civilly treated it is true, but yet without a privilege and almost without a right. (Gover 1871, xv–xvi)

41. Interestingly, as this book was being written, Karunanidhi's daughter, Kanimozhi (b. 1968 in Chennai), rose to phenomenal success, becoming a member of Parliament and representing Tamil Nadu in the Rajya Sabha (the upper house of India's Parliament). Kanimozhi has become well known for her support of women's welfare programs and the transgendered *aravani* community in Tamil Nadu. Kanimozhi, however, does not, to my knowledge, publicly claim *icai vēḷāḷar* status as her father does.

42. http://www.isaivelalar.com/aboutus.htm (accessed December 1, 2009).

43. These cases are found in the following periodicals: *Madras [Chennai] High Court Reports* (1953–2001); the *Madras Law Journal* (1953–1980), the *Andhra High Court Reports* (1961–2001), and the *Indian Law Reports* (1950–present).

44. The proceedings note, for example, that "Ranganayaki and the plaintiff used to give public performance in 'Golla Kalapam' and 'Bhama Kalapam' etc., before the plaintiff settled in married life with the eighth defendant." These are the *kalāvantula āṭa-bhāgavatam* performances that I discuss briefly in chapter 5.

CHAPTER FOUR

1. A prominent NGO called the Weaker Section Welfare Association (WESWA) based in Viralimalai has a page on its website entitled "Legacy of the Devadasi System: Background of Hereditary Prostitution in Pudukottai District" (http://weswa.org/devadasi.htm.) that reads as follows:

> India is a country known for its temples. The gods and goddesses were worshipped with dance according to the Indian tradition. To dance regularly in these temples nobody came forward. So to find and get regularly girls for dancing in these temples they introduced a system called "Devadasi System." Devadasi means 'maid-servant of God.' Originally they were provided with houses to stay and lands to earn their livelihood. Thus they were living a pious, devoted and decent life.
>
> But in the course of the time rich land lords, zamindars and even petty kings lured these dancing girls with their money and comforts and involved them in prostitution. Thus they, in the course of the time became property of pleasure for royal and rich people.
>
> As the number of dancing girls increased and as the landlord and zamindari systems were abolished in India after independence these dancing girls were not entertained by these rich and royal people. They stopped dancing in the temples. The original purpose for which this systems was introduced was lost the deviation of the systems gained momentum they become full time prostitutes as they are not used to hard work in the field and used only to comfort. Luxury and pleasure in

the past. Now they are available to anyone who is ready to pay them . . . There are 80 families in this place involving in prostitution presently. They are often taken to various towns for prostitution. Many rich people visit them also from towns regularly.

2. Murukaṉ is said to have appeared to Anuṇakiri in the form of a hunter, and led him to the temple atop the Viralimalai hill, where he is thought to have composed sixteen hymns to Murukaṉ as Caṇmukanātar that are found in the *Tiruppukaḻ*. Several other Tamil *bhakti* poems are attributed to Aruṇakiri, including *Kantar Alaṅkāram, Kantarantāti, Vēl Viruttam, Mayil Viruttam, Cēval Viruttam, Tiruveḻukūṟṟirukkai*, and *Tiruvakuppu*. Aruṇakiri becomes an iconic figure among *icai vēḷāḷar*s in the twentieth century. Many *icai vēḷāḷar* caste organizations are called "Aruṇakirinātar Caṅkam," and statues of Aruṇakiri have been funded by men from the *icai vēḷāḷar* community. This has to do with their support of the "Tamil music" (*tamiḻ icai*) movement, which sought to revitalize a distinctly Tamil (as opposed to Telugu or Sanskrit) music tradition in Tamil Nadu, and drew in large part from the emergence of Dravidian politics. The relationship between the "Tamil music" movement and Dravidian politics has been described at length by L. Subramanian (2006, 2007), Terada (1992), and Weidman (2006).

3. Other shrines in the temple complex include those to the goddess Maikkaṇṇutaiyāḷ (a small *ammaṉ* shrine located at the base of the hill), the guardian deity Iṭumpan, and a smaller cave shrine for Mīṉāṭci of Madurai and her consort Cuntarēcuvarar. The Caṇmukamūrrti *maṇḍapam* also houses a *palliyaṟai*, or bedchamber, which is used during the nightly *palliyaṟai cēvai* ("bedchamber ritual") in which the god and his consort are ceremonially put to sleep for the night.

4. *Naṭṭuvaṉār*s who were actively performing in the temple and court, and women who had undergone *poṭṭukkaṭṭu* were allotted *māṉiyam* grants. The *māṉiyam* was divided into shares (*paṅku*s), which would be managed internally by elders in the family. In the case of Ramachandra Nattuvanar, he received twenty acres of land as an ancestral service allotment from his mother Nagammal, who also received the same.

5. Ulaganatha Pillai, son of Sivarama Nattuvanar, narrated a story about the brothers, which involved the performance of a text called *Rakunātarāya Kuṟavañci*. The premiere (*araṅkēṟṟam*) of the *kuṟavañci* was staged at the *darbār* in the presence of the king. The role of the Ciṅkaṉ was danced by Ramasvami and the Kuṟatti (Ciṅki) by his wife Akhilandam. Over the course of the performance, the couple divined that the *rājā* would soon become the father of a male child. The *naṭṭuvaṉār* was of course handsomely rewarded by Raja Vijaya Raghunatha Raya Tondaiman who gave him a house, jewels, and eight *devadāsī*s to work with so that his presentations at the *darbār* and Tirugokarnam temple would remain of a high standard. Personal communication, December 27, 2004.

6. Detailed information about Martanda Bhairava is found in Waghorne (1994). In many respects, he was the ideal gentleman-raja; his life is described by Waghorne as follows:

> Now the raja of Pudukkottai no longer spent money uselessly on palanquins, jewels for inveigling wives, or extravagant religious ceremonies. Thos. Cook & Son's

> Information for Travelers, and catalogs for fine leather saddles, silver teapots, tennis rackets, steamer trunks, and of course the latest prices for Rolls Royces are still among the artifacts of this gentleman-raja in the old palace record boxes . . . But this perfect picture of colonialism ended ironically. By 1917, neither His Highness's subjects nor the British could relish his presence; the lovelorn price married an Australian beauty, much to the chagrin of his colonial keepers, who recoiled as he stepped too firmly into their world. (1994, 81)

Native and British dissatisfaction with Martanda Bhairava following his marriage to Molly Fink is also discussed at length by Dirks (1993, 391–397).

7. The story of "Sayimata" Siva Brindadevi (1927–1998) is unique. She was an informant for Saskia Kersenboom's ethnographic work on *devadāsīs* in the early 1980s, and a ritual composition (swing song or *ūñjal*) she knew is recorded in Kersenboom's book (Kersenboom 1987, 160). Around this time, she had just founded the Thilagavathiar Thiruvarul Adheenam in Pudukkottai, on the grounds of the former home of S. Narayanaswami, Muthulakshmi Reddy's father. She became an ascetic sometime in the 1970s. She was the first female head of a Śaiva *ādhīnam*. She was also the president of the World Hindu Women's Organization (WHWO), which she also founded in Pudukkottai in 1984. In 1986, she traveled to Malaysia to inaugurate the second conference of the organization, where she was described as the "sannyasini abbotess of an Indian adheenam monastery" (Thiruvasagam 1986, 23). In 1997, reacting strongly to a performance entitled "Vata Vriksha: Banyan Tree" (1996) by Bharatanāṭyam dancer Lakshmi Viswanathan, she wrote a forceful letter to the editor of *Sruti*, a popular music and dance magazine from Chennai. Her concern was that "devadasis were portrayed in a very bad light" in the dance production, as was her maternal aunt, Dr. Muthulakshmi Reddy. In the letter, she speaks passionately about the stigma of being a *devadāsī*: "[I]t was common to abuse a girl of any community for using even cosmetics by asking her rhetorically: 'Why do you make-up like a tevadiyal?' Applying facial makeup was not the habit solely of the devadasi-s, but the abuse directly or indirectly pointed to them" (Siva Brindadevi 1997, 5). She was known to have discussed her *devadāsī* past quite freely and openly with others. She died in 2000. Today, her disciples run her monastery, which is named after Tilakavatiyār, the sister of the Tamil saint Appar. The monastery also houses a state government-approved English medium school called the Muthulakshmi Reddi Nursery and Primary School. Sayimata's successor Dayananda Chandrasekaran has authored a major biography on her (2003), and has also recently written a book on Muthulakshmi Reddy (2007).

The organization also runs a website, http://sivabrindadevi.org, and a channel on YouTube, http://www.youtube.com/sivabrindadevi.

8. A major biography of Sashiah Sastri was written in 1902 (Aiyar 1902). An engaging, critical discussion of Sashiah Sastri based on the Pudukkottai palace records is found in Waghorne (1994).

9. Joanne Waghorne's work with the Pudukkottai palace records has unearthed correspondence between Sashiah Sastri and the government of India to this effect:

> Next I found it necessary to nail up a secret door which opened directly to the apartments of the Senior Princess and allowing all sorts of characters at all hours of

the day and night. Next I stopped the ingress of all dancing girls who were found in constant company with the Princess . . . (Waghorne 1994, 63)

10. The Madras Devadasi Association wrote letters denouncing the bill that then circulated in the press. In reaction, caste organizations consisting of men from the *devadāsī* community published letters that taunted the Madras Devadasi Association for its justifications of *devadāsī* lifestyles. The letter from the Isai Velalar Sangam in Kadalur is found in appendix 1.

11. The proceedings of these debates are reproduced in MRP, subject file 11 (part III), 561–574.

12. The son of Martanda Bhairava Tondaiman and Molly Fink, Martanda Sydney Tondaiman, was born in 1916 in Sydney, Australia. But there was opposition to his succession of the Pudukkottai throne, and the decision to declare Rajagopala Tondaiman ruler in 1928 was made by the government of India, apparently owing to public opinion (Ayyar 1940, 905; Dirks 1993, 396).

13. MRP, subject file 11 (part III), 574.

14. Pandanallur Kumarasvami Nattuvanar (1846–1907) was one of the most famous dance masters of the Tanjore region. He was the first disciple of Civāṉantam of the Tanjore Quartet. He was also the teacher of Pandanallur Meenakshisundaram Pillai (1869–1954), one of the first *naṭṭuvaṉār*s to teach urban middle-class women in the 1930s–1940s.

15. Chennai-based dancer Padma Subrahmanyam and her late sister-in-law Shyamala Balakrishnan came to Viralimalai in the 1960s to learn this *kuṟavañci* as part of Shyamala's doctoral research on Tamil folk music. Ramachandra Nattuvanar, his family, and his *devadāsī* student Ammakkannu taught them the songs over a two-day period, though an acknowledgement of his contribution is largely excluded from the reworked versions of the *kuṟavañci* as it has been presented on urban stages and television since 1986. There is also another *kuṟavañci* text dedicated to Murukaṉ at Viralimalai, the *Virālimalai Vēlavar Kuṟavañci*, written by one Piḷḷaipperumāḷ Kavirāyar, which exists only in textual form—it has no extant music or choreography. It was edited by V. R. Madhavan, and published in Madras in 1983. Another popular drama was *Kapilai Nāṭakam*, attributed to one Keśavabhārati of Sendamangalam, which was performed not at Viralimalai, but at the Tirugokarnam temple. This is a dramatization of the *sthala purāṇa* of Tirugokarnam, in which a cow who comes to worship Śiva by carrying water in her ears for the temple rituals is granted liberation by the god. It was performed once annually on the day of *āvaṇi mūlotsava* in August–September, by *devadāsī*s and temple priests who would sing the songs of the drama. This tradition is said to have come to an end during the rule of Martanda Bhairava Tondaiman.

16. Ramachandra Nattuvanar's students included nearly all the *devadāsī* of Viralimalai who lived in the early twentieth century. Picchaiyammal (dates unknown), Nallammal (1913–1976) and her sister Ammakkannu (1915–1974), Sarasvati (b. 1922), and Marikkannu (b.1924), all *devadāsī*s living in Viralimalai, were his students, in addition to his own daughter Muttukkannammal.

17. The music troupe that would accompany *devadāsī*s in performance also acquired the name *kañceṭṭu* (the English term "gunset"). This term was used in Tanjore

and Pudukkottai, and usually referred to a band made up of the bellows, clarinet, and *mṛdaṅgam* or *muṭṭu* drum.

18. My interviews and documentation project with Muttukkannammal took place over a period of four years, from 2005 to 2009. These were facilitated by her only student, Hari Krishnan.

19. There is a great deal of controversy around the etymology of the term *catir*. A number of scholars including B. M. Sundaram have noted the use of the Tamil word *catir*, likely a cognate of the Sanskrit *catura* ("clever," "beautiful") in early medieval Tamil sources. Others like Arudra have argued that it is derived from the Telugu *caduru*, referring to a court, *sabhā* or throne (Arudra 1986/87, 30). I am inclined to believe that since the term is always prefixed to the Urdu word *kaćahrī*, the use of this compound to refer to *devadāsī* dance has to be attributed to the courtly multilingualism of the eighteenth century. Thus, while earlier a term like *catir* may have been used in Tamil to refer to dance, the compound *catirkkaccēri* almost certainly reflects the distinctive Tanjorean cosmopolitanism discussed in chapter 1.

20. This is the song "kaṉṉūñjal āṭi-iruntāḷ" in the *rāga* Ānandabhairavī. *Devadāsī*s were often invited to sing these songs at upper-caste weddings, and these concerts were known as *kalyāṇakkaccēri*. A fascinating early twentieth-century collection of "wedding songs" (*kalyāṇappāṭṭu*) in Tamil entitled *Śrī Cāratā Caṅkīta Kalyāṇap Pāṭṭu* (Kaṉṉaiyātās 1922) contains "swing songs" next to the *padams* of Kṣetrayya, implying that these genres were simultaneously performed by *devadāsī*s at weddings.

21. Dated 1820, TSML, 2C/17, also cited in Shelvankar 933, 15.

22. The Hindustānī portion of this song is fairly difficult to decipher. It appears to be written in the loose Braj-bhāṣā style that we see at the courts of Tanjore and Travancore in the nineteenth century. There is also a strong possibility that this portion of the song has come from the repertoire of the Tanjore *naṭṭuvaṉār*s who migrated to Baroda in the late nineteenth century. Gauri (1871–1950) and Kantimati (1872–1953), two *devadāsī*s who lived much of their lives in Baroda, danced a piece sometimes referred to as *madhumatta naṭanam* ("intoxicated dance"), which began with the same words as Muttukkannammal's *mōṭi*. Gauri and Kantimati performed it at the Baroda court with a number of other "entertaining" pieces such as "Rādhā-Kṛṣṇa Naṭanam" and "Pataṅg Uḍāī" (Sundaram 2003, 253). From a formal perspective, the text of the *mōṭi* dance is grammatically "incorrect," but this of course does not diminish its value as cultural capital. Details about this style of Hindustānī language and music have already been discussed in chapter 1.

23. Brown, *Telugu-English Dictionary* (1903), s.v. "*jātivāḷḷu*," 462.

24. This song is not mentioned in the *Jātisvara Sāhityamulu* manuscript but is entitled "vande mīnākṣī tvam sarasija vaktre." It is present in the Telugu treatise *Saṅgīta Saṃpradāya Pradarśini* prepared by Dīkṣitar's descendant Subbarāma Dīkṣitulu, published in 1904.

25. Muttukkannammal's repertoire also includes a large number of songs dedicated to Martanda Bhairava Tondaiman. These include an important *maṅgalam* (song of auspicious praise) in the *rāga* Sindhubhairavī on Murukaṉ at Viralimalai, which ends with a verse dedicated to Martanda Bhairava, plus several *kummi* and *kōlāṭṭam* songs that would be danced by groups of *devadāsī*s in public settings. According to Muttuk-

kannammal, there seem to have been around a hundred compositions in total dedicated to Martanda Bhairava. This is corroborated by Joanne Waghorne, who provides the text of a song dedicated to Martanda Bhairava sung for her by Tirugokarnam Saraswati, a *devadāsī* she interviewed in Pudukkottai (Waghorne 1994, 180).

CHAPTER FIVE

1. The term *abhimāna strī* was used by several *kalāvantula* women in coastal Andhra Pradesh but also appears in turn-of-the-century writing by Tamil *devadāsī*s. A case in point is a Tamil text published in 1911 entitled *Uruttirakaṇikaiyar Katācāratiraṭṭu* by Ka. Añcukam, a *devadāsī* from Colombo, Sri Lanka. In the autobiographical section of the work, she refers to herself as the "*apimāṉa strī*" of Ka. Ciṉṉaiyā Piḷḷai, a wealthy merchant in Colombo (Añcukam 1911, 226; Soneji 2010).

2. The most prominent of these organizations was the AMG India International, established in 1968. I have written about the representations of *kalāvantulu* in the rehabilitation programs of this organization elsewhere (Soneji 2008).

3. Caste associations in some parts of coastal Andhra Pradesh are still quite active. In Duvva village (West Godavari district), for example, Saride Seshagiri Rao and Saride Narasimha Rao head the Kalavanthulu Sangham (Reg. 308/88), which seeks to regulate outsiders' representation of and accessibility to *kalāvantula* women in the region.

4. The first line of the text of the song is *ĕṃto jesināve ĕlamaḍi koṃpamāpitivi, o laṃjamuṇḍa*.

5. For celebratory readings of "Vilāsini Nāṭyam" see Jyoti (2010) and Swapnasundari's own book entitled *Vilasini Natyam: Bharatam of Telugu Court and Temple Dancers* (2010).

6. There are a couple of exceptions to this general observation. One is the case of Annabhatula Lakshmi Mangatayaru, granddaughter of Annabhatula Buli Venkataratnam. Mangatayaru lives in her ancestral home in the village of Mummidivaram in the East Godavari district, but also performs quite regularly in public. She runs a small dance school in Mummidivaram as well. Much of this is due to the encouragement her family was provided by Nataraja Ramakrishna in the 1970s. Another example is that of the young dancer Yashoda Thakore, who did not know that she was from a *kalāvantula* background until after she decided to take up dance professionally. Thakore grew up in Hyderabad, where she currently lives and works. She holds a Ph.D. in dance from the University of Hyderabad, and has recently charted her own social and aesthetic journey in a fascinating essay published in a Telugu-language newspaper (Thakore, 2009).

7. In the *pallavi* ("sprout"), one line of music is repeated over and over again, and the dancer performs specific sets of "choreographed" movement. There are actually three types of *pallavis*: *svarapallavi* (performed to a song consisting of notes, called *svaras*), *śabdapallavi* (performed to a song consisting of rhythmic syllables set to a melody), and *sāhityapallavi*, considerably shorter and performed to a song with lyrics. These three forms of *pallavi* still survive in the *kalāvantula* community (I have see performances of *svarapallavi* in the *rāga* Ārabhi, and *śabdapallavi*s in the *rāga*s Ānandabhairavi and Maṇiraṅgu), and are also found in a set of manuscripts from Viz-

ianagaram thought to be approximately 150 years old (Appa Rao 1952). For a brief note on the *svarapallavi* as a musical genre, see Satyanarayana Rao (1965).

8. An example is the famous *varṇam* in the *rāga* Regupti (Mohanam) "sarigā dānipai," attributed to the composer Karvetinagaram Govindasāmayya (c. 1680–1740). This is a very early example of the kind of virtuosic piece that was later foregrounded by the Quartet. This composition is found in two printed texts, the *Saṅgīta Saṃpradāya Pradarśini* (1904) of Subbarāma Dīkṣitulu (1839–1906), and in the *Abhinaya Svayambodhini* (1915) discussed later in this chapter.

9. An example of one of these "local" *varṇams* is referred to popularly as *pedda bhairavi varṇam*, "great Bhairavi *varnam*," to distinguish it from the other Bhairavi *varnam* (dedicated to King Serfoji II of Tanjore), which I examined in chapter 1. This one, beginning with the words "sāmi vinarā," is dedicated to the god Śiva as Kŏppeśvara in the temple at Palivela in East Godavari district.

10. Composers such as Vidyala Narayanasvami Nayudu of Tirupati (1875–1942) and Neti Subbaraya Sastri (c. 1880–1940), for example, composed *jāvaḷis* that became tremendously popular in the coastal Andhra Pradesh region (Arudra 1986b). The poets themselves had close interactions with the *kalāvantula* women of their times. Vidyala Narayanasvami Nayudu's mother was from the *kalāvantula* community, and he regularly sang for the dance performances of Nayudupeta Rajamma, a famous courtesan from Sri Kalahasti (Chittoor district). I have had the opportunity to see a number of Neti Subbaraya Sastri's compositions in performance, marked by his "signature" or *makuṭa "naupurīśa."*

11. Sastri's evocation of Sanskrit treatises on dance such as *Bharatārṇava* and *Abhinayadarpaṇa* is significant. Most palm leaf manuscripts of the *Abhinayadarpaṇa* were in Telugu script, and were found, like many manuscripts of *Bhāmākalāpam* and the *Gītagovinda*, in the homes of Brahmin scholar-poets who interacted with Telugu-speaking *devadāsī*s. South Indian Brahmin men were involved in the production of courtesan dance as composers, scholar-teachers, and interpreters. Brahmin men were also involved as the scholarly collaborators of *devadāsī*s and *naṭṭuvaṉār*s in some parts of South India. Chetlur Narayana Ayyankar, for example, coauthored the Tamil text *Apiṉaya Navanītam* in 1886 with Panchapakesa Nattuvanar of Tanjore (1842–1902). The silence around much of this nineteenth- and early twentieth-century intercaste collaboration has to do with the fact that Brahmin men were also largely the sexual partners of *devadāsī*s. This, combined with political non-Brahmin assertion and the appropriation of courtesan dance by Brahmins in the middle of the twentieth century, has created serious, palpable caste-based tensions around dance in contemporary Tamil Nadu.

12. The term *kalāpam*, which is one of the most common ways of referring to the texts or scripts for these performances, has several meanings. First, it can simply mean "bundle" or "assemblage," a meaning that is reflected in the structure of the genre as a collection of literary forms such as *daruvu*, *cūrṇika*, and *padyam*, all linked by a single narrative framework. Another meaning of the word *kalāpam* that elaborates upon this idea is "a peacock's tail," where again, each of the forms that constitute the *kalāpam* are seen as comprising various hues and shades, yet all held together by conceptual or narrative uniformity. One of the earliest of such texts that survives in a nearly

complete form is the *Āṭabhāgavatam Bhāmaveṣakatha*, written by the poet Narakuri Nārāyaṇa, under the patronage of Velugoṭi Kumāra Yācendra Nāyuḍu (r. 1777–1804), the *zamīndār* of Venkatagiri (Nellore district), held at the Oriental Research Institute, Tirupati (D1899). By the late eighteenth and nineteenth centuries, the Velugoṭi *zamīndār*s of Venkatagiri were great patrons of courtesan dance. A. Sastri (1922) and Sadāśiva Śāstri (1910) provide accounts of cultural patronage at Venkatagiri.

13. Elsewhere (2004, 74–91) I have proposed a tripartite typology of *yakṣagāna*, *kalāpam*, and *veṣam* to understand the complex metagenres of traditional theater in Telugu-speaking South India. *Yakṣagāna* refers to full-length dramas that tell linear narratives, in which multiple actors play various roles. Examples include the mid- to upper-caste *vīdhi-nāṭakam* (also called *bayalāṭa*) and the *cindu-bhāgavatam* performed by Dalits from the *mādiga* community. *Kalāpam* involves one, or at most two, characters; it has little narrative content but usually explores a particular mood or *bhāva*. Examples include *kūcipūḍi-bhāgavatam* performed by *smārta* Brahmins, *tūrupu-bhāgavatam* performed by the goldsmith (*kammari*) community, and the *kalāvantulu āṭa-bhāgavatam* that we are discussing here. The final metagenre is *veṣam* or *veṣālu* (lit. "guises") in which one character performs a monologue or a scene from a known drama. An example is the genre of *pagaṭi veṣālu*, which include *bahurūpulu* (a more formal, usually upper-caste version) and *jātra veṣālu* (performed at the time of festivals or *jātra*s such as those for the goddess Gaṅgamma in Tirupati).

14. For a discussion of some dimensions of the *kalāpam* or *āṭa-bhāgavatam* genre as social critique, see Jonnalagadda (1997).

15. For example, the famous poet of the Godavari delta, Gaddam Subbarayudu Sastri (d. 1940) composed individual *Bhāmākalāpam* librettos for fourteen *kalāvantulu* in the East Godavari region, including the famed Maddula Lakshminarayana and Maddula Venkataratnam. Atkuri Subba Rao, a contemporary of Sastri, composed similar librettos for the *kalāvantulu* of the famous Annabhatula family of Mummidivaram.

16. In one exceptional, localized instance, courtesan *āṭa-bhāgavatam* was performed on a large scale, and this was known as *navajanārdana pārijātam*. In the late nineteenth century, when Gangadhara Rama Rao ruled the *zamīndāri* of Pithapuram (c. 1877), a woman named Pendela Satyabhama was the primary dancer of the Kuntīmādhava temple there. She participated in the performance called *navajanārdanam* ("nine Janārdanas" [Janārdana is a name of Viṣṇu]), held annually in the *mahāmaṇḍapa* (main pavilion) of the temple. In the *navajanārdana* ritual, usually hosted by the *zamīndār* of Pithapuram, nine *devadāsī meḷam*s would perform *Bhāmākalāpam* for nine consecutive nights. This was done in relay fashion, in which one *devadāsī* would resume the drama where the previous performer had left off. The text of the songs interpreted during the *navajanārdana* ritual thus consisted of a number of individual librettos coming together over the course of the nine night-long performance. On the evening of the tenth night, the tenth canto of the *Bhāgavatapurāṇa* would be recited in Sanskrit, and the local ruler, the Maharaja of Pithapuram [the *zamīndār*] as the commissioner (*yajamāna*) of the ritual, along with the *kalāvantulu*, would receive ritual honors and gifts from the temple. The name *navajanārdanam* is derived from a circuit of nine Vaiṣṇava temples in the Godavari River delta. Although the Kuntīmādhava temple in Pithapuram is oddly not one of the *navajanārdana* temples, it appears to have been the site where such perfor-

mances, in honor of the nine localized forms of Viṣṇu-Janārdanasvāmi, were held. Some of the songs from the text for this performance were dedicated to Viṣṇu as the "Lord of Pīṭhikāpura" (Pithapuram). Several accomplished women artists were called upon to perform in the *navajanārdana pārijātam*. For example, according to Saride Manikyam, her aunt, Saride Chandramma, was brought to Pithapuram by the Maharaja to take part in the *navarajanārdanam* in the early part of the 1920s. The *meḷam*s were carefully chosen by the Maharaja on the basis of the skills and accomplishments of the performers. Today what is left of the *navajanārdanam* survives in the form of a few songs taught to dance teacher Nataraja Ramakrishna by Pendela Satyabhama. These songs obviously represent only a very small portion of the whole gamut of the texts meant for *navajanārdanam* performance.

17. To my knowledge, this composition, like many of the *jāvaḷi*s of coastal Andhra Pradesh, has never been published. Therefore, the full text (*sāhitya*) is fragmented and has been pieced together by Saride Maithili. Her memory of the composition is vague but nonetheless conveys much of the spirit of the text.

APPENDIX ONE

1. MRP, subject file 11 (part III), 482–485.
2. MRP, subject file 11 (part III), 442–443.
3. *Cutēcamittiraṉ*, n.d.
4. MRP, subject file 11 (part II), 72.
5. Date unavailable. MRP, subject file 12 (part II), 90–91.
6. MRP, subject file 11 (part II), 58.

REFERENCES

Aiyar, Kamesvara B. V. 1902. *Sir A. Sashiah Sastri, an Indian Statesman: A Biographical Sketch*. Madras: Srinivasa, Varadachari & Co.

Abhinaya Sara Samputa by Chetlur Narayana Ayyangar and Abhinaya Navanita by Chetlur Narayana Iyengar and Tanjore Panchapagesa Nattuvanar. 1961. Madras: The Music Academy.

Allen, Matthew Harp. 1992. "The Tamil 'Padam': A Dance Music Genre of South India." Ph.D. diss., Wesleyan University.

———. 1997. "Rewriting the Script for South Indian Dance." *Drama Review* 41 (3): 63–100.

———. 2000. "Tales Tunes Tell: Deepening the Dialogue Between 'Classical' and 'Non-Classical' in the Music of India." *Yearbook for Traditional Music* 30: 22–52.

Alter. 1994. "Celibacy, Sexuality and the Transformation of Gender into Nationalism in North India." *Journal of Asian Studies* , 53, no. 1: 45–66.

———. 1996. "*Gandhi's* Body, *Gandhi's* Truth: Nonviolence and the Biomoral Imperative of Public Health." *Journal of Asian Studies* 55, no. 3: 301–322.

———. 2000. *Gandhi's Body: Sex, Diet, and the Politics of Nationalism*. Philadelphia: University of Pennsylvania Press.

Anandhi S. 1991. "'Representing Devadasis: '"Dasigal Mosavalai"' as a Radical Text.'" *Economic and Political Weekly* 26, nos. 11–12: 739–46.

———. 1997a. "Sexuality and Nation: 'Ideal' and 'Other Woman in Nationalist Politics, Tamilnadu, c. 1900–47." *South Indian Studies* 4: 195–217.

———. 1997b. "Reproductive Bodies and Regulated Sexuality: Birth Control Debates in Early Twentieth Century Tamilnadu." In *A Question of Silence? The Sexual Economies of Modern India*, edited by Mary E. John and Janaki Nair, 139–166. New Delhi: Kali for Women.

———. 2005. "Caste and Gender in Colonial South India." *Economic and Political Weekly*, April 9: 1518–22.

Anantha Raman, Sita. 1996. *Getting Girls to School: Social Reform in the Tamil Districts, 1870–1930*. Calcutta: Stree.

Añcukam, Ka. 1911. *Uruttirakaṇikaiyar: Katācārattiraṭṭu*. Koḻumpu: "Mīṉāmpāḷ" Acciyantiracālai.

Anonymous. 1874. *Translations, Copies and Extracts of the Several Letters in which the Services of the Ancestors of his Excellency the Maha Rajah of Poodoocottah are Particularly Acknowledged and Approved by the Governors and other Public Officers of the Honorable E.I. Company and the Nabob of the Carnatic*. Puducotta: Sree Brehademba Press.

———. 1931. "Abolition of Devadasi Service in Pudukotta Temples." *Stri Dharma* 14 (10): 457–58.

———. 2007. "Minor Girl made 'Devadasi.'" *Hindu*, November 6. http://www.thehindu.com/2007/11/06/stories/2007110654390400.htm.

Appadurai, Arjun. 1981. *Worship and Conflict under Colonial Rule: A South Indian Case*. New York: Cambridge University Press.

Appa Rao, Vissa. 1952. "The Vizianagaram Music Manuscripts." *Journal of the Madras Music Academy* XXIII: 153–165.

Arapatta Nāvalar. 1876. *Paratacāsttiram*. Ceṉṉai: Taṇṭaiyārpeṭṭai Ilakṣmi Vilāca Āccukkūṭam. [Tamil]

Arondekar, Anjali. 2009. *For the Record: On Sexuality and the Colonial Archive in India*. Durham, NC: Duke University Press.

———. 2011. "Subject to Sex: A Small History of the Gomantak Maratha Samaj." In *Feminisms in South Asia: Contemporary Interventions*, edited by Ania Looma and Ritty Lukose. Durham, NC: Duke University Press.

Arudra. 1986a. "Javalis: Jewels of the Dance Repertoire." *Sruti* 23–23S: 43–46.

———. 1986b. "Javalis: Jewels of the Dance Repertoire II: Salvaging After the Decline and Fall." *Sruti* 25: 33–36.

———. 1986c. "Bhagavata Mela: The Telugu Heritage of Tamil Nadu." *Sruti* 22: 18–28.

———. 1986/87. "The Renaming of an Old Dance: A Whodunit Tale of Mystery." *Sruti* 27/28: 30–31.

———. 1988. "Telugu Dance Traditions of Tanjore Court." *Shanmukha* 14: 19–23.

Aruṇācala Piḷḷai. 1907. *Abhinayābjodaya Sulocani*. Madras: Śrīniketana Mudrākṣara Śāla.

Assayag, Jackie. 1990. "Modern Devadasis: Devotees of Goddess Yellamma in Karnataka." In *Rites and Beliefs in Modern India*, edited by Gabriella Eichinger Ferr-Luzzi, 53–65. New Delhi: Manohar.

Ayyar, K. R. Venkatarama. 1940. *Manual of the Pudukkottai State*. 2 vols.. Pudukkottai: Sri Brihadamba State Press.

Babiracki, Carol M. 2003. "The Illusion of India's 'Public' Dancers." In *Women's Voices and Musical Worlds*, edited by Jane A. Bernstein, 36–59. Boston: Northeastern University Press.

Balasundara Mudali, R. 1913. *The days of a dancing girl; or, The inner life of India unveiled: a book of revelations in the life of the rich and religious in India as seen through the private life of an Indian prostitute*. Sowcarpet, Madras: Coronation Book Depot.

Bakhle, Janaki. 2005. *Two Men and Music: Nationalism in the Making of an Indian Classical Tradition*. New York: Oxford University Press.

Bautze, Joachim K. 2006. "The Dancing Girl ('Devadasi') of South India in Actual Early Photographs." In *Sahṛdaya: Studies in Indian and South East Asian Art*, edited by Bettina Baumer et al., 201–25. Ceṉṉai: Tamil Arts Academy.

Bayly, Susan. 1999. *Caste, Society and Politics in India from the Eighteenth Century to the Modern Age*. Cambridge: Cambridge University Press.

Bell, Shannon. 1994. *Reading, Writing and Rewriting the Prostitute Body*. Bloomington: Indiana University Press.

Besant, Annie. 1913. *Wake Up, India: A Plea for Social Reform*. Adyar, Madras: Theosophical Publishing House.

Bhabha, Homi K. 1994. *The Location of Culture*. New York: Routledge.

Bhagavan, Manu. 2003. *Sovereign Spheres: Princes, Education and Empire in Colonial India*. New Delhi: Oxford University Press.

Bhima Rao, T. R. 1972. *Nirūpaṇa Guccha* (Part 1). Thanjavur: Sarasvati Mahal Library.

———. 1986. *Nirupanagutcha of Sri Gurudasa*. Thanjavur: Sarasvati Mahal Library.

———. 1990. *Goṃdhaḷāce Sāhitya*. Thanjavur: Sarasvati Mahal Library.

Bhosale, Tulajendra Rajah. 1995. *Rajah Serfoji II (with a Short History of Thanjavur Mahrattas)*. Thanjavur: Sadar Mahadi Palace.

Bhujanga Rau, Raja M. 1904 [2nd edition]. *Vārakāntā: The Nautch Girl*. Ellore: The Manjuvani Press.

Biardeau, Madeleine. 1984. "The Śamī Tree and the Sacrificial Buffalo." *Contributions to Indian Sociology* 18, no. 1: 1–23.

———. 2004. *Stories about Posts: Vedic Variations around the Hindu Goddess*. Chicago: University of Chicago Press.

Blackburn, Stuart. 2003. *Print, Folklore, and Nationalism in Colonial South India*. New Delhi: Permanent Black.

Booth, Gregory D. 1996. "The Madras Corporation Band: A Story of Social Change and Indiginization." *Asian Music* 28, no. 1: 61–87.

———. 2005. *Brass Baja: Studies from the World of Indian Wedding Bands*. New Delhi: Oxford University Press.

Bor, Joep. 2007. "Mamia, Ammani and other *Bayadères*: Europe's Portrayal of India's Temple Dancers." In *Music and Orientalism in the British Empire*, edited by Martin Clayton and Bennett Zon, 39–70. London: Ashgate.

Bourdieu, Pierre. 1984. *Distinction: A Social Critique of the Judgement of Taste*. Cambridge, MA: Harvard University Press.

Bradford, Nicholas J. 1983. "Transgenderism and the Cult of Yellamma: Heat, Sex and Sickness in South Indian Ritual." *Journal of Anthropological Research* 39, no. 3: 307–22.

Bṛhadīśvaramāhātmyam. Ed. T.R. Damodaran, S. Rajalakshmi and N. Srinivasan. Thanjavur: Sarasvati Mahal Library, 1985. [Sanskrit]

Brinda, T. 1960. *Javalis of Patnam Subrahmanya Iyer, Tiruppanandal Pattabhiramayya, Dharmapuri Subbarayar, Tirupathi Narayanaswami and Others*. Madras: Music Academy.

Brown, Katherine Butler. 2000. "Reading Indian Music: The Interpretation of Seventeenth-Century European Travel-Writing in the (Re)construction of Indian Music History." *Ethnomusicology Forum* 9, no. 2: 1–34.

———. 2007a. "Introduction: Liminality and the Social Location of Musicians." *Twentieth Century Music* 3 (1): 5–12.

———. 2007b. "The Social Liminality of Musicians: Case Studies from Mughal India and Beyond." *Twentieth Century Music* 3, no. 1: 13–49.

———. 2007c. "If Music Be the Food of Love: Masculinity and Eroticism in the Mughal *Mehfil*." In *Love in South Asia: A Cultural History*, edited by Francesca Orsini, 61–83. Cambridge: Cambridge University Press.

Browne, Stephen Howard. 1999. *Angelina Grimke: Rhetoric, Identity, and the Radical Imagination*. East Lansing: Michigan State University.

Brunner, Hélène. 1990. Review of *Nityasumangali: Devadasi Tradition in South India*. *Indo-Iranian Journal* 33: 121–42.

Buck, David C. 2005. *A Kuravanji in Kutralam: A Tamil Tale of Love and Fortunes Told*. Ceṉṉai: Institute of Asian Studies.

Burgess, J. A. S. 1883. "The Ritual of Ramesvaram." *Indian Antiquary* 12: 315–326.

Burton, Antoinette. 1994. *Burdens of History: British Feminists, Indian Women, and Imperial Culture, 1865–1915*. Chapel Hill, NC: University of North Carolina Press.

———. 1999. "The Unfinished Business of Colonial Modernities." In *Gender, Sexuality and Colonial Modernities*, edited by Antoinette Burton, 1–16. London and New York: Routledge.

Cabral e Sa, Mario. 1990. "The Evolution of a Community: Devdasis of Goa." *Manushi* 56: 25–27.

Caplan. 1987. "Celibacy as a Solution? Mahatma Gandhi and Brahmacharya." In *The Cultural Construction of Sexuality*, edited by Pat Caplan, 271–95. London: Tavistock Publications.

Cassio, Francesca. 2005. 'Artistes ou concubines? La tradition vocale féminine en Inde du Nord.' *Cahiers de Musiques Traditionnelles: Entre Femmes* 18'

Cĕṃcayya, Darisi. 1952. *Nenū, Nā Deśam*. Vijayavāḍā: Jayanti.

Cēṣacāyi, Mahakavi Kottaiyur. 1928. *Tācikaḷ Tarmam*. Tamil MS no. 6523B, Sarasvati Mahal Library, Thanjavur.

Chakrabarty, Dipesh. 2000. *Provincializing Europe: Postcolonial Thought and Historical Difference*. Princeton: Princeton University Press.

———. 2002. *Habitations of Modernity: Essays in the Wake of Subaltern Studies*. Chicago: University of Chicago Press.

Chakrapani, C. 1992. "The Jogins of Telangana." *Eastern Anthropologist* 45, no. 3: 281–288.

Chakravorty, Pallabi. 2008. *Bells of Change: Kathak Dance, Women and Modernity in India*. Calcutta: Seagull Books.

Chandra Mowli, V. 1992. *"Jogin": Girl Child Labour Studies*. New Delhi: Sterling Publishers Private Limited.

Chandrasekaran, Dayananda. 2003. *Oru Peṇ Tuṟaviyiṉ Camaya Vāḻvum Camutāya Vāḻvum*. Pudukkottai: Thilagavathiar Thiruvarul Adheenam.

———. 2007. *Mātar Kula Māṇikkam*. Pudukkottai: Thilagavathiar Thiruvarul Adheenam.

Charmichael, Amy. 1912. *Lotus Buds*. London: Morgan and Scott.

Chatterjee, Partha. 1993. *The Nation and Its Fragments: Colonial and Postcolonial Histories*. Princeton: Princeton University Press.

Chatterjee, Santosh. 1945. *Devadasi (Temple Dancer)*. Calcutta: Book House.

Chennakeshaviah, N. 1974. "Javalis in Kannada." *Journal of the Madras Music Academy* 45: 155–58.

Chetti, P. S. Ramulu. 1912. *Gandharvakalpavalli: Being A Self-Instructor in Music*. Madras: India Printing Works.

Cho, Nancy Jiwon. 2009. "Prophylactic, Anti-Pedophile Hymn-Writing in Colonial India: An Introduction to Amy Carmichael (1867–1951) and her Missionary Wiritngs." *Modern Language Review* 104: 353–374.

Clothey, Fred. 1978. *The Many Faces of Murukan: The History and Meaning of a South Indian God*. The Hague: Mouton.

———. 1996. *Quiescence and Passion: The Vision of Arunakiri, Tamil Mystic*. Bethesda, MD: Austin and Winfield.

———. 2006. *Ritualizing on the Boundaries: Continuity and Innovation in the Tamil Diaspora*. Columbia: University of South Carolina Press.

Comaroff, John, and Jean Comaroff. 1992. *Ethnography and the Historical Imagination*. Boulder, CO: Westview Press.

Coomaraswamy, Ananda K., and Gopala Krishnayya Duggirala. 1917. *Mirror of Gesture: Being the Abhinayadarpana of Nandikesvara*. Cambridge, MA: Harvard University Press.

Coorlawala, Uttara Asha. 1994. "Classical and Contemporary Indian Dance: Overview, Criteria, and a Choreographic Analysis." Ph.D. diss., New York University.

Dalrymple, William. 2008a. "Serving the Goddess: The Dangerous Life of a Sacred Sex Worker." *New Yorker*, August 4. http://www.newyorker.com/reporting/2008/08/04/080804fa_fact_dalrymple.

———. 2008b. "The Daughters of Yellamma." In *AIDS Sutra: Untold Stories from India*, edited by Negar Akhavi, 217–242. New Delhi: Random House India.

David, Ann R. 2005. "Performing Faith: Dance, Identity and Religion in Hindu Communities in Leicester and London." Ph.D. diss., DeMontfort University.

De Bruin, Hanne. 2004. "The Devadasi Debate and the Public Sphere." In *Folklore, Public Sphere and Civil Society*, edited by M. D. Muthukumaraswamy and Molly Kaushal, 103–111. New Delhi and Ceṉṉai: Indira Gandhi National Centre for the Arts and National Folklore Support Centre.

———. 2007. "Devadasis and Village Goddesses of North Tamil Nadu." In *The Power of Performance: Actors, Audiences and Observers of Cultural Performances in India*, edited by Heidrun Bruckner et al., 53–84. New Delhi: Manohar.

De Bruin, Hanne and Theodore Baskaran. 2002. "Self-censorship as a self-cleansing process." *Indian Folklore* 2 (2), 18–23.

Desai, Kiran. 2008. "Night Claims the Godavari." In *Aidsutra: Untold Stories from India*, edited by Negar Akhavi, 37–56. New Delhi: Random House India.

Devendra Kuravanji by Serfoji Rajah, ed. T. L. Thyagaraja Jatavallabhar. Kumbakonam: Sri Mahabharatham Press, 1950.

Dhere, R. C. 1988. "The Gondhaḷī: Singers for the Devī." In *The Experience of Hinduism*, edited by Eleanor Zelliot and Maxine Berntsen, 174–189. Albany: State University of New York Press.

Dīkṣitulu, Subbarāma. 1904. *Saṅgīta Saṃpradāya Pradarśini*. Eṭṭayapuram: Vidyā Vilāsini Press.

Dirks, Nicholas. 1993. *The Hollow Crown: Ethnohistory of an Indian Kingdom*. 2d ed. Ann Arbor: University of Michigan Press.

———. 1997. "The Policing of Tradition: Colonialism and Anthropology in Southern India." *Comparative Studies in Society and History* 39, no. 1: 182–212.

———. 2000. "The Crimes of Colonialism: Anthropology and the Textualization of India." In *Colonial Subjects: Essays on the Practical History of Anthropology*, edited by Peter Pels and Oscar Salemink, 153–179. Ann Arbor: University of Michigan Press.

———. 2001. *Castes of Mind: Colonialism and the Making of Modern India*. Princeton, NJ: Princeton University Press.

Dube, Saurabh and Ishita Banerjee-Dube. 2006. "Introduction: Critical Questions of Colonial Modernities." In *Unbecoming Modern: Colonialism, Modernity, and Colonial Modernities*, edited by Saurabh Dube and Ishita Banerje-Dube, 1–31. New Delhi: Social Science Press.

duPerron, Lalita. 2002. "Thumri: A Discussion of the Female Voice of Hindustani Music." *Modern Asian Studies* 36, no. 1: 173–193.

———. 2007. *Hindi Poetry in a Musical Genre: Thumri Lyrics*. London: Routledge.

Ebeling, Sascha. 2010. *Colonizing the Realm of Words: The Transformation of Tamil Literature in Nineteenth-Century South India*. Albany: State University of New York Press.

Enthoven, R. E. 1922. *Tribes and Castes of Bombay*. Bombay: Bombay Government Central Press.

Epp, Linda Joy. 1992. "Dalit Struggle, Nude Worship, and the 'Chandragutti Incident.'" *Sociological Bulletin* 41: 145–66.

———. 1995. "Devadasi Mothers and Dalit Reformer Sons: Subterranean Ambivalence." In *South Asian Symposium 1994–94: A Reader in South Asian Studies*, edited by Michilynn Dubeau and Louis E. Fenech, 64–73. Toronto: Centre for South Asian Studies Graduate Students' Union.

———. 1997. "'Violating the Sacred'? The Social Reform of Devadasis among Dalits in Karnataka, India." Ph.D. diss., York University.

Evans, Kirsti. 1998. "Contemporary Devadasis: Empowered Auspicious Women or Exploited Prostitutes?" *Bulletin of the John Rylands University Library of Manchester* 80, no. 3: 23–38.

Farrell, Gerry. 1998. "The Early Days of the Gramophone Industry in India: Historical, Social, and Musical Perspectives." In *The Place of Music*, edited by Andrew Leyshon, David Matless and George Revill, 57–82. New York: Guilford Press.

Flueckiger, Joyce. 2007. "Wandering from 'Hills to Valleys' with the Goddess: Protection and Freedom in the *Matamma* Tradition of Andhra." In *Women's Lives, Women's Rituals in the Hindu Tradition*, edited by Tracy Pintchman, 35–54. New York: Oxford University Press.

Foucault, Michel. 1969. *The Archaeology of Knowledge*. Translated by A. M. Sheridan Smith. London and New York: Routledge, 2002.

Fox, George Townshend. 1853. *A Memoir of the Rev. Henry Watson Fox*. London: Seeleys.

Francis, W. 1906. *Madras District Gazetteers: Madura*. Madras: Government Press.

Fuller, C. J. 2001. "The 'Vinayaka Chaturthi' Festival and Hindutva in Tamil Nadu." *Economic and Political Weekly* 36, no. 19: 1607–1616.

Gandhi, Gopalakrishna. 1983. *Tamil Nadu District Gazetteers: Pudukkottai*. Madras: Government of Tamil Nadu.

Gandhi, M. K. 1942. *Women and Social Injustice*. Ahmedabad: Navjivan Publishing House.

———. 1963. *The Collected Works of Mahatma Gandhi*. Vol. 34. Ahmedabad: Navjivan Publishing House.

Gaston, Anne-Marie. 1996. *Bharata Natyam: From Temple to Theatre*. New Delhi: Manohar.

Geetha, V. 1998. *"Periyar, Women,* and an *Ethic* of Citizenship." *Economic and Political Weekly* 33, no. 17: 9–15.

Geetha, V. and S. V. Rajadurai. 1998. *Towards a Non-Brahmin Millennium: From Iyothee Thass to Periyar*. Calcutta: Samya Books.

George, Glynis. 2002. "'Four Makes Society': Women's organization, Dravidian nationalism and women's interpretation of caste, gender and change in South India." *Contributions to Indian Sociology* 36 (3): 495–524.

Ghose, Rajeshwari. 1996. *The Tyāgarāja Cult in Tamilnadu: A Study in Conflict and Accommodation*. New Delhi: Motilal Banarsidass.

Gold, Ann, and Bhoju Ram Gujar. 2002. *In the Time of Trees and Sorrows: Nature, Power, and Memory in Rajasthan*. Durham: Duke University Press.

Good, Anthony. 2004. *Worship and the Ceremonial Economy of a Royal South Indian Temple*. Lampeter: Edwin Mellen Press.

Gopālakṛṣṇa Yācendra, Velugoṭi Baṅgāru Sarvajña Kumāra. 1890. *Sabhā Rañjani*. Madras: n.p.

Gover, Charles E. 1871. *The Folk-Songs of Southern India*. Madras: Higginbotham and Co.

Green, Anna. 2004. "Individual Remembering and 'Collective Memory': Theoretical Presuppositions and Contemporary Debates." *Oral History Society Journal* 32, no. 2: 35–44.

Guha, Ranajit. 1997. *Dominance without Hegemony: History and Power in Colonial India*. Cambridge, MA: Harvard University Press.

Gupta, Charu. 2001. *Sexuality, Obscenity, and Community: Women, Muslims, and the Hindu Public in Colonial India*. New Delhi: Permanent Black.

Gurumurthy, Premeela. 1994. *Kathakalaksepa: A Study*. Madras: International Society for the Investigation of Ancient Civilizations.

Hancock, Mary. 1999. *Womanhood in the Making: Domestic Ritual and Public Culture in Urban South India*. Boulder, CO: Westview Press.

———. 2008. *The Politics of Heritage from Madras to Chennai*. Bloomington: Indiana University Press.

Handelman, Don. 1995. "The Guises of the Goddess and the Transformation of the Male: Gangamma's Visit to Tirupati, and the Continuum of Gender." In *Syllables of Sky: Studies in South Indian Civilization in Honour of Velcheru Narayana Rao*, edited by David Shulman, 281–337. New Delhi: Oxford University Press.

Hemingway, F.R. 1907. *Madras District Gazetteers: Godavari*. Madras: Government Press.

Hiebert, Julie Hamper. 1988. "Royal Evenings: Sanskrit Poetry of Queen and Court." Ph.D. diss., Harvard University.

Higgins, Jon. 1993. *The Music of Bharata Natyam*. New Delhi: ARCE-AIIS/Oxford and IBH.

Hodges, Sarah. 2005a. "'Looting' the Lock Hospital in Colonial Madras during the Famine Years of the 1870s." *Social History of Medicine* 18, no. 3: 379–398.

———. 2005b. "Revolutionary Family Life and the Self Respect Movement in Tamil South India, 1926–49." *Contributions to Indian Sociology* 39, no. 2: 251–277.

Hubel, Teresa. 2005. "The High Cost of Dancing: When the Indian Women's Movement Went After the Devadasis." In *Intercultural Communication and Creative Practice: Music, Dance, and Women's Cultural Identity*, edited by Laura Lengel, 121–140. Westport, CT: Praeger.

Hughes, Stephen P. 2002. "The 'Music Boom' in Tamil South India: Gramophone, Radio and the Making of Mass Culture." *Historical Journal of Film, Radio and Television* 22, no. 4: 445–473.

———. 2007. "Music in the Age of Mechanical Reproduction: Drama, Gramophone, and the Beginnings of Tamil Cinema." *Journal of Asian Studies* 66, no. 1: 3–34.

Inna Reddy, S. 1998. "Social Reform Movements in Andhra (1920–1947)." Ph.D. diss., University of Hyderabad.

Inoue, Takako. 2005. "'La réforme de la tradition des devadasi: Danse et musique dans les temples hindous.'" *Cahiers de Musiques Traditionnelles: Entre Femmes* 18: 103–132.

———. 2008. "Between Art and Religion: Bhagavata Mela in Thanjavur." In *Music and Society in South Asia: Perspectives from Japan*, edited by Yoshitaka Terada, 103–136. Osaka: National Museum of Ethnology.

Irācu, Ce. 1987. *Tañcai Marāṭṭiyar Kalveṭṭukkaḷ*. Tañcāvūr: Tamiḻp Palkalik Kaḻakam.

Irschick, Eugene F. 1986. *Tamil Revivalism in the 1930s*. Madras: Cre-A.

Jackson, William J. 1994. *Tyāgarāja and the Renewal of Tradition*. New Delhi: Motilal Banarsidass.

Jacolliot, Louis. 1868. *La Devadassi (Bayadère): Comédie en Quatre Parties*. Paris: Librairie Internationale.

Jīvacuntari, Pa. 2007. *Muvālūr Rāmāmirttam Ammaiyār*. Ceṉṉai: Maatru.

Jones, Clifford. 1963. "Bhāgavata Mēḷa Nāṭakam: A Traditional Dance-Drama Form." *Journal of Asian Studies* 22, no. 2: 193–200.

Jonnalagadda, Anuradha. 1995. "Crossed Swords over Andhra Natyam." *Sruti* 134: 13–14.

———. 1996a. "Traditions and Innovations in Kuchipudi Dance." Ph.D. diss., University of Hyderabad.

———. 1996b. "Bhamakalapam Texts: An Analysis." In *Kuchipudi Mahotsav '96*, edited by K. Subhadra Murthy, 78–81. Mumbai: Kuchipudi Kala Kendra.

———. 1997. "Kalāpas: A Study in Social Protest." *Trends in Social Science Research* 4 (1), 79–86.

Jordan, Kay Kirkpatrick. 1993. "Devadasi Reform: Driving the Priestesses or the Prostitutes Out of Hindu Temples?" In *Religion and Law in Independent India*, edited by Robert D. Baird. New Delhi: Manohar.

———. 2003. *From Sacred Servant to Profane Prostitute: A History of the Changing Legal Status of the Devadasis, 1857–1947*. New Delhi: Manohar.

Jyoti, Pujita Krishna. 2010. "Revival of Vilasini Natyam at the Ranganathaswamy Temple, Hyderabad." M.A. thesis, University of California, Irvine.

Kadam, V. S. 1998. "The Dancing Girls of Maharashtra." In *Images of Women in Maharashtrian Society*, edited by Anne Feldhaus. Albany: State University of New York Press.

Kalyāṇasuntaravalli, S. 1958. "Carapēntira Pūpāla Kuṟavañci." *Souvenir of the Twelfth South Indian Natyakala Conference*. Madras: The Indian Institute of Fine Arts.

———. 1961. "Bharata Natya and its Eclipse and Revival." *Souvenir of the Fourteenth South Indian Natyakala Conference*. Madras: The Indian Institute of Fine Arts.

Kamakshee Boyi. 1860. *Native Petition to the Imperial Parliament for the restitution of the Raj of Tanjore, Sewajee [or rather, of his legitimate heiress Kamakshee Boyee] and the restoration of the property, confiscated by the Madras Government*. British Library, HMNTS 8023.dd.38.

Kannabiran, Kalpana. 1995. "Judiciary, Social Reform and Debate on 'Religious Prostitution' in Colonial India." *Economic and Political Weekly* 30 (43-WS): 59–65.

———. 2004. "Voices of Dissent: Gender and Changing Social Values in Hinduism." In *Contemporary Hinduism: Ritual, Culture and Practice, edited by* Robin Rinehart. Santa Barbara: ABC-CLIO.

Kannabiran, Kalpana, and Vasanth Kannabiran. 2003. *Muvalur Ramamirthammal's* Web of Deceit: *Devadasi Reform in Colonial India*. New Delhi: Kali for Women.

Kaṉṉaiyātās, Vēlūr. 1922. *Śrī Caratā Caṅkīta Kalyāṇappāṭṭu*. Ceṉṉai: Me. Kaṉṉaiyā & Kampēṉi.

Kapur, Anuradha. 2006. "Love in the Time of Parsi Theatre." In *Love in South Asia: A Cultural History*, edited by Francesca Orsini, 211–227. Cambridge: Cambridge University Press.

Kapur, Ratna. 2005. *Erotic Justice: Law and the New Politics of Postcolonialism*. New Delhi: Permanent Black.

———. 2010. *Makeshift Migrants and Law: Gender, Belonging, and Postcolonial Anxieties*. New Delhi: Routledge.

Katrak, Ketu. 1992. "Indian Nationalism, Gandhian 'Satyagraha,' and Representations of Female Sexuality." In *Nationalisms and Sexualities*, edited by Andrew Parker et al., 395–406. New York: Routledge.

Kersenboom, Saskia. 1981. "Viṟali: Possible Sources of the Devadasi Tradition in the Tamil Bardic Period." *Journal of Tamil Studies* 19: 19–41.

———. 1987. *Nityasumaṅgalī: Devadāsī Tradition in South India*. New Delhi: Motilal Banarsidass.

———. 1988. "Ciṉṉa Mēḷam or Dāsī Āṭṭam: Songs and Dances of the Devadāsīs of Tamilnadu." In *Śiva Temple and Temple Rituals*, edited by S. S. Janaki. Madras: Kuppuswami Research Institute.

———. 1991. "The Traditional Repertoire of the Tiruttaṇi Temple Dancers" in *Roles and Rituals for Hindu Women*, edited by Julia Leslie. Rutherford: Fairleigh Dickinson University Press.

———. 1995. *Word, Sound, Image: The Life of the Tamil Text*. Oxford: Berg Publishers.

Kesavanarayana, B. 1976. *Political and Social Factors in Andhra* (1900–1956). Vijayawada: Navodaya Publishers.

Kinnear, Michael S. 1994. *The Gramophone Company's First Indian Recordings, 1899–1908*. Bombay: Popular Prakashan.

Kittappa, K. P. 1961. *The Dance Compositions of the Tanjore Quartet*. Ahmedabad: Darpana Publications.

———. 1964. *Adi Bharata Kala Manjari*. Madras: Natyalaya.

———. 1979. *Javalis of Sri Chinniah*. Bangalore: Ponniah Natya Shala.

———. 1993. *Parata Icaiyum Tañcai Nālvarum*. Tañcāvūr: Tamiḻp Palkalaikkaḻakam.

———. 1999. *Tañcai Nālvariṉ Nāṭṭiya Icai*. Ceṉṉai: Music Academy.

Kittappa, K. P., and Ñāṉā Kulēntiraṉ. 1994. *Nāṭṭiyap Pāṭṭicai: Tañcai Carapēntira Pūpāla Kuṟavañci*. Tañcāvūr: Tamiḻp Palkalaikkaḻakam.

Knight, Douglas M. 2010. *Balasaraswati: Her Art and Life*. Middletown, CT: Wesleyan University Press.

Krishna Iyer, E. 1948. "Renaissance of Indian Dance and its Architects." *Souvenir of the Sixteenth South Indian Music Conference*. Madras: The Indian Fine Arts Society.

———. 1966. "Classical Bhagavata Mela Dance Drama." *Marg* 19, no. 2: 4–12.

———. 1969. "Bhagavata Mela Dance-Drama of Bharata Natya." *Sangeet Natak* 13: 46–56.

Krishnan, Hari. 2008. "Inscribing Practice: Reconfigurations and Textualizations of Devadasi Repertoire in Nineteenth and Early Twentieth Century South India." In *Performing Pasts: Reinventing the Arts in Modern South India*, edited by Indira Viswanathan Peterson and Davesh Soneji, 71–89. New Delhi: Oxford University Press.

———. 2009. "From Gynemimesis to Hyper-Masculinity: The Shifting Orientations of Male Performers of South Indian Court Dance." In *When Men Dance: Choreographing Masculinities Across Borders*, edited by Jennifer Fisher and Anthony Shay, 378–391. New York: Oxford University Press.

Krishnaswamy Mahadik Rao, A. 1950. *Loka Geet (Folk-Songs in Mahratti)*. Devakottai: Rajaji Press Limited.

———. 1988. *Saṅgīta va Nṛtya Padeṃ (Sangeetham and Nritya Padam)*. Thanjavur: Sarasvati Mahal Library.

———. 1989. *Korvyāṃce Sāhityāṃce Jinas*: *Dance Pieces in Marathi (Vol. 2)*. Thanjavur: Sarasvati Mahal Library.

———. 2005. *Dorā Dharūṇ Goph Veṇī Paddhati (Piṉṉal Kōlāṭṭam Muṟaikaḷ)*. Thanjavur: Sarasvati Mahal Library.

Krishnaswami Mahadik Rao, and G. Nagaraja Rao. *Korvyāce Sāhityāce Jinnas: Dance Pieces in Marathi by Serfoji Raja*. Thanjavur: Sarasvati Mahal Library.

Kulendran, Gnaanaa. 2004. *Music and Dance in the Thanjavur Big Temple*. Srirangam: Krishni Pathippakam.

———. 2007. *Kuṟavañci Nāṭṭiyap Pāṭṭicai*. Tañcāvūr: Tamiḻp Palkalaikkaḻakam.

Kuppuswamy, and Hariharan, 1996. *Javalis*. Trivandrum: CBH Publications.

Kurucāmitās, K. 1943. *Mēṭrācai Viṭṭu Nāṭṭipurattukku Oṭṭam Piṭitta Tācikaḷ Taṅkap-pāṭṭu*. Kumpakōṇam: Kē. Kurucāmitās.

Kusuma Bai, K. 2000. *Music, Dance, and Musical Instruments during the Period of the Nayakas (1673–1732)*. Varanasi: Chaukhambha Sanskrit Bhawan.

Lal, Vinay. 2000. "Nakedness, Nonviolence, and Brahmacharya: Gandhi's Experiments in Celibate Sexuality." *Journal of the History of Sexuality* 9, no. 1–2: 105–136.

Lawson, Sir Charles. 1887. *Narrative of the Celebration of the Jubilee of Her Most Gracious Majesty Queen Victoria, Empress of India in the Presidency of Madras*. London: Macmillan and Co.

Leucci, Tiziana. 2005. *Devadasi e Bayaderes: tra storia e leggenda*. Bologna: Cooperativa Libraria Universitaria Editrice Bologna.

———. 2008. "L'Apprentissage de la Dance en Inde du Sud et ses Transformations au XXème Siècle: Le Cas des Devadasi, Rajadasi, et Nattuvanar." *Rivista di Studi Sudasiatici* 3: 49–83.

———. 2009. "Du Dasi Attam au Bharata Natyam: Ethno-histoire d'une tradition choré-graphique et de sa moralisation et nationalisation dans l'Inde coloniale et post-coloniale. " Ph.D. diss., École des Hautes Études en Sciences Sociales.

Levine, Philippa. 2003. *Prostitution, Race and Politics: Policing Venereal Disease in the British Empire*. New York and London: Routledge.

Leslie, Julia I. 1989. *The Perfect Wife: The Orthodox Hindu Woman According to the Strīdharmapaddhati of Tryambakayajvan*. New Delhi: Oxford University Press.

Linderman, Michael Christian. 2009. "Charity's Venue: Representing Kingship in the Monumental Pilgrim Rest Houses of Maratha Tanjavur, 1761–1832." Ph.D. diss., University of Pennsylvania.

Thomas, Lowell. 1930. *India: Land of the Black Pagoda*. New York and London: Century Co.

Maciszewski, Amelia. 1998. "Gendered Stories, Gendered Styles: Contemporary Hindusthani Music as Discourse, Attitudes, and Practice." Ph.D. diss., University of Texas at Austin.

———. 2006. "Tawa'if, Tourism, and Tales: The Problematics of Twenty-First-Century Musical Patronage for North India's Courtesans." In *The Courtesan's Arts: Cross-Cultural Perspectives*, edited by Martha Feldman and Bonnie Gordon, 332–351. New York: Oxford University Press.

———. 2007. "Texts, Tunes, and Talking Heads: Discourses about Socially Marginal North Indian Musicians." *Twentieth Century Music* 3, no. 1: 121–144.

Manet, Raghunath. 1995. *Bayadères: Danseuses Sacrées du Temple de Villenour*. Pondicherry: Editions Tala Sruti.

Mani, M.S. 1926. *The Pen Pictures of The Dancing Girl (With a side-light on the Legal Profession)*. Salem: Srinivasa Printing Works.

Manjunath, Chinmayee. 2004. "Reluctant Inheritors of a Tainted Legacy?" *Tehelka*, July 17. http://www.tehelka.com/story_main4.asp?filename=Ne071704Reluctant.asp&id=1.

Mardaan, A. 1959. *Deva-Dasi*. New York: The Macaulay Company Publishers, Inc.

Mason, Caroline Atwater. 1902. *Lux Christi: An Outline Study of India, a Twilight Land*. London: Macmillan & Co. Ltd.

Massumi, Brian. 2002. *Parables for the Virtual: Movement, Affect, Sensation*. Duham, NC: Duke University Press.

Mathur, Saloni. 2007. *India by Design: Colonial History and Cultural Display*. Berkeley: University of California Press.

Mattson, Rachel Lindsay. 2004. "The Seductions of Dissonance: Ragini Devi and the Idea of India in the U.S., 1893–1965." Ph.D. diss. New York University.

Mayo, Katherine. 1927. *Mother India*. New York: Harcourt, Brace and Company.

———. 1929. *Slaves of the Gods*. New York: Harcourt, Brace and Company.

McClintock, Anne. 1995. *Imperial Leather: Race, Gender and Sexuality in the Colonial Contest*. New York and London: Routledge.

Meduri, Avanthi. 1992. "Western Feminist Theory, Asian Indian Performance, and a Notion of Agency." *Women and Performance* 5, no. 2: 90–103.

———. 1996. "Nation, Woman, Representation: The Sutured History of the Devadasi and Her Dance." Ph.D. diss., New York University.

Meegama, Sujatha Arundathi. 2004. "Shifting Bodies: Postcards of 'Nautch Girls' from Colonial Ceylon." Qualifying Paper in the Department of History of Art, University of California, Berkeley.

Meibohm, Margaret. 2002. "Past Selves and Present Others: The Ritual Construction of Identity at a Catholic Festival in India." In *Popular Christianity in India: Riting Between the Lines*, edited by Selva J. Raj and Corinne Dempsey, 61–83. Albany: State University of New York Press.

Menon, Indira. 1999. *The Madras Quartet: Women in Karnatak Music*. New Delhi: Roli Books.

Misra, Kamal K., and K. Koteswara Rao. 2002. "Theogamy in Rural India: Dimensions of the *Jogini* System in Andhra Pradesh." *Indian Anthropologist* 32, nos. 1–2: 1–24.

Mouffe, Chantal. 1992. "Feminism, Citizenship, and Radical Democratic Politics." In *Feminists Theorize the Political*, edited by Judith Butler and Joan W. Scott, 369–384. New York: Routledge.

Mudaliar, Chandra. 1976. *State and Religious Endowments in Madras*. Madras: University of Madras.

Mukund, Kanakalatha. 2005. *The View from Below: Indigenous Society, Temples and the Early Colonial State in Tamilnadu, 1700–1835*. New Delhi: Orient Longman.

Muilwijk, Marina. 1996. *The Divine Kuṟa Tribe: Kuṟavañci and other Prabandhams*. Groningen: Egbert Forsten.

Nagaswamy, R. 1989. "Thanjavur Natya on Canvas." In *Maṉṉar Carapōji Piṟanta Nāḷ Viḻā Malar*, edited by Mu. Catācivam, 16–17. Thanjavur: Sarasvati Mahal Library.

Naidu, Venkataratnam R. 1901. "Social Purity and the Anti-Nautch Movement." In *Indian Social Reform*, edited by C. Yajneswara Chintamani, 249–281. Madras: Thompson & Co.

Nair, Janaki. 1994. "The Devadasi, Dharma, and the State." *Economic and Political Weekly*, December 10: 3157–67.

———. 1996. *Women and Law in Colonial India: A Social History*. New Delhi: Kali for Women.

Nair, P. M., and Sankar Sen. 2005. *Trafficking in Women and Children in India*. Hyderabad: Orient Longman.

Nair, Savithri Preetha. 2005. "Native Collecting and Natural (1798–1832): Raja Serfoji II of Tanjore as 'Centre of Calculation.'" Journal of the Royal Asiatic Society of Britain and Ireland 15: 279–302.

Narayana Rao, Velcheru. 2007. *Girls for Sale: Kanyasulkam*. Bloomington: Indiana University Press.

Narayana Rao, Velcheru, and David Shulman. 2002. *Classical Telugu Poetry: An Anthology*. New Delhi: Oxford University Press.

Narayana Rao, Velcheru, David Shulman, and Sanjay Subrahmanyam. 1992. *Symbols of Substance: Court and State in Nayaka Period Tamilnadu*. New Delhi: Oxford University Press.

———. 2001. *Textures of Time: Writing History in South India, 1600–1800*. New Delhi: Permanent Black.

Natarajan, S. 1990. "Bhagavata Mela Nataka Tradition and Its History at Melattur." In *Melattur Sri Lakshmi Narasimha Jayanti Bhagavata Mela Natya Nataka Sangam Golden Jubilee Souvenir*, 9–19. Melattur: Sri Lakshmi Narasimha Jayanti Bhagavata Mela Natya Nataka Sangam.

Natarajan, Srividya. 1997. "Another Stage in the Life of the Nation: Sadir, Bharatanatyam, Feminist Theory." Ph.D. diss., University of Hyderabad.

Native Petition to the Imperial Parliament for the Restitution of the Raj of Tanjore and the Restoration of the Property Confiscated by the Madras Government. Madras: The Hindu Press, 1860.

Neild, Susan Margaret. 1977. "Madras: The Growth of a Colonial City, 1780–1840." Ph.D. diss., University of Chicago.

Neild-Basu, Susan. 1984. "The Dubashes of Madras." *Modern Asian Studies* 18, no. 1: 1–31.

Neuman, Daniel M. 1990. *The Life of Music in North India: The Organization of an Artistic Tradition*. Chicago: University of Chicago Press.

Note on the Past and Present Administration of the Raja's Chattrams in the Tanjore and Madura Districts. 1908. Tanjore: V. G. & Bros.

Nora, Pierre. 1989. "Between Memory and History: *Les Lieux de Mémoire*." *Representations* 26, no. 1: 7–24.

Norton, John Bruce. 1858. *Topics for Indian Statesmen*. London: Richardson Brothers.

Nṛsiṃhaśāstri, Māṭukumalli Kanakādriśāstri. 1864. *Cĕnnapuri Vilāsamu*. Cĕnnapuri: Ma. Sundareśvara Nāyani.

Oldenburg, Veena Talwar. 1990. "Lifestyle as Resistance: The Case of the Courtesans of Lucknow, India." *Feminist Studies* 16, no. 2: 259–288.

Opinions on the Nautch Question, Collected and Published by the Punjab Purity Association. 1894. Lahore: New Lyall Press.

Orchard, Treena. 2004. "A Painful Power: Coming of Age, Sexuality and Relationships,

Social Reform, and HIV/AIDS among Devadasi Sex Workers in Rural Karnataka, India." Ph.D. diss., University of Manitoba.

Orr, Leslie C. 2000. *Donors, Devotees, and Daughters of God: Temple Women in Medieval Tamilnadu*. New York: Oxford University Press.

O'Shea, Janet. 2005. "Rukmini Devi: Rethinking the Classical." In *Rukmini Devi Arundale: A Visionary Architect of Indian Culture and the Performing Arts*, edited by Avanthi Meduri, 225–245. New Delhi: Motilal Banarsidass.

———. 2006. "Dancing through History and Ethnography: Indian Classical Dance the Performance of the Past." In *Dancing from Past to Present: Nation, Culture, Identities*, edited by Theresa Jill Buckland, 123–152. Madison: University of Wisconsin Press.

———. 2007. *At Home in the World: Bharata Natyam on the Global Stage*. Middletown, CT: Wesleyan University Press.

———. 2008. "Serving Two Masters? Bharatanatyam and Tamil Cultural Production." In *Performing Pasts: Reinventing the Arts in Modern South India*, edited by Indira Viswanathan Peterson and Davesh Soneji, 165–193. New Delhi: Oxford University Press.

Page, Jesse. 1921. *Schwartz of Tanjore*. London: Society for Promoting Christian Knowledge.

Pālacuppiramaṇiyaṉ, Kuṭavāyil. 1987. *Cōḻa Maṇṭalattu Varalāṟṟu Nāyakarkaḷiṉ Ciṟpaṅkaḷum Oviyaṅkaḷum*. Tañcāvūr: Tamiḻp Palkalaik Kaḻakam.

Pandian, M. S. S. 1996. "Tamil Cultural Elites and Cinema: Outline of an Argument." *Economic and Political Weekly* 13, no. 15: 950–955.

———. 2000. "Tamil-Friendly Hindutva." *Economic and Political Weekly* 35, nos. 21–22: 1805–1806.

———. 2007. *Brahmin and Non-Brahmin: Genealogies of the Tamil Political Present*. New Delhi: Permanent Black.

Pandither, Rao Sahib M. Abraham. 1917. *Karunamirtha Sagaram* (2 Vols). Tañcāvūr: Karuṇāniti Vaittiyacālai.

Parasher, Aloka and Usha Naik. 1986. "Temple Girls of Medieval Karnataka." *Indian Economic and Social History Review* 23, no. 1: 63–91.

Parker, Kunal M. 1998. "A Corporation of Superior Prostitutes: Anglo-Indian Legal Conceptions of Temple Dancing Girls, 1800–1914." *Modern Asian Studies* 32, no. 3: 559–633.

Parthasarathi, N. C., and Dvaraka Parthasarathi. 1980. *Jāvaḷilu: Svarasahitamu*. Hyderabad: Andhra Pradesh Sangeeta Nataka Akademi.

Pasler, Jann. 2000. "Race, Orientalism, and Distinction in the Wake of the 'Yellow Peril.'" In *Western Music and Its Others: Difference, Representation, and Appropriation in Music*, edited by Georgina Born and David Hesmondhalgh, 249–282. Berkeley: University of California Press.

Patel, Sujata. 2000. "Construction and Reconstruction of Woman in Gandhi." In *Ideals, Images and Real Lives: Women in Literature and History*, edited by Alice Thorner and Maithreyi Krishnaraj, 288–321. Delhi: Sameeksha Trust and Orient Longman.

Paxton, Nancy L. 1999. *Writing under the Raj: Gender, Race, and Rape in the British Colonial Imagination, 1830–1947*. New Brunswick, NJ: Rutgers University Press.

Penny, Mrs. Frank. 1898. *The Romance of a Nautch Girl: A Novel.* London: Swan Sonnenschein & Co. Ltd.

Perez, Rosa Maria. 2005. "The Rhetoric of Empire: Gender Representations in Portuguese India." *Portuguese Studies* 21, no. 1: 126–141.

Peterson, Indira Viswanathan. 1986. 'Sanskrit in Carnatic Music: The Songs of Muttusvāmi Dīkṣita.' *Indo-Iranian Journal* 29: 183–189.

———. 1997. "When the Love-God Smiles: Brahmins, Courtesans, and the Problem of Satire in Sanskrit Temple Dramas from 18th-Century South India." Paper presented at the Annual Meeting of the Association for Asian Studies, Chicago.

———. 1998a. "The Evolution of the Kuṟavañci Dance Drama in Tamil Nadu: Negotiating the "Folk" and the "Classical" in the Bharata Nāṭyam Canon." *South Asia Research* 18: 39–72.

———. 1998b. "Improvising Kingship in Late 18th Century South India: Interpreting Heterogeneous Discourses of Royal Personhood in the Life of Serfoji II of Tanjore." Paper presented at the Annual Meeting of the Association for Asian Studies, Washington D.C.

———. 1999. "The Cabinet of King Serfoji of Tanjore." *Journal of the History of Collections* 11 (1), 71–93.

———. 2000. "Reading the Temple-dancer as Sati from South Indian legend to Goethe's Poem *Der Gott und die Bajadere.*" Paper presented at the Annual Meeting of the Association for Asian Studies, San Diego.

———. 2001. "Eighteenth-Century Madras through Indian Eyes: Urban Space, Patronage, and Power in the Sanskrit Text *Sarvadevavilāsa.*" Paper presented at the Annual Meeting of the Association for Asian Studies, Chicago.

———. 2002. "Beyond Tanjore City Walls: Serfoji II's Improvisations on Kingship in his 1820–22 Pilgrimage to Banares." Paper presented at the Annual Conference on South Asia, Madison, Wisconsin.

———. 2004a. "Staging Smārta Religion in Marāṭhā Tañjāvūr: King Tuḷajā's Drama of the Wedding of the Goddess at the Mahādevapaṭnam Viṣṇu Temple." Paper presented at the Annual Meeting of the Association for Asian Studies, San Diego.

———. 2004b. "Court Theater and Cultural Politics in Marāṭhā Tañjāvūr: The Argument between Gaṅgā and Kāveri." Paper presented at the Annual Conference on South Asia, Madison, Wisconsin.

———. 2004c. "The Tamil Christian Poems of Vedanayaka Sastri and the Literary Cultures of Nineteenth-Century South India." In *India's Literary History: Essays on the Nineteenth Century,* edited by Stuart Blackburn and Vasudha Dalmia, 25–59. New Delhi: Permanent Black.

———. 2006. "Becoming a Chola Monarch in the Nineteenth Century Tanjavur: The Maratha Ruler Serfoji II and the Brihadisvara Temple." Paper presented at "The Time of the Cholas: 900–1300 CE" Conference, University of California, Berkeley.

———. 2008a. "The Drama of the Kuṟavañci Fortune-teller: Land, Landscape, and Social Relations in an Eighteenth-Century Tamil Genre." In *Tamil Geographies: Cultural Constructions of Space and Place in South India,* edited by Martha Ann Selby and Indira Viswanathan Peterson, 59–86. Albany: State University of New York Press.

———. 2008b. "Portraiture at the Tanjore Maratha Court: Toward Modernity in the Early 19th Century." In *Portraits in Princely India: 1700–1900*, edited by *Rosie Llewellyn-Jones, 40–63. Mumbai: Marg Publications.*

———. 2010. "The Schools of Serfoji II of Tanjore: Education and Princely Modernity in Early Nineteenth Century India." Paper presented at the Annual Conference on South Asia, Madison, Wisconsin.

———. forthcoming. "Speaking in Tongues: Literary Multilingualism at the Maratha Court in Eighteenth-Century South India." *Journal of Medieval History.*

Peterson, Indira Viswanathan, and Davesh Soneji. 2008. "Introduction." In *Performing Pasts: Reinventing the Arts in Modern South India*, edited by Indira Viswanathan Peterson and Davesh Soneji, 1–40. New Delhi: Oxford University Press.

Piḷḷai, Kaṅkaimuttu. 1898. *Naṭaṉāti Vāttiya Rañcaṉam*. Tirunelveli: Union Central Press.

Pillai, Shanti. 2002. "Rethinking Global Indian Dance through Local Eyes: The Contemporary Bharatanatyam Scene in Chennai." *Dance Research Journal* 34, no. 2: 14–29.

Pillai, J. M. Somasundaram. 1958. *The Great Temple at Tanjore*. Tanjore: The Tanjore Palace Devastanams.

Pillaipperumal Kavirayar. 1983. In *Virālimalai Vēlavar Kuṟavañci*, edited by Vē. Irā. Mātavaṉ. Ceṉṉai: Meyyammai Patippakam.

Pollock, Sheldon. 2006. *The Language of the Gods in the World of Men: Sanskrit, Culture, and Power in Premodern India*. Berkeley: University of California Press.

Post, Jennifer. 1989. "Professional Women in Indian Music: The Death of the Courtesan Tradition." In *Women and Music in Cross-Cultural Perspective*, edited by Ellen Koskoff, 97–109. New York: Greenwood Press.

Pranesh, Meera Rajaram. 2003. *Musical Composers during the Wodeyar Dynasty*. Bangalore: Vee Emm Publications.

Prasad, A. K. 1990. *Devadasi System in Ancient India: A Study of Temple Dancing Girls of South India*. New Delhi: H. K. Publishers and Distributors.

Premalatha, V. 1970. *Tiyākēcar Kuṟavañci*. Thanjavur: Sarasvati Mahal Library.

Price, Pamela. 1996. *Kingship and Political Practice in Colonial India*. Cambridge: Cambridge University Press.

———. 1999. "Relating to Leadership in the Tamil Nationalist Movement: C. N. Annadurai in Person-Centred Propaganda." *South Asia* 22, no. 2: 149–174.

Qi, Wang, and Jens Brockmeier. 2002. "Autobiographical Remembering as Cultural Practice: Understanding the Interplay between Memory, Self and Culture." *Culture and Psychology* 8, no. 1: 45–64.

Qureshi, Regula Burckhardt. 2006. "Female Agency and Patrilineal Constraints: Situating Courtesans in the Twentieth-Century India." In *The Courtesan's Arts: Cross-Cultural Perspectives*, edited by Martha Feldman and Bonnie Gordon, 312–331. New York: Oxford University Press.

Rācaveṭikavi. 1864. *Gaṇikā Guṇa Pravartana Tārāvali*. Cĕnnapuri: Mā. Sundareśvara Nāyani.

Radhika, V. S. 1996. "Development of Sadir in the Court of King Serfoji II (1798–1832) of Tanjore." Ph.D. diss., University of Hyderabad.

Ragaviah Charry, P. 1806. *A short account of the dancing girls, treating concisely on the general principles of dancing and singing, with the translations of two Hindo songs* [sic]. Triplicane: Gazette Press. (British Library HMNTS C.131.ff.11)

Raghavan, V. 1939. "Notices of Madras in Two Sanskrit Works." In *The Madras Tercentenary Volume* 107–112. London: Humphrey Milford and Oxford University Press.

———. ed. 1959. *Sarvadevavilāsa*. Madras: The Adyar Library and Research Centre.

Raghunathji, K. 1884. *Bombay Dancing Girls*. Bombay: Education Society's Press.

Raghuramaiah, K. Lakshmi. 1991. *Night Birds: Indian Prostitutes from Devadasis to Call Girls*. New Delhi: Chanakya Publications.

Rajayyan, K. 1969. *A History of British Diplomacy in Tanjore*. Mysore: Rao and Raghavan.

Rama Rao, V. V. B. 1985. *Poosapati Ananda Gajapati Raju*. Hyderabad: International Telugu Institute.

Ramachandran, K. V. 1935. "Dance Traditions of South India." *Triveni* 4 (Jan.–Feb.): 1–4.

Ramachendrier, C. 1892. *Collection of the decisions of the High Courts and the Privy Council on the law of succession, maintenance, &c. applicable to dancing girls and their issues, prostitutes not belonging to dancing girls' community, illegitimate sons and bastards, and Illatom affiliation up to December 1891*. Madras: V. Kalyanaram Iyer.

Ramakrishna, Nataraja. 1968. *Dakṣiṇātyula Nāṭyakala Caritram*. Hyderabad: Viśālāndhra Publishers.

———. 1984a. *Nava Janārdanam*. Hyderabad: Perini International.

———. 1995. *Ardhaśatābdhi Āndhranāṭyam*. Hyderabad: Perini International.

Ramakrishna, V. 1983. *Social Reform in Andhra (1848–1919)*. New Delhi: Vikas Publishing House.

Raman, Indu. 1999. "Vanishing Traditions: Bhagavatha Mela Natakams of Melattur." In *Vanishing Traditions in Music: A Collection of Essays*, edited by Sakuntala Narasimhan, 87–94. Baroda: Indian Musicological Society.

Raman, Srilata. 2009. "Who are the Velalas? Twentieth-Century Constructions and Contestations of Tamil Identity in Maraimalai Adigal (1876–1950)." In *Shared Idioms, Sacred Symbols and the Articulation of Identities in South Asia*, edited by Kelly Pemberton and Michael Nijhawan, 78–95. New York: Routledge.

Ramanathan, S. 1985. *Śāhavilāsa Gtam by Ḍhuṇḍhi Vyāsa*. Thanjavur: Sarasvati Mahal Library.

Ramanujan, A.K., Velcheru Narayana Rao and David Shulman. 1994. *When God is a Customer: Telugu Courtesan Songs by Kṣetrayya and Others*. Berkeley: University of California Press.

Ramaswamy, Sumathi. 1997. *Passions of the Tongue: Language Devotion in Tamil India, 1891–1970*. Berkeley: University of California Press.

Ramberg, Lucinda. 2006. "Given to the Goddess: South Indian Devadasis, Ethics, Kinship." Ph.D. diss., University of California, Berkeley.

Ramesh, Asha. 1992. *Impact of Legislative Prohibition of the Devadasi Practice in Karnataka: A Study*. New Delhi: Joint Women's Programme.

Ramusack, Barbara N. 2004. *The Indian Princes and Their States*. Cambridge: Cambridge University Press.

Ranganathan, Edwina. 1982. "Bhagavata Mela." *Sangeet Natak* 64–65 (April–Sept.): 40–50.

Rangarajan. M.R. 2005. *K. Subrahmanyam: A Biography.* Madras: East-West Books (Madras) Pvt. Ltd.

Rao, Kristen Olson. 1985. "The Lavani of Maharashtra: A Regional Genre of Indian Popular Music." Ph.D. diss., University of California, Los Angeles.

Rao, Vidya. 1990. "Thumri as Feminine Voice." *Economic and Political Weekly,* April 28, WS31–39.

Reddy, Gayatri. 2006. *With Respect to Sex: Negotiating Hijra Identity in South India.* Chicago: University of Chicago Press.

Reddy, S. Muthulakshmi. [1927]. *Why Should the Devadasi Institution in the Hindu Temples Be Abolished?* Chintadripet: Central Co-Operative Printing Works Ltd.

———. 1927. Poṭṭuk Kaṭṭutal: Oru Cāpattītu. Ceṉṉai: Tamiḻnāṭu Pavar Piras.

———. 1928. *The Awakening: Demand for Devadasi Legislation.* Madras: Madras Printing Co.

———. 1930. *My Experience as a Legislator.* Triplicane, Madras: Current Thought Press.

———. 1932. "Andhradesa Kalavanthulu Conference." *Stri Dharma* 15 (11), 608–615.

———. 1964. *Autobiography of Dr. (Mrs.) S. Muthulakshmi Reddy.* Madras: Author.

Rege, Sharmila. 1996. "The Hegemonic Appropriation of Sexuality: The Case of Lavani Performers of Maharashtra." In *Social Reform, Sexuality and the State,* edited by Patricia Uberoi, 23–38. New Delhi: Sage Publications.

Report on Public Instruction in the Madras Presidency for 1875–76. 1877. Madras: The Government Press.

Robinson, Thomas. 1831. *The Last Days of Bishop Heber.* New York: T. and J. Swords.

Rose, Nikolas. 1996. *Inventing Our Selves: Psychology, Power, and Personhood.* Cambridge: Cambridge University Press.

Row, T. Venkasami. 1883. *A Manual of the District of Tanjore in the Madras Presidency.* Madras: Lawrence Asylum Press.

Rudisill, Kristen Dawn. 2007. "Brahmin Humor: Chennai's Sabha Theatre and the Creation of Middle-Class Indian Taste from the 1950s to the Present." Ph.D.diss., University of Texas at Austin.

Sachdeva, Shweta. 2008. "In Search of the Tawa'if in History: Courtesans, Nautch Girls and Celebrity Entertainers in India (1720s–1920s)." Ph.D. diss. SOAS-University of London.

Sachdeva-Jha, Shweta. 2009. "Eurasian Women as Tawa'if Singers and Recording Artists: Entertainment and Identity-making in Colonial India." *African and Asian Studies* 8, no. 3: 268–287.

Sadāśiva Śāstri. 1910. *Velugoṭivāri Vaṃśacaritramu Leka Veṅkaṭagiri Rājula Vaṃśacaritramu.* Cannapuri: Śāradāmba Vilāsa Press.

Sadasivan, K. 1981. "Devadasi Strike." *Historia* 1, no. 1: 111–118.

———. 1993. *Devadasi System in Medieval Tamil Nadu.* Trivandrum: CBH Publications.

Said. 1978. *Orientalism.* New York: Vintage.

Sambamoorthy, P. 1939. "Madras as a Seat of Musical Learning." In *The Madras Tercentenary Volume,* 429–438. London: Humphrey Milford and Oxford University Press.

———. 1955. *Pallaki Seva Prabandham: Telugu Opera of Shahaji Maharaja of Tanjore*. Madras: The Indian Music Publishing House.

Sampath, Vikram. 2010. "My Name Is Gauhar Jaan": The Life and Times of a Musician. Delhi: Rupa & Co.

Sankaran, T. 1970. "A Javali and Swarajati of Sri Tirupati Narayanaswamy Naidu." *Journal of the Madras Music Academy* 41: 238–241.

———. 1982a. "Dharmapuri Subbarayar." In *Glimpses of Indian Music*, edited by Gowry Kuppuswamy and M. Hariharan, 23–25. New Delhi: Sundeep Prakashan.

———. 1982b. "Pattabhiramayya." In *Glimpses of Indian Music*, edited by Gowry Kuppuswamy and M. Hariharan, 142–145. New Delhi: Sundeep Prakashan.

———. 1984a. "Kanchipuram Dhanakoti Ammal." *Sruti* 11 (September 1984: 31–32.

———. 1984b. "Mana Ramaniah and his 'Essencu.'" *Sruti* (March 1984): 41.

———. 1986. "Women Singers." *Kalakshetra Quarterly* 8, nos. 1–2: 58–65.

Sarangapani Ayyangar, P. S. 1956. "The Devadasi System." *Souvenir of the Ninth South Indian Natyakala Conference*. Madras: Indian Institute of Fine Arts.

Sariola, Salla. 2010. *Gender and Sexuality in India: Selling Sex in Chennai*. London: Routledge.

Sarkar, Tanika. 2001. *Hindu Wife, Hindu Nation: Community, Religion and Cultural Nationalism*. New Delhi: Permanent Black.

———. 2009. *Rebels, Wives, Saints: Designing Selves and Nations in Colonial Times*. New Delhi: Permanent Black.

Sastri, Alladi Jagannatha. 1922. *A Family History of Venkatagiri Rajas*. Madras: Addison Press.

Sastri, B.V.K. 1974. "Kannada Javalis." *Journal of the Madras Music Academy* 45: 159–166.

Śāstri, Devulapalli Vīrarāghavamūrti. 1915. *Abhinaya Svayambodhini*. Kākināḍā: Sarasvati Mudrākṣaraśāla.

Satish Kumar, M. 2005. "'Oriental Sore' or 'Public Nuisance': The Regulation of Prositution in Colonial India, 1805–1889." In *(Dis)Placing Empire: Renegotiating British Colonial Geographies*, edited by Lindsay J. Proudfoot and Michael M. Roche, 155–174. London: Ashgate.

———. 2006. "Idioms, Symbolism and Divisions: Beyond the Black and White Towns in Madras, 1652–1850." In *Colonial and Post-Colonial Geographies of India*, edited by Saraswati Raju, M. Satish Kumar, and Stuart Corbridge, 23–48. New Delhi: Sage Publications.

Satyanarayana Rao, Y. 1964. "Javali." *Journal of the Madras Music Academy* 35: 224–27.

———. 1965. "Swara Pallavi—Jakini Daruvulu." *Journal of the Madras Music Academy* 36: 105–112.

Seetha, S. 1971. *Sivakamasundari Parinaya Nataka*. Thanjavur: Sarasvati Mahal Library.

———. 1981. *Tanjore as a Seat of Music, during the 17th, 18th and 19th Centuries*. Madras: University of Madras.

Seizer, Susan. 2005. *Stigmas of the Tamil Stage: An Ethnography of Special Drama Artists in South India*. Durham, NC: Duke University Press.

Śeṣakavi. *Tañjapurī Mahātmya*. Ed. T.R. Bhīmarāv. Thanjavur: Sarasvati Mahal Library, 1979.

Shankar, Jogan. 1994. *Devadasi Cult: A Sociological Analysis*. New Delhi: Ashish Publishing House.

Sharma, V. Venkatarama. 1930. "Bharata Natya." *Journal of the Music Academy Madras* 1, no. 1: 32–37.

Sheshagiri Rao, B. n.d. *History of Freedom Movement in Guntur District, 1921–47*. Ongole: Prasanna Publications.

Shelvankar, R. S. 1933. *A Report on the Modi Manuscripts in the Saraswati Mahal Library, Tanjore*. Madras: University of Madras.

Shirgaonkar, Varsha S. 1995. "Dancing Girls of the Peshwa Period." *Quarterly Journal of the Mythic Society* 86, no. 4: 61–67.

———. 2010. *Eighteenth Century Deccan: Cultural History of the Peshwas*. New Delhi: Aryan Books International.

Shiva Kumar, N. D. 2009. "Finally, an End to Devadasi System." *Times of India*, January 23. http://timesofindia.indiatimes.com/articleshow/msid-4023672,flstry-1.cms.

Shortt, John. 1867–1869. "The Bayadère; or, Dancing Girls of Southern India." *Memoirs Read Before the Anthropological Society of London* 3: 182–94.

Shulman, David. 2001. "Poets and Patrons in Tamil Literature and Literary Legend." In *The Wisdom of Poets: Studies in Tamil, Telugu and Sanskrit*, edited by David Shulman, 63–102. New Delhi: Oxford University Press.

Shureef, Jaffur, and G. A. Herklots. 1832. *Qanoon-e-Islam, or The Customs of the Moosulmans of India*. London: Parbury, Allen, and Co.

Sinha, Mrinalini. 1995. *Colonial Masculinity: The "Manly Englishman" and the "Effeminate Bengali" in the Late Nineteenth Century*. Manchester: Manchester University Press.

———. 1999. "The Lineage of the 'Indian' Modern: Rhetoric, Agency, and the Sarda Act in Late Colonial India." In *Gender, Sexuality, and Colonial Modernities*, edited by Antoinette Burton, 207–221. London: Routledge.

———. 2006. *Specters of Mother India: The Global Restructuring of an Empire*. Durham, NC: Duke University Press.

Siva Brindadevi, Saimata. 1997. "Devadasi Dancers." *Sruti* 149: 5–6.

Soneji, Davesh. 2004. "Performing Satyabhama: Text, Context, Memory and Mimesis in Telugu-Speaking South India." Ph.D. diss., McGill University.

———. 2008. "Memory and the Recovery of Identity: Living Histories and the Kalavantulu of Coastal Andhra Pradesh." In *Performing Pasts: Reinventing the Arts in Modern South India*, edited by Indira Viswanathan Peterson and Davesh Soneji, 283–312. New Delhi: Oxford University Press.

———. 2010. *Bharatanāṭyam: A Reader*. New Delhi: Oxford University Press.

———. 2011. "*Śiva's Courtesans*: Religion, Rhetoric, and Self-Representation in Early Twentieth-Century Writing by *Devadāsīs*." *International Journal of Hindu Studies* 14, nos. 1–3: 31–70.

Sontheimer, Gunther-Dietz. 1997. *King of Hunters, Warrriors, and Shepards: Essays on Khandoba*. New Delhi: IGNCA and Manohar.

Spear, Jeffrey. 2000. "Of Gods and Dancing Girls: A Letter from 1802 Madras." *Wordsworth Circle* 31, no. 3: 142–149.

Spivak, Gayatri Chakravorty. 1994. "How to read a 'culturally different' book." In *Colonial Discourse/Postcolonial Theory*, edited by Francis Barker, Peter Hulme, and Margaret Iverson, 126–150. Manchester: Manchester University Press, 126–50.

Sreenivas, Mytheli. 2008. *Wives, Widows, and Concubines: The Conjugal Family Ideal in Colonial India*. Bloomington: University of Indiana Press.

Srilata, K. 2002. "Looking for Other Stories: Women's Writing, Self-Respect Movement and the Politics of Feminist Translations." *Inter-Asia Cultural Studies* 3, no. 3: 437–448.

———. 2003. *The Other Half of the Coconut: Women Writing Self-Respect History*. New Delhi: Zubaan-Kali for Women.

Srinivasan, Amrit. 1984. "Temple 'Prostitution' and Community Reform: An Examination of the Ethnographic, Historical and Textual Context of the Devadasi of Tamil Nadu, South India." Ph.D. diss., Cambridge University.

———. 1985. "Reform and Revival: The Devadasi and Her Dance." *Economic and Political Weekly* 20, no. 44: 1869–1876.

———. 1998. "Culture, Community, Cosmos: Two Temple Orchestras of Tamil Nadu." *Sangeet Natak* 129–130: 3–15.

Srinivasan, N. 1984. "Kulaviḷakku Tīpāmpāḷ" and "Dīpāmbā Mahātmyam." *Journal of the Tanjore Maharaja Serfoji's Sarasvati Mahal Library* 33: 1–18.

———. 1985. *Mahākavisaptaṛṣipraṇitam Mohinīvilāsakuravañjināṭakam*. Thanjavur: Sarasvati Mahal Library.

———. 1999. *Vāsudevakaviviracitāni Saṃskṛtapadāni (Sanskrit Padas by Vasudeva Kavi)*. Thanjavur: Sarasvati Mahal Library.

———. 2006. *Tamiḻicai Pāṭalkalum Nāṭṭiyap Pataṅkaḷ (Vācutēvakavi Iyaṟṟiyavai)*. Thanjavur: Sarasvati Mahal Library.

Srinivasan, Priya. 2003. "Performing Indian Dance in America: Interrogating Modernity, Tradition, and the Myth of Cultural Purity." Ph.D. diss., Northwestern University.

———. 2009. "The Nautch Women Dancers of the 1880s: Corporeality, US Orientalism, and Anti-Asian Immigration Laws." *Women and Performance* 19, no. 1: 3–22.

Sriram, V. 2007. *The Devadasi and the Saint: The Life and Times of Bangalore Nagarathnamma*. Ceṉṉai: East-West Books (Madras) Pvt. Ltd.

Strandberg, Elizabeth. 1980. "A Tanjore Marathi Letter in Modi Script to Chr. F. Schwartz." *Acta Orientalia* 41: 17–25.

———. 1983. *The Modi Documents from Tanjore in Danish Collections*. Wiesbaden: Franz Steiner Verlag.

Stocqueler, J.H. 1858. *A Familiar History of British India, from the Earliest Period to the Transfer of the Government of India to the British Crown in 1858*. London: Darton & Co.

Stoler, Ann Laura. 1995. *Race and the Education of Desire: Foucault's History of Sexuality and the Colonial Order of Things*. Durham, NC: Duke University Press.

———. 2002. *Carnal Knowledge and Imperial Power: Race and the Intimate in Colonial Rule*. Berkeley: University of California Press.

Subrahmanya Sastri, S., ed. 1942. *Saṅgīta Sārāmṛta*. Madras: Music Academy.

Subrahmanyam, Sanjay. 2001. *Penumbral Visions: Making Politics in Early Modern South India*. New Delhi: Oxford University Press.

Subramanian, K. R. 1928. *The Maratha Rajas of Tanjore*. New Delhi: Asian Educational Services [1988 reprint].

Subramanian, Lakshmi. 2006. *From the Tanjore Court to the Madras Music Academy: A Social History of Music in South India*. New Delhi: Oxford University Press.

———. 2007. "A Language for Music: Revisiting the Tamil Isai Iyakkam." *Indian Economic and Social History Review* 44, no. 1: 19–40.

———. 2009. *Veena Dhanammal: The Making of a Legend*. New Delhi: Routledge.

Sundara Raj, M. 1993. *Prostitution in Madras: A Study in Historical Perspective*. New Delhi: Konark Publishers.

Sundaram, B. M. n.d. *The Advent of Marathi Lavani in Tanjavur*. Unpublished manuscript.

———. 1994. "Marathi Lavani in Tamilnadu." *Journal of the Indian Musicological Society* 25: 56–74.

———. 1997. "Towards a Genealogy of Some Tanjavur Natyacharyas and their Kinsfolk." *Sangeet Natak* 124: 30–41.

———. 2001. *Harikatha: Its Origin and Development*. Bangalore: Vidvan R. K. Srikantan Trust.

———. 2002a. *Marapu Vaḻi Paratap Pērācāṉkaḷ*. Citamparam: Meyyappaṉ Tamiḻāylakam.

———. 2002b. *Varṇa Svara Jati*. Thanjavur: Sarasvati Mahal Library.

———. 2003. *Marapu Tanta Māṇikkaṅkaḷ*. Ceṉṉai: V. Raghavan Centre for the Performing Arts.

Sunder Rajan, Rajeswari. 2003. *The Scandal of the State: Women, Law and Citizenship in Postcolonial India*. New Delhi: Permanent Black.

Suvarchala Devi, K.V.L.N. 2001. *Āndhranāṭyam: The Lāsya Dance Tradition of Āndhras*. Hyderabad: Abhinaya Publications.

Svejda-Hirsch, Lenka. 1992. *Die indischen devadasis im Wandel der Zeit*. Bern: Peter Lang.

Swapnasundari. 2010. *Vilasini Natyam: Bharatam of Telugu Court and Temple Dancers*. New Delhi: Swapnasundari.

Tambe, Anagha. 2009. "Reading Devadasi Practice through Popular Marathi Literature." *Economic and Political Weekly* 44, no. 17: 85–92.

Tambe, Ashwini. 2009. *Codes of Misconduct: Regulating Prostitution in Late Colonial Bombay*. Minneapolis: University of Minnesota Press.

Tañjāpurīmāhātmyam (Viṣṇusthalam). Ed. S. Rajalakshmi. Thanjavur: Sarasvati Mahal Library, 1986.

The Tanjore Palace Crown of India Remembrancer. Madras: C. Foster and Co., 1879.

Tarachand, K.C. 1991. *Devadasi Custom: Rural Social Structure and Flesh Markets*. New Delhi: Reliance Publishing House.

Taranath, Anupama. 2000. "Disrupting Colonial Modernity: Indian Courtesans and Literary Cultures, 1888–1912." Ph.D. diss., University of California, San Diego.

Taylor, Diana. 2003. *The Archive and the Repertoire: Performing Cultural Memory in the Americas*. Durham, NC: Duke University Press.

———. 2006. "Performance and/as History." *TDR: The Drama Review* 50, no. 1: 67–86.

Te Nijenhuis, Emmie, and Sanjukta Gupta. 1987. *Sacred Songs of India: Dīkṣitar's Cycle of Hymns to the Goddess Kamalā*. Winterthur: Amadeus Verlag.

Teluṅku Ciṅkāra Jāvalikaḷ. 1924. Ceṉṉai: Tiruvoṟṟiyūr: Śrī Rāmānujam Accukūṭam.

Terada, Yoshitaka. 1992. "Multiple Interpretations of a Charismatic Individual: The Case of the Great Nagasvaram Musician, T. N. Rajarattinam Pillai." Ph.D. diss., University of Washington.

———. 2008. "Temple Music Traditions in Hindu South India: Periya Mēḷam and its Performance Practice." *Asian Music* 39, no. 2: 108–151.

Thakore, Yashoda. 2009. "Khaṇḍālu Dāṭina Telugu Kaḷa." *Eenadu Newspaper*, December 23: 10.

Tharu, Susie, and K. Lalita. 1993. "Empire, Nation and the Literary Text." In *Interrogating Modernity: Culture and Colonialism in India*, edited by Tejaswini Niranjana, P. Sudhir, and Vivek Dhareshwar, 199–219. Calcutta: Seagull.

Thiruvasagam, N. "Malaysian Women Take Charge." *Hinduism Today* (January 1986): 23–24.

Thurston, Edgar, and K. Rangachari. 1909. *Castes and Tribes of Southern India*. 7 vols. Madras: Government Press.

Thyagaraja Jatavallabhar, T.L. 1950. *Devendra Kuravanji by Serfoji Rajah*. Kumbakonam: Sri Mahabharatham Press.

Tiyakecar Kuravanci. 1970. Edited by V. Premalatha. Tanjavur: Sarasvati Mahal Library.

Tulpule, S. G. 1973. *Marāṭhī Bhāṣecā Tañjāvarī Kośa*. Puṇe: Vhīnasa Prakāśana.

Tusan, Michelle Elizabeth. 2003. "Writing Stri Dharma: International Feminism, Nationalist Politics, and Women's Press Advocacy in Late Colonial India." *Women's History Review* 12, no. 4: 623–649.

Ul-Hassan, Syed Siraj. 1920. *The Castes and Tribes of H.E.H. The Nizam's Dominions*. Bombay: The Times Press.

Underwood, Dhana. 2002. "La Bayadère: La femme représentée et la femme représentante de l'Inde coloniale au XIXe siècle." *International Journal of Francophone Studies* 5, no. 2: 85–94.

Vaikuntham, Y. 1982. *Education and the Social Change in South India: Andhra, 1880–1920*. Madras: New Era Publications.

Venkata Rao, N. 1978. *The Southern School in Telugu Literature*. Madras: University of Madras.

Venkataramaiya, K. M. 1985. *Tañcai Marāṭṭiya Maṉṉarkāla Araciyalum Camutāya Vāḻkkaiyum (Administration and Social Life under the Maratha Rules of Thanjavur)*. Thanjavur: Tamil University.

———. 1987. *Tañcai Marāṭṭiya Maṉṉar Varalāṟu (History of the Maratha Rules of Thanjavur, Mackenzie Manuscript D 3180)*. Thanjavur: Tamil University.

Venkataramaiya, K. M., and S. Vivekanandagopal. 1989. *Tañcai Marāṭṭiya Maṉṉar Mōṭi Āvaṇat Tamiḻākkamum Kuṟippuraiyum*. 3 vols. Thanjavur: Tamil University.

Veṅkaṭasundarāsāni, Ulsūr. n.d. *Bharata Kalpalatā Mañjarī*. Xeroxed copy from the Saraswati Bhandara Library, Mysore.

———. 1908. *Rasikajana Manollāsinī*. Mysore: G. T. A. Printing Works.

Venkita Subramonia Ayyar, S. 1975. *Svati Tirunal and His Music*. Trivandrum: College Book House.

Vijaisri, Priyadarshini. 2004. *Recasting the Devadasi: Patterns of Sacred Prostitution in Colonial South India*. New Delhi: Kanishka Publishers.

———. 2010. "In Pursuit of the Virgin Whore: Writing Caste/Outcaste Histories." *Economic and Political Weekly* 45, no. 44: 63–72.

Visvanathan, N. 1980. *Tyāgeśapadeṃ (Thyagesa Padas of Shahaji Maharaj)*. Thanjavur: Sarasvati Mahal Library.

———. 1985. *Sabdam alias Tala Solkattu of Bharatam Kasinathakavi, King Sahaji and Narana Kavi* [Captam eṉṉum tāḷaccoṟkaṭṭu paratam kācinātakavi, maṉṉar cakaci, paratam naraṇakavi ākiyōr iyaṟṟiyavai]. Thanjavur: Sarasvati Mahal Library.

———. 1999. *Bhoṃsala Śāharāju Sāhityamulu (Tiruttalappataṅkaḷ)*. Thanjavur: Sarasvati Mahal Library.

———. 2000. *Uṣāpariṇaya Nāṭaka*. Thanjavur: Sarasvati Mahal Library.

Visvanathan, N., and N. Srinivasan. 1993. *Sītā Kalyāṇamu*. Thanjavur: Sarasvati Mahal Library.

Viswanathan, T. and Matthew Harp Allen. 2004. *Music in South India: The Karnatak Concert Tradition and Beyond*. New York: Oxford University Press.

Visweswaran, Kamala. 1994. *Fictions of Feminist Ethnography*. Minneapolis: University of Minnesota Press.

Vivekanandagopal, R. 1998. *Thanjavur Marathi Lavani Songs: Tañjāvūr Marāṭhī Lāvaṇī Vaṅmaya*. Thanjavur: Sarasvati Mahal Library.

———. 1999. *Modi Documents in the T.M.S.S.M. Library*. Volume 1. Thanjavur: Sarasvati Mahal Library.

———. 2006. *Marāṭhī Pāḷaṇā Saṃgraha*. Thanjavur: Sarasvati Mahal Library.

Volga, Vasanth Kannabiran, and Kalpana Kannabiran. 2001. *Mahilavaranam/Womanscape*. Secunderabad: Asmita Resource Centre for Women.

Waghorne, Joanne Punzo. 1994. *The Raja's Magic Clothes: Re-Visioning Kingship and Divinity in England's India*. University Park: Pennsylvania State University Press.

———. 2004. *Diaspora of the Gods: Modern Hindu Temples in an Urban Middle Class*. New York: Oxford University Press.

Walker, Margaret Edith. 2004. "Kathak Dance: A Critical History." Ph.D. diss., University of Toronto.

Wallace, Jo-Ann. 1998. "'A Class Apart': Josephine Butler and Regulated Prostitution in British India, 1886–1893." In *The Body in the Library*, edited by Leigh Dale and Simon Ryan, 73–86. Amsterdam and Atlanta, GA: Editions Rodopi.

Walthall, Anne. 2008. "Introducing Palace Women." In *Servants of the Dynasty: Palace Women in World History*, edited by Anne Walthall, 1–21. Berkeley: University of California Press.

Weidman, Amanda. 2006. *Singing the Classical, Voicing the Modern: The Postcolonial Politics of Music in South India*. Durham, NC: Duke University Press.

Wheeler, George. 1876. *The Visit of the Prince of Wales: A Chronicle of His Royal Highness's Journeyings in India, Ceylon, Spain, and Portugal*. London: Chapman and Hall.

Wheeler, J. Talboys. 1878. *Early Records in India: A History of the English Settlements in India*. London: Trübner and Company.

Whitehead, Judith. 1998. "Community Honor/Sexual Boundaries: A Discursive Analysis of Devadasi Criminalization in Madras, India, 1920–1947." In *Prostitution: On Whores, Hustlers, and Johns*, edited by James E. Elias, 91–101. New York: Prometheus Books.

———. 2001. "Measuring Women's Value: Continuity and Change in the Regulation of Prostitution in Madras Presidency, 1860–1947." In *Of Property and Propriety: The Role of Gender and Class in Imperialism and Nationalism*, edited by Himani Bannerji, Shahrzad Mojab, and Judith Whitehead, 153–181. Toronto: University of Toronto Press.

Zvelebil, Kamil V. 1987. "A Devadasi as the Author of a Tamil Novel." *Journal of the Institute of Asian Studies, Madras* 5, no. 1: 153–155.

———. 1994. "Kaṉaki Purāṇam: A Nineteenth Century Poetic Biography of a Ceylonese Devadasi." *Wiener Zeitschrift fṃr die Kunde Sṃdasiens und Archiv fṃr Indische Philosophie* 38: 251–65.

———. 1998. "Paracurāma Kavirāyar's *Tēvatāci*." *Journal of the Institute of Asian Studies* (Madras) 15, no. 2: 1–14.

INDEX